Other Poetry Collections by Mark Spitzer

Poetry Land, Salmon Press, 2023.

Cryptozarkia, Cornerstone Press, 2023.

Airborne and Unbelieving, Audience Askew, 2023.

Leviathan, Hot Tomato Press, 2022.

Inflammatosis: Polemic Poetry, Incendiary Prose,
and Other Extremes of Love and War 2008–2018, Six Gallery Press, 2018.

Glurk! A Hellbender Odyssey, Anaphora Literary Press, 2016.

Crypto-Arkansas, Spuyten Duyvil, 2013.

Age of the Demon Tools, Ahadada Books, 2007.

The Pigs Drink from Infinity: Poems 1995–2001, Spuyten Duyvil, 2006.

Motorhead, Bone World Publishing, 1998.

The Notch of the Sorceress, Bone World Publishing, 1998.

Junkyard, '58 Buick Press, 1998.

En Délire (bi-lingual chapbook), Derrière la Salle de Bains, 1997.

Angry Young Man Rants, Oedipus Press, 1994.

Fish Stories, Spectrum Press, 1994.

Poetry School, Spectrum Press, 1993.

Creatures, Redneck Catfish Books, 1992.

Alley Life, Spectrum Press, 1991.

Poetry Books Translated from French

The Genet Translations: Poetry & Posthumous Plays, Polemic, 2015, 2010.

Films Without Images, Blaise Cendrars, Green Integer, 2013.

Divine Filth: Lost Writings, Georges Bataille, Creation Books, 2009, 2004.

From Absinthe to Abyssinia: Selected Miscellaneous,
Obscure and Previously Untranslated Works
of Jean-Nicolas-Arthur Rimbaud,
Creative Arts, 2004.

The Collected Poems of Georges Bataille, Dufour Editions, 1999, 1998.

OVERKILL OMNIBUS!!!

The Collected,
Selected,
Unapologetic,
Überfluous,
Posthumous Poetics of

Mark Spitzer

1972–2022

with introductions by Paul Hoover
and Garin Cycholl

SPUYTEN DUYVIL
New York City

ISBN 978-1-959556-32-9

Library of Congress Cataloging-in-Publication Data

Names: Spitzer, Mark, 1965- author. | Hoover, Paul, 1946- writer of
    foreword. | Cycholl, Garin writer of foreword.
Title: Overkill omnibus!!! : the collected, selected, unapologetic,
    überfluous, posthumous poetics of Mark Spitzer, 1972-2022 / Mark
    Spitzer ; with introductions by Paul Hoover and Garin Cycholl. Afterword by Richard
Blevins.
Description: New York : Spuyten Duyvil, 2023.
Identifiers: LCCN 2023036017 | ISBN 9781959556329 (paperback)
Subjects:
Classification: LCC PS3569.P558 A6 2023 | DDC 811/.54--dc23/eng/20230808
LC record available at https://lccn.loc.gov/2023036017

to Lea Graham Spitzer
who will not appreciate all the verse in this Mea Culpa Magnum Opus
but who is nevertheless incarnations beyond
all the poetry I've ever conceived
and the absolute love of my life

Carry my name in spirit
and take me on your pilgrimage

CONTENTS

Prelude to an Overkill

I write this foreword knowing I have weeks to live
and that I've always wanted to see as much of my poetry amassed
together as possible
in one, monstrous, overwhelming cinderblock of a collection

Hence, what we've got here
contains previously censored work
resurrected experiments
bastard verse, bombast
and manic rants just as much
as the breakthroughs and the best
       (arranged roughly chronologically
       according to theme/style)

I've always loved tracing the chrysalis of poet juvenilia
i.e., the shwagg of Rimbaud and where that all went
and I define my own such formative works
as occurring between 7 and 25

Therefore, this Mongo Hail-Mary Fatty
looking back on almost everything except
what I don't wish to recall and what's still in print
       (since it would be a jerk move to muscle in
       on work that's currently being marketed
       by publishers who've invested
       in my imagination)

Some of this work has been published before
Some has never been seem before
Some has been lost for decades
Some is incomplete, unrealized
       fragments, ephemera

I regret not being able to find a high school poem
entitled "Forbidden Melons"
but beyond that I don't regret much else

I've lived a fuller, more colorful, more adventurous, more rewarding life
than most people ever get
& this is what I want to leave
as literary legacy.

MARK SPITZER
SLOAN KETTERING CANCER CENTER
NYC
XMAS 2022

OVERKILL
OMNIBUS!!!

INTRODUCTION I

As the reader can judge from the book's title, this volume of collected poems is ambitious in design. It contains almost all the poetry Mark Spitzer has written in his fifty-seven years of life, and numbers over a thousand pages. It is labeled as posthumous, because, sadly, he is soon to die.

In "Prelude to an Overkill," he announces that the manuscript contains "previously censored work, resurrected experiments, bastard verse, bombast, and manic rants." He has also included formative works, written from the age of 7 to twenty five. As the manuscript everywhere shows, Spitzer values personal experience, particularly events of childhood, which he recalls with wonderful clarity. His influence is Rimbaud and the Beats, which allows for, and even demands, what Allen Ginsberg called "opening secrecy." Ginsberg also once said, and it's true for the personal mode in general, "I know it's a real poem if it embarrasses me." Honesty is a dazzling. It can also be searing. One of Mark Spitzer's youthful poems begins:

> I know I'm a stupid son of a bitch.
> Me and Jerry should get the fuck out.
> They just beat that poor bastard
> Till he puked and shit and died.

One of the clichés of poetry workshops is "less is more," which demands the well-made poem, perfectly crafted and measured. Wallace Stevens defined poetry as "what suffices," and Robert Creeley as simply, "an act of attention." Spitzer insistently follows the demand of "more is enough." He is most comfortable when telling it all. That urge can be seen in his youthful Puck series ("Puck / babbled to the rodent masses / on the arithmetic of space"), in which we encounter another hero of expansive poetics:

just like Walt Whitman
cruising though the universe
making love to all losers and lovers and loners
with a Transcendental
Emersonian boner

It's also in the Puck series that we first encounter one of Mark Spitzer's guiding obsessions: fishing. But his was not an easy catch of bluegills in a farm pond. It was the dangerous battle with muskellunge, northern pike, and gar, which are sharp-toothed and monstrous in size.

I start with sunnies
move on to crappies
then bowfin and sheepshead and carp and suckers.

cuz there's a world of species
beneath me, behind me
inside of me
and ahead

An intensity of knowledge and craft enter into the fishing poems, exciting the syntax and shaping the line-breaks. I see some influence of the Objectivist poets, at least with regard to poetic technique. But Spitzer's spirit remains, always and forever, that of a youthful Beat, with its mood of celebration and discovery.

The setting of his early work is Minnesota, where he was raised:

Naïve, But So What?

I'm not a hobo or tramp
   but I know how it feels
to hear far-off train sounds

   that drawn out whistle
      cutting across still night

                humming like a tuning fork
                      blaring lonely and sedate

                It's like the drain of plasma
                    listening to that wavering wail
                    knowing the drone
                of all other loners
                        calling me

                                to breathe deep.

On a neighboring page, there's a poem about a sex scandal in Jordan, Minnesota. Beyond that, a recipe for turtle soup. In "Out of the Boundary Waters," Jesus and Buddha have taken up fishing but "they couldn't even catch a sunny," meaning sunfish. Returning home, Jesus drives the car 85 mph, with "Buddha snoring in the back." Use your poetry measuring instruments on these soulful stanzas from "Between Fall Lake and South Basswood":

        but I know the shallows, the murky black waters
            and I know the summer
                hunger of feeders

                    and the first case proves it
                        an enraged pike strikes

Fishing is a quest, and so is driving a car. However, fishing's quest takes you into depths that include the subconscious:

        so I released the beat creature back to the milfoil
            and the alleys of the underlake
            and as I watched it descend
                like a shrinking slash of gold
                    the sun glanced off its sheen
                    piercing
                        my eyeball

The San Francisco poet Jack Spicer believed that poetry was related to magic, thus the creation of his Magic Workshop. We know instinctively when literary magic appears; it's physical, then ephemeral, then a tender scar in memory. This magic is what Mark Spitzer has been seeking from childhood unto death. To write, you have to descend:

> which is why I went beneath
> > the Twelfth Avenue Bridge
> > > because this is where the creatures were
> > > and this is where

> > > > > I made museums.

Mark Spitzer has published eighteen collections of poetry, edited the *Toad Suck Review*, and written books of creative nonfiction about monster fish and the teaching of creative writing by "investigative" means. He has published the novels *Viva Arletty! Our Lady of the Egrets* and *Chum* and translated from French *The Collected Poems of Georges Bataille* and *Divine Filth: Lost Writings of Georges Bataille*.

It has been a full and active life, out on land and under water. We can be grateful for this monstrous new book, writhing on the hook like a Northern Pike, and that lasting glint of light in his eye, with its secret knowledge about to be made public.

PAUL HOOVER
EDITOR OF
POSTMODERN AMERICAN POETRY:
A NORTON ANTHOLOGY
AND THE ANNUAL LITERARY MAGAZINE
NEW AMERICAN WRITING

Introduction II

"our gar hearts"
: the collected poems of Mark Spitzer
by Garin Cycholl

On the road or mid-stream, Mark Spitzer is a poet of itinerant place. Conversations with time start and stop around a catch in the poet's throat, a recognition of a deeper American poetic journey—one set to a Beat impulse and as unruly as water running its course. The poems utter persistent jokes beneath a wider shout that resonates against memory and place. Amidst "Notes of Despair," Spitzer recounts, "yesterday I threw Herman Melville into the Seine / Today a potato". Things are at hand as they shift, fly, or sink, even time itself. Spitzer measures "American standard time" within such loss. These poems are not so much lamentation though as a recognition of breath chasing place gone lost.

This sense of lost American spaces ripples through "The Real," a sequence of journey poems. Watching trucks fly by on I-90, Spitzer's companion, Jules, rises and affirms:

> "Whatever's out there"
>   she tells me
> "I want to be in it
>   when I die"

> and I agree
>   passionately
>   and understand why
>   my mother cried
>   twelve years back
>   in Yakima, winding
>   into the orchards
>   of desert gorges
>   the geography of her birth

Stung within that elegiac sense of American place, the poet resolves "to drive this Mobius highway / but it's way too early / for eternity". Jules's "it" crouches outside time; the poet's "it" sits just beyond "windshield time." Spitzer's poems restlessly seek movement within that "it"—the movement of waters, memory, sound, and road. "Restlessly" in the sense that his musics re-sound that space which rests, as Ed Roberson puts it, "at the far edge of circling the country." A "west" that exists beneath or beyond the map. An "east" that's been put down for the night. Along that compass of a distinct American "here," Spitzer echoes the Beats' own deep hesitations about living in the rented space of the Americas (perhaps retold in the cadence of a marketer schooled on Ginsberg). As Spitzer "dreamchases" Legeia Poe, another co-journeyer, he writes:

> america weans her young on miller beer
> linoleum and lithium
> and video
> and plutonium
> and concrete
> and neon
> and pop tarts
> and pop art
> and interest rates
> and money down
> and america
>
> calls this beauty

The poet screws this way and that, here and there; he seeks himself, an American "wildman" along the highway's wide places, their songs overheard on someone else's radio. He fishes for forms. Sounding the waters glancing against memory and pantleg, he pieces out the language across the recollection of journey and page. These poems scratched over time, Spitzer's country is "The Real":

America, I seethe, is a web of these
    different places in between:

        a fucked up friendship here
            a slit-wrist lover there

Against these losses, the poet sometimes detours into a surrealist's west, pure product of America gone somewhere outside the map—space of testing ground, dry streambed, light slipping the horizon, and dreamed up ex's—the "twisted" narratives of "the nation." As Spitzer tells it,

Dog Priests salvaged that whiskey on your dreadful breath. Tumultuous, the warriors dance; my friend Ohio, we are sensible of energies...Meanwhile, Africa believes; sweet Beatitude bleeds; and the pigs drink from Infinity.

Or in "Trans-Amerigo Sound-Vision Sutra for Scotty Lewis Exit 192":

Kansas I see your rolling golden abdomens
sigh-grinding sky

  those deeper darker deltas
    thrusting from creeks...

            because DIESEL! ARBY'S
                BREAKFAST DELUXE!
                because LA QUINTA! and
                JESUS IS REAL!

What is as "real" as a roast beef sandwich soaked under a heat lamp, Ohio, or "JESUS?" The poet remaps the country across the page. Sounds disappear in space and echo. Can the poet bring them back from memory? Amidst "The Real," it is an ancient fish in hand that calls Spitzer back into this world. Lifting the fish up out of a space of itinerant floodwater along the Little Missouri, Spitzer writes:

a very strange fish—supposedly extinct
               yet still I held it
                           felt it, saw it
                                     twitch its gills
                                                 across the lifeline of my palm
it was a living fossil
               supposedly gone
                           since the Pleistocene

Time slips within a potential horror, a fish liquidated in time but now at hand. A fish that seeks the place of water against the no-place of disappearing water. Or, within the poem's resonance, an ancient fish in an ancient place—as ancient as sound itself. This fish is real. For Spitzer, it makes us as real as the emptied sounds that we eventually become. In his writing, Spitzer celebrates the gar. Among the "Sutras," he writes, *"our gar hearts / sump for your wampuslore"*. So much of these poems (and ourselves) depend on the existence of these "trashfish." Spitzer writes, "this freaky fossilific fish / once dominated the continent...until the settlers & their demons / came colonizing..." ("Ode to America's Most Persecuted 'Trashfish'").

With the fish, Spitzer takes deep American time in hand. His subject is this deeper memory that resides beneath sound, mapped on the page and measured in lines. Amidst waters that have been dammed and drained, these poems are at work *"carving Time, running gulfward / plentiful with fishes"* ("The Real").

Memory rises. Its own distinct sense of time is dreamed through Spitzer's writing, but also hard-seeps from land to poem. Spitzer owns his language, a language takes you somewhere. Away from the forgetting within a still-life of "comfort" motels and "perfect" French fries. Into endless road and the finite stare in a bar across from the Omaha bus station. "Like a picture of nothing" this sound catches its own American time. In "Cardinal Sin," the poet himself goes fishing.

...but I still didn't want to go home to my empty mancave
so I grabbed my fishing pole
and my tackle box
and some worms

then went to this spot behind Furniture Row
it's a holding pond for drainage from Target and Best Buy and
                                        Home Depot and all that
all the parking lots and gutters and ditches empty in here and then it flows
down to Lake Conway

anyway, there was rubble on one side
suburbs on the other
the sky was oranging and
I figured when it got dark
I wouldn't catch shit

but when it got dark
I suddenly caught
a small yellow bullhead

    it was cool...

Fisherman that he is, Spitzer leans into that crouched America, its current, waiting
for the language to strike.

PART 1

JUVENILIA

1972–1990

February

February is cold
February is winter
February is snowy
February is 1972

When Curtis Was Younger

and I was too
and he lived in Iowa
we used to search through the woods
by his house
full of rattlesnakes, snapping turtles,
guinea pigs, lizards, salamanders, red poisonous
frogs, tree frogs, horned toads, badgers and
scorpions.

Then Curtis moved
to the dry, hot city of Albequerque
and lived in a crude, square concrete pueblo
and there were thorns in the grass.

A tumor grew in his head
as we visited him that summer.

I played with his younger brother
while he laid in bed with tubes up his nose.
And I only talked to him.
Andy and I swam in the pool
while Curtis just watched
and I talked less to Curtis
because swimming was better.

Andy and I hiked up a mountain
while Curtis sat in a lonely room
soaking up radiation
and I hardly even thought of him.
I only saw his bald head and scrawny body.

After Curtis died
I tried to feel sorry.
I tried to feel sad.
I tried to feel angry,
but I just felt guilty.

I Used to Dream in Black and White

No colors did invade my sight
Visions barely vivid day or night
Slow slogs in a cadaverous display
For one thing I was dreaming paranoid
Before, drunken stupor could hide my fears
Temporary escape could fill the void
I thought I was judged by baleful peers
Groping blindly, felon inside the gloom
Nocturnally running, seeking to hide
To dwell in light seemed hard in my closed tomb
From the obscuity I wished to glide
But now I dream in red, green, orange and blue
And all the shades are another hue.

An Unsocial Tomb

I wished for a quick explosive death
to envelope my companions
as they maneuvered their doomed crafts
mutely trying to survive
on the parasitic video game

I discovered myself
clenching my fists
impatiently wanting to live
in their ignorant prison of solitude

Together we isolated ourselves
by staring hypnotically
among the beeps and flashings
wondering what we would be doing now
without this lonely infection
that breeds like maggots in a fish head

Senseless are friendships
built around the widowing video game
and weak are the slaves
who can't think of anything else to do.

Powerless, Helpless Again

I was hauled off to Minnesota Fabrics
despite my "trouble-making" whines
and "unreasonable" protests,
and was forced to endure
another sentence of ultimate monotony.

While my mother bargain-shopped curtain material,
dress patterns, zippers and thread,
I crawled through caverns
beneath tables and racks,
amidst lost buttons and dust bunnies,
occasionally encountering another me
dulled beyond comprehension
searching for escape
from the nightmare of "innovative mothers"
who reigned complete emotional control
over their kids.

Sometimes I'd find a dur-dur tube,
which was a cardboard cylinder that rolls of fabric
come wrapped around,
and I'd press it to my mouth
and walk around trumpeting:
"durrrrr-durrrrr-durrrrr-durrrrr…"
the Minnesota Fabrics boredom dirge.

Once I came face to face with
a monolithic pile of dog shit;
a festering island in a sea of urine,
beneath the miscellaneous table
(25 cents per yard).

Another time an injured fruit bat
tumbled out of a dur-dur tube of maroon flannel
and screeched until I poked it into a paper bag.
I was apprehended
trying to smuggle it to the parking lot.
The clerk thought I was making off
with stolen lace
or fabric crayons.

Eventually I'd become too familiar
with the linoleum tiles of the building
and all the dark corners and dur-dur tubes
ceased to amuse me.
I'd end up as a lump of kinder protoplasm
slouched next to somebody's wheezing grandmother

on the fiberglass chairs by the check out lanes,
waiting for existence to conclude.
I'd drift into scowl-limbo
until the never-expected voice
of my mother would arrive
like a pardon from the governor:
"Now let's go to Red Owl."

THE WORST DAY IN TOAD HISTORY

I

The entire Minnesota cult had converged.
For 50 miles along Highway 61.
They were lined up in rows three hundred toads back
Poised and chirping, croaking with hormones
Waiting for the legendary midnight signal
Which would trigger their traditional orgy
Andy they would flow in reptile waves
Across the gloss of the two lane tar stretch;
Hopping, marathoning, rioting rebels celebrating;
Storming the Bastille for their species' conception.

Then somewhere on the toad front
The Midwest's greatest bull toad
        barked a guttural battle cry.

BRRRRRRRRRAAAAAAORRRRRRRRRRRRRRRRRRRRRRRRRRRRK!

II

Windshield wipers slap with Tull;
Our heads nodding hard with kettle drums
And the wild flute energizing our flight.
We race north with the Rock Island
Winding our way along the Mississippii,
Legs stretched forward, relaxed in the heat.

When we round the bend the pavement is gone
Replaced by a swarming rusty entity.
And we hydroplane, fisthtail, skid and spin.
Two showering headlights illuminate
A massive, gravel sludge of popping pyramids
Rolling across the road and under tires.
Kent hits the accelerator, digs in for traction
Spraying thousands of toad limbs in pureed arcs—
Finely ground pebbled skins, digits dismembered, warts
Blended in the midair spirals of toad-matter spatter.

III

We come about, plow onward through the mush
Radials slick; full of four million doughy post-vertebrate souls
Sliming and slipping in swells of stampeding croakers
Vents clogged, grill plastered, under-frame saturated
By the hamburger of Nature squished together
Destined on that sacrificial night
To fill our omnipotent tread.

SON OF A BITCH IN THE BIOGRAPHY SECTION

I know I'm a stupid son of a bitch.
Me and Jerry should get the fuck out.
They just beat that poor bastard
Till he puked and shit and died.
        "You ain't no crooks!"

I know I'm a stupid son of a bitch.
You ain't never seen no shit.
You see Mitch kill that punk
Write on the wall "peeg?"
P-I-G, peeg! With the guy's own blood.

Sixteen of us in one fucking boxcar.
Mitch, though, he slept in a dumpster
Cuz it was full of paper to keep warm
And the other three, they got sent to the hospital.
        "You ain't no crooks!"

One son of a bitch died a year later.
I ain't never gonna find that spot.
Pigs don't even know bout them.
Burlington Northern, spension bridge, dirt road forks
Ten miles or a day into the canyon...
Follow the piles of green-brown shit and busted glass.
Sons of bitches live there
Catch pheasant with grain from the tracks
Eat crab apples and muskrat.

Ugly fucking one-eye kids with pusin sores
Born with syphilis and gon'rea.
Some those fucks ain't been out for six years
Cuz they'ze stupid sons of bitches
Criminals, sick fuckers, shit-for-brains
Ain't seen a cig for three years
Don't know no more the taste of gutterbutt
Or Irish Rose, bottle of Phillips gin.
        Shhhhhhhheeeeeeeeeeee-it!

Don't tell me shut up!
Go on... kick my ass... try it!
Try it... WHITE TRASH!
I'll kill you...
I know I'm a stupid son of a bitch.
Don't matter none to you:
A body down at the river.
Don't matter me none neither.
I seen plenty a dead fuckin' dogs.

IDIOSYNCRASIES

My birthday present this year:
A haircut by Russ.
For 23 years it's always been cut
By my mother or sister
And not by Russ.

I know what it's like
When Russ cuts hair:
Sensemilla and cognac
Reggae thumping house
"Family haircut time"
My father calls it.

I show my dad
My 23rd car.
He sits down in the bucket seat
Which is all the way back.
His knees are not bent.
"Your clutch is too tight!"

I see Russ' coffee-jaundice skin
He breathes guac in my face
His fingers worm in my scalp.
My ears retreat into my head.

Sometimes Dad comes over
Drives up to the house
And stands on the horn.
I'm there every time
Reading on the steps.
I don't tell him stop.

Everything's hysterical.
They're passing the pipe.
Russ jokes about the women he fucks.
My dad and stepmother laugh
Do yoga and dance.

"Something's definitely wrong;
Your clutch is too tight"
(Ass on the edge of the seat).
It's the 23rd tight clutch
In 23 years.
I don't tell him stop.

UBIQUITOUS GANGRENE

My roommate returns with 40-weight oil.
He enters the kitchen and utters a moan.
"Oh no! Return of the lentils!"

At first they were bags; dry grains and beans.
Split peas and vegetables were added
And the stew began to simmer.
Then the leaden, emerald bulk began to swell
And I had to call in reinforcements
Of now permanently tainted yellow pots.
A bloating pea-green ocher mutation
I scooped the slag into mixing bowls
To occupy the space of future frozen pizzas.
A sallow lentil tinfoiled Atlantis—
Dormant now—sepia peat in suspended animation.

I eat it for breakfast, take it to school.
It's with me at work in Tupperware.
I wish it would form into balls
That I could carry around:
Bright green lentil-mass moons.
Because it orbits me daily
In swamp goulash style.

Bruce doesn't like curry
Celery, garlic, carrots and rice.
They haunt the refrigerator and hog all his Teflon.
They make the place smell like some hippy's pad.
He once swallowed a few globs
And declared it his nemesis.
He's fettered to a lease
That makes him nauseous.
Trapped in a bronze-green gorge
Filling with eternal onion-infested lava
Up to his stretching saffron-stained neck
Submerged in jaundicy lime tinted slime.
Salt and pepper and open windows can't dull
The infinite and merciless volcano spewing
Neon glops of veggy madness.

Lentilphobia does not stir muddy eddies in my mind.
I laugh as he scrambles to the phone
And dials his mother in Denver.

    "Mom. He's driving me crazy!
    I need macaroni and cheese.
    I can't breathe in this joint.
    They aren't natural.
    Why can't he cook in neutral tones?"

And as he grabs his face and cries
I roar laughter from the threshold
Walk in with a fresh batch steaming
Sit down on the couch beside him
And laugh so hard I spit lentil missiles
At his fetal wracking body.

MOTORCYCLE FOR SALE

I

The gashed sod healed
A boulevard spruce grows here.
I bought it for 150 dollars
At 17.
This tree's predecessor
Was run down by a
1968 Bondobird
Out of control
Racing.

Neighbors raking leaves
Witnessed the lawn slaughter;
Saw its carcass get mangled
Beneath the tranny.

II

Power poles do not surround
A "new boulevard tree"*
Forming an iron alloy shell.
Boulders are not linebackers braced
To absorb two tons of steel impact.
No ditch, no moat
No logs or guardrails.
Lightning can strike twice
From a driveshaft sky
With an oilpan thunderhead
Leaving floorboards and exhaust
To descend in its wake.

This boulevard spruce cringes
Not at the prophecy
Of her sap smearing the sidewalk
Her trunk shattering; wood chips and sawdust
<u>Uprooted and snapping</u>, spine suddenly splitting

* Police Report, October 30, 1982.

Limbs splintering and branches crunching
Lacerating, helpless, deafening instant
Knots plucked fluidlessly from callow sockets
Impaled through the grill
Dragging and skinning barkless woodmeat
Scraping its dough into the blacktop.
This boulevard spruce flinches
Not at the vision:
Roots yanked, crippled, pale
Nerves exposed, white-hot and raw on the curb.

Naked branches: Oblivious to the threat
Of ripping rabid bumpers
That have records of shredding
Into limp fibers pulpy
The sprouting stems
Of sibling saplings.

She dreams, planted on this greensward strip:
Zephyrs erotic thrill her leaves;
Adrenaline gusts flex her boughs.
          Thriving spruce
Tacks into the wind.

III

I goose the throttle
pull into the street.

BEATER

Drooling over her quarter panels
Scenting the stock cast iron ticking
                veiled by a forbidding hood
I'd await with full case and funnel
3000 miles of turnover
                to change the oil.

Ratchet ready, I'd jack up the front.
Inch my crawler into the heat radiating below
One palm caressing the scattered porous
Nicks and dings on the chrome
The other socketing the plug
Loose from its hold on the block.
Gentle paced rhythm
                to not strip the thread
The pan grazes and lubes fingers rich.
Growling, the slimed ratchet tenderly rocks;
Vibrations felt deep in the loins of leaf springs flexing.

zzzzzzzzzzzzzzzzzzzzzzzzzzzzzzzzzzzzzt...
zzzzzzzzzzzzzzzzzzzzzzzzzzzzzzzzzzzzzt...
zzzzzzzzzzzzzzzzzzzzzzzzzzzzzzzzzzzzzt...

Ball bearings of the tool
Midsummer-dance manic, packed in grease.
A trickle trails incandescently down the wrist.
Beads on the underbelly collecting—I sweat.
Arching, sooth stream, translucent—freed
Feverishly filling the familiar pan.

I twist off the filter, finish the task
Jack down the body, hop in the cab
Burn rubber through the drive, blast into the street
Wracking the shocks for 3000 miles:
My unconscious victim;
Maintained by an impatient odometer;
Asceptic to one
Junker's loss.

THREE DAYS WITH A SCHITZO

Coffee/No-Doze hard-boiled eyeballs.
Oatmeal mind distilled by
"Mammy! Mammy! Mammy!"
Unceasing lunatic raving "Mammy!
Mammy! I am Walt Whitman, Mammy!"

He chucked the anti-depressants in Olympia and flipped
Mammied all the way to Two Dot, Montana.

In Highway 12's ditch we stopped for a piss
Then spotted the accordianed farmhouse
Hurtled barbed-wire with outstretched arms
"Mammy! It's me, Walt!"
To the outhouse's punky frame grave
Kneeled and thrust his head down the pit
Emerged lungs full and vibrant with scent.
"This used to be where a family shat!
And it smells like lye. It smells like lye!"

Leaping like a lama
He cleared the plain with one graceful bound
"Realism Mammy! Wow realism! REALISM Mammy!"
Rust and dust converged, billowed up from the earth
When he tore an Edsel's door off its pins
And an infant cheered in victory
To find the shell's vinyl intact
As he thrust his open palm through the upholstery
Grabbing a handful of ochre, sandstone foam
Crumpling it in his fist to cereal dust
He smeared it into mustard on his chest and neck.

Again his lungs filled with some divine breath:
"I love you Edsel! Mammy I love you! Realism! Oh
Realism! Mammy! I am Walt Whitman!"
He wept and pirouette leapt
To a rotting mound of moss-covered shingles
Diving and clawing for the richest and dampest
Producing one garnished by mildew and moist.

Scraping black beetles and salmon earthworms
Spider egg sacks and isopods possum
He swallowed the frosting and licked his teeth
Declared to Big Sky the proclamation:
"Food of the gods from Montana soil!"
Then passed out drenched in euphoria
And for two days
he slept.

PUCK

He laid upon the rocks up North
His scalp and back conducting warmth
The slabs—his skull—concretely spun—
Apricot filtered nimbus sun.

A rolling mist from the flexing disc
A lapping current consoled the risk
Of worrying about a beatless heart.
The waves of space distilled apart.

Sandstone layer—his eyeballs danced
The only life in an acid trance.
Horizon flow on translucent fringe
Velvet pines on a moaning hinge.

Luminous, fluid, black light dome
Royal meniscus, floating home.
Both you whisper in symbols mute
Comatose drowse hears woods' flute.

Vital time blasts the groin and spine
Shocks the cliff—his whole supine…
A balance here of life and death
Control each lone desperate breath.

With a rush from lung to heart to throat to brain,
Muscle and bone contemplate the pain
They never knew, or felt, or saw or heard,
But clench crazed will and vision blurred.

All that matters is in the waning mist,
And a human is crushed by Nature's fist.
Breathing is restored, and fingers twitch,
Unearthly chaos in a body mixed.

My limbs are scarred by some design,
Blood-red real as sacred wine.
Grapes sanguine, combined in pulp,
The Lethe-fed roots
                                deflesh with gulp.

Forty Thousand Digits to Puck

Pretext

the narrator is a thirty-one-year-old unemployed guy
still living at home

reflecting on Puck, a thirteen-year-old "rehab kid" obsessed with math

Anyway, the narrator's parents (who are good democrats and friends with Puck's parents) had forced the narrator to take Puck fishing up in the Boundary Waters of Northern Minnesota in order to get Puck to "communicate," or else (so the parents tell the narrator) the narrator "should reevaluate his financial situation."

Part I: The Calculus of Fish

"It's a matter of millimeters!"
    Puck tells me

        washing down his medication
        with Old Milwaukee

            "If they see it, they'll take it!"
            he says

                and casts his spoon into
                another likely spot

      where calculating creatures
        lurking for silver

                Puck rambles on about the position of pupils
                determining the focus

                      of feeding northerns

                                                            scanning the surface

        "Cuz all fish have a range," Puck tells me,
                "of what they can see
                        and what they can sense
                                which is their Vector!"
                                                            he exclaims

                                        staring into the cattails where
        pointing out a purple grackle

                                        Puck acts as if
                                                this is some sort
                                                        of warbler
                                                                of distinction

                                *

Then he goes on
telling me "All fish can be determined!"

                as he grabs his abacus
                and dives into a squinting world
                of sliding logarithms,
                trigonometries and theoroms

                        and emerges
                                with 4.3:

                                "the probability for the strike
                                of an active hungry pike
                                facing due east in Horsefish Lake..."
                                                        he tells me

                                *

Meanwhile I work to free a snag
                my own spoon dangling three feet beneath the hull
                        flashing in the algae

        and when I lift my leader up

an eruption sprays my face:

    cuz suddenly, a lunker
        is writhing between my feet
            slapping the keel with its tail

        a snaky
        blue
        northern

        equaling
        4.3

    *

But
    "This fish does not exist!"
    Puck resists

    "The odds do not support this fish
        Grounded on Hypothesis!
            This fish is an Inference!"

    *

Still   I string the creature
    which weighs at least five pounds

        and as I hang it in the lake
            Puck up front, starts to break

            into a sweat
                pressing fingertips into his skull

    *

Which is what his psychiatrist
told him to do
if the Insect King came back

Which   according to Puck's father
wasn't supposed to happen anymore

Because   according to Puck's father
the freak outs were over

That's why I'd been provided
a deluxe station wagon
one canoe
two life preservers
a tackle box
a tent
some freeze dried food
a budget

and an extra vial of lithium
for his son Puck
who I took
cuz of family
and the fact
that we both wanted muskie

*

Besides, Puck's father had assured me
his son had recovered

from tracking the digits
of his own private pi:

3.1415926...

the result of circumference
divided by diameter

a figure which Puck
kept padlocked in his closet

till the day the Amboy Dukes regrouped
and came to play Fort Wayne

Part II: Enter the Nuge

It had happened three months prior
when Puck's father had commissioned me
to take his son to see the Nuge

       so there we were
       at the Fort Wayne Coliseum

            when suddenly Puck
            broke away, jumped on stage
            grabbed the mic

                        and howled from the bowels
                        of his puberty throat

"ANGST-RIDDLED TEENS OF THE INDIANA CORNSCENE LISTEN TO ME!
    I'M PUCK AND WE'RE FUCKED!"
            my "responsibility" suddenly
            chicken-littled
            at me

                        and twenty three thousand kids with zits
                        not to mention six security guards
                        one reconstructed rock and roll band
                        and the Wild Man himself

                            Ted Nugent

   And then Puck howled again

            "BEWARE THE MISLEADING COMPUTERS OF THE SIXTIES
                STILL PUMPING OUT PI TODAY!"
                he yelled
                and fell

                into the rhythm of the Amboy Dukes
                    jamming behind him

           *

"TODAY! RIGHT NOW! IN GOVERNMENT LOTS!"
Puck rocked
"WE GOT TRAILERS PACKED WITH NOTHING!
WE GOT BOXCARS FULL OF BUNK!
DECADES OF PAPER!
DECADES OF INK!
DECADES OF TREASON!"

the concert cops
approached Puck screaming
"OPEN YOUR EYES! PI IS A LIE!"
But suddenly the Nuge stepped up
dressed in silver rawhide
and holding one hand
up toward his henchmen
he told em

"Hey, Whooooooooaaa! Let's hear this kid out!
Let's let this kid ride the storm out
Like the fallout
Of a MotherFucking
Rocking Rolling
Youbetchyer Ass
Nuclear Winter, Baby!"

and the crowd went Gonzo
as Puck kept howling
"UNPLUG THE DECEITFUL COMPUTERS OF FICTION!"

and the drummer combusting
thundered percussion
while Puck on his hearth
cried to the tempest

"RECYLE THE WASTED PAPIRUS OF PI!"
OR WE'RE ALL GONNA DIE!
WE'RE ALL GONNA DIE!"
he hollered to the sky
to the stars
the Galactic Expansion...

as the Amboy Dukes kept on blasting
behind him
and the Nuge

who knew things were coooooool
cuz this is what he saw:

one feral teen unleashing
some crazed bengal inside
beyond Basic Hendrix
and Fundamental Page

some crazed bengal
more like Zappa
more like Floyd

now howling out what Steppenwolf
had been trying to say

cuz that crazed bengal inside him
it was something the Nuge
knew
could handle a twelve string

of an electric Fender Stratocaster
with a whammy bar
and a built in synthesizer

"GOVERNMENT PI IS A GOVERNMENT HOAX!"
Puck croaked

while the Nuge, right beside him
wired on adrenaline
backed him up on geetar

squelching distortion
blasting impassioned

And the slam dancing crowd
the auditorium rumbling

The tremors, the humming
the Richter scaling

  And Puck letting rip
  spraying spit
"GOVERNMENT PI WAS DESIGNED TO KEEP US IN LINE!"
  launching forty six thousand fists
      pounding the marijuanaed air

   with the sign of the Devil!
    the epitome of Metal!

    one pinky, one thumb
    protruding from each
    set of knuckles
    666ing
    thrusting

      the highest honor ever
      bestowed on any newgod

      by any pimpled pack
    of concert rockers

Till suddenly Puck was ejaculating
  "GOVERNMENT PI IS A SCANDALOUS QUOTIENT!
   WE ARE ALL SHACKLED IMMACULATE!"

   and

  "GOVERNMENT PI! GOVERNMENT BOGUS!
   GOVERNMENT PI IS REPUTED CONTINUOUS!
    BUT IT'S A SPAWN OF IGNORANCE!
    BLOCKING US FROM REACHING NIRVANA!"

  then the Nuge kicked it in the ass
  soloing hyper, mach-speeding fingers
  rifting like Icarus soaring skyward
   the audience chanting
    "PUCK! PUCK! PUCK!

PUCK! PUCK! PUCK!"

the focus of twenty thousand
butane flames
saluting a martyr

"PUCK! PUCK! PUCK!
PUCK! PUCK! PUCK!"

protesting the manacles of a society fettered
by a mythical figure

"CUZ REAL PI IS DIFFERENT!
he suddenly shrieked
REAL PI IS FINITE!"

and suddenly
eight hundred stoners
in rows 1 A, B and C
through rows 9 A, B and C

permanently lost
all hearing forever

though nevertheless
the mob kept chanting
"PUCK! PUCK! PUCK!"

And the stadium trembling, all girders shaking
"PUCK! PUCK! PUCK!"

just like that Who concert, the aisles jampacking
"PUCK! PUCK! PUCK!"

And the masses panicked
and ran amuck
stampeding each other

then FOOOOMP!
one incensed wave of adolescents
was running from the clouds
of crowd-control tear gas

released from the smog of the National Guard
storm trooping in, cracking skulls
and the Nuge
just kept playing

Part III: Puck Goes Live on NBC

Before going on Letterman
the Nuge alerted
the producer of a national show
that a man in his band needed a hand
spreading a word that had to be heard

and so Puck was flown to Hollywood
to tell the world that nobody should
believe the dogma of government pi
which, according to the Insect King
ain't eternal

"Because,"
Puck told Letterman Puck told the world
"Pi quits on
the forty thousandth digit!
It just stops, kaput! That's it!"

he told the camera He told the audience
"Because infinity is propaganda!
And propaganda is conspiracy!
And conspiracy is data!
And data rules!"

Puck expounded
and broke out his abacus
and began his demonstration
on how to apply Pythagoras
and how to square root this
in league with the frequency broadcast to him
telepathically by
the Insect King

and "Mysterious Insect King, people"
        Dave responded
the zoom zooming in
showing him
rolling his eyeballs

                "And who exactly is
                this Insect King?"
                        Dave asked Puck

who conceded
        that the Insect King
        was the kingpin
        behind the distribution of canned goods and kerosene
        to mercenary out in the Rockies
        constantly in contact with
        the mothership

                "I see"
                the Letman returned
                        then inquired "What
                        is the purpose of the Insect King?"

                        to which Puck responded
                                "He's awaiting rocket fuel
                                with nothing to do
                                except bother me
                                with the truth about pi!"

                and "hmmm,"
                        hostguy sighed
                        and replied
        "let's take a break people and we'll be right back
                to hear more from this young man
                who claims that pi
                        is absolute"

but Puck never returned
        he went to the restroom instead

where he held his head
                blithering that he
                                never wanted to be

the patsy of the Insect King
who never should've been revealed to him
                        an intelligence just too much
                                    for the human brain to handle

                an intelligence capable
                of driving people
                to consider the limits
                            of digits

                    which was driving him
                                to the Continuum
                                        and out of his
                                                freaking mind

Part IV: Puck Chills for a Spell

then Puck lived in a nice white place
        with nice white people
                who treated him nice
                        telling him he was a nice boy
                            and nice boys don't
                                    compute pi

        they took away his abacus
                hoping he would concentrate
                        on more appropriate activities
                                for a depressed teenage boy

                                like stamp collecting or muscle cars
                                    or comic books or masturbation

but Puck didn't give a rat's ass
        about anything except
                his muse the Nuge

                and numbers

                        and fish

                          from which

                            was born the inspiration

                                to lounge around in his pajamas

                                configurating formulas

                                for landing trophy muskellunge

                                on Raven Lake near Canada

so using statistics
        applying probability
                Puck used geometry
                        and what he knew of biology
                              in gamefish populations

                he wrote on the walls he wrote on the doors
                      he wrote on the ceiling he wrote on the floors,
                          scrawling divisions
                              until finally he lost all compassion
                                  for proving that the digits
                                      of a certain Grecian ratio
                                        were terminal

thus Puck was judged "healthy"
by a committee
who agreed it was time
for the boy to go fishing

and instead of continuing

to mess up their walls
Puck was encouraged
to work on his math skills

also   during psychoanalysis
         Puck had told to his therapist
         that the Insect King
         had finally repaired the mothership
         using methanol for fuel
         then split

So Puck was released
and certified "competent"
but only under the condition that

         if he go a-fishing
         he go a-fishing
         with a "custodian"

                  aka
                  me

Part V: Puck Gleans the Cosign

to determine the planes a muskie can envision
at twilight in the Boundary Waters
out of Eely Minnesota

(which is where I fried a pike
in butter over coals the night
Puck delivered his lecture

         to the ground squirrels on
         the physics of Einstein's lies
         regarding relativity)

Puck explained
         "E does not = mc^2!
         E = mc PI!"

but the mammals just chattered
at Puck who shattered
      the calm of the lake
      with a voice meant to break
      their chipmunk trust in him

      "And speaking of the Insect King!"
          Puck suddenly flared
      "He's now back on Earth!
      Trading in integers!
      With the Koreans!
      For Plutonium!
      With which to reach light speed!"

and quivering, Puck
      sat on a log
and shivering, Puck
      slid wooden beads
and stuttering, Puck
      babbled to the rodent masses
      on the arithmetic of space

"Which!"
      Puck related
          "Is the volume of a solid
          due to the vacuum warping time"

          "Which!"
          Puck declared
              "Is the erosion of planets
              alias the elephantiasis
              of screaming electrons!"

      "Which!"
          Puck raved
              "Whirl like Sisyphus
              that guy in hell
              due for retirement
              tomorrow at DAWN!"

then Puck went on
about the computations
of peripheral vision

      "Which!"
         he asserted
            "Is a trait of all muskellunge.
            And the reason these creatures
            pull up to their prey
            ride alongside
            coil into an S
            and snap like a viper
            frequently missing!"

            "Which!"
                Puck professed
            "Is why there's always a factor
            to consider when calculating
            the algebra of muskie DUSK!"

          then stepping up on the log, Puck ordained
                "Therefore
                to pinpoint the way a muskie would gaze
                to avoid the glare of the setting sun's haze
                you must skitter a jitterbug
                on the line of the norm!"

            Puck stormed
         "Because this is the hour
         ripe with strikes!
         And this is the hour
         to reckon the cosign
         of the Big One!"

hearing this, the mammals scattered
as Puck became lost in a tempest of beads
clicking and clacking
his abacus smoking

just like Walt Whitman
cruising through the Universe
making love to all losers and lovers and loners
with a Transcendental
Emersonian boner

Puck was riding the jet stream of gelatin madness
he was pressing his fingertips into his skull
reeling, spinning, murmuring, humming
portending Big Ones violently coming

forty thousand gone galactic signals
surging in his cranium
burning like uranium

Then blacked out
fell off the log
and conking his nugget
he woke up
sat up
glimpsed a chipmunk
and whispered to it

"1 in 2.3…

at 110 degrees…"

Part VI: Puck Extrapolates a Muskie Mutant

Rising nonchalantly beneath the blasted maple
Puck picked out a jitterbug, grabbed his pole
and meandered to the shore and cast
his buzzbait at an obtuse angle
divisible by five

"I've placed my lure"
    he informs a duck
        "along a ray extending forty meters
        parallelling the lily pad hypotenuse
        which is the edge of the vector
        scanned by all feeders"

                <<and>>

    a silver belly broke the surface
        splashing diamonds in the distance

                <<and>>

Puck's line wet tight
    Puck played
        Puck fight
        a skinny ten incher
        toward the bulrushed shore

           where he landed it and grabbed it
              like a three inch chub
                 or a common white sucker
                   awaiting the barb

I looked at the fish
    it was cobalt with white tiger stripes
        like a zebra pattern painted on a weenie
        it was a hybrid
        tiger muskie

"Like I said"
    Puck swaggered really cool
"the trajectory of twelve pound test
launched north by northwest
can stimulate a muskie's iris
causing it to sneeze

and so it sees
the glimmer of a lure!"

"But this aint a muskie"
I quipped
and flipped the northern
browning in the pan
"It's a crossbreed and
it isn't legal
not even
a yard long"

"Fuck Fishing Laws!
Fuck Fishing Ethics!
Fuck Thirty six
Fucking Inches!"

Puck spat
"I'm a member of
the Metric System!
This is my
muskellunge!"

and he took out his blade
and he stabbed it in the brain
and he scaled it and fileted it
and threw it in with mine

where it fried
until it was crisp, until it was done
until he offered me half
the flesh of his fish
and I accepted

just so he
got less

Part VII: The Forty Thousandth Digit

After dinner and the dishes
we digest and hang our food
light some farts and go to bed

though waking up to pop more pills
he leaves the tent
while I'm asleep
and in my dream
I hear his piss
sizzling on the embers

and I also hear the drone of bugs
rising with the sour stream
which I follow through the trees
forgetting Puck on Raven Lake

where finally waking in the morning
I find his down bag next to mine
still empty and unslept in

so figure he's out jigging
bullheads off the bottom

but when I rise and look outside
I find the birds are chirping manic
perched above his body rigid

in the Alumacraft
his sarcophagus
all scrunched up
like a swastika

one tangerine life vest pillowing his head
swollen purple

"Puck, you're an asshole

I tell his waxy complexion
not because I have to get his body home
but because he used my stringer when
he could've used his own

undoing the tourniquet
I wind it up and stick it
in my pocket with
his abacus
he died clutching
like a crucifix
birdshit splattered
on his chest

then laying out
a green plastic tarp
I pretend it's a tortilla
and Puck is the beans
as I slowly roll him
into an eggroll

Part VIII: Lugging Puck's Butt

For the next three days
   I see no bodies on the water
      as the two man canoe
         fishtails and wanders
            crossing lakes
               with no power in the bow

it's impossible to troll or drag live bait
   and portaging becomes a nightmare
   of muskeg and hornets and nettles
   and thistles and ticks and burrs

   as I haul first the canoe, then the gear
   and then the tarp
   which I drag like a log
   for rods and rods

                    carving grooves
                    in the mud

                                        sometimes with Puck's feet
                                        sometimes with his head

until just north of Rattle River
I meet a Christian youth group
passing by in kayaks
singing songs to God

                    and though I want to spoil their trip
                    I decide to forego showing them
                    my burden in the bow

                    so stroking on against the wind
                    I paddle onward
                    toward Long Lake

                                        a flooded valley
                                                ten miles long
                                        all of it
                                downwind drift

but first I have to get there
and so I put my mind on auto
and paddle and paddle and paddle and paddle
crossing lakes clogged with milfoil

                    then acid rain and thunderstorms
                    lightning striking
                    spruces on the shore

where I see a great pine hit in the tip
and see it superheat
and all its bark shatter
and know

                    it could've been me

                    but I am drenched
                    instead

the hours pass, my muscles ache
it drizzles as I sniffle
in the increasing wind chill
catching some flu
all veins blue

as a headache throbs
as my fingers blister
as an earache starts up
and I consider

                              how the keel cuts much smoother
                              when one centers all cargo
                              J-stroking on each side

so shifting Puck
between the thwarts
          I grab a squat on his back
          and find the zigging
                    ceases zagging

                    making it possible
                              to trail a weedless
                                        crayfish lure

and finally
fishing instead of fretting
          conducting lightning or
          getting ill
          I lose myself
          in applauding bass

          now I'm trolling
          reeling
          casting

I dig a moose
 and a bunch of blue herons

the sun comes out
and I thrive on ultra
violet rays

just like Tarzan, just like Thoreau
just like Grizzly Adams and
the Buddha, feeling
like a Zenguy

then reminiscing
my freshwater fish
history

      I start with sunnies
      move on to crappies
      then bowfin and sheepshead and carp and suckers

cuz there a world of species
beneath me, behind me
inside of me
and ahead

there is no final
six hundred rod portage
there is no uphill
climb along a swamp
notorious for
mosquitoes lusting blood

which is why the Chippewa
named that marsh
Two Dead Men

no
there are only creatures

and way more than

forty thousand.

LAKE OSAKIS

Kris is coming down from Fargo, I am coming up from Minnie
      in my father's two-tone
          orange/white
            van
                my yellow canoe
                    (*Das Lümpencraft*)
                    up top

        I write and drive
             at the same time
cut through corntowns
      here comes one now

                    water tower to the left
                    steeple to the right
                    one weathered sign

               "Welcome to Freeport
               Dairy Capitol of the World"

still

         I don't see no cows
         I don't see no ports
         and freedom
                            is relevant

                America:

                          godblesser
                            cornsoul...

                  . . .

Now that town is gone
Now Osakis

          bait shops

                    camping
                    cabins

                                        I stop for gas
                                        taxidermied bass
                                        black ellipses
                                        on their backs

                    (bass ain't
                    like that)

                                            . . .

Post office
Kris there
we head off for the cherry access

                    muddy ruts
                    cattails
                    brush

                                        we smoke up
                                        drop in
                                        float out

                                            . . .

apricot sunset
                        metallic
                                    tinged pink

            low sky
                        birds fly

                                    swoop

                                        dive

            Kris and me

we fish in the eye of a vast bird plane

thousands around us

heading toward us

they just keep coming

Kris is

covered with insects

soft moths

me too

good bugs

the birds are feeding but the largemouth ain't

we swill Miller

paddle back

cook brauts

. . .

and the Milky Way is rare tonight
the late August
Midwestern welkin
golden

we can see for centuries

. . .

Up North, this is the season

we freeze in

                                        the sometime

                        our childminds

                        try to find

                                              before we die
and when it happens
we're always surprised

                                        . . .

tonight you can see as far as you
can imagine
space has never
reached so far
summer has humped, we gotta wear gloves

                                    dockie hats

              we

                        smokum doobie

velvet eddies
in our lungs

                        cop comes

                                        . . .

"Can't camp here boys. Private Property"

                        "Awwwwww," Kris says, "Hey!
                              Ya got any panfish
                              in this lake?"

"Yeah   big ones   out deep"

"Wow!" Kris howls, "I'm from Fargo!
He's from Minnie!"

"Minnie?"

"Yeah! Minneapolis!"

"Oh," cops says

(Kris has
control of him)
"What they biting on? Chubs? Crawlers?"

"Crawlers"

"You gotta boat?" Kris asks
nodding fast

"Yeah," cop responds, "All loaded up. Gotta get out."

"So," Kris says, "where can we camp?
We don't wanna spend
forty five bucks?"

. . .

Walleye Saloon

"Ladies Night"

(they drink   2 for 1)

ain't no ladies though

just fish

on walls

three pound crappie
hunchback sunny

                              buck busts also

"Look at that badass mudderfucker"
                    Kris yucks
       "he used to be King of the Forest
                              running around
                                        always getting laid"

              "Yeah," I say, "but now he's on the wall
                    cob webs in his antlers"

                                        we drink tappers
                                        shoot pool

eggs hover
                    in clear gallon jars
                              turkey gizzards also

                                        locals never eat em

                    but we do

                                        and we love em

                                        . . .

There's a guy   Farm Accident Guy

       I name him this in my mind

              Farm Accident Guy
                              has a slash
                                        across his neck

                                                  his flesh
                                                       is red
                                                  the tissue
                                             has no beard
                              growth on it

Farm Accident Guy comes over
tells us where the bass are at

                                                           "Thanks man"

                       "No problem"

                             . . .

Morning

          the sun

                 flat and oblong

                             molten orange

     Kris boils black grit coffee

                       I smell stinking dogshit

       "Some dogshit"
               I tell him
                  "stinking"

          we eat

             donuts

                             . . .

Maple Lake

            shoreline

                     casting spinners

   the water's warm
             our breath is hanging

white like

the mist in the air

WHAM! spinner gone—

Damn! hand me another

THWACK! a bass—

little bugger
but still

I keep it

we work the shoreline

THHHHWHAP!

Big Bass!

SPALLASH!

tail slaps

northern now

YEEEHAAW!

big and green

long white belly underneath

then

nothing

it starts to rain

. . .

The Sportsman's Cafe

not even one

puny perch on the wall

coffee tastes

like a sock

but pie looks good

bananacream

we eat eggs instead

overeasy

white toast
hashbrowns
$2.25

. . .

tomorrow will lobotomize

the yolky taste

of this breakfast

tomorrow I start making

for another world.

PART 2

POETRY SCHOOL

1990–1992

SLAVES

I captured all species of sunfish
abducted perch, bullheads, painted turtles, small bass and crayfish
I took snapping turtles, quillbacks, leeches, dogfish and snails
snatched suckers, box turtles, carp and pike
I kidnapped water beetles, baby blue jays, grackles and garter snakes
heisted lizards, sparrows, rabbits, mice, grasshoppers, pollywogs
        fruit bats and toads

then took them home
put them in coffee cans, aquariums, terrariums
cardboard boxes, metal cages, gallon jars and
chicken wire

they were given names like Sunny, Raggedy Tom, Micky Mouse, Splat
Snapper, Chucky, Tweety, Fred and King Kong

I fed them
watched them
played with them
and buried them in the worm garden
back by the trash cans

they were the happiest
pets on the block.

Almost Frogs

Back when I rode a banana seat Huffy
I went with my onion sack/clothes hanger net
and plastic yellow five gallon bucket

to Mother Lake
a swamp on Airport Property

That day I captured 400 tadpoles
and brought them home to show my dad
who said
"pretty neat"

The bucket sat in the garage for a few days
while the bubblehead creatures treaded clockwise swirls
a nervous soup of fat inky commas

Then my mom told me to do something with them

Because it was a long ride back to their marsh
and knowing that they wouldn't survive
in the fast running creek waters across the street
I dumped them in the alley
where they dried into 400
flat black periods

still
this memory always ends
in an ellipse

...

Aquarium Tyrant

Sunny
who was caught in an onion sack net
in Minnehaha Creek
was an army green warmouth sunfish
vertically tiger striped

He had a belligerent upturned jaw
the odious sulking frown of a fish
who'd been neglected and deceived as a fry
and his mouth sported the sadistic twist
of a serial killer

Sunny was a pugnacious runt
three years old
but only half an index finger long
his growth was stunted by goldfish food
and ten gallons of claustrophobia

Here are some words describing Sunny:
malevolent
vicious
maniacal
bitter

Sunny's madness
lorded the aquarium
he bullied his subjects with threatening glares
guaranteeing mutilation
sometimes he'd twitch
just to watch other fish
lose control
of their bowels

When Sunny paced his battle arena
the tank inhabitants huddled behind aerators
awaiting slaughter

There was no anticipating the wrath of Sunny
nobody would stand up to him
not even the armored crayfish
who were bigger than him
but cowered beneath their rocks
avoiding Sunny's snapping jaws
or his skull he used like a battering ram
driving it into the kidneys of
minnows and perch

Here are some more words describing Sunny:
melancholy
neurotic
manic depressive
vindictive
misanthropic
existentially orphaned
Machiavellian

Sunny dwelled in a world of unresolved agonies
Sunny was driven by the lust for bloodshed
Sunny massacred goldfish
because he loathed their luster
and sappy expressions

Then one day
Sunny made a break for it
he jumped out of the tank
and I found him on the hardwood floor
dry and curved like a Frito
an oxidized finish coating his body
like a thin veil of chalk dust
his eyes were frosted ivory opaque
he had been lying there for forty minutes
I had to peel him off with a spatula

I swished Sunny back and forth in the aquarium
forcing water through his gills
which is how to jumpstart a fish
who has passed through
the threshold of death

Sunny revived
and continued to rule the tank
but with the ghostly complexion of vengeance
and glazed blind eyes like white hot pearls

We never threw Sunny out
we allowed him
to terrorize us.

RHODIE

There once was a bat faced Chihuahua
with a greasy black hide
and the coarse haired body of an emaciated piglet

That hoary old cur
had nothing better to do
than drag its worm infested ass around on the carpet
terrorizing children for sport

When I would go over there
the slightest twitch launched Rhodie's mood swings
I'd find myself scrambling up the staircase
its piercing yap fangs
snapping after

At that time of life
all menaces
were bullies
and gargoyles

and Rhodie
was both.

EXISTENTIAL DECISION

when I was nine
I saw my grandfather in the backyard
white exploding Einstein hair
bony varicose legs
he was staring up
at the power lines

I had just returned from the creek
with a blue plastic tub full of crayfish
and as I crossed the lawn
to show him my specimens

I found myself crawling
then sneaking
then holding the largest
crustacean

its gnashing pincers
were reaching toward a snaking vein
on the back of his
old man calf

I paused for only a second
I would be lectured
I would be grounded
no tv for a week

now
when I envision the flailing
and leaping
and the subsequent questions
I couldn't answer

I realize why the Stranger
shot the Arab.

Awaiting New Legislation

In the spring
when the carp used to come up Minnehaha Creek to spawn
it was only a few inches deep in the shallows
their gold finned backs rose above the water
as they motored across broken glass and gravel

Mike Adlesman and Mark Flackney
when they weren't punching me in the nose
used to splash after migrating schools
hurling bricks and cinderblocks
leaving bashed corpses in their wake
which floated and rolled downstream
to get hung up in root snags
or beached on muddy sandbars

Carp
are rough fish
which means garbage fish
because they eat the eggs of game fish
and take up space in lakes and rivers
there's a law that says
it's alright to leave them
gasping on the shores

but I'm waiting for another law
which allows us to do the same
with bullies like Mike and Mark
who are just as non-native
and just as invasive
as any species
deviating from
its natural range.

HER BREATH SMELLED LIKE MOTHBALLS

Old Mrs. Michelson
with her dirt gray netted mass
                    of widow hair
used to lecture us
on why to not run through her yard

sometimes
while she was hanging pale laundry
we cut through
faster than she could turn around

she used to wear faded thin linen frocks
which hung like limp tents
her skin was dry and rubbery
and her face was dusty like bread dough

to us
she was nothing but a bag of death
guarding a gateway
                    to nothing

which was
                    all she had

us cruel little shits
didn't understand that
        we despised her for what
        she projected
or rather what
        we translated

it took me thirty years
to finally finish this poem
        half satisfactorily
and not a damn
                thing has changed.

(revised 2022)

WAITING FOR THE YELLOW SHELL OF GREEN VINYL ANGST

in Minnesota
winters sucked

frozen hair
thirty below
tongue chunks stuck
to iron poles

    —Mark Overbee bloodied
     my nose once a week

    —I got in a fight
     with some kid named Christian

    —almost killed a kid
     by shoving him under a bus

then came junior high
and the bus stop hierarchies
the coolest kids went all the way to 15th
while the nerdiest waited on 10th and 11th

Rick Bishman punched me in the eye
so did John Jacobs
both their dads
were cops

plus
there were popping noises
in the inner ear
and everyone
had acne

I still don't understand why
there were only two
suicides.

ALLIGATOR GAR

I'll tell you why
alligator gar intrigue me:

it's because I found a belly up carcass
washed onto the mud shore
of the Minnesota River

it was white and pale
with diamond shape scales
it was also snaky
and streamlined
like a pike
and it had that toothy
reptilian head

I nudged it with my supermarket thongs
it was softer than a dead
fish should be

but here's what really
intrigues me about
alligator gar:

they don't swim north
of the corn belt
and they can't travel
through time.

(postscript: this poem was written at a time
when I didn't know the difference between alligator gar and other gar species
irony is that this popular misconception
is something I'm now constantly working to correct)

GUT-CURDLING CHIMERA

Once I met a water beetle
so huge and scary
and so far from its habitat
that it reached my backyard
through special selection

this water beetle was
a dry dirty creature
gray pointy furry flat
cockroachy and armored looking
maybe six inches long

it was under the picnic table
I saw it approaching my bare toes
and then it kicked into high speed

my mother grabbed a spade
and split that rat sized bug
it lay there chopped open
its skin thick as melon rind
its insides yellow green and meaty
all those legs clawing
                    grasping
reaching for a grip
        on some kid's
    tender skin

I then grabbed that shovel
and hacked its twitching bits
into the earth

chopping my newest nightmare
into chop suey
so I'd never witness
its horrific
strangeness
again.

Some Call It Elusive Rubber Lizard Karma

I was six
and I had this green rubber lizard
my sister and I each had one
and we lived on Minnehaha Parkway
and there was a walk-a-thon going on
mostly teenagers
in worn denim
they were marching for peace
and I was shaking my lizard's grimacing maw
at them

then a girl with stringy hair and rhinestones
grabbed my toy
and flung it into the pedestrian masses

I retrieved the lizard
and the next day I buried it
along with my sister's identical rubber reptile
thinking
He he he, pretty sly

because she was scampering around the house
crying for her creature

when I went back to dig them up
it was the start of a twelve year search
and a lifetime of head scratching

I moved a shitload of soil
but never found
those rubber lizards

go figure.

WE MADE IT

The event of my childhood
was the Spitzer Family Driveway Debut

the concrete was covered with black plastic sheets
and the backyard was swarming
with hippies and students
professors and neighbors
musicians and children

the sailboat was packed
with bottled beer and Shasta
there was a popcorn machine
and a spectrum of banners
hung from the roof

at sunset
the jug band burst into blue grass
and my nuclear family
ran with the tarps
unveiling an earth brown
avocado ocher
swirling whirl

pupils dilated
mouths uttered "Cool!"
"Psychedelic!"
"Far Out!"
"Fantastic!"

and the ten o'clock news
came to film it

that night
everyone else
had blacktop.

HIGHWAYS

Used to be
we'd take Highway 12
to the West Coast

it was a two lane blacktop road
winding through blue spruce forests
into ocher red badlands
across brown earth prairies
then snaking through gold rock canyons
and down into gulch desert vista

the towns
were named Big Stone City
Roundup, Two Dot, Culdesac, Naches, Packwood, Mossrock

now there's Interstate 90/94
four to six lanes of trans continental
freeway
Minneapolis, Fargo, Missoula, Seattle

all heading to
the same place

with a lot less stopping
in between

and what that stopping
always starts.

Below Pepin the Weather Changed

Caught in roiling Mississippi night spray
daggerboard jammed in the well
squall edge running us down
lightning striking shore and bluffs
pines exploding in white light
flashing impressions in negatives
he shouts
"Drop the jib goddamit!
The wind's too much!"
frothing waves break three feet tall
slapping us airborne
mast creaking
bowing
sail snapping whipcracks
boom swinging back and forth
invisible in black wet

water rushes over deck
bobbing logs, deadheads, snags
scrape by unseen
gouging hull

he wrestles the rudder
growling
"Custody week
And I bring him out here to die!"
I wait to hear
"Keep your head down!
Watch out for the boom!"
but he's silent until
I hear him say
"There's no sense in this"

and under the thunder
he whispers
"Let's ride the storm"

so that's what
we do.

After Wanting to Be a Comic Book Illustrator

and being pubescent
and feeling angst
I went for the opiate of sci fi
and somewhere along the line
saw a paperback on the school library shelf
with a picture of a bronze hero heaving bare chest
holding a fleshy warm mass of coltish voluptuousness
there was a fight going on
with giant multi-limbed lizard men
swinging gleaming swords and razor sharp battle axes

I read about how this earth guy was on the lam
and all of a sudden he was an outlaw in the Martian underground
and because of the differing gravity
he was able to leap for hundreds of yards
and hoist refrigerator-sized boulders over his head

I read it all without stopping
knowing I was experiencing something
beyond the universe of Green Lantern

meaning I had passed through
the threshold of no return

even though
I sometimes do.

THIRTEEN

Hunting on Bob Kennedy's farm
was an activity invented for custody
I just wanted to stop pushing through the freezing woods
I liked just standing there
looking around
through white breath air

though I can't say I didn't
want to kill anything

I was such a poor shot that I could never hit
a moving target

and then
I saw a few snow birds
huddling
and I blew them
the fuck away

there's no other sound like a shotgun concussion
jarring the ear drum

now
thinking of those feathers
fluttering in the gray
shimmer of smoke
brings back that shock

I learned how to kill
and how to hate
trudging through the snow
on Bob Kennedy's farm

and I accepted it.

WE CALLED HIM DOOKIE

though his real name was Tom Sendeki
he was a six foot four, two hundred twenty pound
    checkered polyester, snap button shirt
    larva of flesh
who always wore fat ass Wrangler stretch denim jeans
and pop bottle bifocals

He drove a brand new Camaro with white bucket seats
    compliments
of mommy Visa and daddy Mastercard
while the rest of us drove Novas
    station wagons, Mavericks and Darts

Dookie's house had metallic puce wallpapered halls
a hot tub, a VCR, satellite t.v. and
La-Z-Boy loungers with vibromatic options

Upon entering Dookie's doorway
guests were greeted by the grinning grotesque
of Ronald Reagan's pink lacquered head

Dookie's parents were from Texas
his mom wore a tent of sequins
and served us Dolly Madison

Dookie claimed his Camaro was the fastest car in the city
but all it had was a standard 350
with single exhaust

Dookie got into taking white crosses
that's when the race riots broke out
between North High and Washburn

Dookie was commissioned
to chauffeur the warriors
and the trunk of his chariot
was laden with guns, knives, nunchucks and bats.
They went out "hunting for nigs"

Then there was the Hub Mall rumble
Dookie was busted by the Richfield Police
but his parents had connections
and the cops let him go

    Now Dookie is a partner
in his father's construction company
they build townhomes in cornfields
creating suburbs
      without trees

There's a word for these
in the dictionary:
"slurbs."

MOTORHEADS ON THE EDGE

Us motorheads
were a bunch of South Minneapolis white boys
going to high school and living at home
where there were driveways
to park three hundred dollar junkers
and garages to adorn with hubcaps and license plates

we'd spend our time spreading Bondo
installing four-barrels
cruising the lakes
blasting Van Halen

and drinking 3.2 beer
that somebody's older brother bought us
from Food & Fuel
on a Friday night

four or five lanky guys
who otherwise would've been home
sticking pinholes in zits
were jammed into rusty Chevelles
or beat Cutlasses
we'd go over to the Hub shopping mall
where hotrods and beaters
sat idling with hoods raised
their owners leaning against the grilles
smoking cigs
sporting shades

sometimes
there'd be a drag race
two cars full of sweaty adolescents
five motorheads in each
ten pairs of sunglasses in all
lined up at the Lyndale entrance to Crosstown West
the light would turn green
there'd be a bunch of brake stand white smoke
the neighbors would be shocked awake
by shrieking rubber and roaring V8s
to test the quarter mile

a bunch of hormone raging kids
crammed into a steel shell
past ten smoking pot
often meant
skidding out of control

but in those days
being out of control
was having control
and we all escaped death
at least a hundred times
but never wiped

until Greg Little rolled in Wisconsin
bashed his head through the windshield
and died in a ditch

then
all of a sudden
having control
meant Toyotas and
and baby snot.

IDIOTS HAVING POISON CONTESTS

I have a chink in my shin
from swinging a timber axe all fucked up

I'm lucky that's all I have
left over from those Leach Lake days
when fifteen guys used to get smashed
chopping down trees when we couldn't even stand up
blowing shotguns off with double vision
driving 110 between bars and
puking in the parking lots

cigs and chew
cases of Strohs
mirrors striped
with lines of coke

we'd get hammered
and play with weapons

all of us
complete morons
testing the limits
of what we'd be given

as if what we'd be given
wasn't enough.

Driving Like a Jackass

I'm in the passenger seat
driving up the canyon with a guy
who screeches through every turn
like back when I was 16

when it was cool to cut
through a hairpin so fast
and the hubcaps went screaming
into the ditch

that was the year
I drove my mother and sister
through the redwoods in her Dart
on winding cliff road 299
banking so hard
the tires sang

but now
the canyon swerves
and shrieks again

this time sounding
like the Nuge.

THE NIGHT FLETCHER FINALLY PAID

I've never met anyone
with a smarter mouth than Fletcher

he used to work
in the hospital cafeteria
when a feeble old woman asked him
where the soup was
and he replied
"Over there, bitch"

I also remember
once at White Castle
he told the cashier
"give me one slider
a slab with vinyl
two gobblers
and a pack of nails"

then one night
at Cedar Lake
drinking Old Mill with some guys
the cops came by
told them to get lost
and Fletcher said
"Suck my dick, pig"

but instead
they cuffed him to a tree
broke six ribs
knocked his teeth down his throat
and busted his nose
with a baton

his smug sneer however
remains to this day
same twisted curl
on the edge of his lips

but not always followed
by what you'd expect.

Scoring Pot

Back when a dime bag cost ten bucks
all you had to do was go to Portland Avenue
between 27th and Lake Street
and head into the low income
black family complexes
where all the white kids
were exiting

you knocked on the door
said dime or quarter
or even nickel

they also had
or single joints for a dollar
that shwagg as brown
as dead grass

the door would open a crack
and if a bag full
of sticks and beans
wasn't passed to you
they'd let you in
to stand there watching
some baby screaming

at a spider web shattered wall
or a television blaring blue fuzzlight
the dealer expertly
rolling a Leroy (extra thin)

the next week you'd come back
to a door boarded over
but down the corridor
there'd be letter jackets
backpacks
a line in the hall
same stuff
same price

but after a while
it became almost impossible
to buy on Portland Avenue
the police were always idling with
those tall black generic tires

but sometimes you
could go around back
and they'd slip it through
a hole in the screen
which was risky

it got to the point
where I'd hear flat out
we don't sell to whitey no more

that's when dime bags
went up twenty bucks.

GRANNY AND THE METAL HEADS

I know a bunch of metal heads
who live in a house
next door to an old woman

when I'm at the metal head house
I look out the window and see
the old woman's window
there's a lamp in there
with a floral shade

sometimes the old woman
sits in the window
staring into the metal head house
watching them
doing bongs
until they pass out

then
when the metal heads wake
she waves with a smile
full of cookies
and tea.

BREAKDOWN

My steering was feeling loose
and each time I hit a pothole
the whole right side would shudder
so I got under there
and yep
it was the sway bar
the shock absorber thing needed tightening
so I started wrenching

it was more of a suspension problem
than steering

anyway
it's fixed now
and the bumps aren't felt so hard
that is
until it goes
out again

and it
surely
will.

INTERNATIONAL HARVESTER

A garbage man named Tom Smith
bought my primer orange Scout for 85 dollars
the hardtop was held on by electric cord
and duct tape
you could only get in through the windows
and you got high and sick on exhaust
even when
the lid was off

that's why I used to roll down Flagstaff
grinding the calipers
it was better ending up at the bottom
with burnt brakes
and brain cells

seems like all my cars end up this way
chassis rusting
frames corroding

in Tom Smith's
backyard.

SURVIVAL

I had this '68 Charger
a real Bondo buggy
bought it for fifty bucks
without any seats
tranny
or engine

I got a 318 and an automatic
out of a '67 Plymouth Fury III
which I bought for $65
and I got the bucket seats
out of a Road Runner

they went in crooked
and looked like bat ears
coming at you

when I got that Charger together
it kept breaking down
all over town

I slept on many residential streets
walked to too many service
stations in the night

eventually I sold it
to some country guys
who were impressed by the heater
"Feel that heat
It's a Mopar alright!"
they said

then five years later
I saw that car parked
in Southwest Minneapolis
same rough body
same mag wheels
some crooked seats

it had 2 x 4s strapped together
for leaf springs
and a log for
a front bumper

it was
a Mopar alright.

FREAK ACCIDENT

I knew this guy
who was riding at night
without a helmet
and he turned to say something
to his passenger

at the same time
one of those mongo hoary moths
the size of a fruit bat
was out for a flutter

ear met moth
at sixty miles per hour
and insect tissue
bug juice
and fur pelt
got lodged
crammed
smushed
into inner ear

stuck in his skill
like the wick of
a Molotov cocktail
it screamed and buzzed
its most desperate cry
into that guy

it must've felt
like a drill bit boring
sonic death
driving
vibing
into braincore

but all he told me
was he went to the hospital
and the doctor removed it
with a tweezers.

CREATURISM

I've always played with creatures
>   stalked creatures
>   >   captured creatures

>   and all the time
>   >   I've been telling people
>   >   >   I appreciate creatures
>   >   >   >   creatures have rights
>   >   >   >   >   creatures
>   >   >   >   >   >   over people!

Meanwhile
>   I terrorize creatures
>   >   imprison creatures
>   >   >   and salivate the fluids
>   >   >   >   of their flesh

>   >   but then again
>   >   >   to really love something
>   >   >   >   you have to know
>   >   >   >   >   how it dies.

CREATURES IN TREES

long the erosion of creekbanks
  root tangles descend
     tapping straight to the source
      of foliage moist

          where muskrats bore dens
           beneath twisting foundations
            beyond fusiform curtains
           where turtles dig in
             to sleep for the freeze

       this is where tiny sunfish hide
        the bullheads hunker and the crayfish climb
         this is where bowfin
          tread sulking in shadows
           where yellow perch nibble
            snails from tendrils:

                 the root hairs, the fibers
                  siphoning streamways
                 through sapways

        a resin   that's driven
         through the rings of heartwood
          to bursting buds
           burning green their instant
     here, in the upper strata
      grounded in oxygen
        there are different strange creatures
        visible in the shimmer
         of ripples reflecting
           the currents, the bloodline
         of trees   that feed
           through the slow suck
            of amber.

I Think That I Shall Never See

Granted
I was all flipped out on purple heads and stems
but still
the rusted brown bark
that crumbled off that fallen spruce
I straddled
was the most beautiful bark in the wild

despite gigantic wolf spiders
I dug my nails into that tree
spread my fingers along its contours
filled my shirt with its dust
placed wet bark in my mouth
sucked the earth from its pulp
crying because
it let me love it
in that moment

and I loved it
back.

FRONT RANGE VESUVIUS

this old-timer cottonwood
                        explodes from the loam
         a massive, gnarled eruption of rough bark
                                  tons of knotted densewood tentacles
                  mushroom-clouding the sky
                                       as two thirds more the Medusa
                  grapples toward the mantle
                                        poised frozen
                                                paralyzed
                        for a split second millennium

         timber too weighty for the tree to support
                           fallen monster limbs lying fractured
                  embedded in centuries of soil
                                    its own punk-rot, leaf-mulch and pulp

                  there were rabbits in history
                                          eagles and toads
                  they scattered when these ancient arms
                              blasted the earth
                                        cracking the sky

                              and it's all still there
                                       over the fence
                              across the ditch

                                               outliving
                              almost
                                               everything.

TREE TRIMMING

This morning
I was watching the trimmer
up in the locust
with ropes and straps
and I was also looking at the lawn
strewn with sticks and twigs
I asked him how he decided
which limbs
got to live

he told me
dead wood always goes first
but then there are the bogarts
branches crowding other
hoarding all the light

he said they had to be cut
to maintain harmony
and then he fired up
his O so melodic

chainsaw.

LIVERWORT

This moss grows like emerald brain flowers
sprouting out of rock pores
it is the fresh lichen of youth

but then with age
moss curdles black
and eventually
the scorching orb
toasts it gold

black and gold death moss
but still
more alive than its stage
the rock

moss has the liberty to be
and die
you see
and you got to be organic
to be free.

Fly Agaric

this mushroom is the prototype of evil fungi
it is the incandescent crimson
              ivory speckled spore
                  of sundry toadstool myths

damp button gleaming lethal
     this scarlet amanita
          is as deadly as it looks

pushing through the ferns and ivies
        of rain drizzled aspen
           these swollen
        blood luster multitudes

          these murderous melons
               these full gilled umbrellas
                    of venom

                       send a message
                         just growing there
                          everywhere.

WESTERN YELLOW BELLIED RACER

In a ten gallon tank
I dominate
an olive
mudgreen snake
winding around
a gnarled poplar root

it's elongating toward the screen
once again
tracing the rectangular perimeter
nudging for gaps

the tongue
an instant hiss of blackflame
flickers
and the racer presses
its bony head
into an upper corner
it strains
arches

but *Desolation Angels*
weighs on the lid.

Western Yellow Bellied Racer II

As I finish drafting
    a night poem about the snake
        that friends tell me
            should wind through saltgrass and live moss
                I glance through the lamp-lit glass
                and

it is looking my way
    holding two polished beads
        in obsidian glare

the racer stares
    it knows
        I gaze upon its strangeness
            which it
                was hatched into

but then it twitches
    coils back
        there never was
            a reptilian peer

for hours
    its diamond scaled length
        ticks and constricts
            pulsing breath
                underbelly plates
                    stretch slow
                        slither and roll

    Dawn
        and I know why I'm serpent-captivated
            it's because no one can ever
                fully snare
                    such alluringly strange
                spinal
                  twisting
            contours

                    when every word
                        is apocryphal.

THREE ORPHANS BLINDED BY NAPALM

Kowalski laughs at the snake
shoving its head beneath
a spongy tuft of dry moss

Kowalski says the snake
looks like the drummer
from Grand Funk Railroad
playing live in the Chicago Coliseum
1971.

MOLDY CARP

Some elderly carp weigh twenty or thirty pounds
they have scales the size of guitar picks
and when you float up next to them
in the warm waters of the cattails
they ignore you

this is either because they rule the murk
          or they have ick

you can tell if a carp has ick
because its head looks like a football with mold

there's not much you can do with an old muck carp with ick
      except watch it swish
        slow and gray gold.

SLIME

I'm through killing birds
and I won't shoot a rabbit
but I will clean a fish
and when I'm done
I'll have its blood beneath my nails
its dried scales stuck to my wrists
and the smell in my skin

there ain't no better way to be
than going through the day
covered by the scent
of what you love.

FECES SPECIES

Shit can be incinerated
gasses can be converted
and engines can burn the ideal

I mean
this is how individuals
are supposedly empowered

But as a group
        we suck the black blood
of anemia

the land is a parking
        lot of waste

        Duh!

Behemoth Bloodsuckers

I've only heard of monster leeches
they get up to twenty inches long
I imagine they look
like strips of liver
their brown spotted bellies
corrugated with ribs

lunker leaches lurk
deep beneath cattail stalks
amidst the bones of missing children

it must be that
these leeches are too slippery to grasp
and they kill whatever they catch
draining bodies livid
—only runaways
ever see em.

Manatee Eden

Somewhere in the world
(I saw this on tv)
there's dead sea desert
so dry the terrain is webbed with fissures
cacti don't even grow there

There's a crack in the vast
boomerang shape
it stretches for four hundred yards.
This spring fed rift is full of pond water
lush vines and ivies creep up the banks

For some reason
two manatees live in this freshwater crevice
they are bulbous elephant skinned creatures
with spatula tails
and heads like sacks of dough.
All they do is float there
sucking algae
living the way
we'd all like to die.

Dugongs Being Free

Manatees
aquatic leather skinned apparitions
gaseous mammalian bloat bags
phlegmatic elephantine
animated underwater intestines
bovine organisms of blue mud nakedness
being lazy
masticating
tropical
vegetation

what else
is there to say?

Another Non-Biodegradable Consequence

No predator preys
on "the Mississippi white fish"

I've seen them drifting beneath the Lake Street Bridge
flat and wrinkled
ribs exposed
rubbery round mouths frozen in open gasp

they float through the locks and dams
following Huck Finn's route down the river
where they end up in the Gulf
of Mexico

their slack hides get hung up on coral
bottom feeders and crabs leave them alone
not even bacteria can eat through their skin

But at least someone
got their spawn on.

Erosion

for centuries, creeks meander
gnawing mudbanks
as cattails and bulrush
bog in the swing
of sharp reedy grasses
lacing the loam
webbing back the spill
of sod clumps that crumble
exposing decades in ocher
striped rusty with gravel
layered in gray clay
remembering past storms
locust and fire
tornados and drought
in the swirling grit currents
which wash with the roil
slow grinding miles
the fine teeth
of creeks.

TRIBUTARIES

in Midwestern Julys
        there are slow roiling rivers
             cutting through cornfields
                    wandering the prairies

the animals born here
        blend with the clay

      blue herons perch still
            on rough bark and limb snags

        lead-yellow carp backs
           roll spawning in dry reeds

          mud-honed muskrats
              wind through root tangles

           and brown-striped deer flies
                swarm the humid afternoons

these murkwaters are fertile
              with currents
     and creatures
           their nests
    as well as their graves
        dark as the churning earth
         always eroding
             flowing
                downstream.

CALLISTO WE EKE

We're the erosion of windstreams
                    caressing the ice planet—
sweeping the orb's albescent contours
                    into porcelain moonpearl

See us from afar, dub us polishing zephyrs
but enter the atmosphere and you shall see fissures:
    continental rifts lace the shattered face
        And as you descend to the skin of the stratum
            note landscars etched deep with myriad canyons

Sweep down in valleys abandoning gravity
    rush with us through crag labyrinth carvings
        sanding down jagged glacial peaks
            crumbling silver bluff edges

And we the tempests don't make love with the surface
        our ragged tooth blades drag troughs through its flesh;
cyclones scour razored lowlands

    azure prairies with fang rubble gorges
        ravenous whirlwinds grind ivory beneath us
            jet current wakes lash crystallized badlands

Devouring this carcass while piling up mountains
    we jettison sparkling silt
        forming diamond dust dunes of foundation

Now this distant glazed sphere does not appear frozen smooth
    It's too cold to visit with organs and blood
        too turbulent for those who can't race with the storm.

Naive, But So What?

I'm not a hobo or a tramp
but I know how it feels
to hear far off train sounds

that drawn out whistle
cutting across still night
humming like a tuning fork
blaring lonely and sedate

it's like the drain of plasma
listening to that wavering wail
knowing the drone
of all other loners
calling me

to breathe deep.

SINCLAIR STATIONS

In a way
this green brontosaurus
has been resisting Evolution
for decades

these gas stations have remained pretty basic
regular, unleaded, premium
oil, air, maps
mechanic on duty

they aren't gussied up like 7-Elevens
they aren't extinct
like Skelly

so why are they worth mentioning?
Hell if
anyone knows.

TEXACO STATIONS

There used to be so many funky old Texacos
out in the desert
out on the prairies
wind worn with
red metal stars

but now it's fiberglass city
convenience-o-rama mentality

Corporation!
Corporation!
Corpse Station!
Discorporation!
ruling more
than just the oil.

THE BENEFITS OF SLOTHFULNESS VS. BEING A WATER BUFFALO

I would rather be a three toed sloth
rather than a water buffalo living in the African savannah.
A three toed sloth lives where it's lush
and a three toed sloth doesn't do much
but mosey around all day
hang upside down
and roll rocks over
looking for succulent bugs

A water buffalo
on the other hand
spends its time standing around
in blazing ultraviolet rays
sucking up mudwater
ribs sticking out
birds squatting on bovine rumps
pecking at parasites and the eggs they lay

A three toed sloth lumbers in the shade
it has no predators
because sloth meat is not palatable

water buffalo
however
have to contend with buzzards
who circle in shimmering heat
squawking
"DIE!
DIE!
DIE!"

You be the judge.

Alley Life

Never before have I considered
the culture of this graveled two rut road

I know there's a bag lady from Russia
who walks a butterscotch barrel shaped dog
and sometimes clean colored joggers pant by
being healthy
there are also raccoons
that waddle down this alley
eating fallen apples and digging through garbage
at night
their eyes are gold discs

and then there's the trash men
who come in different trucks
on different days
to pick up different loads
of domestic refuse
it makes me think
there's a garbage conspiracy
going on.

Biking Guys

These two guys just stopped over
decked out like superheroes
in fluorescent colors
styrofoam helmets
Spandex
goggles
and there were numbers and letters
all over their clothes

we sat around
and then they got on their bikes
they balanced there without moving forward
twisting around
pedaling backwards
then cruised on up the alley

I was left wondering
if I'd just been visited
by beings from the future.

Fastfood Consequences

Locked in a dime stall
at the Uptown McDonalds
one pink-haired white-faced punker
pumped full of Southern Comfort
drowns puking
in the turlet

or maybe
she choked

someone's mom bangs on the door
baby has to pee.

High School Geek

Ruby zits
waggly bobber head
Chess Club

Maroon highwater cords
calculus text
wizard of PRODOS

Alone at the lunch table
beat up at the bus stop
masturbating into a tube sock

There's a handgun in a locker
meant for exploding his forehead

We produce
nerds of bad aim.

Denver Strip

After working at MOTORS
he walks down the street to POOL/BEER
has a few beers
shoots some pool
walks to the corner of RESTAURANT and MOTEL
enters RESTAURANT
and waits for a ho
then walks across the street

in the morning he goes to 7-Eleven
gets a coffee, a TYLENOL
and some rolls from
SANITARY BAKERY

enuff
said.

SCREED SCREAMED ON THE DENVER MALL

Oh stimulating, virile, verdant world of business
Oh universe of lunch time martinis and gibson onions
lap top computers and personal pager happy hours
conversation orbiting Madonna and the Broncos
lipstick smeared menthol cig butts
smiling hostesses sporting after dinner breath mints!

Oh fastfood world of Rolex wristwatches
Oh rushing to health clubs for executive exercise programs
treadmills and jock itch
whirlpools and rub downs
fake nails, manicures, sparkling rock digits
wing tips, pumps, sensible shoes
hair spray, pseudo lashes
    lawsuits!

Oh magnificent, glimmering, crystalline utopia of business
Oh artful, philosophical, soul searching religion of crisp

                                        cotton
                                    undershirts
                        panty hose and high heels
heavy perfumes and cellular phones
three hundred dollar gold plated monogrammed pens with LED readouts
Cover Girl makeup, Cuban stogies
    deodorants and colognes leaping from underarms
        screaming clairvoyant the pickled presences of perfumed pits!

Oh fantastic, vibrant, gilded, godly realm of business
Oh glamorous entity of shellacked, scalp molded toupees
hair enmassed and constipated into buns
American Express Gold cards
kids aspiring to be stockbrokers
grappling to mount the three piece pedestal
    of numbers and graphs
enrobed in snazzy suits and fashionable ties
wound up like bleach fibered mummies
    in Arrow shirts and swanky evening wear!

Oh vast, golden, fertile era of business harmony
Oh ethereal forest of fax machines and Xerox copiers
dancing to the Wall Street orchestra playing Dow Jones symphonies
while waltzing to the neon lit noon time downtown hustle
then slam dancing through megamalls!

And the fartbag swarms flowing in and out of busses, subways, cars
greasy, sweaty meat organisms brandishing the quivering finger
through tinted windshields
en route to rave about consumer products and prime time television
    over Big Macs and Whoppers
cursing and honking in rush hour traffic jams
desperate last minute facial tune ups in rear view mirrors
    with goopy waxes and plasti-paints
traveling home to VCRs, satellite and cable
dreaming of new friends named Yes Sir and Big Guy!

Oh marvelous, poetic, romantic life of business splendor
Oh cosmic milieu of sterile dreams, lackluster imaginations, limp lusts
pale, flaccid yearnings
glorious investments
immaculate airports
fabulous embossed stationary
polyester golf slacks that rise above the navel!

Ohhhhhhh business life
you're all a bunch of Amway reps!

STEVENS PASS

You see them VW busses over there?
yeah
those white mounds
covered by three feet of snow
them snowbirds been here half the winter now

Out here
at Steven's Pass
I'm the Maintenance Engineer
my job is to keep the lot clear

But then I get them hippies coming in here
in the middle of the night
they park their vans anywhere they please
play guitar, drink booze, smoke that pot
have orgies

Far as I'm concerned
they're parked in the wrong spots

You see those orange cones over there?
that's where they're supposed to park
and they're supposed to do it in nice neat rows
but they don't

So
the way I see it
they ain't got no right coming up here
parking all over the goll-damn place

Soon as my alarm rings
at 6:15 a.m.
I'm out of bed
and firing up the truck
Now you just take a look
at this here official Washington State machine
it's got four wheel drive, winch up front
studded snows, CB radio
and a 351 Cleveland—

ain't nothing like a Ford V8 for torque
    Anyways
don't matter if them hippies got their trannies in gear
don't even matter if they got the emergency brakes on
they ain't asposed to be there
and I'm in charge

What I do is
I ease my front bumper up
to their Grateful Dead stickers
and I drop her in low
put the pedal down

I shove those damn kids up to the orange cones
where they would've parked in the first place
if they had any sense in their heads

Once one of them long hairs leapt out
popping around in his sleeping bag
like a ding-dang Mexican jumping bean
screaming and hollering
that I ain't got the right
... skinny little sucker

Hell
there ain't nothing they can do
if I want
I could get the state patrol up here
faster than they could yell
"Charles Manson for President!"
them punks would be busted in no time flat

Let me tell you
when I was a nipper
me and my buddies
all we needed was a jug of corn whiskey
and we was set
but kids now days
they got to go and blow their brains out
on that

LSD

and that acid stuff too
they rob Loaf 'n Jugs and jump off bridges
the guys go around raping women
and sometimes men
the gals go around getting pregnant
all the time
they're the ones responsible for all them abortions going on
and another thing
they got sharp tongues
sharp tongues and smart mouths

that's why I got to put them
        in their place.

GEORGE BUSH DEVOURS LARD

george bush goes to truck stops
sits down at the grill
orders one pound dollops
   of coagulated
         gelatinous
               bacon grease
                   sludge

he eats it bare handed
smearing it all over his face and neck
flashing back to the way it used to be
when he was a fourteenth century
flemish peasant dreg
   born leprous
wandering from town to town

    begging for scraps of rancid meat
and handfuls of grain
   spoiled by ergot
chased by vengeful packs of abused curs
stoned and spit at by children
laughed and mocked by merchants and soldiers
avoided by all travelers, peddlers and vagabonds
forced by law
to shake a gourd-fashioned rattle
to announce his diseased presence

Oh that silly george bush
he slept on church steps
in the gray plague dawn
and was kicked in the kidneys
by infuriated bishops and priests
envisioning demonic miasmas arising
from louse infested rags

and george's lips and gums rotting
mouth teaming with twelve
   different kinds of gingivitis

cavity blackened teeth falling out
one eye swollen
    sealed with golden crust
rats gnawing on gangrenous toe stubs
frequent loss of bladder control
haunted by waves of diarrhea
relentless facial spasms
digging through festering gutter garbage
seeking abandoned heaps of lard
tossed out of inns
    by indifferent
        scullery maids

Stinking
    animal
        fat
           is the fruit
              of our leader
                      it's his nectar
his thousand points of light
he spreads it like lotion
    on open pustules
shampoos it into his scalp
wolfs it into intestines
    where salty, pasty coats
    carpet his pallet
    tongue and throat
        and melt slowly in
           the depths
              of his bowels.

SANTALOPE'S AFTERMATH

One day Kris Kringle's elves
will conquer genetic engineering
they'll cross Santa with a reindeer
to create a highly efficient Santalope
capable of hauling his own goods
through the Christmas sky

Then   all the unemployed unskilled reindeer
Dancer and Prancer and Comet and Cupid
will be loitering around on Larimer Street
red noses and cigs
stubbled cheeks
reeking of urine and vomit
muttering
"shoulda formed a sled hauling union"
thinking
"never thought the old bastard would screw us like this
leaving us penniless and uncared for"
wishing
"shoulda seen it all coming
shoulda read the signs"

adding
"Santalope dropped our health benefits
initiated mandatory piss tests
Rudolph got shitcanned for traces of crack
but hey, he flew hard and he led the team
never missed a Christmas Eve"

so now they're living
the futile lives of welfare mammals
hung over shot up skid row stags
shuddering from DTs behind dumpsters
tracks all the way down to their cloven hooves
blindly reaching for bottles of cheap wine
standing in line itching at bedbugs and lice
waiting for the only solace of the season
an exhausted and insincere
"Merry Christmas to you"

from the volunteer nurse
vaccinating for syphilis
with the compassion of
a hash slinging
cafeteria grunt worker
and what do these cervine survivors find
in their stockings?
Nothing but a brick
of government cheese!

ONCE FERAL

For me
it would be interesting
to delve down glare singing pupils
past gnashing canines
into the psychic core
of a manacled frothing wild kid
captured in a Bavarian forest
flung in a cage
and carted off to the town square
of an eighteenth century
German village

it would be insightful
to experience
being exhibited
wearing nothing but the hide of my half brother
with whom I used to hunt rabbits
but because of competition for some she-wolf in heat
I ripped out his jugular cord
and ate him raw

and I want to know what it's like
for it to be miserable wet with melting snow
and what it's like
for the tavern doors to swing open
releasing waves of drunken fatmen in lederhosen
and how it is
when they poke me with their canes
commenting to each other
on my odds for survival
in the Russian woods

and having to listen to them laugh
because I scavenge bugs, earthworms, rodent carrion
anything that is soft and meaty
that slides down the gullet

they hold their guts
and HO HO HO HA HA HA
breathing bratwurst in my face

I want to understand what it's like
to be the brain trapped within that scowl
to seethe beneath that rippling brow
twitching with knots of human tissue
to be behind that incisor
baring grimace
that shudders like bowstrings
pulled taught to their limits
because then I'd comprehend
why that wolfboy
is driven to contain all his quivering muscles
until he can't take all the prodding
and laughing and spitting
and he leaps forward clawing
with such force
that his forehead smashes between the bars
and in that instant rush of rage
and with the sudden shock of pain
I might discover what propels that kid
to continue thrusting and forcing
his skull through those bars
so he can twist a mouthful of neck flesh
or a goiter
from the throats of his tormentors
but since that ain't the case
this is as close
as it gets.

SOMEONE ASKED ME WHAT I LIKE TO THINK ABOUT

I like to think about two Homo Robustus cave dwellers
meeting for the first time
while gathering larvae and grubs beneath mossy logs
they examine each other
tawny fur, slouchy posture, protruding jaw
jaundice rotting teeth

then one bares its fangs and the other grabs a rock
they charge each other shrieking
clash and hurl themselves to the ground
and because of a nearby volcano erupting
there are earthquake fissures opening
slamming shut without warning

many cave people have been swallowed before
specters of earth devoured tribe members
haunting primal dreams

I like to imagine Celtic Pagan warriors of the eighth century
with mustaches like scrub brushes
and helmets like huge chrome thimbles with nose plates
riding along with human head garlands
dangling at their sides
they bring these trophies back to their villages
hang them on the door jambs
neighbors come by to congratulate the warriors
slapping them on the back
telling them "Hey, nice going"

then there's a feast to honor the druids

And I like to think about 1976
when I led the annual Fourth of July parade around the block
on a lime Huffy one speed
peddling frantically
trying to stay ahead of the other kids
Uncle Sam was coming up on my rear
Betsy Ross wasn't too far behind
I was dressed as a bald eagle

cardboard yellow beak
flannel feathers flailing
then my pedals got out of control
they spun beneath me
like the steel blades of a fan
and I went flying down the hill into the alley
hit a row of garbage cans
a fence
my balls slammed down on the crossbar
and when I awoke from the pain
there was a circle of red, white and blue patriots
gathered around me
violet lips
bicentennial bomb pops stuck in their maws

I like to envision a nineteenth century pioneer farm family
spotting a swarmcloud of locusts on the prairie horizon
and I like to imagine the one they call Pa
running to the barn to get the horse and cow
then leading them to the house
where the one they call Ma
wipes the sweat from her brow
because she's busy stuffing rags under the doors
and in the chimney
to keep out the insect invaders

the cow and the horse become nervous
the buzzing cloud descends
the cow backs into a cabinet
Ma's collection of china teacups
brought over on *The Mayflower*
tumble to the pinewood and shatter
the horse is prancing around in the pantry
jars of preservatives crash and explode
children cry
they don't have much

in fact, the two girls have to share a tin drinking cup
and then sunlight disappears
the window panes darken with clawing, gnashing
arthropod underbellies

the air hums
the bugs dig through the mortaring mud
between the logs of the wall

Ma grabs a broom
starts swatting at them
Pa grabs the horse
the children try to calm the cow
And I like to think that gum
when swallowed
sits in your stomach
an insoluble clump
for seven years

I like to recreate the fire safety film
they showed us in fourth grade
there was this blond crew cut boy
from 1962
and we were supposed to empathize with him
he looked like someone named Billy
fresh off an episode of *Flipper*

we went through an average type day with him
met his whole nuclear family
and went with him to school
where he pledged allegiance to the flag
we met his teacher and classmates
played with all his little white friends
but Billy didn't listen very well
he played with matches
and that night the house blazed to the ground

only Floppy lived
Floppy was a wiener dog.

North American Roadkill

Fat Daddy skyscrapers block the sun
marching armies pack the soil
satellites and radar signals hoard the wind
all water is to be bleached and filtered
education sucks
art is a waste

Culture died in America
its bloated belly reeks in the sun
maggots squirm in pus under blood
this is the underside of an animal
that ran across the highway
terrified by its own shadow.

Ain't No Nausea No More

When parents beat their kids I think "um"
when AIDs patients die I think "oh"
when governments torture people I think "hmm"
when war mongers bomb cities I think "fuckers"

when somebody punches me in the nose
I smell the blood
and taste the mucus

but the only time I ever want to throw up
is when I get the flu

if the world's like me
we've lost touch with our guts.

POSTMODERN PURGE!

Last night I drifted limbo till dusk
floating down the dirtwater canals of some neural Amsterdam
watching subterranean brick walls and back doors passing by
knowing the muffled reverb of torture
was reaching my ear
veiled in the drone
knowing that haggard lesion riddled prostitutes
abducted as children from small towns in Spain
were zombie-swallowing businessman cum
of West German fat dads on their way back from Prague
knowing that emaciated junkies
surging with euphoria
were draining pain sobs into mattresses and skin
moaning corrosion
gasping last phlegm songs
knowing that runaway puberty buskers
purple haired flame spitters
who lie on busted green bottle glass
in the kerosene fumes of noon
were getting swastikas tattooed
on their eyelids
their foreskins and labias
pierced by nails

So I took to the littered allies of sanguine light
kicking syringes and soggy rubbers
cringing away from display windows
howling images of twelve year old boys
chained and strapped
lapping testicle sweat off ogres and mastiffs

Then
dragging my duffel down the steps
of a Heinekin hash bar
I stared at the already rolled sticks on the shelf
but went for a gram
of Afghany blonde
and stoned myself
past Pluto
and into dawn.

My Soul Is a Yam

a rich burnt umber tuber root
writhing beneath the topsoil
peeking above the strata.

I am immaculate!

He Sank Back in His Chair Like Christ and Sighed

There's this guy Darrel
in the plate glass cube where I work
he's studying Traffic Management
from the economic
government guy perspective
and I asked him
Hey, how's your reality?
and he replied
I don't know
so I asked him why
and he shrugged

I asked him if he felt disconnected from his environment
and he said he didn't know what environment meant
so I asked him what was the text book
he was reading
and he said
I don't know
and then he said
words.

THE DARREL SAGA CONTINUES

I ask him
Don't you think it would be better here
if the place was a moist jungle atmosphere
with palm trees and ring tailed lemurs
and he says yeah
so I say
Look out the window

there's a ten foot tall rubber tree on a dolly
and he says
You ARE NOT bringing that tree in here
and I say
why not?
I want it in here so it will influence me
and he says
No way
you ARE NOT moving plants

and so I say
You got to have the tree in here
not out there
and he says
The tree stays out there

so then I bring a small fern in
and Darrel says
I DID NOT want you to do that
and I respond
I want to be in a lush den of vegetation
I'll put it back when I'm done
I tell him
To be the green
you got to have it here
or else you don't absorb its light
so then what color are you?
You're a pale flaccid color
and he says
Then I'm a pale flaccid color
and he is.

I Sit Down and Write Furiously

muttering
breathing hard
and when I get done I look up
and Darrel's staring at me
like I collect body parts

then I realize I'm feeling crazed
therefore
I must be wearing a crazed expression
so I check my face
with my mind
and yep
that's how I look

Darrel says
That plant is not
helping you.

You Got to Be Organic to Be Free

Darrel says
what are you doing
with that plant on your lap?
I say I'm living the fronds
he says
What do you mean living?
I tell him
You got to be organic to be free

That's what all these arguments
with Darrel
are about.

PLATTE BAR

Everywhere I go
I talk to my tape recorder
and then I went to the Platte Bar
in North Platte Nebraska
the toughest bar I've ever been in

in one corner   Mexicans
in another corner   Native Americans
in another corner   redneck

everyone yard
workers for
the Union Pacific

the air was yellow with smoke
there were a lot of rolled up t-shirt sleeves
and tattooed biceps

the story reached my mom
about how I was telling all this
to my tape recorder
when I heard a voice say
"Hey, what are you? A Narc!"

she wanted to know
if I learned anything
from the silence that followed
and almost getting
beat the fuck up

I told her it just made me sad
which is not what she wanted
to hear.

WRITING IN THE CORNER

The Other exists
in Louisville Colorado
when I'm in a corner
of the Track Inn

the Other exists
in Louisville Colorado
when he has to show it's poetry
to be left alone
like a scabrous leper

the Other exists
in Louisville Colorado
when he's accused of being a cop
and all he's doing
is trying to be
away from the city

the Other exists
in Louisville Colorado
when he has to buy strangers beers
to keep from getting
his ass kicked
from here to Duluth

correct me if
I'm wrong.

BOMB ON PARADE

On television
there's a welcome back parade for the troops
one of the floats
features a spectacular
star spangled rocket
with a bulbous warhead

the crowd applauds
waves flags
cheers Hurray!
Hurray for blowing
the shit out of people!

clap, clap, clap, clap...

imagine
that.

TRUCK STOP

Somewhere in Iowa
a cornfield was paved completely over
and an empirical truck stop was erected
it looks like some sort of a station for starships
hundreds of trucks converge toward the center
parking in radiating lines
like the emanating tendrils
of a child's illustration
of the sun

at the core are treasures
the foremost being the holy grail of caffeine
others being
hearty meals, country western tapes
magazines, boom boxes, video cassettes
prophylactics

the most interesting gadget
is a machine that looks like some sort of blender
which plugs into the cigarette lighter
it's a nose hair trimmer
and there is a diagram on the back
of how to stick it in your nostril

now
I can't get the vision out of my head
of all those well fed truckers breaking away
from various mother ship nipples
rolling out onto the interstates
feeling the cool breeze of the road
up their noses.

MEETING A FAMOUS POET OF COLOR AT THE E CONCOURSE

thinking
yeah, happy to see things getting better
sometimes
but discouraged this ain't
utopia yet

I step back from the urinal
and it flushes

there are electric eyes
in the tiles.

Welcome Home Mike

the signs say
at the Denver airport
and it looks like the Fourth of July
with all the flags
the plastic mass production ones
as well as genuine year round
front porch Old Glories
with bronze plated eagles
mounted on pole ends

Mike's mothers and sisters
all bleach blonde extra mascara
wear perfumes that can be smelled half a block away
and his brothers sport purple satin jackets
"Doug's Towing" and "Coors"
embroidered in gold

there are two girls
thirteen or fourteen years old
clomping around in high heels
revealing the top forty percent
of new breasts
chewing watermelon flavored gum
snapping bubbles
while waiting for Mike
to get off the plane

that's the way it is
this side of the Gulf War

4-17-1991.

OYSTER SPIT

every masturbation
every wet dream
is the ghost of Walt Whitman
        sneaking from the netherworld
and poking us with his
little sizzler.

TOWELS

I took my dripping face into my room
and reached for my towel
but then realized there were two towels
and to be sanitary
I had to pick the proper one

looks like another
temporary
stage.

ABOVE TREELINE

Deep heliotrope
star scattered welkin
coyote waves wailing
embers crackling
plates strewn
around the hearth

the spaghetti is cold
we're naked and sweating
as something erupts
and flesh ripples
and collapses

chianti swirls
as she heaves deep sleep
into my shoulder

the moon glow separates
white hot orb twins hover
bore
through the cumulus gauze
of an elongated horse skull

its eyes merge back
the head dissolves
an owl calls

and all that's left
are lungfuls
of evergreen resin.

JERKING OFF
I REMEMBER THE RUBBERLESS NIGHTS OF OUR LOINS

I

masturbating I gaze
  the white arching stream
    it's been a long time I've seen
     hot jettisoned beads

II

usually
  I secrete in my sheets
    emitting fluids not pooling
     the petals of rippling
      roseflesh

        that sometimes other place
         I'm rarely graced to be

III

glimpsing the geyser
  I conjure gone nudescapes
    lost scenes
     peaking bodies
      naked
       in heat

IIII

below
  breast heaves flood
    the webs of my palms
     as those sculpted loaves
      bloom up from above
       our wailing
        pulsing
         inferno

    until another seismic creature
     is birthed in the magma

IIIII

unsheathed
      I withdraw at the saddest time
            the clawing time
                when tissue melts
                        into itself
                soldering cells
                        in animal fusion

IIIIII

      I lay wet
            across the valley of her spheres
            and fire along
                the spinal line

                      to the shoulder blade basin
                      liquid pearling

IIIIIII

she lifts her head
        giggling the distance
           the accuracy
              and I laugh too
                 as if there is victory
                    in approaching the nape

           as if some molten beast
             didn't die
                from exposure.

AWKWARD MOMENTS IN FUCKING

1

after months of getting each other off
    in cars on couches
        we found ourselves
            rolling on the carpet

    so we made a list:

        1. brush teeth
        2. turn off lights
        3. undress each other
        4. finally do it

2

the next day in the pharmacy aisle
    we decided on three
        boxes of twelve:

            ribbed, sleek
                and regular latex

    which was a commitment to thirty six rubbers
        or thirty six fucks

            which she couldn't admit
    to the male cashier
            so we waited for the hag
            at register 3

3

then came the clompings
    my ceiling, the creakings
        their floorboards, the snappings
            erratic sleep
    valerian root

                    but we kept on fucking anyway
                        waking up crabby
                            aspirins and headaches
                                '   though always horny
                                        for more

        4

then came the night my first poem published
        she brought champagne
                which I drank the brunt of
                        until sloppy drunk
                            I told her the subject
                                was her

            so we stayed up all night
                    naked and fighting
                        about lines like these
                            which she'll never see

        5

way above treeline
        the tent got soggy
                and drove us outside
                    for unusual sunburns

                    which the hunters at dawn
                        couldn't help notice
                            even her nipples
                                flushed in the dusk

        6

toward the end of July
        she lost inhibition
                it was the night I'm not
                supposed to remember

            but I do
                even though
                    "it never happened"

7

her parents detested
    my unprincely ways
        to them I was just
           some impulsive drifter
             hanging around
               to yank her pants down

       and oh yeah
           our friends weren't supposed to know
           we were humping

8

sex with X
    was always such a sweet
           cramp in the gut
           like the howls of an ulcer

  and after three rubbers
      I should've known
         we both should've known
           and by the fourth I'm sure
         we were aware

                of thirty six fucks
                going nowhere

    but still
        knowing never stopped us
        knowing never stopped

                 nothing.

Hotel Eastern

weary drivers
      besogged campers
            we yearn a shower
                  some clean sheets for sleep
                        a bed to sleep till noon in and

      counting our dollars
            a western pink neon beacons us

she sits behind the streaming windshield
      while I go in
            to the lingering smell
               of incineration

      there are pleated
               periwinkle
                    curtains in there

and an old guy sitting stiff
      in an avocado lounger
            scowling smalltown decades
               at a fizzling black
               & white tv

      he is bald with a bloated gut
            wearing suspenders and
               a polyester shirt
                  looking like
                        a rural
                          oldporchman

      the kind who grinds out hundreds of butts
            growling as he waits for squirrels
               with a stainless steel rattrap

      until finally some kids walk by
            on their way to play
               video games

and the codger explodes
      "CUT OUT THE GRAB ASS
           AND GIT OFF MY LAWN!"

I approach the old fart
   Carson har hars

    "TWENTY FIVE DOLLARS!"
        the curmudgeon barks
"CLEANEST ROOMS AROUND!"

      I tell him maybe
         we'll be back

   "WON'T FIND ANYTHING
    CHEAPER IN THE ROCKIES!"

so we sit in the car
    necks stiff from backroading
      while behind the plate glass
        bathed in the flamingo glow
          he blazes a gargoyle
            of gnarled constipation

      pupils burning through the rain
        like hypodermic needles
       piercing us
          with the feud of his squirrel wars

    commanding
    demanding
     us to enter
    his vacancy

        endure the pungent odor
         of corridor mold
  and crawl into those linens
        and Hump!

"YOU GET IN HERE!" he finally explodes
"YOU GODDAMN KIDS, YOU GET IN HERE
AND START HUMPING GODDAMMIT!
I GOTTA HOTEL TO RUN
I GOT CARSON TO WATCH!!"

          and that's it
          we drive away
            leaving him rigid
              gripping
              the armrest.

Shacking Up with Aphrodite

I've been told
there are good naked people
and bad naked people

      meaning some physiques
                                  spur suicide
      and others don't feel
                        so comfortable
                                        exposed

     well
        if this is true
               then I lived with a woman
                      who was an Olympian naked person

                         her body was streamlined
                         dunefully curvacious

        everybody
               male and female
                   wanted to see it
                      twist and arch
                        baring the rare pink
                              of nude valley blossom

and many did
        because businessmen with boners
               wolfing down patty melts
                    paid for the strut
                       of nubile voluptuousness
                          across wetbars
                              at lunchtime

     but later
           when we were waking up with cats
                    she was posing for four different
                    art departments

eating breakfast
        I'd feel all drooly
            and hollow
                and lost

        sometimes that anatomy
            shot cramps to my gut
                like the sudden slow spread
                    of spiderbite venom

then she'd veil
    those statuesque breasts
        and warmflesh thighs
        and go off to class

                where she'd shed down to
                the bodyscape I
                    aligned myself
                        to nightly

    and sketching   painting
            they'd strive to capture
        her contours because
            they were also
                        clinging
                            the instant.

IN YOUR EYES I SEE HIM LYING SHATTERED

We do it standing up
        slick lather
           spray
               shudder

      and I hold my finger on that spasm point
           and come because you leave the shower
              the house, the planet
                      in a shrill wave

leaning into tile
      my eyes trace rivers down your thighs
              while I hold you
                  in your swoon

      meanwhile, beyond the wall
         the hermit hears your cry
            and sees you woozy too

             in fact
        he sees everything I see
       even your
            returning gaze.

Hypothetical Last Time Ever

she said I'd never seen her naked before
        that always she was veiled by sheets
            that showers didn't count
                that my vision of her, that night
                    doesn't not exist

and she did not cry
        I want you IN me!
        I want you IN me!
            thrusting her pelvis spaceward
                her ass bouncing
                    against the futon

and joining
        the moist sultry sanctum of her inner loins
            I did not
                kneel between perspiring thighs
                    fingertip poised on her nub
                        triggering the dynamo
                            into ecstasy death throes

and she did not tug
        my shoulders down
            and sliding in
                catalytic juices
                    did not squish
                      incandescent

and electric fluids never merged
        and flashing tongue currents
            and swirling charged lips
                did not uncouple
                  to gasp
                    to breathe

and there was no wet
        no thick tepid wet
            no thin slippery wet
                no salty sweltery
                  drying
                    in the night.

A Poem for Those Who Ain't Getting Laid

An unusual thing happens
      when people press their flesh together
         first they get all sweltery
            then all moist pored
               and glisteny

                       strange body scents
                       permeate the air

until eventually there's
      a psychic Vesuvius
         because of all the rubbing
           and secreting
              and fluids smearing
                 pubic regions

                       —genitals
                           become Dynamos!

      fornicating beings moan
         now they are different than an hour before
           driving to their place of sex

        now they are patients
          lolling from anesthesia
            sharing
               spinal
                 spiral
                    spasms
            revealing
                    vast chasms.

CENSORED

It's always surprising
      how people pretend they never sweat
             and clung
                  and thrust
                     themselves
                         into each other

    how mammalian flesh
        wallows to root

           how bodies excrete
              their fluid selves

      how animals writhe slick
         and glisten with liquids
    absorbed into pores

        how brine is tasted
          savored ingested
            all the time

          yet in the aftermath
             in order to function
              nothing

                ever

                    happened.

She Slit Her Wrists but Lived by Accident

It was predictable
 the way she'd melt
  spotting strollers
   the way she really
    needed me inside her
     her fix

  how she'd peak and cry
   sobbing out omens
    lamenting a life
     without me:

    someone's brother
     she latched onto
      some guy she liked drinking with
       looking at
        exchanging whispers with

  some guy she prophesied
   brown eyed infants with
    yet couldn't fathom
     the torn jeans of

      Man!

  she'd cry so hard
   I'd cry myself
    crying and fucking
     at the same time

  every slow slide in
   a howling savored suicide
    every slippery slide out
     a muffled awakening
      in some psychic dungeon

      anyway
      I hear she's happy
       now that they've upped
        her lithium.

DEMISE OF THE THIRD SCOUT

the summer she left, came back
   and left again
               was the summer my U-joint
               went out on the mountain
                           and vandals smashed a rock
                                       through my windshield

it was the summer we fought
   on the phone, wrote letters that snarled
               it was the summer I slept with another
               and my driver's side door
                   fell into the street

      by the end of that summer
         my alignment was wobbling
                   and I discovered my lug nuts
                   loose on the rims

then she came back and we started again
   my steering gears broke
      the battery fried
               the differential began smoking
               and so we decided
                           to give it a break

         now it's been 5000 miles
            the V8 running smoothly
               until a few nights ago
                   when we played Scrabble
                   and fell into bed

                  where sweating and sliding
                  we came together
                     once more
                        for the death of my car.
                           (for K.W. Durango)

Epithelium Rose

peeling petals, I slide with the slick
   into sepal dew
      and wiggling silk lips
        to the calyx, quivering
           deep dark and pink

     and here, in the bud
      there are tremors radiating
       from the tendrils
        to the root hairs
         igniting
            like wetflames
      this is the most beautiful blossom there is
        the only flower
         I desire.

Maximus Poem

Oral sees
      the quintessence of flesh
            at the Trailways Depot
               in North Platte
                    Nebraska

    faded jeans
        soft seams
            arise from a fiberglass bench
            and soar
          to a unisex restroom
           forsaking

                            aging
                            dentists
                            gaping

                          in wake of suicide loaves

but soon!

    La Gluteus blossoms
              from bathroom
        and glides avec
            the underswoosh
                of curving cotton fibers

      and mounting Greyhound passenger stairs
          orphans
             poor Oral
                eternal
            . . .

                  Bawling
                  Neural
                  Laceration!

Oral flees
      to the Sabine sanctuary
      of ammonia washed tiles

the ceramic confessional
of waxen pupils
that stare up albino
watching men weep

and Oral beholds
water still swirling

whirl

pool

ing

whorl
pull

ing

she
had sat
on that plastic horseshoe

like a magnet
it draws Oral down

where

a fleeting derriere
the silk of Venusian Meatgrace
had pressed flush to the U

and Oral gives in
lays his lips down

a phantom
is kissed.

THE LUNATIC SHOW

It's more than terror
        it's the duneful smooth rollings
                whispering "kill yourself dreamer
                        forfeit the vision
                                sculpt in your lies"

        meanwhile
                wet woman skin haunts me
                        as I paint warm flat granite
                                pressed to the breasts
                                        of Phaedra spread naked
                                                beneath a bleached sky

the tongues of space lick beads from her spine
        the white hot currents ebb her dry
                and I feel a numbing radiation
                        burning from the steel
                                of a sneaky little vandal
                                        hiding in my entrails
                                                slicing organs with his blade

                                                and jacking off
                                                on the pancreas!

        it's the slit wrist jester
                vying for my attention
                        the third time this week

he strokes his penis
        squeezes his balls
                syrupy liquids
                        splatter and squirt
                                his whole body jerks

        then Phaedra rolls over
                and tiny pools shimmer
                        translucent on her skin
                                my gape reflecting back
                                        at least a hundred times

"OVER HERE! OVER HERE!"
the madman howls
mixing fluids in his palms

"WASTE YOURSELF! WASTE YOURSELF!
HONEYDEWS NEVER LAST!"
he cries hysterical
spraying spittle
smearing galaxies
in his loins

until suddenly I'm applauding
like a trained seal
barking out praise
for swirling blood and semen

which is much more mesmerizing
than evaporating flesh.

LACERATION

I remember a frozen december
  laying naked
      pressed together

          beneath down quilts, we made love
           melting into a pool
             of flesh sweating tears
            mourning the years
               gone tomorrow

    and with dawn
             we scraped the icy pane
        staring out
           at the frosted other side

        she took the cats
        and I got the truck
          and drove off

            wondering when will I die
             from not bleeding to death?

NIGHT DRIVE

I like being the only one up
  in the world
    but tonight every second
      the frozen road
        scorches

halogens shimmer
  families in black
    I have to
      can't

      eighty below wind chill
            blows ice through the dash
floating across Iowa black
            I sip styrofoam coffee
      watch the mirror
        the interstate
              Minnesota

          having just left the cats
          having just slept my face in her breasts
      both crying last night
            and now
heading into Missouri
    Georgia
    Miami
            places I've never been
              nor wanted
                  to be.

GASPING, THE MAMMAL
GULPS ITS FIRST ZOO BREATH

it's the birth of a beluga
  captured on Kodak
      by a thousand flashbulbs
        bursting their welcome

      "a magical moment" NBC tells us
        "an aqua ballet between mother and child"

          the crowd applauds, waves aquarium banners:

              "Hurray for the mom whale
                nudging the young whale!
                Hurray for the babe whale
                    gleaning the surface!"

gasping, the mammal
  gulps its first zoo breath
      gags, gurgles
        sinks to the bottom

          EMTs dive in, fish out the carcass
          CBS and CNN
              show CPR
                happen before us
                  everybody wonders
                      why it died.

DESTINY OF THE CREW CUT KID

when I was ten and watching
  scrambling daycampers splashing
      after laughing counselors I

          saw in the hogpile one
            trampled crew cut kid go down
              kicking meekly, buckling
                beneath a thrashing wave of skin

                  the children didn't sense
                    any flesh beneath their limbs
                    they just Yahooed oblivious
                        howling "Git the Counselor!
                        Git the Counselor!"

so wading out there, I reached down
  felt a wrist and tugged him up
      unconscious, limp
        spitting lake

      and dragging him
        toward the shore
          the kids continued
            chasing counselors

              meanwhile, Crew Cut
                was collapsed on the sand
                  coughing, racking
                    whimpering, when he
                      woke up groggy, looked at me
                        said nothing
                          rose
                            and wandered away

though I did see him a few more times
  shuffling between
        the busses, the games
      the various tents

with a look on his face
like a cat that gets up
trots to its food
waggling its head through every room
just making its way

to the litter box
or some warm spot
never glancing at its
environment

once I tried to talk to him
but mouth half opened, glazy eyes
he gazed right through me
fingering his
lower lip

I told him I wonder
What if I
had never been there?
What if he
was still down there?

but he could only answer Yes
or No and so

years later, I saw that same
brain damaged cat expression on
a milk carton, it seems

he disappeared entirely
from earth, one day
at Camp Away-a-Day
I guess

Darwin was right in this respect:

the population of crew cut kids
has decreased exponentially.

TRAFFIC GUY

having just smoked a bong, I shake off the rush
  and drive back to work
        to protect and serve

            for the cops
                who give me a Motorola radio
                and an orange plastic vest
                and position me
                    in the middle of an intersection
                        to make Buff fans turn left

            but many are hammered on Adolf Coors
            and many are adrenalized
                on first downs and touch downs
                and fumbles whereas
                    others are just assholes
                        looking for head-butts

I find myself
  growling notes in my tape deck:

        "O belligerent sports masses!
          O after game violence!
          O football, a Celtic game
            once played with human heads!"

meanwhile
        radio voices
                cry for assistance:

        a meter maid's harassed
          by a trio of drunks
                pissing on her Cushman

            an overdosed fratboy
            suffers from seizures
                at Hot Dogs 'n Beer

and there's a stalled semi on Broadway
where an old man's passed out
in a Le Baron
all the while
I gesture to the left
explaining

"No, you can't turn right!
No, you can't argue!
No, you're part of a system!
Tough Shit, piss ant!"

then a fat Texan approaches
tells me I gotta smart mouth
and prophesies the coming of He
who shall knock my block off
like he should

I tell him to get
the hell out of the street
I tell him to fuck off
and lose some weight
as another neat guy
in another Z-28
sneaks past my orange cone
guns his V8
and gives me the finger

and I'm a cop
Yep, a fucking pig
deputized immaculate
by the University of Colorado
Police Department
stoned rabid, incensed
shouting into the radio:

"Some Bastard in a Camaro
Coming Your Way!
Give Him a Ticket
He Disobeyed Me!"

but no one responds
   because other parking nazis are howling the air waves:
         one woman wails for barricades
           the paramedics can't locate the Chrysler
             lightning strikes the Armory
              and the Fire Department is on their way

then to the right, another Buff fan rips by
   burning rubber on the asphalt
      same chromatic shades
      same middle digit
        and I'm pointing back
          aiming my antenna at the proletariat hordes
            threatening eternal
           incarceration
              chastising my tape deck
                calling it the names
                  their fingers
                    stab in my face

static crackles
   there's a four car accident at Taco Bell
      medical help
          required immediately!

            and finally it happens
            another neat guy
            in another Z-28
              lays a strip past my orange cone
                and snags a loogie
                as he goes

                    I lose it, froth irate
                     kick one size 12 dent
                     in his driver's side door

kick it so hard   I hear the hollow   impact of metal
kick it so sudden   picnicking alumni   twist toward the screech

           as he slams on the brakes
            and emerges in the street

one six foot three jarhead
with knuckles like lug nuts
and teeth clenched
like the grille of
a charging Camaro
"Way to go!" someone in the throngs shouts out
"Way to go, Traffic Guy!"

No Names Have Been Changed to Protect the Guilty

Officer Von Leigh
howabout that night
you and your team
of rookie cops
raided our house
three hours after
the party was over?

we were sitting around
five undergraduates
watching a giant ant
destroying a city

when
without a search warrant
your platoon came stormtrooping in
and tore through our rooms
searching for drugs and stolen tvs
but all they found
was one wilting stalk
of Minnesota green

so then they decided
to kick everyone out
they barged into a room
Vic and Angie were fornicating
and because she had large mammaries
you raped her every orifice
with your salivating oglers

and when I tried to shut that door
you grabbed me by the nape
and something from your childhood
                    SNAPPED!

you tried to thrust
a 19 year old boy head
through a solid plaster wall

you tried to smash my skull
like a cantaloupe
you bacon fat bastard!
but you didn't
squish my brains through splintered bone
because I wasn't ready
to be another kid murdered
by the Minneapolis Police
and dumped by the river
I resisted   remember?
you burgermeister
                    of bratwurst!

you wrenched my neck
threw me through a door
and aiming for my molars
punched your fist
through the partition

but because you had trainees that night
you cuffed my wrists green
          and took me downtown
instead of to the Mississippi
like you did Mark Thorston
who was bludgeoned to death
by vagrants
                    my ass!

Officer Von Leigh
I wonder where you are
have you been exonerated yet
for beating up kids?
are you still driving around
looking for teenage skulls to bash?
and do you still live
in Richfield
          (yes, I looked you up)
with your black eyed wife
and belt whipped children?

what's it like
trapped inside a polyester wrath
navy blue   hating the world
despising an adolescence
you can't crush
like a pumpkin?
So here's a suggestion:
next time you get pissed off

    kill yourself...

                                pig.

To Officer Potter of the Cincinnati Police Department, Who

stopped a woman for a moving violation
  led her to a parking ramp
    and felt his hard on throbbing so

        ordered her in his back seat
          clawed her panties off her thighs
              then stuffed them down her throat and jammed
              his cock inside

Officer Potter, I would like some information please
      Did you cuff her first then
        beat her senseless afterwards
        or was it the other way around?

        and did you shove your pecker in
          something warm, something alive
          though dry, not wet
            because no vagina is ever wet
            for you?

                and did you do this, Officer Potter
                    for the same reason a split
                      knuckle mechanic
                        kicks a fender or

                did you grow up accustomed to
                  your sisters forced to masturbate
                    your alcoholic father?

Officer Potter, you have had the following thoughts
    in the following order:

        1) nobody respects an Officer of the Law
        and 2) just a little pussy... that's all I need

Officer Potter, a citizen cried
  beneath your billy club
      pressing purple
            the tendons of her neck

as you grunted, farted, squirted
then pulled out limp because
this is the price America pays
to keep the general peace:

one reported inner city pigrape
for every dozen committed

well, Officer Potter, it seems to me
that what we see is the way it is

and what we see are your pale buns
clenching as you shoot your wad
gritting, squinting, whispering
"bitch..."

so anyway, Officer Potter, you are going to jail
where you will meet a big black man
who will ram your head in the toilet
growling "Motherfucking
Whitetrash
Honkeycop!"

while you whimper
as he fucks you

Officer Potter,
enjoy your next
twenty years.

American Bile

Back when I was arrested by the Secret Service for
  writing hate letters to the CIA
      FBI and President
        I only suspected the shadow government
          of mass slaughter
            genocide torture

      "Why'd you write those letters?" they asked
      and that's when I learned
        Americans can't write about
        what really ticks them off
        without some thugs
          coming to their house
          their school their work
          to make them shut
          their mouths

"Because," I told them, "I want to be on
    The List!"

      "What list?" they asked

      "You know, the list of those opposed
        to secret murders like
               JFK
                  RFK
                    MLK
                      El Salvador
                          Etcetera"
"Why would you want to be on that list?"

      "Because," I shot back, "I don't wanna march around
      chanting, thrusting signs around!
        And I don't wanna get beat up
        by polyesters pigs no more!
        And I want to be counted
          among those who take the risk for me
          so I don't get silenced
          in my sleep!"
"Well," they told me, "there's no list like you suggest
    but we'll be happy to put you on another list:
      the U.S. Marshall's directory of

possible assassins. You see
each year the President receives
2000 anonymous death threats and we
like to keep handwriting samples
of those who pose a threat to him"

so they made me copy
in printing and in cursive
these patriotic anecdotes:

"The Constitution protects the country"
"The President is for the people"
"In God we trust, America
the beautiful"

then pledging allegiance, they let me go
to consider my rebellious behavior but I
decided that they
didn't just blow Kennedy away
those fascist civil servants they
blew the brains out of all of us
they assassinated the freedom of my generation
before we ever had any
Goddammit!

so to the next Godbless-America Vietnam vet who tells me
"You punk kid, I fought the gooks
so you can smoke your smack, your crack
your holy pot"
I say

"Thanks for the buzz, you brainwashed motherfucker
it sure makes it easier not to taste
the blood you splattered for the warlords.
Can I please have some more
chemicals please?
I'm starting to wake up and I just
might teach your kids
to write about what twists their guts!"

. . .

and so I wait
and so all of us wait
for guns to send us home.

Secret Service, Here's Something Else for My File

And what about squawfish
  the western trash fish
    whose upstream runs are dammed?

      even the Navajos don't give a damn
        concrete means jobs
            and people want bitchin' Camaros
            and townhomes
            and remote control

            and to crawl inside cubes
            and crowd each other
            and breathe germs
            and infest each other

who needs the Japanese?
who needs the Americans?
who needs anybody?

                    I want to kill the President

                    I want to kill the Fat Daddies

                    I want to kill the Europeans

                    I want to kill the orphans

                    I want to kill the Third World

    the first kingdom
      the only kingdom
          is the animal kingdom
          and the rest
                  is a ghetto!

JAMAICA, NO PROBLEM

when the booze cruise brought the tourists to
  the island smoking ganja we
      cut more lines, slammed more rum
      then paused to watch
        a Jamaican kid

          kicking sand, sprinting fast
          but not fast enough
             to flee four guys

               who caught him, held him
               then proceeded to stomp
                 his head, his skull
                 sucking up
                   dry white sand

"Haw! Haw! Haw!" the tourists guffawed
  an excellent fight, realistic blood

    "Haw! Haw! Haw!" they yucked away
      these Canadians, these Japanese
        these blind Swiss
        on holiday

          laughing as a carcass
            got hauled away
               for stealing chicken

             and someone cried out
                  "Jamaica...
                No Problem!"

    Bullshit!

  his wide wet eyes had been locked on mine
    bugging as they gasped for vision
      like the lungs of
        a choking victim

it was the piercing look a deadboy casts
    when his heart has stopped
        but his brain's still ticking

                                and so
                    the ocean was the place to go
                    snorkeling amidst the coral where
                        I gazed amazed at the patterns ingrained
                        in brain coral while
                                the tourists partied on
                                in a cocaine haze

                                one less mother
                                fucker in the world.

Rural Pimps on TV

in Jordan Minnesota
the highest structure is the water tower
and the second highest
is Saint John's Church

here, it seems
they had a sex scandal
a family named Cermak
was prostituting children

uncles were in on it
aunts were in on it
      moms, dads
grandparents
it was all going on
in a trailer park

then the public schools found out
and television crews
filmed elder Cermaks
getting handcuffed
      and taken away

they looked languid
      and pale
like wandering monks

and in the background:
one of those water towers
silver and cylindrical
cone shaped on top

a construction of the railroad.

RV ROMANS IN ALUMINUM SIDED CHARIOTS SECRETING LACTIC LUST

descending from their Winnebago Olympus
a larded family from suburban Milwaukee
steps to KOA earth
as would a bovine herd
of bloated jolly Armstrongs

legs of gelatinous wobblepork
arms of varicose blubber
they erect a pygmalion shrine
to sanguine slabs o' steak
   draining
      on sizzling
        grease-capped coals

moo moo mooing
they strut about the charcoal
digestive acids bubbling volcanic
   then the first kiss of Pepsi nectar
   the initial caress of cupcake bliss
      opiates tantalizing
        intestinal linings

there is orgasm of esophagi
like new-to-puberty boys
ejaculating in Sears cotton undershorts
at the sight of candy-lipped school girls
bopping promiscuous pendulums
   the mutton of pale skin veiled buttocks

thrive carnivores thrive!
devour!
cataclysm glutcattle cannibals
of salivary nymphoglands
everstarving the fast fuck of food

   metabolism my ass!

THE OLD DAYS

Orgg
Homo Australopithecus
wakes
          to the dawn screech
                    of reptile birds

Orgg
ambles from his cavern
          grunts down to the first volcano
                    remembers
                              forgetting his club
                                        so decides on a rock
                                                  to wield
                                                            in his next mortal combat

Orgg prophesies
          battling taloned mammals
                    or perhaps
                              the hominids of the meadow
                                        who chew roots and fronds

but instead
          Orgg meets a behemoth
                    jungle roving salamander
                    hissing
                              in its eggful nest

so Orgg conks it
          on the cranium
                    and the last amphibian
                              gasps
                                        gurgles
                                                  perishes.

The Truth About God

God exists because
        somebody's pa
                was working beneath a 72 Nova
                        when the jack stands collapsed
                                and somebody's ma heard the crash
                                the howl
                                        the hubcaps rattling

        and she ran to the garage
                prophesying nightmare
                        only to discover
                                hubby's legs slack and splayed

it doesn't matter how they were thrown together
        why they stuck together
                there's a chassis settled on her bed partner
                        dinner partner
                              pew partner
                                        he's squashed beneath two tons
                                            pinned by a tranny
                                                  murdered by Chevy!

        but somebody calls 911
                runs back to the garage
                and jacks the bumper up

meanwhile, ma prays and prays
        swings deals with God
                promises to always believe
                        foreverandever
                              to crusade for Christ
                                    and John the Baptist
                                        all the saints
                                              swears

        to push religion on her bridge partners
                to Push! Push! Push!
                        like the Krishnas she turned away last week
                      If only! If only! If only!

Please! Please! Please Virgin Mary!
God! God! God!
Keep somebody's pa alive!
ALIVE!

then somebody raises the car
an ambulance arrives
the paramedics do their paramedic things
sirens
emergency room
machines with clear plastic tubes
and the verdict...

Hubby lives!
HUBBY LIVES!

so you see
there is a God
somebody's ma knows
and don't you ever tell somebody's ma
she vowed slavery
to air.

There Was a Beat-to-Shit 68 Firebird

bleeding puddles at Red Nelson's

Buy Sell Trade
Cash for Cars

and being seventeen
masturbating car scenes
I was driven by the fendered curves
the vented hood
and especially the chrome beak
streamlined to cleave
all asphalt ahead

like the wink of Red Nelson
a man of dazzling plaids
a man who proved to me
that Bondo is sculpture
that quarter panels are thighs
that two bucket seats
                    worth 250 each
could've been sold
to a hippy

but Red had saved that car
for some teen seeking wheels
some teen who reminded him
of himself

so I gave Red Nelson money down
and drove that junker off the lot
dual white clouds
        billowing out from behind

it was the smog of bad rings
but it looked like burning rubber
and so I put the pedal down
until the tranny whined
a sonic rumble grew
and

                    BAM!!
the engine blew
            a rod through the block
and hot oil sprayed
                    rippling brown waves
all over the windshield
obscuring everything
except one loser kid with zits
        wincing back
                    in the glass

DIAPERISM

I have no yearn to be a childmaster dad
    to passion hug a fleshmass of unblossomed me-genes
        a pale wrinkled skinbag of leaking, bawling liquids
            to spend my dawns id-sculpting
                controlling, cleaning, teaching, amusing
                    a brain-thing that will grow to admire
                        or detest
                            or be indifferent to
                                its genital parents
                                    the world—

and why should I try
    to trial and error cultivate
        a sack of plasm-bound entrails
            who black night cries from boogie man horror
                the terror tears of not knowing nothing?
                    an infant who later
                        grows to howl from playground fights
                            and sidewalk scrapes
                                plus the wall staring aloneness
                                    inherent in the brand stripes of shoes

and then the much more lacerating sting of half-life
    involving slack shouldered, novice father moi
        paternal pessimist
            patting sobbing offspring's back
            declaring

        "I'm so sorry son/daughter
            it's all part of life
                that is
                    getting all ga-go and gooey
                        over another vulva jettisoned oxygennaut
                            whom you think you love
                                but you don't
                                    because you still don't know nothing yet

        "you were thrown together in the hot brine of loin lust
            your hand holdings and pelvic squishings
                were merely the preliminaries of pain

so now you feel like you wish you were dead
because you're alive and misery hovering
the angst horizon of Empty and Lost"

What would I do
haggard I-pa of the burnt past future?
I'd tell that kid

"now you know
we're all orphans and fucked
now you know
that living is standing death
the slow funeral of self"

yeah, I'd never make Dad of the Year
I couldn't tell the truth
I couldn't tell that person
that there was a point I dreaded slobber and poo
the excretions of you

that there was a time when the prospect of fatherism
rode on the same plane as hospitalness
and prison
that the he/she/it prophesy
of uncrystallized spermatozoa
testicle-circulating my seminal
angry young man tubes
was once as welcome as syphilis

and that the affection I now have for you
O spore manifested drool monster
is daddy sympathy
formed from feeling your failures
and tracking your creep evolution to ego
sans Pampers!

because only after you shed those plastic shit drawers
only then
was I able to feel comfortable holding you!

but it's the truth, you see
and say twenty years after birth eruption
how could I deny to that adult
that I thought and wrote this
unless I lie?
which I will

and then I'll even laugh off this poem
telling him/her
I was just being
dramatic.

The Rats at Lock and Dam #1
(A historical Landmark)

I

chewing a salted nutroll
on a Mississippi culvert
I jig for smallmouth
schooling in a swirl
of waterlogged sparrows
were milk cartons and bottles
bob in the froth
kicked up by the churn
of coal-loaded barges
awaiting passage

this is the railroad of the river
buoyant in the sluice
like a dead carp
excreting fluids
through osmosis of steel

upstream
muskrat are brown
they eat fish and freshwater clams
constructing dens
with green reeds and limbs

but beneath the Twin Cities
their pelts are stained black
and slickened by the current

here
they're called sewer rats
and have evolved a different diet
they screech through the foam
winding like water snakes
scavenging sugar
in milk duds and gum
and the sweet decay
of carrion

II

beneath me now
in the gush of bilgewater
colored gasoline
nine or ten rodents
chatter up at my nutroll

so I toss in a chunk
and a scrawny female leaps
exposing six swollen teats
hairless and tender

like her belly
thrashed open
by a flurry of talons
as if she were fruit

the whole pack squeals and rides her down
like a wig of squirming ropetails
the sinking Medusa descends
disappearing
in a spectrum of oils
sealing smooth
on the surface

then ten feet toward shore
the victor emerges
and swallows the morsel
again

the other rats, however
return to tread spirals
craning their necks
up from the blood
shrieking for more peanuts
and nougat

but I fling it on a passing mound
floating in the creosoted berth
and packing my tackle
I rise like the mammals
that migrated north
centuries ago.

Into the Boundary Waters

once I went way in
with Jesus and the Buddha
there were moose in the marsh
and loons in the bays

beyond Mad Snapper Lake
we discovered an island
with granite shelved cliffs
which I scrambled with Buddha
as Jesus
canoed off
for the Big One

meanwhile
naked, we dove
into cool liquid jade
ate wild blueberries
our bellies sunburning
all afternoon
until Jesus, empty handed
paddled back with the moon
lamenting two spoons
lost to a pike

that night we made Aunt Jemima
and had a flapjack competition
I beat them both
with my rounded, sturdy
pancake of perfection

then I worked my way around the island
casting a spinner off every lichened rock
the water was swarming
with steel blue northerns
of which I caught six
and one
that looked like the muskie
no one ever sees
but everyone knows
is out there somewhere.

To Make Snapping Turtle Soup

1. slosh through a cattail bog
searching for a jagged mossy boulder
trailing one gray tail
thorned with white spikes

2. menace it with a 2 x 4
and when it clamps on
chop its head off
with a razor sharp axe

      (do not miss)

3. bury chomping turtle jaws
three feet beneath the soft earth
and piss on the dirt
to discourage the dogs
from digging it up

4. split its breast
with a wedge and a sledge
gut it and scrape
all flesh from the shell

5. boil turtle strips
until tender
in beer

      (for a century old reptile
      this may take half a day)

6. throw in parsnips, potatoes
zucchini and sage

simmer
      its decades.

HOLES DRILLED IN THE ICE

atop six feet of solidified lake
on a twenty below Sunday
AM Vikings bleat
      touchdowns and fumbles
from plywood huts

in the White Bear Lake distance
a red flag pops up
I trek through wind chill so frigid
there are inner ear snappings
     spit
       freezes in flight

and peering through slush
I see a rising white blur
in the frozen blue throat
it's a crappie
I figure

but a northern erupts
from an ice water geyser
and slapping down on the snow
its oval spots bulge

so I lug the pike
to Roy and the others
and though I deny it
someone breaks out a camera

No, they say
You caught it!
a flash goes off

              Kodak.

SAINTS OF THE MISSISSIPPI

St. Paul dumps
chemical waste
into the river
Huck Finn went down

St. Paul spews
caustic tons
but only gets caught
when there's an election

St. Paul says sorry
pays the fine
opens an annual valve
crud gushes out

St. Louis looks north
says What the hell?
            We're already poisoned
parks freights
            on trestles

St. Louis drains
tankers in tributaries
            steel bladders
horse pissing
            toxins

and downstream
kids leap from banks
catch crawdads and catfish
make love
            in alluvial currents.

First Lunker

after all those crayfish
bullheads and sunnies
I finally came upon a northern
that couldn't elude me

serpentine
brown and green
it was stranded in a puddle
the creek gone dry
the first big fish
I ever foresaw dead

so scooping its head
into my onion sack net
I dragged it up on the gravel
where it tried to flip back
but I held it down
with my clothes hanger hoop

not knowing how to gaff it
or knock its skull with a rock
I held that pike
until all its mucus
went from slimy
to sticky
to dry

then my mother
came and found me
still pinning that gasping pike
still drowning it
in orange twilight haze

she went and got
the big yellow bucket
and the red buck knife
which I opened and poked
into its brain

for my father who gutted
and scaled the creature
and my mother who wrapped it
in tinfoil, placing
all of its inches
including the head
into the oven

where she baked
its white feathered meat
its predator seasons.

THE ALL INTRINSIC OMNIVORE MIND

first there was the Big Bang
and space began to radiate
expanding like bread dough
at almost light speed
forever

                *

then came
the slow roiling Crow River
which I drifted with deer flies
stopping only for fungus
on naked dead elms

the cornfields were flooded
and the carp had escaped
the winding churn
of cut banks and clay beds
driftwood and cattails

they were tearing at tassels
pulling up roots
exploring
new planes of black mud

while miles in the distance
farmers with rifles
set beads on gold backs
the crack of their twenty twos
carrying for acres
each shock
passing through the flesh
and ringing
                in the hull.

Romance of the Northern Pike

the Saxons dubbed them pike
        after the ancient weapon
    and the Celts called them Luce
        meaning wolf of the water

    up by Canada
        they wander the lakes
            never staking out territories
              like their cousins
                        the muskellunge

pike are carnivores
    befinned
        they vagabond
            from April to June
                splashing in the shallows
                    from sunset to sunrise
                    fertilizing roe

    by noon however
        they're crossing the lakes
            swimming wild spirals
                in streamways and rivers
                    seeking soft flesh
                      for their fangs to tear into

        feeding to seed
            devouring to spawn.

DOGFISH

heat lightning beyond
                    jagged Olympic black peaks
        the Sound shimmers burnt orange
                        and I recline
                                saltwater etherized

            thunder concussions
                        the apricot night glow
                my heart surges
                            and I haul back
                                        set the hook
                                feel the barb embed
                                                in cartilage

rain
    the drag whines
                    and I fight a creature up
                            into the crackle
                                of microorganics
                                            phosphorescent
                                                    azure

                        it kills me.

Wrapped Up in Bacon

my mother always asks
Do you remember that northern
I cooked up in bacon?

and every time I answer
            Yeah Mom
and think of that interstate lake
and that snake of a northern
caught on a grasshopper
plucked from the grille
of the 69 Chevy

I also remember the grizzled drunk
who told me, Hey kid
Throw back that minnow!

and my mother responding
Maybe if you weren't so intoxicated
You could see the proportions!

but the guy just swooned
on the dock
he didn't punch her
into the lake

which was impressive
having never known her power
over anyone else

then later that night
we camped on Long Lake
in a state I can't recall

and my father told me
there were hundreds of Long Lakes
while my mother grilled the fish
wrapped up in bacon

so I called her last week
asked if she remembered
that bacon wrapped pike
Yes, she said, it was Dickinson, North Dakota
The 75 Valiant
After your father

You mean, I asked
There was no Long Lake?
No wavering drunk?

Maybe, she said
I've cooked hundreds of northerns
Wrapped up in bacon.

STUCK ON BIG SANDY

1

he wakes me one night
three days before custody
"pack your gear" he tells me
"we're going up to Big Sandy"

then he drives the El Camino
and we listen to a tape
of him and his buddies
playing bluegrass in the basement

I ask him to turn the music down
but he doesn't hear me
and again he doesn't hear me
when I tell him "Dad
you're a horseshit father"

2

at dusk we reach the lake
and spray each other down
then portage through the thistles
and a peeling stand of birches
where sliding into marshgrass
distant leaping largemouth
slap ripples through the rice

and suddenly, I feel it
in the flex of the keel
he's stretching out
getting ready to blow
the same harmonica riff
he plays every summer:

WATER TEE TIE TOE!

the notes rise up in shockwaves
coursing through my calves

into the point of a barb
in the center of my fist
and squeezing even tighter
I lodge a lure
into my thumb

3

which we take to Skelly Gas
and run beneath cold water
as he holds my hand in his
pulling with a pliers

but it won't come out
so we wait for the nurse
who gives me three shots
which warm the flow
of an icy sliver
sliding through the meat
appearing beneath the nail
the bronze tip
of a needle

4

and later in the lily pads
the bottom is a moonscape
cratered with the gravel nests
of hungry spawning bluegills

sunfish after sunfish
they tumble in the bilge
burnt orange breasts
swollen with muscle
and roe

meanwhile in the stern
he strums and sings the blues
as silhouettes of sunnies
weave feeding through my shadow

"Hey!" he yells "Get that wound
Out of the lake!
You'll get an infection!"

but instead I watch the bluegills
nibble on my digit
until suddenly they scatter
as his six string hits the hull

resonating with a steely twang
that seems to make
no sense at all.

Bigmouth Buffalo

buffalo fish
are gold/brown and carpy
sometimes fifty pounds
sometimes sixty

in floodtimes they ascend
Iowa rivers
swarming the corn rows
rifling husks

farmers go out
with pitchforks and clubs
take potshots at dorsals
with twenty twos
and four tens

buffalo spawners
die by the acre
their bodies roll downstream
beaching in furrows

the survivors however
gestate down south
waiting for the rains
for a few years
as "gourdheads"

the populations grow
the females swell
and then once again
they break from the bayous
racing the current
into the heartland
into the soil.

Jelly Fish

something so slick
        something so wet
                cannot sting

        its scientific name
            Medusae
                is dogma

man-of-wars
        trailing orange coils and streamers
            are another creature
                invented to protect
                    the fingers of children

        but young purple sea jellies are different
            iridescent they slide
                through saline seas
                    washing up on the sand

                you can hold them in your hand
                    you can trace their ribs
                    with the tip
                          of your tongue.

STURGEON

there are myths of inland sturgeon
      reaching twenty four feet
            there are accounts of water skiers endoing
                and speedboats flipping
                        on surface lazing sturgeons
                            beyond a rod long

but actually
      these fish
            never exceed a canoe

      vacationing Republicans
            are the shamans of our time
            they desire monsters
                to blame for their blunders

          they desire scapefish
                as long as their yachts.

BOWFIN

grindle, grinnel
       cypress trout
mudfish, dogfish
       these are bowfin

I hooked one once
in the Mississippi River
off the entrails of a sheepshead
which it struck like a sandshark
twisting beneath
opaque in the foam

until it broke from the sluice
shooting six feet in the air
driving spaceward
like some primal dynamo
then back to the froth
then out again

for forty five minutes
I played the drag
and cranked that reel
fighting a fish
alive in the sky
as it beat itself bloody
on the spillway concrete

then ignoring my protest
Kris Hansen climbed down
and squeezing its eyes
into its skull
he heaved the whole fish
over his head
up to the asphalt

where jackhammering death throes
I stabbed its boneplated head
again and again
poking steel
into its brain

but it refused to admit
the river had stopped.

Last Sediment

Go to Hansville
    to Point-No-Point
        where game anglers trail squid
           for coho and king

head down the channel
    past Skunk Bay
        to the rainforest rampart
           of Foul Weather Bluff
              and tracing conifers Soundward
              follow the spires

        to the froth gauzed kelp beds
           where slick olivine sculpin
           pacific tomcod
              and ratfish and dogfish
                cross vast duned planes
                of musseled rubble
                  scavenging
                  decay in the silt

    this is the bay of Twin Spitz

           scatter

              me here.

OUT OF THE BOUNDARY WATERS

circling the island
landing blue northerns
I howled every strike
          even fourteen inch snakers
rubbing it in
because Jesus and Buddha
couldn't even catch a sunny

returning to camp
with my stringer of pike
          (and maybe a muskie)
this prompted Jesus
to blaspheme about Mary
while Buddha, hysterical
rubbed his fat belly

then a black thunderhead
          appeared on the spires
so we set out stroking
          for Crooked Lake Harry
paddling and portaging
          to beat the storm

it took two humid days
to reach the Impala
and the filets in the cooler
smelled funky and sweet

but Buddha used to work
in a halibut cannery
and he sniffed my meat
          declared it unspoiled

so Jesus driving 85
Buddha snoring in the back
we cruised through Duluth
past roadkill on the highway

to my mother, in Stillwater
waiting
          with bacon.

Viscera

I

if I could twist language into a fish, this page would be flesh
      and you would be pressing
           a stainless steel tip
                between the eyes of a pike

II

the silver cleaves
  the skin and the meat
      the incision deepens
         the blade touches down

         and pausing

             you sense the tension
               between metal and bone

                  and telling yourself
                 it's only a pink
                     fish organ

                 you press down
                     snapping the skull

III

as the knife slides
         inside its mind
            igniting the spine
               sparking seizures

            one charged arc
              burns its last flex
                  into your grip

        you clench the creature
          you grasp its spasm

                                        it bows, it slackens
                                                like the tendons
                                                        in your forearms

                                                                but only
                                                        for a second

        IV

because now comes the friction, the scaling
            the peeling of its shingles

                        as you lift
                                row upon row
                                        of its long smoky cobalt

                                        scraping the northern
                                                from the base of its tail
                                                        to its red feathered gills

        —WHACK!—

                        there goes the head
                                you see live striations
                                        pigments deep
                                                in the meat

                —POP!—

        you puncture its anus
                slit it to the thorax
                        then gut it and scrape
                                the cavity's lining
                                        your fingernails filling
                                        with thick spinal blood

            and there

                        at the end of the ribcage
                                exposed to first light

you see the luminous gland
oblong and turquoise
translucent
the gonads

V

and in your own intestines
there are acids reacting
devouring
something like hunger
but not

you reach
the end of my poem
ask so what?

feel whatever you feel
and forget.

Between Fall Lake and South Basswood

I

at the end of Four Mile Portage, I slosh through the muskeg
        while game anglers with radars
                prime outboard motors
                        listening to country
                                and waiting for the truck

                for days they've been casting
                        and camping and trolling
                                for days they've been fishing
                                      the drop offs, the deep spots
                                          yielding nothing

and as I stare at the fishermen there
        attaching bass-busters like pom-poms
                my toes sink into the mire
                        where I prophesy muskrats
                                in quest of pale flesh

                nevertheless, I wade further out
because wild rice and cattails
                              harbor carnivore lunkers
                                  and I know that they're out there

"Ya won't catch nothing that close in!"
        an old fat Texan yells to me

        but I know the shallows, the murky black waters
                and I know the summer
                        hunger of feeders

                                and the first cast proves it
                                  an enraged pike strikes

II

three northerns, six largemouth later
    I am slimed to my limit
        and there are no specters
            voracious in murk
                only meatpounds
                    of fishflesh
                          strung to my beltloop

"Goddammit Son!"
    the old fat Texan yells at me
        "I been depth-finding for days, gotta new sonar
            and now some kid with a Zebco
                pulling out big ones!"

adjusting his headphones, he fires up his bass boat
    and listens for fishsongs
        blipping in the bay

        "too bad for you"

                I hear myself say

                (but he doesn't hear me)

so crouched in the thistles
    I gut two-foot long creatures
        blood and scales
            drying on my forearms
                mud caking
                    a new skin on my shins

                    thinking this is the way
                    fishing should be.

Beneath the Surface

drifting sunset
        on a birch-groved
                lily pad lake
     I was fishing for red ears when

       beyond my reflection
              I glimpsed
                    a chromy white flash
                 gone in the instant
                        it glimmered

        though from this split-
                    second blur
          I knew what it was it was

       a twenty inch pike
              on a stainless steel stringer

              the kind with chain link
              and clips

then the wind blew my canoe
        into the cattails
     and I saw it in the ripples
                      expanding around me

   already I was heading
       back to that spot
   already I was searching
       that spark
              and spotting it

      I was diving to the bottom
          chasing some crushed can of Schlitz
      or a lost license plate

but it wasn't litter in my head
    and I couldn't not waste
      the last rays of dusk

so shedding my clothes, I leapt and I dove
        beneath the vegetation

                and

        as in the vision
                discovered the silver
                        stringer entangled

                        in the stems   and the northern
                                slack and albescent
                                        paralyzed
                                        brain dead

Stupid Fish!

        I wanted to strangle
                                its elongated throat
                choke up its confession
                why was it there?
                why did it do
                        this to me?

        certainly not
                for this poem, I'm still
                strangling that pike still writing to air
                        trying to make sense
                                of its weird pale death

                I tell myself
                        it was just some creature
                                some fisherman lost
                                I tell myself

                                this is the most
                        I can do with that.

Mating Habits of the Smallmouth Bass

1

sweeping craters with his tail the male bass prepares
                   the gravel commencing
                               his search for a ripe female

        then spotting one treading plump in the cattails
                    he steers her to his lair
                       where

           pressing even closer he blocks her retreat
                    swimming jerky circles

2

together they churn; the spastic dance
        together they scatter the jettisoned eggs
               revolving orbits in the nest

                  until her urge is to stay in the shallows
        thrashing spirals in the semen

3

but then the male bass breaks heading out for deep water
        gathering distance to snap at her tailfins
               when she comes racing after
                   quivering for the finish
                   of whatever it was
                          when they swam shuddering
                             together

4

the male smallmouth though, has other bass to spawn
        and so he twists   in the chase
               driving his jaws
                   into her gillwork
                        until she swims

                                    reluctant from the rushes
            which again, he scans seeking more swollen females
                  to force to his crater to fertilize once more
                              sometimes impregnating
                                        as many as four bass

          5

then just as sudden as the spawning
            the bay starts to swarm with sulking angry male bass
                  pacing craters
                              guarding something
                                    they can't understand

                                          yet continue to feed on

          6

finally however, the smallmouth young are hatched
            and the spawned mothers hungry
                  approach for the flesh
                              of the black bronze fry
            and that's when the fathers start flaring their fins
                  to make themselves monsters
                              in the eyes of the mothers
                                    who back off
                        but not from the thought of eating their own
                                    they flee torn fins
                                    they flee what they know.

SIMULTANEOUS BASS

up by Forest Lake
     my father lied to a whining camp counselor
        who told us we couldn't fish off the spit

         he told her we were friends
          of the family that we
            had driven from Corvallis
            1800 miles away
               to angle off this point

        so brushing on by
          we baited our hooks
            and casting past the bathers
             both our rods bowed

    together we played
         one lunker largemouth toward shore
          sure that our lines
          had finally been crossed
          sure that our decades
           had finally merged
            in something as absurd
             as a fish

yet nothing could be more serious
        for two men bound by digging worms
          creaking docks, boats and tides

        my father and I
         we are used to sitting silent
          staring blankly at black mountains
           we are used to cold night winds
            sweeping steely off dark waters

         the weather never penetrates
         we have waited decades

but as I watched him wading backwards   I could tell by his steps
      his balance was off

and by the arc of his rod
                    I knew his memory too
he was giving the bass
                              too much slack

              which was something he had taught
                                        me never to do

        and already he had forgotten this
              is the surest way to lose a fish

          and already something freon
                ran coursing through my bloodways

              to think that he would lose the fish
                to think that I would have to reel it in alone
                                        because he couldn't
                          do it anymore

but I was wrong   we both were wrong:

                          it wasn't one
                      monstrous fish
                              we hauled twisting
                                through the lily pads

        it was two fat green bass

                                    each mouth gaping
                                        the size of a fist

            until "HEY!"
                          a sudden voice
                                      shattered the shoreline
                    and we turned to see
                    an old man in britches
                              emerging from the birches
                                    shaking a dustpan at the sky
                                    howling

            "This is my camp and this is my water!
              And I ain't never seen
                        you two before!

so packing our tackle
we walked back to the Dodge
but the old timer stopped us
and tapping out a menthol
he lit up and said:

"You boys are liars
but I'll tell ya this...

ya sure do know
how to fish!"

then smiling two rows
of yellowed false teeth
he blew smoke on our catch
and told us to get
the hell off his land

which we did
with two trophy fish
we thought were one

and that was the last time
I fished with my dad.

I Beat Buddha to Nirvana

the Buddha
      sat cross-legged
            on granite
            watching me fish
                  the wild rice of South Basswood

I was casting my Mepps
                  into crystalline water
        it was rare to see
            my spinner way out there
                    with a dark silhouette
              racing for silver
               and striking
                  in the daylight

in that instant I knew it was the Big One
    the lunker I'd dreamed of
        for over two decades
            the muskie I knew
              I'd someday latch onto
              battle
               and lose

the water was rich, a gold iron luster
    as the fish passed beneath me
        barrel-rolled twice
            white tiger stripes
              flashed by in copper

                  like seconds, like hours

                  its length too enormous
                  to measure in inches

and then with a twitch it snapped the leader
        heading out toward deep water
            as its dorsal rose once
                cobalt
                  then never
        up on the rock, I heard Buddha gasp
        he was still straining
            for that seventh level.

Beneath 3M

I saw it primeval
a fossil survivor
glumming on the shore
of an industrial marsh
one rusty spoon
dangling from its jaw

the dogfish was scaled
a gray olive-brown
one orange spot
glowing on its tail

which meant it was male
at least twelve years old
maybe twenty

       it's impossible to tell
       when they get this old

so lowering my worm
in front of its face
it lurched like a viper
gulping down the whole leader
even the sinker

there was no way to hold
that splashing, thrashing
grand-daddy dogfish
suddenly remembering
the cold burn of steel

like a missile it shot
alive from the froth
skyward, flaring
its fins, its gills

whip-cracking girth
with a lash that could've
blackeyed a human
or knocked out a tooth

and all I had was six-pound test

which it wound itself into
plummeting spirals, back to the shallows

where once in the water
it jerked our connection
snapping the line

and swam off
as dogfish do

skimming the surface.

No Fish Suffers Like a Creek Carp

1

they spawn in September
swim upstream in packs
gold bellies grinding
the gravel, the glass

2

urban bullies
emerge from alleys
and descend on the creekcarp
with cinderblocks
and brick chunks

3

splashing after the spawners
they bash fish slime
into fish skulls

Creek carp, they claim
are rats in the stream

Creek carp, they claim
think unimportant things

Creek carp, they claim
eat shit

5

which, in part, is true
carp vacuum the silt
and they don't always
spit the shit out
this is what they're built for
this is why they die.

How to Catch Big Rivercarp

at sunset in August
            take 1 friend to the Mississippi River
                        spray each other down with Off
                                    bait hooks with canned corn
                                    and cast out
                                                in the current

            then sit on a sunbleached log
                        drink 1 bottle red wine
                                    or 1 six pack dark beer
                                                watch barges
                                                            guffaw

when a carp strikes fight it to the sand
                        haul it up on the beach
                                    unhook
                                                and release

                                                            (this is a bonus)

            rebait and cast out
                        recount the scales of the creature

                                    translucent and amber
                                                like guitar picks
                                                            but bigger

                                                            watch barges
                                                                        guffaw.

BULLHEAD DEATH

wherever there are culverts
        there are kids with firecrackers
                blasting the skulls
                      of black bullheads open

            across the asphalt they're strewn
                  like pink-brown carnations
                          flesh blossoming
                                from exploded gill petals
                                  tissue curling
                                        and drying
                                  on the tarmac.

YELLOW BULLHEAD STORY

it was the most pathetic fish I ever met
        it looked more like
                an inner-city
                      bottom-feeder
                              than a cornfield lake bullhead
scars ran its length its belly was tumored
        whiskers were severed one eye was poked out
                parasites hung
                      from its lopsided jaw
                          welted and rashed
                          down to its tail
                                shredded and mangled
                                    just like its dorsal
                                      healed crooked
                                      and sealed
                                      with a solidified knot
                                          of translucent
                                              calcium
so I released the beat creature back to the milfoil
        and the alleys of the underlake
                and as I watched it descend
                      like a shrinking slash of gold
                              the sun glanced off its sheen
                                  piercing
                                      my eyeball.

SCANDINAVIAN GRANDPARENTS WITH PEEN SCOOPS

eelpout is burbot
    lawyer and ling;
        a freshwater cod
            slick-skinned and long
                abhorred on the shores
                    of Midwestern lakes
                        for intercepting bait
                            meant for lake trout
                            and walleye

except in Winona   where there are ice fishing contests
        in which old parkaed husbands
            and snowsuited wives
                sit on overturned buckets
                    staring through slush
                        debating the flesh
                          of an eelpout

      "It's acrid, not edible"
          argues someone's gramma
        to someone's grandpa
            who claims "No, it's oily
          not flaky"
              according, that is
                to his cousin Sven
             who once cooked an eelpout
                in Wisconsin   youbetchya!

and so every winter these anglers return
    to sit and jig huddling
        in ice huts, in trucks
          rehashing the pouts
            of the previous season
                switching subjects sometimes
                    to the Vikings or Packers
                  but mostly just waiting
                      with whiskey, a fish bat
                        and subzero patience

              for eelpout
                  to happen.

Beneath the Twelfth Avenue Bridge

when the Wagner brothers weren't up on the keystone
    snagging goobers, calling me pussy
        I'd stray from the sun
            enter the underbridge dank
            and inhale the waft
                of bitter human piss

there were words on the walls
    like NIGGER and FUCK
        and there was broken bottle glass
            scattered amidst
                the condoms and tampon
                  applicators strewn
                  like dead fish on the gravel

sometimes stalagmites
    would drop on my hair
        shattering with a splash
        of light fluid crystal

and the swallows of the girders
    were screechers and swoopers
        they'd dive-bomb my face
            while the bats just hung there
                motley and fleshy-eared
                  wrapped in black skin
but beneath worn tires, cinderblocks and bricks
    in rusty cans, in rotten shoes
        there were broken-claw crayfish
        gnashing raw meat

and all along the limestone walls
    at the base of the arch
        there were torn lesioned bullheads
            skin flaps peeled back
            sour milk flesh
                exposed to the current

which is why I went beneath
    the Twelfth Avenue Bridge
        because this is where the creatures were
        and this is where
        I made museums.

On Maroon Vinyl Stools

up north, there are taverns
            with crescenting northerns
                        lacquered and mounted
                                    on pinewood stained walls

                                                red/silver spoons
                                                            dangling from jaws

    up here, I drink beer
                chew corn nuts, gnaw jerky
                        gazing past walleye
                                    crappies and bass

                                        watching these
                                                    beer clock scenes:

        a metallic green pheasant
                    struts through the cornrows
                                its brown stripy belly
                                        ruffled and muscled

            a burly Hamms bear
                        ambles revolving
                                    sky blue waters
                                            shimmer like diamonds

and scanning the counter, there are pickled pork hocks
                preserved and submerged
                        in clear gallon jars
                                reflecting back
                                        the worn ruddy faces
                                                which remember the weather

        these old men of sun and wind
                    are experts on live bait
                they know crawlers, they know leeches
                        they know fatheads
                                waterdogs, jumbo chubs

these old men, they filet their prey
with the precision of surgeons
they are used
to catch and release

and me
making up stories
of them and their glory

meanwhile, I flick
tiny scales off my wrists
staring back at them
and their fanged trophies

half these lunkers
sport brass plaques
recalling lakes, recounting weights
renaming the big ones
that didn't get away

I don't belong here
this is why I stay.

JOHNNY DARTER

you see this spotted bronze minnow
                        only in flashings
                                  they're there
                                        then they're not
                                                suspended in fluid

          one of their forbearers must have known
                   how it was to remain
                             hovering alluvial
                                        drifts of debris

this ancestral darter must've made some minnow vow
                   to break from the algae
                             into backwater currents
                                      and mossy rock rapids
                                      into creeks that flow
                                                steady always

          because now
                       you can't catch
                                      what you can't see
    and johnny's too fast
                                      for gillnets and pails

                       with the twist of his wake

                           he carves grooves in the silt.

SUNFISHOCIDE

I remember looking up
       from my bucket of bullheads
           quillbacks and perch
               as I stood with my net
                    in the bend of the puddled
                       creekbed gone dry

          as if unfocussing from hours of whittling
              my back bent stiff, my eyes resisting
                 I beheld a strewn corpse field
                    of gold bellies curving

                            like woodchips, their sheens
                               fading slowly

I told myself these are just
       common bluegills just sunfish I culled
           from the deep spots because
                          they got in my way

                their deaths mean nothing!

                       they are like bugs!

      then scanning the gravel, the multitudes scattered
          I can't remember
                scooping the live back

         I know only my decision

             was based on the if

            of a late summer storm.

A Stringer of Sandpike is the Machinery of Hell-Fire (1838-1899)

this is the epitaph of the Saugering Minister
    of the lower Wabash River
        who used to row upstream
            in water so roily
                yellow froth slid
                    like a watersnake winding
                        through the rough weave
                            of river roots
                                lacing the mudshore

    on Saturdays he'd drift, trailing a creekchub
        watching the banks for possum and raccoon
        and riverclam shells
            lodged in the redclay
                like porcelain shards

passing cattle, he'd scan for the hunchbacks of dungheaps
    where grackles perched pecking   for thin skins
        ribbed and translucent

            until the strike of a sauger
            shocked him back
                every single time

    then sitting up, he'd set the drag
        and fight a creature to the surface
        where he'd land it   and string it
           and hang it in the Wabash

    and this (according to his sermons) was a bonus because
        drifting lazy downstream, gazing up
        at the revolving sky
            he never expected to catch a sauger
            he never expected
                    anything

the congregation, however, expected hell-fire
and they could always tell if the fishing was good
because the pastor's smokehouse
was upwind of town
and the thick scent of hickory
on a Saturday night
always meant brimstone
on Sunday

but then one dusk, around turn of the century
whole families in backyards found themselves slapping
fat brown mosquitoes
and everyone rubbing
rising white welts

and nobody saying
nothing until

the emergence of stories, of which there were many
remembering the boat, beached in the reeds
remembering the minister
but not his name

and, so they say, his bones are still out there
still unrecovered
still lost to the world
but not
to the sauger.

THE TWISTER

sometimes anglers
        battle deep water lunkers
                never even glimpsing
                        the torquing forces
                                bowing their poles

these creatures are never walleye, never pike
        always they are muskie
        and always opaque
                      blurred beneath fathoms

except when mounted
        in Leech Lake taverns
                where the average summer catch
                    is a muskie per day

but not in July
        1955
        when a sudden tornado tore through town
        and plucked a Plymouth
                from the asphalt
                    then carried it out
                        six miles on the lake
                              where finally unwinding
                              a Chippewa family
                              was lost off Bemidji

                            (the Muskellunge Capitol
                            of the World)

legend has it however that divers descended
        but all they discovered
                was the vehicle settled
                    on the bottom
                        and no bodies
                              were recovered

still, a flare gun was fired
        commencing a contest
                in which sixty-six

                              trophy fish
                                        were landed on bucktails
                                                  and spinners

so then one day at the local cafe
          I caught the Mayor eating breakfast
                    an asked why them muskies
                              back in the 50s
                                        struck so intensely
                                                  and basically

                    he blamed the fluky weather

          which made the lake all foamy and green
                    and eerie with a certain light
                    a light, he told m,
                                        that brings the big ones
                                                  to the surface

but I wasn't satisfied with this

                                        explanation of fish
                                                  being all frenzied

                    and so I told him "Ludicrous!"
                              and he got pissed
                                        went red
                                                  and said

                    "Look kid, I'm eating my breakfast!
                                        If you want answers
                              go ask the shaman!"

          but the shaman wasn't home

          and so

                    I left Bemidji with nothing but a story
                              which, if you ask me

          is more than just enough because
                    when it comes to catching muskellunge
                              the truth is always
                                        just as elusive.

Muskie Cult

I'd heard of a place
        a smalltown up north
                the map called it Mud Dog
                        so I decided to go there

                            to see their record muskellunge
                                supposedly mounted
                                        on cedarwood walls

it took two humid days
        drifting downstream
                through logjams and deadheads
                and overgrown ivies

                for thirty-one miles
                        on the Windigo River
                              I paddled and ruddered
                                    and cut through the clutter
                                          till suddenly
                                                on Sunday
                                  a swell rose
                              swishing beneath me

                and gazing down, I saw a long silhouette

but knowing refraction plays tricks on the eyeballs
                I dismissed this illusion
                            as a family of otters

                and paddling onwards
                                    I came to a dock:

                it was the landing at Mud Dog

                        where

                  half-hidden in cattails
                a weathered sign read

"Pilgrims! Welcome!
Fishing Forbidden!
Population 24."

"hmmmm..."   I muttered
                    and tied my line
                                    to a piling
                    then walked on down
                to a gray faded building
            where out front
                        an old man
                                sat cackling
                                                so I told him up front

    "There ain't no such thing
            as a muskie reaching
                    twenty-one feet!"

to which he replied:

        SONNYBOY! You don't know nothing!
                Leastwise about lunkers!
                So come on in
                        to the Mud Dog Saloon!
                        And git yerself a gander
                        at the Big One on the wall
                                the one that we call
                                    Spotted Jesus!"

        I went on in
                    and met the Sheriff
            and the local bartender
                    and they showed me a creature
                    two pool tables long

        but I was still skeptical
                it wasn't symmetrical
                    it sagged in the middle
                        and it wasn't as girthful
                            as a muskie
                                should be

so I peered in closer
and saw the expert shingling

it was the taxidermy of twenty-one pike
layered in whitewash
puttied with Bondo

"This Fish is Bogus!" I exploded

to the Sheriff who admitted
it was

"Designed as a prop
to bring in the tourists
who came in past summers
but not anymore"

"However!" he added
"Such a fish
does exist
cuz this is
an effigy of it"

"Of what?!" I demanded

and he took a swig
lit up a cig
and told me "Kid
on Sundays after sundown
there ain't no strangers allowed in town
cuz this is when the members
of the Mud Dog Baptist Church
offer rodents to the river
singing songs to God"

downing my beer   I wandered outside
bid goodbye
to the crotchety old guy
then walked down to the dock

and shoving off

I entered the currents of a creature
              at least a rod long
                    that is
                  according to the folks
                    of Mud Dog

                              a town which makes sense
        when it's spelled

                    backwards.

THE OLD WOLF

there is no living muskellunge
       as monstrous as the Old Wolf
          who dwells beneath twelve feet
             of frozen Lake Katoma

                  "The Official Coldest Place
                     in the Upper Midwest"

         where wood-chopping thunks
                       chime for six months
            and exposure is instant
                     and quicker than windchill

This is Wolfgar Wisconsin
       and the predators here
          have evolved extreme genes
             and the weaker are merely
               calories

                    providing heat, providing speed
                     for the Old Wolf
        who once was timed with a radar gun
          striking a piglet on a rope
          at 112

         and twice he's been speared in the moonlight
           once back in 1922, and then again
              in '62
and of course there are photos
                    fogged in the distance
        as well as videos
                  of unconvincing footage
       which is why the University of Wisconsin
            (Platteville)
          conducted a study in which
               66
               anglers were attached
        to polygraphs and asked
            about this

                                        mysterious fish
     and surprisingly

          75 percent
                    gave similar descriptions
                         of a broken harpoon
                                   lodged in the left gill

                    however, there are skeptics
                              (mostly the wives
                                   of the local members
                                   of the Rod n' Gun Club)
               who claim that the Old Wolf
               was born in some cabin
               on some fishing weekend
                    when Lloyd Schrodermier
                    drunk on whiskey
                         convinced his buddies
                         to start a conspiracy

     But if you ask me, it really doesn't matter
               if the Old Wolf is real
               or if he's fiction

                         because up north in Wolfgar
                              it takes a lot of energy
                              for a story to survive

                         which is why the Old Wolf
                              will never die.

Nick Norman's Logjam

upstream
        on the Minnesota/Wisconsin border
            there's a monument which remembers
                an angler and his prey
                    who were taken away
                        from a place know today
                            as Nick Norman's Logjam

        "The Official Site
        Of The Unofficial Capture
        Of The Unofficial World
        Record Muskie"

                            (a fish which never made it
                            to the scales in Duluth)

but me and Donny Brewer, we know the truth
 cuz we seen the creature
  one day when we was out shooting b.b. guns at turtles and squirrels
   down on the banks
                of the Upper St. Croix

                where out on the driftwood
                we saw Nick Norman
                      puffing on a Lucky Strike

Yep, it was him alright

        the same white-bearded leather-faced oldman
            who runs the Skelly station northeast of town
                selling chew to minors
        and there he was, scowling like a curdog
                reeling in a frogplug
                with Missy

                    his little wife of sixty years
                      sitting stiffly next to him
                        sewing lace on doilies when
                          WHAMMM!

Nick's whole pole
        bowed into an arch

                and a geyser erupted
                        from the river's blackskin

                                as a creature flumed skyward
                                        spraying silver

                                                        shimmering ivory

"TIGER ALBINO HYBRID!"
        the oldman cried
          wide-eyed, shaking
                cranking his drag
                  falling back in the snag
                        clutching his rod in one hand
                                his heart with the other

                                while I gaped the creature
                                emerging longer
                                        than a refrigerator

                                and thicker than
                                        a fifty-five
                                                gallon drum

                                it hung

                                airborne, twisting

        like porcelain, ghostly

                but fine-scaled

                and white-fleshed

                        had fangs

                        and one

red
bloodred eye

gleaming electric
like a lightbulb

right where Nick had hooked it

until SPLASH!

it crashed
back to the foam

"NO SLACK! NO SLACK!"
the fisherman snapped
leaning back grinding the sprocket
fighting a creature
snagged in the socket

while me and Donny Brewer
perched in a willow
sat dangling feet
chewing tobacco

spying down on Nick
cussing at the fish
calling it

a "NO GOOD
DING-DANG
STINKING CRANKBAIT THIEF!"

and a "WEASLY
TWO-BIT
POUT-LOVING
SCALLYWAG FISH!"
and a "LOUSY
OVERGROWNED
REDHORSE BOTTOM SUCKER

JIST A-SUCKING UP

MUD N' CRUD!"
to which Missy responded
"Nick Norman, you quit that fishing!
You'll get a hernia Nick!
They'll put you in traction!
Just like Mr. Grubervitch!
Think of the children!"

but Nick wasn't fixing on letting the Big One
break away like some crappie
hooked on a fathead
Nope!
he barked out instead

"MISSY HONEY! THE CHILDREN ARE 54 AND 56!
SO FERGIT MY DAMN HEALTH
WHEN THEY'RE THE ONES
GITTING GALLBLADDERS OUT!

AND HURRY UP
AND TAKE MY DAMN PICTURE!
CUZ WHEN I LAND THIS LUNKER
THEY'RE GONNA TAKE MY MUG
AND PUT IT ON T-SHIRTS!"

so Missy snapped the instamatic
shocking Nick's complexion pale
bathing him in white light glow
Sparking
Flashbulb
Seizures!

"Nick, Nick!" Missy shrieked
"You won't survive another, Oh,
Put down the pole Nick!
Put it down and pray
So we can meet in heaven Nick!"

"TOO LATE FOR THAT PLACE NOW!"
Nick Norman howled
paralyzed from the waist on down

shivering convulsions
trembling spastic

"AND BESIDES, I AIN'T GOING NOWHERE WHERE
A MAN'S GOTTA DRESS LIKE A SISSYBOY
AND PLAY THE HARP TA GIT BY!

GIMME MONSTERS FOR ETERNITY!
I'LL CATCH EM FOREVER!"

"Why Nick Why?!" Missy cried

"Why?! Why?! Why?!"

"CUZ!" Nick Norman spat "I DONE HOOKED ME
THE GREAT WHITE MOTHERFUCKER!!"

AND MISSY DARLING, I'LL TELL YA THIS!
I AIN'T LETTING NO WHOPPER MAKE OFF WITH MY TACKLE!
ASPECIALLY THIS ONE!

YUP! I SEEN HIM BACK WHEN I WAS SIX
AND I HOOKED HIM ONCE AT SEVENTEEN
WHEN HE TOWED ME DOWN TO TAYLOR'S FALLS
THEN HAULED ME BACK UP HERE AGAIN
THEN BROKE MY PAPPY'S STURGEON ROD
AND STOLE MY BIGGEST JITTERBUG!

SO NOW MISSY HONEY,
NOW THAT SONUVABITCH IS BACK FER MORE!
I BEEN WAITING SEVEN DECADES!
SO THIS TIME MISSY HONEY
I'M GONNA RIDE THAT BADBOY DOWN!"

"Oh my God, he's gone insane!"
Missy Norman wailed hysterical
"Somebody call 911!
I'll pay a hundred dollars!"

and that's when Donny Brewer, trackstar of Moose Lake Middle School
dropped from the branch and took off running
for the Ranger Station
two miles away

meanwhile, the muskie
                    dove beneath the bark-peeled firs
                    horsing like a Clydesdale
                        as Nick up top
                                for twenty minutes
                                grit his dentures snarling:

"ALBINOOOOOOOOOOOOOOOOOOOOOOOOOOOOOOO!!!"
    YOU LISTEN UP AND LISTEN UP GOOD!
    YOU AIN'T GOING NOWHERE SEE!
            ME AND YOU, WE GOTTA SCORE TO SETTLE!
            JUST TRY AND GIT AWAY!"

            "Please, please, please!"
            Missy Norman begged her husband
                    "For the love of God Nick
                        Give up the fish!
                        Don't end up like Grubervitch!"

but Nick just scrunched his face all up
    like a big old snapping turtle
        pulling its head
            inside its shell

                    then striking out
            "MISSY PUMPKIN! I LOVES YA DEARLY
                BUT I JUST CAN'T STAND
                    YER PERSISTENT NAGGING!
                        SO GIT YER BUTT
                                TO THE TRUCK!
                AND GRAB THE JACK HANDLE
                    UNDER THE SEAT!

                AND WHILE YER AT IT
        GIT THE TWENTY-TWO
                                                TOO!"

    Nick Norman demanded
        to Missy who acted
                leaping logs like a runaway doe
            up to the lot where the brown dust rose

from the Moose Lake ambulance
driving 85
"Hallelujah! Hallelujah!"
Missy screeched above the sirens
four doors swinging open
Donny Brewer jumping out

then the Mayor
then the Sheriff

then a pair
of paramedics

and a newspaper reporter
from Superior

all of them hightailing it
down to the logjam
to see their local fisherman
torquing up the muskellunge

"WATCH THIS! WATCH THIS!!"
the old man spat
and wound up
coiled back
yanked forward
and let rip...

"The Old Slingshot Maneuver!"
the reporter cried
"Which I ain't seen since 69!
It's a Celtic technique
developed by Goths!
Used for hoisting
big rivercats up!"

but it weren't the nose
of a mudcat that rose
like a five gallon bucket
Nick winched up

Nosireeeebob!

it was the curved underjaw
of the Tiger Albino
glazed slick with mucous
smooth as enamel

"GODDAMN!! GODDAMN!!"
Nick Norman hacked
streams of sweat
running down his back
tendons stretching
in his neck

"MISSY!" he yowled
"YER MY LITTLE PANFISH, WE BEEN MARRIED SIXTY YEARS
SO IF MY DIRTY LAUNDRY MEANT ANYTHING THEN
SET YER BEAD AND SET IT NOW!
SEND THAT BASTARD BACK TO HELL!"

and Missy obeyed, blasting a hollow point into its skull
right as it shot, alive from the froth
rocketing spaceward

crescenting

then plummeting back
spasming death throes
belly-up

in the Upper St. Croix

And that's when the EMTs climbed down
and tried to take Nick's pole

but he wasn't ready
to be rushed to the city

Hell No!

he kept on reeling

he kept on smogging
                              ordering them medics:

"HEY YOU TWO, MONKEYBOYS!
WHATCHYA GONNA DO, PLAY POCKET POOL ALL DAY?
          MAKE YERSELFS USEFUL!
                    GRAB THAT THERE JACK HANDLE!
                         AND LEND A HAND PRONTO!
                              DANGNABBIT!"

so sliding black iron in through its gills
          they gaffed the beat creature
                    hauled it up on the logs
                         spread it slack on one stretcher
                              Nick Norman on the other
                                   then proceeded to brain it

                         just as the old man
                                   started to mutter

something about gods alive in the river
          ...

          something about how
                    ...

          it looks like now
                    ...

                    the time done finally come
                              ...

                    fer an old shit-kicker like hisself
                              ...

                    to upgrade
                              ...

                              from a Zebco

then gasping, gurgling, spitting up bubbles
          Nick twitched twice

went rigid

       then slack

           and blacked out

               forever

     (so they say)

but what they don't say is how them medics
    drove off the bridge

       because of some freak sudden squall
          sweeping down the river valley

            just as the ambulance
               was crossing the St. Croix

    with Nick
       the fish
          and the reporter
               from Superior

           who me and Donny Brewer
             discovered
               an hour later
                  washed up on the logjam

"Kids," he wheezed
    "I was down there with Nick Norman
      and I swear to God
        I actually seen him
          awake from his coma
            when we hit the water

           as did the muskie
             who was only knocked out...

    and the next thing I know
      we was settled on the bottom

and the doors, they strained
and the river, it burst in...

and that's when Nick, in the chaos
lurched into the current
and grappled that muskie
in a triple half-Nelson..."

and then with his last

few seconds of breath
the reporter leaned forward
swooned and went pale

though he managed to whisper
the ending to this tale:

"Kids," he said, "the legendary Tiger
Albino Hybrid
is still down there
with Nick Norman...

scowling cantankerous
smoking his Luckies
not letting go
just riding that muskie...

somewhere in the depths...
of the Upper St. Croix."

IN CORNFIELDS THERE ARE CONDOS

in lakes there are landfills
  and where there would be creatures
    there is concrete

      and Euro Disney
       one third the size of Paris
        a Japanese tourist haven

         for people to swarm
          because they can't all be
           wrecking the same place
           at the same time

             and people think
             this planet will last?

              and people think
              the earth can be saved?

     these are the signs that forever is spoiled
      these are the telltales of

             the fucking end.

Cosmos

was a nature photographer
  we used to visit in Iowa
    because he lived with Eleanor
    and her kids

    Cosmos collected creatures
     he had tiger salamanders
      rattling diamondbacks
       luminous green Andean snakes
        blood-red Mexican tree frogs
       soft-shelled tortoises
         jagged snapping turtles
          turquoise iguanas
         shaggy tarantulas
           and a badger named Pancake
           that slept in the hallway

Cosmos also had a live World War II bomb
  balancing on the mantelpiece
    a red-headed nude
    painted on the shell
     which the children
     were forbidden
     to touch

    once a scorpion escaped
    and there was a dollar reward
     for whoever discovered it
     and Andy cornered it
     under the sink

that's the night Curtis was sick
  dying from cancer
   coughing in his bunk
    till dawn

    when Cosmos suddenly appeared in the doorway
   his balls hanging out
    silhouette trembling

and he kicked the badger
screaming
"STOP COUGHING! JESUS CHRIST!
STOP! FUCKING! COUGHING!"

I'd never seen
Cosmos
so ugly.

At Western Bob's
House of Hashbrowns

a guy walked in drunk
it was Richard Brautigan

he sat down in a booth
and began writing about
how beautiful he felt this morning
because he had been inside
some woman twice

then Sasquatch ambled in
he was drunk too
but not as drunk as Brautigan

they embraced
and both of them cried for blossoms
opening for the prow of a new ship

it was embarrassing

so I got up and left
(I was drunk too) and drove
to Fort Wayne Indiana
where nobody makes love
and cries about it later.

Sasquatch Encounter

Between windshield wiper slaps
his silhouette appeared
hulking on the highway

Bigfoot was illumed
by my high beams
and when I skidded to a stop
I could see he was at least
twelve feet tall
    with ratty
          matted
               rain-soaked fur

his head was the size of a watermelon
cords stood out in his neck
strings of drool swung from his beard
    and his slimy
          purple
             gums
                 were quivering with bludgery

like a raging orangutan
he beat his breast and roared like hell
then batted my bumper
into the ditch
    that sad sorry sonuvabitch
    what a drama queen!

so I threw the car into reverse
backed up
then put the pedal
        to the metal
    as he howled
          disemboweled
             orphan rage
          eyes ablaze
             in blacknight drizzle

I hit him hard in the knees
my hood crumpled
the radiator burst
but I put him out
of his misery

I console myself however
with the fact that he
was just another overgrown ape
        in need
of a hug.

And Barbara, that "Bitch"

word I cringe at, though wield, a weapon
  like her fist, her sex
    she thrust at me

        Barbara, almost stepmother
          I saw her in a nightmare
            green skinned and cackling
              riding a slow tortoise, laughing
                because she made it to this place
                  beyond the dim lit kitchen on 16th
                    where she sat naked and pale breasted
                      studying Sociology
                        arguing

        "This is my house
            and if I wanna strut my flesh and pubis
              then why the fuck shouldn't I?
                certainly not because my lover's son
                  is here for visitation!"

meanwhile, I was fourteen with zits
  and a rabbit named Buckeye
    who pissed and left small pellets
      in the basement where I slept
        on the shattered skin of a black plastic couch
          erupting yellow foam

          it smelled like kitty litter down there
            beneath the dripping pipes, the silverfish
              the exposed pink
                insulation and

                Stupid Jenny's stupid toys
                  her Barbie dolls, her plastic fruit
                    her sock monkeys—

Stupid Jenny was
  Barbara's finger sucking daughter
    a whiner and a liar

and only part of this poem because
she accused me of holding a gun
to her temple, whispering

"You're a little bitch
and I'm gonna blow
your fucking head off"

but Stupid Jenny was merely psychic
she read my fantasies
I have never called anybody "bitch"
except for Barbara Elliot

who left her diary out for me to find
entries about
"That snot-nosed ingrate Spitzer kid"

"Ingrate!" one of the many words
I learned from Barbara like
these four words she screamed at me:

"You! Artificially! Inseminated! Bastard!"

words I carried for over a decade
words that conjured a freak in the mirror
words that never appeared on 16th where

rules were posted for future stepchildren to obey
like House Rule Number 4:

"Each member of the community shall
receive 16 hugs per day"

however

there were no rules for Barbara who
ran naked and flame haired
stabbing for my father who
hid in the basement the night
she burst in
flashing knives, flashing flesh

howling "FUCK ME NOW YOU FUCKER!
FUCK ME NOW IN FRONT OF YOUR SON!"

and it wasn't too long after this
that my father broke down and left
for New York to recover from
whatever curse she cast
on him while I

tortured bugs in Civics class
hoping he would never come back
because I wondered if

wishing he would die meant I
was just as crazy, though

I wasn't angry, not
like I am now, I think

I won't end up a mess like him
hung up on psychopathic women

like Barbara, that bitch
who scared me into never
forgetting, so never
forgiving, so always
hating, always
writing rants like these
which tend to end
(more or less)
acidic with this message:

Barbara, I remember everything
this is what I do now
and as long as I'm alive I will

remember you exactly.

Anal Poem to Be Screamed at Telemarketers

The doctors say it's all aggression:

I suckle and bat my mother's breast, then grab it
    a handle on a runaway baby carriage
there are tendernesses I don't receive
    and condescensions I don't desire
        I am rewarded by my lover's nightmare
            of castrating triumph
                she shakes the trophies of her gender
                    before my grinding fangs!

I am an Oedipal freak gnashing ice cubes
    brandishing my penis
a lead pipe with which I bluntly punish my partner
    beating her with jerks and thrusts
        because I don't understand
            her smaller claws
                unsatisfied by the touch
                    of plastic dolls
                        with tap water urine!

My shoulders are yanked and held to make her a mom.
    Narcissistic bowels resist their function
        filling the enemy's inferior loins
            with feces and piss!

She yearns a phallus bludgeon and remembers
    some dry and genital drilling enema
        and cries and moans and webs her fingers
            in the small of her flashback
                father's spine

                each is reborn in our nemesis parent.

The verdict is we're all imperfect fucks in a sodomy orgy:
    heterosexual homosexual bisexual biological fuckers
        thrown together in a jar of steaming egg jelly
            while the whole of society
                slithers in the oil
                    of stranger bellies!

Take us to a planet of inhuman orifices
        formless flesh
            unrelated, sexless, emotionally homogenous!

Circumcise away
    our paranoias and perversions.
        Lobotomize our mother-father-nextdoor-neighbor specters.
            Shoot torpid jism in our veins
                and distill the plasma of our hatreds!

        Voyeurs of the Apocalypse
    watch us make love to manholes and fire hydrants
        while excreting our fluids
            into the drains and sewers
                of a planet rid

            OF PEOPLE RASH!!!

THE TRUTH ABOUT LOVE

I

Having slept 10,000 nights, having known a family
            some women, some places
                  some fish

        having ejaculated the word
                  in the animal instant
                        and having lost all sense
                              because of this

            I somehow made it to this page
                  to claim that love exists
                        just as much as America
                              or the speed of light

II

granted, however
    there are "intense feelings"
          (see section IIIIIIIII)
              but for the most part
                    people suck like leeches
                        attaching to humans
                              who suck each other
                              into oblivion

                              because they believe themselves to be
                              another part
                                    of something they're not

"leech" is a word
              which means a pagan surgeon
                              Sabbath witch or bleeder;

          someone who sucks black blood
              like a lecher
                    sucking for the Spanish word for "milk"
                          his mother never gave him
                              by stalking random schoolgirls home

                and fucking their puberty
                on some neural mattress

    which is something we all do to different degrees
        as we feed on orifice dreams
           sucking strangers in our sleep
              with the passion of
                an army of nuns
                    clutching Jesus to their breasts

III

it's not bad to suck
    or be sucked
        or be subject to
           the laws of suction

              that's just the way it is

    even before a child is born
        it gestates in the amnios
           sucking food
              through an umbilical tube
                until it's born
                  a mammal:

        a creature born to suck
           the nipple of its mother

              a creature born to suck
                udder milk and lactose

              a creature born with lips
Every day
    sucklings suck
        sucking sucrose to survive

    every day
        sucklings suck
           evolving into children

                            who suck for reasons
                                    to keep on sucking
                                            into adolescence

                    where questing hickies, seeking kisses
                                    sucklings dream of sucking face
                                            before they even know
                                                    their hormones howl for more

        IIII

those who get erections
often think of blow jobs
which have little to do
with exhaling air

frequently in wet dreams
she crawls between the sheets
she is known as Succubus
and she goes to work
sucking throbbing members
stroking pulsing shafts
till the pearly geyser fountains
signaling
success

        IIIII

we suck the rush of sweat!

                                        we suck pools of brine!

        we suck rippling flesh!

                                        we suck the musk of pits!

        we suck hidden knee pits!

                                        we suck quaking neck pits!
                                            we suck each other's spigots!

we suck tit!

    we suck cock!

        we suck pubis!

            we suck clit!

            we suck fluids
                produced in bowels
                    squeezed through pores!
                      smeared on face!

                        we get pubic hairs
                        caught between our teeth!

IIIIII: Eco-Suck

Hey you, sucking dry the water
        sucking dry the derma
            the globe is our last bosom
                and you're a greedy feeder

                secreting concrete
                  through an urban ooze of Disney Worlds
                    shopping malls
                    and scabs we call the City

where lampreys in the ghettos lurk
  sucking for groceries
      sucking for booze
        sucking for cigs
          sucking for drugs
            sucking for lawsuits
            sucking for welfare
              and sucking for swastikas
                that make them feel adopted

meanwhile
        masticating cattle graze
            sucking bald the grasslands
                sucking bare the prairies
                    as junkies in the suburbs
                        stumble through the crust n' pus
                            addicted to the mineral suck
                            the timber suck
                              the oil suck
                          the loam suck

              and the suck of the Fat Daddies
                who pay banana pickers
                    fifty cents a day
                        and promise not to slaughter
                        whole villages of workers:

      the vampire hordes
          of vampire lords
              sucking tundra for McDonalds
                Burger King and Hardees
and the front porch codgers of Duluth!
  sucking up lungfuls
        of oxygen and space
            sucking up atmospheres
                inside their poisoned organs
                where gastric acids
                    produce the gasses
                        released in the subtle
                        lift of a cheek

     Yes! it's true!
          the exhaust of breathing bodies
             crammed in colonies
                mix with monoxides
                    turning skies to gauze

overpopulation is a premature crack baby
        embryonic beneath
           a gossamer frock

                    the swiss cheesed ozone is a plutonium sponge
                        pissing toxins on the slums
                                where one humongous
                                    proletariat ass
                                        lounges like a shit eating fly
                                            sucking Slurpees, sucking Coors
                                            sucking HBO, sucking cable
                                                sucking Schwarzenneger
                                                    sucking porno
                        sucking up almost everything
                                except for the erection
                                        of home sites built on landfills
                                            paving all ancestral soil

for our successors
            not yet born with birth defects
                    HIV and random spasms

            who'll be a race of bitter mutants
                    coughing blood
                            allergic to the asbestos dawn

        a generation counting down
                the shriveled death of Earth
                        and lamenting
                                            the breast
                                                of a leper!

        IIIIIII

some people suck butt

it's a practice known as felching
akin to gerbiling
or fisting
or greased up doorknobs
turning in the bunghole

here's how it works:

someone comes
in the colon of his lover

then makes a taco with his tongue
and sealing lips to sphincter
the semen is delivered back
in a sudden burst of methane

IIIIIIII: The Suck-Conscious

humans are mammalian suck-machines
      sucking for succulence
            in the excretions of Others

          when pressed together naked
             soft and fleshy structures
              easily align

                    igniting catalysts
                      beneath the epidermis
                       where generating juices
                     we squish with lubrication
                           so as to merge
                           in the surge
                     of orifice-song

simultaneously
      heaving lungs suck air
         and pumping hearts suck blood
           driving the suck of cells
              through a labyrinth of hoses
                 arteries and tubeways

                     supplying limbs with motion
                     making it possible to suck

                       different things
                       in different places

for the stimulation of the eyes
        positioned in front of and above
           the body's major suck hole

> so we can see
>> the skin of what we suck
>
> so we can remember
>> the meat of what we suck
>
> so we can forget
>> why we suck

IIIIIIII

all across the planet
> throughout History, throughout Time
>> organisms have sucked
>>> for nourishment and sustenance
>>> for pleasure and
>>>> the hell of it

> Jesus sucked the crucifix
>> the holy grail
>>> and a handful of nails
>>>> George Washington sucked so much
>>>>> he had to get false teeth

Shakespeare sucked his quill
> Einstein sucked $E=mc^2$
>> Teddy Roosevelt sucked the red sands of the Badlands
>> and Cleopatra sucked her asp

> Ben Franklin sucked 10,000 volts
>> Mary Queen of Scots sucked a thistled crown
>>> All Aztec priests everywhere
>>> sucked the rising sun
>>>> and Nordic Thor
>>>>> sucked his hammer

Allen Ginsberg sucked Neal Cassady
 Margaret Thatcher sucked Great Britain
> Gloria Vanderbilt sucked the hag masses of the 17th century
> and the hag masses sucked dirt

Jimmy Page sucked his twelve string
Menudo sucked the Apocalypse
Sophocles sucked Oedipus
and Buddha sucked Nirvana

Walt Whitman sucked Emerson
Emerson sucked the transparent eyeball
the transparent eyeball sucked Nature
and Nature sucked Zapata

Zapata sucked a gun belt
Picasso sucked the Cubist movement
Helen sucked a Trojan horse
and Tommy Kramer
(aka "Two-Minute Tommy")
sucked as a quarterback
because he lost his scrambling passion

Adam sucked Eve
Eve sucked Adam
Adam sucked Batman
Batman sucked Robin
Robin sucked the Joker
the Joker sucked Alfred
and Alfred just plain sucked

Mohammed Ali sucked, Confucius sucked
Black Elk sucked, Bigfoot sucked
Pope Paul sucks, george bush sucks
I suck, you suck

everybody sucks

because sucking is
the human condition

IIIIIIIII: An Example of How "Intense Feelings" Spark Mirages of Love

if you're wondering about Freud's fifth case study
      History of the Infantile Neurosis
            lemme tell ya
                about the Wolfman

he was an Austrian infant
      whose parents didn't care enough
            to bounce him on their knees
                or count his little piggies

      and so this kid formed a fetish
            with the ample buttocks
                of the bent over scrubwoman
                    who came once a week
                      to polish the tiles

from behind the oven he'd peek at her seams
      stretching and flexing
            swelling with yellow

    until one afternoon
      in the master bedroom
            the master was discovered
                  snorting like an incensed boar
                  riding the hindflanks
                    of the help

                    who got fired on the spot
                    and so

     with no anus to grace him
        the boy collapsed
             uncomfortably numb
               reeling in his mother's bed

which is where the family doctor advised
      the sick child should sleep
          because he was dying
            from a mysterious non

contagious virus

that no physician
in all of Vienna
could identify
or treat

and sometimes at night
the child would awake
to gaze through a fog
and see a primal dog
rocking the mattress

it was his father, the master
gripping his mother from behind
ramming his penis
into her rectum
both of them grunting
both of them growling
the violent conception
of another

which is how it appeared to sonnyboy
who figured that bastards are born
from the bungholes of mothers
fucking like canines
and howling like hounds

hence, he grew up haunted
by recurring dreamscenes
of six big wolves
perched in a tree
each nape rippling
bristling with nightmare

that's how the Wolfman
became known as the Wolfman
because he couldn't see intercourse
any other way

thus, the Wolfman
       often asked doctors
              for permission to defecate
                  on their foreheads

but back to the point:

when the Wolfman was going in and out
       of sanitariums
              he'd run from every dog he met
                and every human too

especially at 5 o'clock
       when depression set in
          for a one hour funk
              in which everything sucked

                  except for the thought
                  of slitting his wrists

so searching asylum
        the Wolfman hid in synagogue
               regiment and silence

and uniforms that bound his breast
     as he marched circles in his room
       thumping the floorboards
         like a Nazi

until finally the master
     couldn't stand the stomping
       every day from five to six
         so he sent for an analyst
           to solve his son's psychosis

the doctor's name was Sigmund Freud
   who specialized in digging bones
     in catacombs of psyches

and he went spelunking
   in the Wolfman

and surfaced with this skull:

During childhood
the subject was stalking a swallowtail
which he chased to an evergreen bough
where it landed and opened
its bright yellow wings
forming the shape
of the letter V

"Voila!"
            Herr Doctor Freud exclaimed
            and explained how nightmares
            are spawned by symbols
                        and colors

                        like the Roman numeral number 5
                            which triggers the stretch
                            of a thin yellow dress
                        that orphaned the Wolfman
                                    eternal

hence, the patient
        completed his treatment
                and became known as the prototype subject
                    of Anal Retention

            as in Erik Erikson's
                bloated boyhood patient who
                    impregnated himself
                            with the prospect of a turd-baby
                                forged for the return
                                of an affection his parents
                                        never gave him

the Wolfman, however
        was dammed by a different constipation:

        his chambers were packed by neural feces:

        the obstruction of an imagination

276

                    suckled on an empty teat

                            suckled on the offal truth
                                which is:

    human beings are full of crap
        human beings are full of bile

                the cargo of all mammals
                    the waste of what we suck

                        and not just through intestines
                        but through all associations

                            unconsciously swallowed
                                into our systems

                                then processed and jettisoned
                                    as stools of the ego

                                    or "intense feelings"

        and so, you see
                Lacan was right:

                        Lack rules all
                            as Freud implied

                            because "love"
                                    as demonstrated by the Wolfman

                                is born from shit

    IIIIIIIIII

mind you, I'm not saying love sucks;
                        since love is not a physical thing
                                it can't do anything

    what I'm saying is

we suck and cry
shit and sigh
and never wean
until we die

which brings me to the ending
of this angry young man rant
an assignment for a final
in a graduate workshop class:

"Tell the truth about love"
ol' Reg Saner said
and twenty wannabe writers
scrambled for their pens
to compete for a grade
to show we understand
why anybody gives a damn
what a page
has to say

and so I say this:

here at Poetry School
attempts are made to write
about what sucks
and what doesn't

while we sit in circles
ragging on each other
about what sucks
and what doesn't

as we sneak behind each others' backs
making lists of those who suck
and those who don't

basing these judgements
of course
on the idea of "accessible poems"
demonstrating certain functions
as well as certain suctions

like the suction of suffering
     and the suction of language
       and the suction of consistency
         and the suction of connections
           which display a learned passion
            for successfully pulling
              people into paper

       otherwise, we're told
        our poems suck

          otherwise, we discover
          nobody gives
            a fucking shit

     And that
       fellow mammals
           is the truth about love.

The Notch of the Sorceress

1

She is Hazel Bane
 nineteen years old
  with flaming copper hair
   and an orange plastic vest
    directing traffic
     in the Pacific Northwest

and as I pass her on the shoulder
 I can't help glancing over
  at the strange shallow groove
   on the end of her nose:

"The Notch of the Sorceress"
 some chroniclers call it

        it's a remnant of history
         a vestige of witchcraft
          and there it is
           on a highway construction worker
            holding a slow sign
             so I stop

"Get going," she says, "move that heap"
 but another voice answers
  lower, gruffer

  and up on a bulldozer
   I see a hardhat guy
    eating a sandwich
     and he yells

        "You tell em, tits!"

and the next thing I know
 the seventeenth daughter
  of a seventeenth daughter

is sitting in my Buick
giving me orders

"Drive this piece of shit"
she tells me
and gives hardhat guy
the finger

2

we drive down the coast
and camp in the wagon
where she shows me her forearm
branded with a pentagram

"Five points for five dreams
five people who died"
she tells me
"what do you think about?"

so I answer "Ratfish
with stingers of venom
and Ted Nugent playing live
to thirteen thousand
inner-city drop-outs
like Rimbaud

whose great motley bear
drooled with bruised violet gums
his eyes on the silver
and crystal of the cabinets"

but Hazel just laughed
and looked in the back
where boxes of books
prompted her to ask
if I was some sort of scholar
or what was the deal?

So I told her about wildmen
those rare hairy in manuscript borders
abducting maidens in their sleep

and I told her about knights
with lances and swords
slaying wildmen in
the name of the Lord

which is why they rampage
solo through the woods
smashing nothing with their clubs

but this was not the answer
to Hazel Bane's question
and so I confessed
that chasing pagans
was my passion

because I'm a guy
obsessed with heretics

and so we had Aunt
Jemima for dinner
and she said she'd eat pancakes
for as long as I fed her

and laughing at that
she leapt into the back
the sun went down
and she began breathing deep
until coyotes howled
and we both fell asleep

but minutes later, I awoke to a KRASH!
it was the sudden crushed metal
of a late 60s car:
four tires shrieking
two tons of steel
skidding off the road
wrapping around
a power pole

but the panorama was clean
 and the Cascades were still
  and so was Hazel
    except for her eyelids
     dancing REM spirals

then I knew:
it was a red Chevrolet
 1800 miles away
  and Greg Little
   a guy I never liked
    was dead

3

in the morning we burned
 Hazel's orange plastic vest
  and I gave her a sweatshirt
   and tried to describe
     the sound of shattered glass
      spraying the highway

I told her I knew
 she had telepathic powers
  that she was some sort of earth daughter
   receiving nightmares
     like an antenna
      and bleeding dreamscenes
       into the dark

and she said this was true
 that an Impala had rolled
  in some Midwestern ditch
   like Minnesota
    or Wisconsin

though she didn't know who
 the body belonged to
  but she wouldn't have dreamt it
   if it didn't mean something

so we kept on driving
 silent through the morning
  until finally she inquired
  why wildmen are loners

and so I warned Hazel
 to watch out for monsters
  because wildmen are shaggy
  and wildmen are crazy
  and they ain't very good
  at cohabitating
   but enough about me
   what about you?

which led her to describe
 the Goddess of Acid
  who she worshipped at thirteen
  by dropping eight hits
   for some guy with an Albert

"which," she said
 "is a chain that dangles
  from scrotum to foreskin"

"which," she declared
 "is the art of piercing"
  something she used
   to be into

   until her left nipple
    got infected and grew

"with scar tissue" she added
 "so it looks kinda funny"

then hopping in back
 she lapsed into a nap
  and watching the reflection
  of my sweatshirt on her

I felt a hardhat
　forming on my brow

　　as I pictured the lift
　　　of sleep-heaving breasts

　　　and the mystery nipple
　　　　solid with the possibilities
　　　　of witchcraft
　　　　and flesh

　　4

the Idaho rest stop was on the barbed-wire edge
　of a vast tuber field
　　where in the dark
　　we laid a tarp
　　　and played wrestling games
　　　rolling across lumps
　　　we thought were potatoes

but nothing really happened
　until idling diesels
　　cock-a-doodle-dooed us
　　and we awoke
　　　to witness a horizon
　　　　of sun-baked dog pylons
　　　　jettisoned from the bungholes
　　　　　of constipated canines
　　　　　like the bon-bon tufted poodle
　　　　　not twenty feet away
　　　　　quaking its flanks
　　　　　for its owner
　　　　　a fatman
　　　　　coaxing
　　　　　　with a donut:

　　　　　"Come on, George!
　　　　　You can do it!"

and this was the scene of our very first kiss

5

at Yellowstone Park
I was half dressed and waiting
watching her wind down the trail
from the green-black firs

then sliding through flaps
into blankets and down
she peeled her jeans
and flowed into me
and everything
was warm
  damp
soft

6

in Kodaka South Dakota
 lightning strikes a pine three campers away
  as she straddles me manic
   like the thunder around us
    exploding spruces in the park
     flooding the tent
      bright orange with the storm
       as her flesh
        flashes
         in amber

then looking up
 I see colors I know
  I'll never forget
   as she throws back her head
    and a long tousled mane
     rides copper and wild
      down the arc
       of her spine

to her hips
 where her knees
  splash on the mat

to the tempo
  of a noise
   like a sponge
   squishing
    between us

the negative burns like a chemical bath
  the tent blazes and flares
  her body goes slack
  as two glowing breasts
  fall to my chest
   with the shudders I hold
   in the small of her back

   which shiver
   and dwindle
    until all that is left
    are two sets of lungs
     heaving the breath
     of a different
     new tongue

   7

it was wet
with wandering waves
and drizzling beads
that settled with the scent
of a bitter carnal musk
that lingered the vapor
of burned body chemicals
excreted from genitals
mixing with sweat
and lathering the dermas
of two lean horny bodies
humping and pumping
and slapping out skinsounds

ahhhhhhhhhhhhh
the apricot dusk

8

baptism is
a briny fuck

9

"You're my raving lunatic"
  Hazel whispers in my ear
   "banished to the wilderness
     forced into exile

          and if you're afraid of motorcycles
            I pledge to ride them in my dreams"

"And you're my schitzo Sybil"
  I tell Hazel
   "casting spells
     bewitching me eternal

              and if you don't like me smoking pot
                I pledge to smog it in my brain"

and as the storm begins to pass
  I pull the blankets
   over the swell of her ass
    as she drifts into slumber
     breathing deep steady lungheaves

and in the puddles in the tent
  I lay awake into the day
   watching the notch
    of the sorceress
     twitch
          counting the pancakes
                    we haven't yet ate

until finally dawn blooms
  and shedding soggy layers
   we crawl out in the mud
     emerging like steam

to scavenge some kindling
 to start a fire
  with which we fry
   two perfect
              flapjacks
which we devour
 driving into Minnesota
  to my duplex I rent
   from John Berryman's widow

who gives us some cats
 and a rubber tree plant
  left by her husband
   who jumped off the bridge

so naming the kittens
 after warlocks and witches
  we watered the plant
   and shared a toothbrush

and then one day
 I asked her to marry me
  and she said I was sweet
   but that's all
    she would tell me

10

after six months of two-backed beasting
 we were still going hard in the flickering haze
  of menstrual constellations
   projected from candles
    she made and arranged
     on her altar
      with incense
                and mugwort

and watching her nude
 flow like oil through the rooms
  we awaited the signals

of the virgin lunar phases;
the determining tides
of our animal synthesis

but I had a different apogee
on the night of the eclipse
when seven planets were due to align
in harmonic convergence:

we were grooving in the strobe
of smoldering nettles
and we were deep in the strokes
orchestrating our grind
to the moans in her marrow
(according to the Tarot)
as voices were conjured
and she crooned cryptic lyrics
born from the spirits
of tricksters
and sisters
and such

until symphonies
of suction
merged with the poundings
of slickmeat and pubis
as she started to jerk
like a blasphemer being stoned

Gotta pull out, gotta pull out now!
I thought
but Hazel cried "No!"
so we raced with the storm
and convulsed in the froth
for another half hour
as she uttered gone names
of dead women and shamans

which gave her strength
to tug on my hips
like an epileptic howling

from the fangs of Apocalypse

my drive however
was spawned by impulses other
like the quest of wild boars
nosing the loam
for the tender young fungus
which fools the crazed fucker
into triggering the wave
of the Amnios Surfer
shooting the tubes
of gnarly tidal breakers
crossing the wash
of sweat-streaming bodies
hanging ten with his toes
and flexing those neck cords
bulging and pulsing
like hoses for sirens

until the heavens of millennia
converged out in space
and she wailed out a deathscream
which rattled the windows
and shook the foundation
informing us both
in the dynamo instant
that she'd broken on through
to the cosmic command
of Discorporation!

and if Hazel so chose
to shatter her matter
then that would be it
for the organic order
of a nubile creature
who'd lose all her moisture
in the mammalian suck
of my saline currents

but suddenly, the celestial worlds

all in a line
  like a string of planetary ducklings
  all trailing a big yellow momduck
  shifted in their drift
    as the solar system quirked
    like the ever so slight
    bend of a reed

and sizzling incandescent
 Hazel bowed
  and blasting a shockwave
  into my chest
    she launched me from her breasts
    into the plaster of the ceiling
    which I smacked without feeling
    then fell down beside her
    as we lay phosphorescent
    radiating on the quilt
    like two rifts of lava
     bending serpents in the air

            11

"I got herpes," Hazel tells me
 and I look at my crotch
  then up at her

"We gotta use condoms," she says
 and hands me a pamphlet
  concerning the lesions
  which appear
   three times a year

"with the comets"
 she adds
  "and I feel em coming on
   you might get infected"

so grabbing a Trojan
 and donning it proudly
 I told her I'd love her
  foreverandever

even if she
had HIV

You Betchya!
I didn't want pustules
all over my penis
so I protected my member
with a sleek golden rubber
and never
        ever
            got VD

12

again I ask Hazel to be my wife
and again she responds
that we have cats
and a rubber tree plant
so what more do I want?
so set the alarm
for nine o' clock—

and again Hazel drifts
deep into sleep
while I lie awake
watching the notch
of the sorceress
twitch

she's having a dream
her eyelids dance
but I can't guess
at what she's seeing now

Hazel has learned
to control her dreams
no longer do they leak
from her sleep

            like the death of Greg Little
            a guy I never liked

Hazel's eyelids start to jerk
 Hazel whimpers "No I can't"
 Hazel moans, shakes her head
  mutters "No
   you don't understand"

so I kiss Hazel on the notch
 and she whispers that witches
  belong in covens
   and to leave her alone
    because can't I see
    she's asleep?

13

that winter solstice we met the monk
 who briefed us on chakras
  and Kundalinian ways:
   like Tantra
    and pressure points
    and herbs for wild sex

so then we went home and she fired up the altar
 arranging skullcap and bones
  across galaxies of sage
   until apolune waxed
    with the sandalwood fumes
     which meant it was time to illume
      the amaranth candles

so contracting our sphincters
 twenty times each
  we brushed lavender auras
   forming glow-melons
    of human radiation
     which led to yab-yumming
      sitting cross-legged
      in the lilac glow

meanwhile my fingers
traced streamlines down thighs
seeking the fleece
of warm downy heather
where bittersweet berries
clustered on vines
climb rich earthen banks
to watercress springs
and it's clement
in the climate
of supple-winged lilies

then peeling gentle petals
I slid with the slick
into sepal dew
and wiggling silk lips
toward the calyx
quivering
deep dark and pink

where gyrating slightly
I massaged just a bit
spreading the nectar
rimming the border

and raising her hips
she guided me in
to the slippery slide
of the crescenting drive
where my fingertips followed
an inner-ridge hollow
to a labial lapel
where resting tranquil
on the tip of the bud
a slow flood of magma
oooozed in our spleens

but we didn't start working
the molten mass up
because the monk had instructed
to press down on the spermway
damming the surge

so we ummmmmmmmmmmmmmmmmmed
and we oooooooooooooooooooooomed
and it went on for hours
as the candles called forth
the undertow powers
which rose with the rays
of a deeper heliotrope

causing her head
to fall to one side
launching the orbits
of her Titian mane
carving arcs
in the dark
swinging
like a grass skirt
alohaing strangers
in the murmurs of ballads
emerging in Latin:

"*scutellaria…*
verbena…
lobelia…
echinacea…"

Hazel moaned
her eyelids flickering
like violet flames
purple and pinking
as she swooped in the swoon
of a woman I knew
I had never
met in my life

"*salamandra…*
esturjon…
molos…
tartaruca…"

Hazel gasped
  until suddenly I was kneading
  the leprous grayflesh
    of some ancient Sabine crone
    howling out a grocery list
    of increasing creatures:

there were lizards and preybirds
 armadillos galore
  reptiles nocturnal
  and even a herd
   of those miniature horses
    primitive and forgotten
     not much bigger than dachshunds
      stampeding amuck
      from the lips of the hag

who sat on my lap
 bouncing on my balls
  screeching and cackling
  yellow teeth glistening
   one tumorous brown mole
    the size of a cupcake
     springing from a wartfield
     rotting her chin

     where one
               giant
                    curly hair
                         was twisting in thickness
                              like my dinner
                               which I puked askew
                               but kept on fucking anyway

I fucked for the ceasing of species!
 I fucked for the death of the shrew!
  but mostly I fucked
   for the return of the nymph
    who finally came back
    and pulled me in further
     to the bowels of her trance

where crackling loinspasms
charged our structures
altering molecules into
helium gasses
as rippling wetflesh
enveloped the rest
of the fallopian scheme

and I abandoned my hold
on the seminal gush

and levitating, we rose
together off the mattress

and hovering, we came
in Mobius fathoms

everything flowing
into the soundlessness

of womb butter

14

and somewhere
maybe in Romania
maybe on Venus
Hazel is crying

so I ask through her dreamhaze
why she is weeping
and she tells me she's not
twelve years old and getting raped
on the cold stone steps of juvie
by Mr. Rumpee, the counselor of all
A to H students

and then she whispers
there are gulls in the sky
and even an eye

floating in a pyramid

and she is up there with it
riding a chopped hawg
across a highway of thunderheads

rumbling combustion
to the olive fields

of Lesbos

15

but first she goes to Nicaragua
to dig a foundation
amidst the bananas
for an abortion clinic
with Nellie

a self-proclaimed
militant butch dyke
who told me I was a parasite
sapping the powers
of the woman she loved

so during that winter, Hazel gone
I decided to hermit
working the night shift
writing *The Wildman*:

a manuscript intended
to be an apocryphal atrocity
eighteen hundred pages long

and I grew a beard
and I didn't go out
in the sharp leaden snow
I just stayed inside
drinking bad coffee
and typing up phonebooks

plus stupid letters to Hazel Bane
 like "Isn't life neat
  due to the size of the planet
   and its proportion to space
    which is almost as vast
     as the next sixty years

     that is, as long as we have Geiger counters for pets
      to warn us when to don our asbestos
       so to stroll arm in arm
        in the plutonium rains?"

to which she responded
 that this was nonsense
  and what about the orphans
   bleeding in the streets?

    And what about the Third World starving?
     And what about empowerment?
      And equal rights?
       And sexual freedom?
        And Nellie and I
         are doing fine

         16

the cats were pissing in the rubber tree plant
 and I was incensed at her mother
  who waddled into the wave
   streaming off the plane
    and stood there like a riversnag
     as passengers flowed all around them
      banging luggage
       like oblivious penguins

but at least her parents drove us home
 while I blithered in the back
  because Hazel was gaunt
   and her nose was now pierced
    by an unfamiliar sapphire

stuck right through the split
in the notch
of the sorceress
and once at our duplex
she couldn't wait
to call up her coven
to organize a coming out day
for women like Nellie
and anyone else
who wanted to join

and speaking of the mastiff
she moved into our house
and slept on the couch
and no one ever asked me
if this was alright

which it wasn't, of course
because what was I supposed to do
and where was I supposed to crash
when all I'd do was lie awake
watching Hazel in her sleep
dreaming scenes I'd never see?

which was the case
for eleven straight nights
after Hazel came home
and lemme tell ya:

I wasn't a zombie
because of sex

17

in the spring I got busted
for driving all swervy
and when the officer approached me
I couldn't stop blubbering
from being awake
for almost two weeks
drinking booze while Hazel snoozed

all the while
   writing *The Wildman*

and so the policeman took me to jail
 for intoxication
  but I was let out on bail
   with a year's probation
    when the judge discovered
     I was merely insane

however, he told me
 there was a condition
  I was to honor
   for my freedom:

I was to undergo analysis
 by a court appointed psychiatrist
  because society
   doesn't need
    furry freaks like me
     running free
      in the streets

"Because this is America, young man!
 Not Borneo!"

18

Dixie was the shrink they sent me to
 who asked me if paper was laudanum

so I showed her *The Wildman*
 which was the size of a tombstone
  and the weight of a dead man
   and she took my tome home
    and came back next week
     her hair a medusa
      of tangles and snarls
       her eyes wide and bloodshot
        larger than eggs

"Jesus Christ!" she exploded
"This forest is veiled
  in ivies and vines
    where no one can find you!"
    to which I replied
      "Or Get In My Face!"

then Dixie said
 I had an attitude problem
  and to lay off *The Wildman*
  and to Jesus Christ
   stop chasing pagans!

I tried to object
 but Dixie wouldn't hear it
  she said my manuscript
   had made her an insomniac

and then she advised me
 that witchery would be
  the death of me
   so I should stop
    pissing her off!

I told her I wouldn't
 I told her I couldn't
  but she said I had to
   because I was driving her
    psychotic:

"With heresy, a lethal obsession!
  And sorcery, which enhances depression!
   And get a shave! And get a haircut!
    And get involved with something else!
    And go home, march into your house
     and kick Nellie
       the hell out!"

19

then I won a prestigious award
 and got a grant
  to do research
   in Europe

which is what I did
 as quick as I could
  because ever since I booted Nellie out
   Hazel had taken
    to calling me "Kraut!"

so I flew off to Amsterdam
 and began tracking Celts
  through lower Bavaria
   then up into Hungary
    but not Scandinavia

        because a fever consumed me
        and I began to hallucinate
        underwater creatures

            like ratfish and squid
            and dogfish and skates
            swimming through the streets
            of Buda and Pest

until a telegram came
 from Hazel who said
  she was sorry she
   called me a Nazi
    and she wanted to meet me
     at Heathrow
      in London

        where things
        were supposed
         to be better

which they were
 in a hostel in Brighton
  where visions of bullheads
  wound through my brain

  as I lay with Hazel
   who said I was tripping
   and told me to shut up
   and sent me behind

and so I put my mind on auto
 making love to Hazel Bane
 who didn't know
 why she came
  except that now
   she hated Nellie too

which is something she expressed
 as we pressed our flesh
  together in bed
  the evening she

        triggered depth charges
         in my head
          shocking my fish
          belly up in her sea

20

Renaissance wildmen existed in Britain
 and I discovered a slew
 in the archives of Oxford

where deep in a crypt
 our vestments stripped
 we screwed in the tombs
 of the rodent voyeurs
  who chattered and chirped
   as our organs worked
    while spiders crawled
    all around us

then in Mumbles
 it was a bronchial fuck
  we were sick and we did it
   standing up in an oilslick
    coughing out phlegmsongs
     looking like one pink stork
      hacking in the distance

after this, we went on to Dublin
 where an irate scrubwoman
  heard noises in our room
   so drove us from her bed and breakfast
    accusing us of hosting Satan
     in an underworld orgy
      of gargoyles and vermin

but at least the Irish coppers
 took us to the slammer
  where we were given a cell
   that smelled like urine
    with one cot
     and two clean sheets
      where we lay entwined
       in a 69
        wondering who
         was screwing who

21

then questing Merlin
 a prototype wildman
  we thumbed through the lowlands
   picking blessed thistle

I was searching the broom
 for the castle of Orson
  the last Gaelic stronghold
   of the Teutonic druids
    driven across Europe
     like cattle and Jews

and when finally we reached
the burnt out remains
the ramparts were smeared
with Cheez Whiz and feces
and swastikas and beer cans
were strewn all about
a hearth full of porno
someone had burned

still, a weathered bas relief
of Jack of the Green
the Celtic vegetation spirit
was carved in the stone
almost obscured
in the grappling grapes

but Hazel didn't give a rat's ass
about the father of wildmen
and she told me these walls
had no spirit in crumble
as she swore on her pentagram
that no infidels
                    ever
                            lived here

but I said there had been
and I said that they were
the most authentic heathens
to ever live anywhere

then pointing at the keystone
I told her that these were the pagans
and that Jack was their Odin
to whom they gave sacrifice
centuries before Christ
and centuries after

then Hazel said she wanted a motorcycle
either a Triumph or a Norton
or a Harley or Ducati
but not a Yamaha
or a Suzuki

"No Fucking Way!" I exploded
 for the third time that week
  and again I explained
   my history of wipe outs
    and how they still ache
     when fronts move in

      like she did
       the night I smashed my bong for her
        and laid its shards
         upon her altar

then breathing hard
 we tore off our clothes
  and Fucked and Fucked and Fucked and Fucked
   until I felt contractions
    way up in the uterus
     until I felt her teeth
      bite into my neck
       until she spat blood
        in my face
         screaming

          "HEY GODDAMMIT!
           I WANNA BE A DYKE ON A BIKE!"

     22

Hazel flies back
 leaves me in Limerick
  and I am consumed by a big mental scene
   like Stephen Dedalus on ludes
    as I ride trains and boats and planes alone
     haunted by fleshscenes
      swirling with nicotine
       yellow and acrid
        three nights awake
         hunkered like a fetus
          umbilicaled to the same
           cycle of questions
            umbilicaled
             to death

then arriving back in Minneapolis
 I taxi to our duplex
  and find a Triumph 750
   leaking oil
    on the drive

and bursting up the stairs
 twelve pounds lighter
  I scream about helmets
   protecting the beauty
    and about the Aegean
     destroying everything
      as I collapse on the futon
       begging to be released
        from whatever curse
         she cast on me

Hazel sits up
 tells me to calm down
  kisses my forehead
   calls me her wildman

But I Am Not A Wildman!
 I Am A Madman!
  ripping tufts
   from my head
    frothing rabid
     and babbling about
      gray blue birds
       rising to the mouldings
        bleeding for a fix
         of an opiate more deadly
          than crack

Hazel tells me she's sorry
 and really she loves me
  as she pulls back the sheets
   inviting me in

where once again
 the sorceress tempts me
  where once again
   I feel the smooth yield of dunes
    into innerflesh rouge
     as I slide in a swirl
      of erratic ellipses
       as the rhythm of thighs
        squeezes me oblivious
         squeezes me insane
          bewitching all that remains
           resolving
                      as always

                                          nothing.

PART 3

VAGABONDAGE

1993–1996

THE REAL

1

winding these night roads
      I drive with Jules
            tell her I dread the Interstate
               the asphalt neverending

America, I seethe, is a web of these
      different places in between:

            a fucked up friendship here
               a slit-wrist lover there
                   torn ligaments, drug abuse
                      warrants in three states

"don't be so melodramatic"
      Jules tells me
            "bitching's too easy"

            I drive on
               west with the landscape
               the only thing
                   that ever seems to change

2

up past Cheyenne
      we smoke hashish
            and the lunar light
               thins the night
                   as I babble on in the indigo:

"wax nostalgia?"
      what the hell
            is "wax nostalgia?"
               as in "waxing and waning?"
                   as in "to wax with the moon?"
                   the moon

                              glowing down on us
                                    illuminating these
                                          roadscenes
                                                I used to wish
                                                      would roll into Forever

"Jules," I say
        and tap her knee
                but she has drifted
                        into memories

        3

we left on Highway 12 when I was 6
        cruising west through early
                autumn Minnesota
                        into the fertile
                                browndirt Dakotas

        it was a hundred degrees
                the windows were open
                        but even the humid
                                summer currents

                couldn't burn the amber
                        tassled cornrows fluxing by

                like spokes
                        like rapid seconds
                                like pages in a story
                                        unfurling, though the story
                                                hadn't started yet

        the fields measured
                time with speed

                        55 miles per hour
                                into the Badlands
                                        into the future

4

the Badlands were named
    during the Depression
        from the eroding edges
            of the Dustbowl's scattered galaxies

where in the early Seventies
    I saw motley betusked bisons
        standing mammoth with their calves
          amidst gopher populations

they were near Medora
    where we wound
        into Theodore Roosevelt
        State Park

where I found an injured fish
    stranded in a sandbar puddle
        of the Little Missouri
          bleeding

it was
    a very strange fish—supposedly extinct
      yet still I held it
        felt it, saw it
          twitch its gills
             across the lifeline of my palm

it was a living fossil
    supposedly gone
      since the Pleistocene

it was ten to twelve
    inches long
  I can still see it
    silver, rough scaled
      its tail tri-lobed
        its skull plated

was not
destroyed in the Ice Age

as the Safeway animal encyclopedia
attested it to be

though already I had thrown it back
to the river where
underwater
I saw it tumble over gravel
away from the murky
shoreline there
into clear mindscape where

for over two decades
it lived like a myth
and thus, I know
and I tell you this fish

does exist
somewhere in the ripples
of the Little Missouri

5

"You're calm tonight"
Jules tells me
breaking my
reverie

"I thought you'd be
raving The Apocalypse!
or ranting The Republicans!"
she says to me
driving north
up into Billings

"Nope," I respond
distractedly
"I'm only wild
when Extreme's around"

"Oh," Jules replies
          and glances at my sling
                    "and do you blame him
                              for your broken wing?"
          "Yep," I laugh
                    and lapse back
                                        into the past

6

I gnawed holes in vinyl
          until I tasted metal
                    rusting up beneath the panel
                    of the 69 Chevy

          a wagon with a wayback
                    a sister sitting next to me
                              a father up front, blasting harmonica
                                        and a mother frowning next to him
                                                  driving solemnly ahead

I gnawed holes in vinyl
nose pressed against the glass
and watched rolling foothill prairies
change to sharper
chiseled dermas:

          horizons more glacial
          more cut by dead sea
          leaving creeks
          at the bottom of vast valleys

I gnawed holes in vinyl
waiting for first mountains
ever seen through my child eyes

and suddenly
monolithic snowcapped peaks
impossible yet actual
poised against the August dusk
apricot luminous

surrounding us
surrounding these
Purple Mountain Majesties

I hoped the coast would never be
I didn't see
how it could ever be
I wanted to ride
for eternity

7

but here
on the Great Plains
these are the Badlands

and Jules
long and leggy
is sleeping next to me
her flesh
lavender in the reaching sky
flickering gold

as star streams shimmer
            split
                        second
                                    eons
                                                in the hour

the Continuum, like opium
fills my lungs
with the ether of infinity

8

ahhhhhhhhhhhhh...

I pop another valium
to kill the pain and drive on
into the distant velvet

maybe everything
never was

9

Jules awakes
rises on one elbow
breathes deep
looks out the window
sees silhouettes
rushing by at 75
affirms the beauty
she can't see

"Whatever's out there"
            she tells me
"I want to be in it
            when I die"

and I agree
                        passionately
                                    and understand why
                                            my mother cried
                        twelve years back
        in Yakima, winding
                        into the orchards
                                    of desert gorges
                                            the geography of her birth, and now

                all my insides twist, choking
                        I want to drive this Mobius highway
                                    but it's way too early
                                            for eternity

        10

Jules drifts
back to her visions
and as she dreams
I climb the rising divide
tires humming in the moondusk

these are the blasted stone walls
the rocks I once saw
twenty two

                          years ago
still red, still granite
they are the thresholds of my journeys

but now, vague
they are silent obscure ghosts
formless on I-90

no one else is alive tonight
my beams sweep steely guardrail serpents
hissing next to me

and Jules moans
soft in her sleep
like a kitten, purring
remembering warm
forgotten places

11

a week before I lived in Boulder
drove south on Highway 93
past Rocky Flats, the plutoniumed soil
into Golden
Colorado

I was with a woman
strangely named Ligeia Poe

Ligeia Poe:
my student, my fantasy
half Apache
half mysterious
Hungarian royalty

and all around us as we drove
traveling the gone bottom of the canyon
I became inspired by the blood of bards
        inventing verse

in my veins

        so wooed her heroically
        conjuring great rivers
        carving Time, running gulfward
        plentiful with fishes

and as the red rocks rose, so did my prose
my fiction, my song
my dazzling creatures

I painted lost species
strange sculpin, lungfish, sturgeon
coelacanths

and as the kingdom appeared before us
we became the fate-torn lovers of my mindtales
both of us radiating
like nuclear fission

but now
Ligeia Poe
is the siren of my dreams
because, alas,
my plans had been set
to white stallion onward
to Seattle, to dwell
with Extreme

                    my enemy, my friend
                    my destiny in the Northwest

and so, in Golden
I kissed Ligeia's high cheekbones
and drank a trickle of her tears
reflecting spectrums
of what could've been

and I drove
west with Jules

and just as always
Ligeia Poe is in my dreams

12

at 4 a.m. the onyx night
is vibrant, the moon is full
incandescent
white light shining
blue honed
iridescent

for five days now
this lone pupil
has been burning down on me

outside last night
I lay awake till dawn
shredded muscles in shoulder blade
swelling in socket

this was the consequence
of one freak accident
involving Extreme, he
    unbalanced me

      pushed me over
      and I toppled
      into a state so dumbstruck

        I wandered home
        like an urban drunk

to lay reeling in the backyard
cringing in the moonglow
sharp pains like shards
slicing through arm
     I am heading his way

           again

13

Extreme, he
       apologized profusely
           paid for x-rays
               gave me codeine
                    (and Demerol
                         and Tylenol 3s
                             and these
                                     numbed the sting
                                         in sling)

then setting out for Sea Tac
       Extreme told me

               "Impulse, just a few days
                     and we will meet in Washington
                           and into the Apocalypse we will Rock!
                                 and your slung arm will heal in salt breeze
                                       sweeping off the sea where we

      will fish and bike and hike and smoke and joke
          and snort and pop and grub and swill
              and booze and cruise for maidens who
                   will massage that poor
                        unfortunate shoulder
                        all the while, strutting nubile flesh about

        and trust me, you won't feel the pain"

and then he smiled that smile
       he smiles to everyone
            that smile that says
               "You are the only one"

and Reader, if you're thinking "fool,
       he fell for it"
                 well then
             you're damn right I did
                that's his magic
                   so how could a romantic

not embrace it?

how could I
a believer in gone creatures
ignore this spirit?

14

Jules and I
    arrive in Seattle
        and I drop her off
            at her hotel

    "take it easy," she advises
        "Extreme can be
            dangerous, selfish
                and it takes an athlete
                    it takes a maniac
                        to keep up with him
                        though I don't know why
                        any sane man would want to"

then here, beneath Ranier
I drive I-5 between the Cascades
and the craggy, misted
Olympic blackpeaks
which mark the Sound
my only god

and driving on
to the edge of the world
I find myself hysterical
laughing uncontrollably
as if my life means nothing
which means I can do anything
because what the hell
do I have to lose?

15

the edge of the world
        begins in Ballard
                at an address where I wait
                        for Extreme

"he'll be back in an hour"
        a scrawny junkie tells me
                "have a seat, watch some t.v."

so I sit down and gaze at his arms
        pale white tatted blue
                red needle tracks
                        dotting main vein

"You a friend of Extreme's?"
        I ask his hypo
                dermic needle
                        lying on the coffee table

"known him ever since
        I forgot who I was"
                his skull face answers
                        adding "that bastard..."

"Oh," I respond
        zoning into tube
                a wavy black and white
                    staring out at me

there's nothing else to say

16

some Scottish band
is jamming on pipes
an electric guitar
leaps in wailing
and the camera glides up
with the gulls

to the jet stream
MTV following
the haze of the shoreline

the beach grows duney
then rocky
then cliffy

a city appears
alone in the country
like a thistle, solo
thorned and protected
and the band rocks on
as if this concrete
is the heart of glory

meanwhile I wait
in Ballard for Extreme
I wait in Ballard
for me

to change into
another me.

Dreamchasing Ligeia Poe

149172

Ligeia
somewhere
a   continent
of   potatoes
lies   dormant
veiled   beneath   a
fertile   umber   topsoil   sea

Ligeia
I   intend
to   gather
these   spuds
spray paint them gold
and   erect   a   pyramid
to shatter all egyptian egos ever

which skeptics may claim
is an impossible feat
but I say it ain't
cuz   look
I just
did

it twice

(1 thousand
and 20 miles to go)

and once upside down

149246

Ligeia
Idaho oldies
crackle on a.m.
there's a fruit pie on the dashboard
and brights are flooding
the rear view mirror

my skull fills with wattage
my whole brain squints
like an albino exposed
to UV rays

(7 hundred
and 7 miles
to go)

Ligeia
one nocturnal hermit
back behind the sockets
dims the shutters
and drives
forever

149440

Ligeia, beware
I savor the scent of roadkill skunk
staining the air with a bitter musk
something you can taste
something

that doesn't smell like anything
ever released from any mammal's asshole
something

that charges the night with glands

Ligeia, beware
I also enjoy raw oysters
liver, gizzards
moon pies, red wine
dinosaurs n' cheese
nectarines, novocaine
pork hocks, octopus
cow tongue, squid
THC, LSD
the sultry essence of an athletic woman's
hidden pits
beads of sweat between the breasts
briny wet
rippling flesh
and everything else
that makes your father
grip
his armrest

(7 hundred
and 47 miles
to go)

149459

Ligeia

great truck tire strips
beached on the shoulder
like momentary sea cows

I glimpse them in the instant
passing headlights sweep their girth

there are otters also
seals, dugongs
tortoises, armadillos
wart hogs, lemurs
sloths and penguins

Ligeia, these
are the vulcanized creatures
of blacknight Idaho
applauding our collision
of nightmares

(7 hundred
and 28 miles
to go)

149600

Ligeia water everywhere

I am deep in the storm
avoiding truck ruts
rainbow glazed with oil and rain

and as the wipers metronome
Lou Reed singing: "Americans
don't care too much for beauty/they
shit in the river/dump
battery acid in the stream"

I can't help agree

america weans her young on miller beer
linoleum and lithium
and video
and plutonium
and concrete
and neon
and pop tarts
and pop art
and interest rates
and money down
and america

calls this beauty

(5 hundred
and 87 miles
to go)

Ligeia, us
ain't american

149662

Ligeia
walked into a ruraltown
utah cafe
and thunk up a poem
old as the great
salt lake

it goes like this:

when a guy with gilded shoes can't ditch
the angry gapes of slack jawed
sideburned cowboys sucking
black coffee then

toxic waste, crack and AIDS
don't exist in the West

nevertheless, I sat down and ordered
biscuits n' gravy

then broke out my anthology
of French poetry
all the while
drinking the same joe as them

(5 hundred
and 25 miles
to go)

Ligeia, america
still believes in commie fags

149771

Ligeia, Wyoming
is miles and times
measurements that don't exist
when syllables do

and the earth is turning red
Colorado red
and there is something of the flesh
alive beneath sharp grass

(4 hundred
and 16 stanzas
to go)

MEN WITH BOOZE, SHOULDERS SLUMPED

there's a posture one assumes
 in Omaha Nebraska
  across the street
   from the greyhound terminal

it's 1:00 in the morning
 and nobody's speaking
  even the bartender
   stares silent at the bottles

                like a picture of nothing.

RUSS

Russ gets up
scratches butt
and slides a Hungry Man
salisbury steak t.v. dinner
into the oven
with all the grace
of a rapist.

Overtime Dreambanes of the Sphincter Sphinxes

the asshole guards
at the Plymouth County Workhouse
sit and sweat grease
from damp, stained, polyester pits
as they read pro wrestling magazines
in the jaundice glow of forty watt bulbs
at card tables
with Fritos
and Mountain Dew

the asshole guards
their job is to look up and grunt
at the weekend criminals
promenading the ceramic stage
and spreading their cheeks
until a nod
sends them along

so the asshole guards can return
to the glossy steroid meat heroes
despite having traveled
the colons of convicts

the asshole guards
drive home at midnight
thinking Hulk Hogan, Mad Dog
thinking tag team action
battle royales

they whistle to AM
switching stations
like surgeons and morticians
like proctologists
passing like turd cargo ghost ships
packing the goulash
of sleep limbo scenes

the asshole guards
they get this all pooped out
from their minds

we all take our day sights
to bed.

KNOW THE MENU

White Castle is White Asshole
or just plain Asshole
but sometimes it's
Wipe Asshole

a hamburger there
is a slider
or an asshole
and a cheeseburger there
is a slider with cheese
or a slider with vinyl
or a cheese asshole

a turkey burger
is a gobbler
a turkey burger with cheese
is a gobbler with glue

not to be confused
with a pigeon 'n pus
which is a chicken burger
with cheese

meanwhile
French fries are nails
ketchup is blood
mustard is piss

it just goes to show
nothing good ever happens
in an asshole.

School Paste

In first grade there were the paste eaters
digging into their shoe boxes
shoving past crayons and markers
going straight for their stash
of chunky white glucose matter
of which they dipped their first two fingers
slipping up the slag of elementary school ambrosia
which they discretely slid under their tongues

school paste was sweet and fatty
like Oreo centers
it stuck to their pallets
dissolving slowly

I didn't get school paste
I got flour and water
mixed by my mother
in a blue plastic bottle
originally meant for soap bubble stuff

my paste got crusty on top
it hardened like plaster
it was yellow

then a paste eater teased me
he said my family couldn't afford school paste
so I conked him on the head
knocked him unconscious
with my cylinder of mom's
homemade paste

the teacher sent me to the principal
who asked if I had problems at home
they always asked that

but it wasn't lack of attention
it wasn't child abuse
it was them
the paste eaters.

DAVID TOURTELOTTE

was 3 rooms away
sitting in a beanbag chair
reading *Mad Magazine*

I had a raquetball in my hand
and was a poor shot
I figured that if I aimed
for his head
I'd hit the wall

so let rip
a 66 mph fastball
and knocked him upside his head
broke his glasses on his nose

he had to wear a wad of adhesive
            tape after that
but he didn't tell
            my mom.

I am a pig and she is a princess

up in the mountain
palace kitchen
staring at her
black lab

"Doesn't my black lab
have a perfect body?"

                                   she asks me

"Yes," I tell her
"You should show her off
more often"

"Yes," she says, "I should
more often."

To a Mountain Gal

Dear Melinda,

Thou art so Swedish for my poppy in the glimmer of my last long dawns. How I nimble brinefully, breathing for those honeycombs of dew. Though in the weantime, my wren, your lashes flicker dimmer and so does the booze.

By yet you have no doubt heard of my not coming Boulderwards. But know: this be because of one jetsam (and one silly jetsam only, O coysome kiddo): your luminous olivine trace.

You see—when again my madful eye did view the bliss of mountain morns in sun with cats and dogs and distant hidden cacti, it was you (askew, and winking Monalisalike) and so I knew: it was the sparkle of your pure pearl baby made me wanna cross the Plattelands Tuesday—but note:

     not just for those instant ripple waves of rhythmic warmflow, secret in the squeak of moonbutter nights, but rather—behold: there are orphans of no-joy whom we all harbor and indulge

                             (little pricks...)

     And so I grit and spit and tick with this along with what you muse on too: that knowledge of the never-nymphs fluting with all mythos.

         Ack, Besmirchable Dreamscenes!

     Witness with your cantaloupes how I would sooner scatter a gaggle of glitter to the vast Ukranian wombfields, MELINDA: our small Elmos must never

                            ever
                               agulate!

        Ciao Mein,

            your sad houseboy gone to Prague
            in the shadow of the blimp of love...

TRIANGULAR WOMAN PAINTING

the dwarf dreams corridors

damn the wild sharp bitter splashings

and mad a rock cracks into

such honey drunk slippery sounds

that savage pressing Christlike

your yellow girl dolphined dizzy

twisting slick in hip-sweat

and blubber spit lips

and smell

and hair, Jesus!

the pure ravaged vile thighing incense

the gulp pup sleeping.

GOLDEN GALACTIC ARSE PAINTING

Dear Friends, the neighbors dialed 911 in April and she hired a bloody yucca. A week later we escaped a burnt out dirt-green Anasazi containing 31 pounds of magic insect jasmine, in Norway where girlie shows cry out: "I am a very rare pet!" Then in May the entire faded festival dreamed we relied on a red century of orphan language. We expect ancient ruins in the rubble.

LUSTY GREEN LIZARD GUY PAINTING (WITH CONDOMS)

madstractions:

it happens

there are body-snipers in the birches

. . .

fearing not the silvered skulls
of decomposing pastures ain't
part of the picture

there's a soft flesh crescent in the belly of
the tangerine machine

. . .

I been in France

I been in Morocco

I been in Spain

I been insane

(New York also)

HEY KIDDO

I like your body
your dawn sea-body
my reflection in it

and I like its rolling flex
its fleshy stretch
the rising waves within it

I like its sculpture
I like its shape
I like its arch
the fire inside it

and I like the feel
of the swell
within it

I like the full of it
I like to fill it

(black flashes, passing between us)

I like
your fluid dawn-body
I like its tide
lifting beneath me

already gone
your gone sea-body

the moment it's in me

I like your gone
sea-body

your dawn sea-body
your gone sea-body
lifting beneath me
already gone.

V.TR. TREMBLER

O naked aspen lady
with your nubs and nips
and nubile contours

in French you are a verb.

Dear Vladamir Hamster,   sept 19, Paris

      that distant blaze i spoke about has now been extinguished by yet another dull and gaseous funk from the machine; here in france, all expatriates died from suicide—and the rest went back to the Phone Co. I am alone here like our phantoms everywhere; those with meter in their theater can't afford to screw the muse—now a rapecase; Ack the stench; get me a clothespin!

      Thus I send you Lautreamont instead; past translations in the public domain. I also send the shrapnel of my queer morning in Paree when I awoke in a proseful mood so started pulling tomes off the shelf and picking from their vast mass of constellations. Call it spontaneous chaotic anti-somethingorother birthed from Plato's gone Teutonic Ludicrosity sans breakfast though of course with some sorta intended underlying strata of order and not just rebel bile ennui, angst and despair, the greatest undiscovered stitchery of syllables since that of Beats in heaven dead.

      I am here for an instant maybe longer.

Manifesto 1349

in the school of sensible nonsense

                                                                              visions

          make sense to the imaginer
                              and their connections are linked
                    through wordplay

                                        it is self delusion
               to the point of practice
                         on paper
                                   achieving
                                        something
                         more

                                                       than nothing.

A Warmer Slagfish Not Tomorrow

I, however, the blue sleepwalker, abhor the methods of the slaver, his determined and vigorous biological slaughter; Kennedy remembered the ambush of young days. On the eve of his departure, I blame your pleasure; it is easy to imagine other tribes. Lo: a lump of cowshit in our coffee.

&&&&&&&&&&&&&&

For the Egyptian in the Emerald light, Napoleon stood naked, his worn pants squealing wild with hurry.

Flashbulb armies toiled and sweated. The Boy-Girl excess, the whole dog-doctor coffin glory, the entire other half strip-tease synod of it—and no creature yet had pressed the final button of our ape-past.

(butchers killing flies, another case of bourbon deluge, Panama Farm...)

So all that year no second brood did stretch its breast upon the iron stairway. Which was which? Whose sauce is this?

DECLARATION:

There is soft body gall

                           ashen-gray
                           berserk-sane

                                         probed frigid

      in your shadowed empty hells

               "Speak"
                      she nodded

                              complicated

                       and the country was perplexed

even the sleepers cherished her fishing
yet still the Aleutian was wet in my hand
              if you want to make a slave, Anglo-Blackfoot,
            take a Turk
                 reclaim your constant decapitations

      All the Bulls have no Balls!

      in Austria, ages ago, when the waitress was sparking Darwin-like, incomprehensible in her high spiky heels, the terracotta people laughed condemned on Devil's Isle… and the blowpipe flashing light into every possible and impossible direction…

Twisted Forever,

Lady Nebraska reared her rotting contraband. Her sharp barbs had grown ample with milk—whereas McCarthy and his slander were colonial to consider the Iraki in the corner. Abruptly, the Dog Priests salvaged that whiskey on your dreadful breath. Tumultuous, the warriors dance; my friend Ohio, we are sensible of energies.

Your sister is a good humane intelligent girl. Exhausted, the egoist brushed against the sun. Big unfamiliar looking blobs went squatting down before the Goddess: "Goddamn Your Kidneys Sir!"

Meanwhile, Africa believes; sweet Beatitude bleeds; and the pigs drink from Infinity.

Beauty Lust of Poison Dead
She Sweet Liquid Morning

....many young tongues prowl the rushes

for strange white ivy soundings

daring their way to the sunlit sea....

O descend impearled

my iron lawn

flay your amber sex immense

fashion spiny axles.

NAKED JELLY BABIES

Suspicious correspondents continue to gaze

across climactic mercury days

And you Lady Midnight

already wiggling

have traveled this far in confident ignorance.

We are awaiting the tragic

Lotus Weasel and Otter

Fixed amidst the crimson

now that we love death.

Scraps Glued to the Back of an Envelope

XI

eastwards through the hills

red-spot fluttered by

X

crowded of ants

one such made a rolling

VII

myriad leaves

Lilliput

sunset

VIII XI

orchids

white light

winding

wings.

ANOTHER ENVELOPE

lying about unearthly

                       glistening

     clusters of the finest muscled fungus

                             soft in the jungle

                                     forgotten.

A THIRD ENVELOPE

    dead leaves

          neglected specimens

      astounding

       jaws.

   Awkward green creatures.

Then suddenly yellow landscape

        wilderness

           sea water

              sweat.

A Thousand Nudists Were Sitting on My Couch

We were watching the Hundred Year War
pretty soon Barbe-Bleu would be born
and then we'd all eat tootsie rolls

At noon I tobogganed to her house
human undulations paved the way
salmonberries slid through our worries
feasts of liver pâté

Oh my glimson glittercouch
ta de ta de ta dum ta dum
fo mi fo mi fo me baby
9.8 meters per second
squared

I fell to the ground in the shape of an X
while cars were made of cardboard there
picking up seashells
in the street.

THEN SUDDENLY THERE'S VIOLENCE LIKE ALWAYS, RENÉ STANDING IN THE DOORWAY

I can feel the malnutrition
lack of vitamin C, broccoli

     *

Beauty flutes above the traffic
makes the night more beautiful than silent

     *

it makes me sick that we gotta get sick

     *

I want to kiss her on the lips
                    ... that's all.

(Now)

looking back on what I once
thought was movement
(or a movement)
I see a buncha pathetic white kids
desperate to connect with something like
religious fanatics, we stood in the rain
letting the weather drench us

It was worth it though, for
the concept of magic—the rush
of that instant affirming
that we just won't
rot for nothing

This however has been said
a million and 12 ways before—but
not by me yet. And you
(idea of Opposition reading this) (Ha!)
you can't shut me up

that is,
                    unless you kill me

But what I'm saying   it ain't really worth
the trouble of that... now
is it?

                              Anyway, it's nice to give up
                                    like the rest of us.

Dry Humping Beauty

so I had my hand on the soft wet sex of the angel—Yep—it was right there between her hot thighs—and she was pulling on my hips and grinding with those oceanic movements—though our clothes were on and we were lying on the bed where the pulse-pulse surge-surge of torpid jism rising skyward in me spun me—and it wasn't so much that I didn't wanna make a mess in my jeans so walk around France smelling like brie, but moreso, it was the pure vulgarity of the moment: I mean, I couldn't just cream upon unspeakable sweetness (cuz I'd ruin something, I'd ruin Everything) and so I pulled back from her tremoring lips and desperate sweat—and I didn't shoot my pathetic madwad. Nope—I just lay there instead, wishing I was dead, for glimmering to bone her

. . . .

Later on, I write and type, smashing my head on the table, straining to capture all I left out—like those flowing woman waves flashing on her save-me-from-my-lonely-self/no-go-away/no-come-back-and-fuck-me-all-the-way-to-the-heart-so-I-can-see-me-gasping-back-in-your-blue-eyes face! and all that suicide & the sea sorta stuff—but just ended up with one scrap of red-inked paper:

"ego loses beauty again."

NOTES OF DESPAIR

...when I'm crazy again I'll write like the damned stacking up demerits...

...there's power in hating what's become of yourself.   Sometimes I wish I was dead.

(That's impulse though)

O warmbreast take me back against
your flesh and pet my head!

yesterday I threw Herman Melville into the Seine
Today a potato.

Truth is
I gotta be sad and mad and crazy
and LOSE!   it's the way I write best
and that's what I have to give
to this miserable world
where beauty's just a memory

Ohmygoditshappenin
I went off mad and got even madder
getting even madder also.
so I gotta turn Madfate around
rid myself of Impulse
or else I kill myself
there's no other way
to live by

NO!

not even imagine
going back and doing Lily

NO!   DEATH!

STORY   OVER

STOP   NOW

I wish I had a god to pray to

but we are all alone

TRAGEDY

the trick is to avoid it
joining it is too damn dark

OK—I'll go crazy again
but just for a bit...

Impulse Banished Himself in his Mind

"I'm not afraid of anything you're not afraid of"   (Kiddo says)

(then)   "When are you going to make me your wife?"

                                        (she asks—tilting back,
                                                    looking up at him)

                                        (in all seriousness)

"We'll go with the fish farm idea"   (Impulse answers)

        "We'll go out there in our beat up boat
                and dump in big buckets of worms"

        "...trout farm..."   (she replies)

                        (like a happy, content
                                                etherized patient)

                "...trout... faaaaarm......"

        "Yeah, Kiddo"   (he says)

        "But let's farm tiger muskie instead
                    We'll introduce muskellunge
            to the Australians..."

        "I love you,"   (she tells him) (again)

"I love you so much it hurts... ...I love you...

... I love you..."

"...yeah..."   (he gulps)

"...I know..."

"...i feel so evil loving you..."

(Impulse tells
                   a piece of paper).

Dec 6 or 7 or 8,

Hey Kowalksi, I guess the enclosed yaller sheet fell out of last letter: you can figure out where it went.

today I'm bummed out for first
time in a few months cuz
monologues in brain, thinking things
I don't wanna think and
scaring self as if
there's no peace cuz if there is it's an illusion.

it's dangerous to hide in your work
but then again, it's fucking deadly being alive.

Love, your pal,
                   Impulse.

P.S. i'd rather be vague than specific. Hope you're riding a beautiful illusion.

P.P.S. last page ripped in struggle with gal.

[yaller page]:

...so George brought me a buttload of breakfast on a tray: giant oatmeal with bananas, a tangerine, mega-apple and bread too, all because (I reckon) the bullshit publishing scene is going purdy purdy fer me and that's what he wants: a "Writer in Residence" who aint sitting on his butt, and the big news of late I guess is this: was walking down some pee-smelling steps by the Beat Hotel a few days ago and suddenly I'm looking into the eyes of the Ginsberg—Yes—Le Fat Daddy hisself looking up at me recognizing him in the instant Yup—and he sees the shock in my eyes, he sees me registering his eyes) (be-spectacled), and that thin jewish nose, and those thick slit lips—and he old and gray awaits my response—though I just shift my gaze to his golden boy beside him instead, looking at me also, and then they're past me and moving on and so I shout out...

> "O PERT BUTTUCKS
> UPRAISED FOR MY MASTERFUL RAPE
> WHICH WERE MEANT FOR A PRIVATE SHIT
> IF THE ARMY WERE ALL!!!"

> —and he, he just kept on
> walking.

The "Wave of the Future"

Originally, I was gonna title this piece "I Should Warn Ya," but really, it's too late now.

You see, they're doing away with The Book. Yep. What they're doing is, they're taking Books, and they're putting em on disk: IBM disk, Mac disk, ASCII disk—and they're conspiring to make little hand-held Gameboy computers to put these disks in, so you can sit on the bus and punch up "a book," "any book"—on a plastic fucking toy.

And the reason I know this is cuz I sold your soul. Yup. No "poet" in the world has sold as many poetry "books" to "them" as me, and there's more coming out. That's right! I'm the Pioneer Poet of Electronic Publishing and I let them exploit me and I did it many years ago, and ya know what? I ain't even made ten bucks yet.

    And that, Poetry Lovers

                                is the price of your pathetic soul.

HAUL

I

I saw the best imaginations of my generation destroyed by stagnance—though well-fed and "making it," living in the sprawls of suburban Denver landfills, Minnesota trailer homes and treeless Puget planes—driving AM/FM/CD machines to Universities for degrees, and/or cube rooms in the City, if not scramming to bend over for some grunt job: slobbing paint, sweating scrubbing herniating torquing hauling always, hauling something: hauling furniture and boxes, microwaves and documents, paperwork and doilie—broomsticks, deodorants, ice cream, corndogs, cocaine, cogs— machinery: Hauling, Hauling!—the Mobius stairways—hauling by the hour, for the Dollar, hauling grass and hauling ass—hauling with a collar—of numbers: like 19%—compounded quarterly for Citibank and Visacard, Mastercard and Student Loan, for the never-rent and ever-buzz, for health insurance, gasoline, computer chips, "Technology"—and no time for madful dawns and all night orgiastic revelry—cuz Family!—and Bossman!—and going bald with anecdotes which fizzle in the glow of remote control, eyeballs jabbing juice (O.J. that is) at us, not contemplating nothing, and not even trying—to get Busted, Man!—for just having fun!—US: like a buncha old phlegm-hacking crewcut bastards with matching plaid blankets all lined up in wheelchairs outside some gone war-home with the giant word of "CONVALESCENT" hovering above—cuz this, People, is what we're hauling for: we find Freedom in our basements—on exercise equipment—with joysticks—but it's worth it, isn't it? I mean: to haul (up and down, and all around, across town) rather than howl (in the angel-headed hipster sense)—cuz really, what has whining ever really given us... besides poetry? And what, really, has poetry ever done for us!?

II

Lemme tell ya about "Beat Poet" Allen Ginsberg—who once ran howling in the night-streets, yowling that he'd heard the Great Prophetic Voice of Blake address him like some sorta Jesus—or was it Walt Whitman?—Anyway, he, now, "Most successful poet of the Century" (influence-wise) teaching like some portly Balzac at Naropa, with readings in New York and London, Tokyo and Paris—he, partying with Dylan and the Beatles, Kerouac and Burroughs—he—he (Old Gray Ginsberg) was recently seen passing a hat at Penny Lane—which is a pink-haired, pierced nipple/upper-lip and eyebrow, teen honky hang-out off the mall in Bouldertown—where, he (Famous Ohmster) was passing the hat to get some dough in order to go somewhere south like Mexico, or Argentina (where, I can only imagine) verse is meant for Revolution—cuz (down there) ink stinks of feces and piss and the gangrene pits of bulldozed stiffs, like in Salvador and places like that, where, each day, thousands of graves fester up a death stench us Western anglo motherfuckers will never ever understand, that is—until our own Apocalypse, when the Pacific will open up in one big toothless smile of blood and gums like some haggard grotesque godmonster about to chow down what it's just thrown up (starting with the soupy goopy chunks of L.A.) the point being: huh, what? Ridiculous! Jolly Cheese Death! Forget this!

(unfinished...

                                   forever...

                   unfinished...)

VAGAVISIONS

Yesterday on St. Germain (night-time) I found a beat up cripple lying mugged at some bus stop in a puddle of his own piss. His pockets were all pulled out and his head was on the dogshit concrete. A cop walked right by him.

Then today, a wino gestured, grunting at me. I was trying to eat a banana at a triangle square across the street from where that mugged guy lay last night (till I gotta nuther cop to go on over and check him out... maybe dead, who knows?)

Anyway, the wino, he wouldn't stop grunting at me—so I got up and moved away, and he, with all the time in the world to spend trying to communicate with whomever he so chooses—he got up and followed me, then sat down on a bench next to a smartly dressed black woman reading a paper with her legs crossed—so grunted at her—and she, shocked, jumped up and shot away with all her jewelry jangling.

So now he sits alone on bench. From ten feet away I can smell his reeking cheapwine. He smokes a cig and grunts at anyone who passes by. Sits with his legs crossed.

And somewhere (behind some building, beyond some wall) there lies another alcoholic with his broken teeth, and his forehead finally smashed in... brains spilling into the street.

Today is his birthday.

Happy birthday, you fucking piece of shit.

STORY OF THE BOOZE

now I'm no millionaire so I certainly
wouldn't have gone out and spent a week's wages
on this booze but Karl would, he
bought it for me
we went to the liquor store around the corner
and he told me to pick a whisky

well it was all fancy whiskey
each bottle cost more than a cow in India
so I looked for the cheapest booze
and picked it, then Ted
drank half

Scotch whiskey, though, is an indulgence
Scotch whisky should only be sipped by publishers
V.I.P.s and world-famous literary artists
not Ted

therefore
I contribute this Christmas booze to
the Sylvia Beach fund for
entertaining royalty and scholars

Happy New Year George.

MOE

Moe came in with his kids
I hate Moe and Moe hates me
he left his kids in a room and went away
I went in to see them
they were 2 and 3 with blonde hair and wide eyes

Hey, I told them, your daddy is a homosexual
do you know what that means?

They shook their heads no

Well, a homosexual gets it up the butt, I told them
you see, your daddy likes to get drunk and fuck other
little kids' daddies, he sucks on their pee-pees too

the kids looked like they were about to cry

But you shouldn't judge your daddy because he doesn't always do
your mommy, I told the little nippers, these days it's
okay to be a homo—not like 40 years ago when sodomy
was either a sickness or a crime or a sin

now the kids were happy again

What you should judge your daddy on, I told them
is by how many friends he has
does your daddy have many friends?

they shook their heads no, sucked their thumbs

That's because your daddy is a loser, I said
do you know what a loser is?

Yes, the 3 year old nodded

I guess she'd heard the word around the house.

FRENCH LESSON

In France
 a teacher is a lecturer
  and the word for nobody
   is personne.

BIG SLABS OF MEAT

sometimes
walking down greek alleys
avoiding the eyes of restaurant guys
trying to sell you a sandwich
is like avoiding
the eyes of a whore.

TO FIND GOOD BROWN BREAD

just stroll through the street
of rotating meat:

gargantua.

SHUT UP FOR POETRY

It's funny to watch the poets of France
  they stand up on chairs when everyone's drunk
   fulfilling the stereo
    type that they are

At the beatnik joint around the corner
  guitars are playing and everyone's singing
   as the Poet composes his face serene
    and patient with reverence
     like all those before him
      who dared to bring
       their poems
        to Paris

          the lyrically loyal quiet the house
           "SHUT UP FOR POETRY!"
            somebody shouts

a bilingual tempest ensues
 "Silence!" "Shuddup!"
  "Claquez Ton Bec!"

then after a moment
 of respect for the Poet
  whose mission it is
   to divine a cliché
    he flowers forth
     his vivid bouquet

          blooming with words
           like "roses" and "birds"
            as the French love to do
             until "Turds!"

"Merde!" howls the Poet. "Merde Alors!
 Mon Frere! Mon Pere! Mon Derriere!
  Brulez-Moi! Enculez-Moi!"

and Voila! Fini!
 the Poets steps somber
  down to the ground
  drowning his gaze
   in the depth of his beer

"Pierre!" we shout
 "Hurray For Pierre!"

meanwhile, over at St. Michael
the new poetry of France
 explodes in the Metro
  splattering bodies all over the place

we see soldiers, stretchers
copters, smoke
 people bleeding
  beneath Notre Dame

      what it means though
      nobody knows

          not even Pierre
         already plucking
         verbs from the air

            like everyone there
           taking this scene
           and making it
           their own.

France Is Fucked up

Not since Hitler, a standstill like this:
  Paris has stopped:

    The metros are on strike
    The trains are on strike
    The Post is on strike
    Telecom threatens
      and so does the power

this country with the best healthcare in the world
  wants to retire at 55

  no space for students
   they smash computers
    burn their own books
     "Like Prague in 1968"
      according to *Le Figaro*

police squads scream through the gridlocked dawn
 blue lights flaring
 sirens blaring
  military vanloads
   offloading everywhere.

but at least there's been
  no bombings for a week
    though nuclear testing
     is still ongoing
       as gargoyles drain
        the acid rain

then last night en route to the Bastille
  (which, now, is he opera house)
   followed 10,000 protesters stabbing the sky
    with pink triangles, blowhorns and whistles
     lying down in the street
      jamming the system

NO CHIRAC! went their chants
NO CHIRAC! NO CHIRAC!

a cop came over
asked What's up?

an eerie army answered his question:
five green trucks abreast
hissing hoses from gutter to gutter
faceless like Vader
orange lights glowing
blinking like eyes in the chlorine mist

then later at Shakespeare
I give him this image
to some South Korean writer
adding the fact
that there were no horses
in this parade
so they must've been spraying
AIDS away

he told me I couldn't
go spreading this image
just cuz I think it
he said my duty
was being objective

I said truth
is what's important
and that we need lies
like peace needs crime

which led to more ire
and wine

this, however, is beside the point
France is fucked up
but so is the world.

DEMISE OF THE BEATNIK JOINT

Chim comes in, backpack on
  just back from Spain

  Hey, I say, where you been?

I been at the base of things
  he replies
They are fascist down there
  they put me in prison because I am black
    and had me a white chick
      but I got out
        and got out fast

So we go to the neighborhood beatnik joint
  where a mustache guy looking like Zappa
    rolls a spliff with chunks in it
      and it goes around

                to Simon with his big Brit voice
                and mad Dr. Frankenstein hair
                singing Delta blues
                        (he knows all the Dylans)

while Just-Got-Out-Of-Jail Guy
  sticks his face
    in every face
      trying to get
        punched in face

and Constantin's stoned with moonglow eyes
  nodding toward Old-Pipe-Smoking Lady
    spouting off about Slut Mother Mary
      and showing us her tits

        plus, there are gals on tables
        dancing with their asses
          but Chim just sits there
          eyes misted

puff puff puff
glug glug glug…
and the next day
the cops stop by
tell us no more music
no more poetry
no more 60s
in the 90s

Chim objects
they haul him off
he is at the base of things.

OCTOBER VERTIGO, KIDDO IN PARIS

I would've understood Rimbaud quitting cuz he couldn't do justice to the Beauty—but he ceased for reasons too soon.

Kissing Kiddo is the most beautiful thing I've ever known. Her movements roll like waves in the night of all the words that go against the reasons I choose to write... including the words I choose to write with... as she brims beneath me, my over-indulgent poetmind (vain enough to call itself this) overflowing something...

Kiddo: her face is angled up toward mine, and her lips are parted slightly... parted with something... something quivering... on some distant brink... something so vague and fragile it can't be expressed. All it can be   i   s unattainable...

...and there she is so much the girl in my arms that the instant makes me wanna cry or die or hide, just to know I know—I know how I feel...

...and the instant, also, it makes me wanna black out, makes me wanna quit smashing, iambic, my head on the table... forever... cuz words (*lightning strikes me!*) can never go this far... cuz words (Run! Run! Food! Kill!) are only animal calls which evolved into language...

...and though syllables sometimes flow into music, Kiddo is all music... so it's impossible for me to capture her, a portrait of her... what surges in her, swells and emerges, swims between us... and holds us together choking my lungs and spinning my head...

I am torn for gratuitous reasons. My purpose here on planet is idealistic and naive: to show how music (the music of words) can approach and touch what kicks and concussions the blood pumping muscle. But another purpose also is to just fucking live goddammit! And to fucking love! And these are things which will never join and never work together to the degree of the "passion" I've tricked myself into dying for so I don't die for nothing...

Kiddo: her Beauty is the Beauty of the rolling sea, and it makes me dizzy to be involved with it. Thus, I write the suicide letters of centuries, disguised as praise for the ocean... I write... shit.

BEAUTY SLEEPS ALL NIGHT

I wrap myself around her naked self
to protect her from the cockroach hordes

    cold: they crawl softly
    up and down my spine
    I flick them off

and warm: she doesn't even know
they're there. Beauty
sleeps all night.

LAST BATH IN PARIS

Beauty in the bathtub inviting me in
    says the most
        profound thing:

      "...if you can love somebody
      in spite of their differences,
       then that's the most important thing
          I think..."

and I am blowed away; I didn't know

                she could be

                    so beautiful.

The Colorado Rockies Are Faraway from France

I loved her naked beauty

    all that warm
      womanflesh

                  wanting me
      to love her back
           and I did
    never figuring
      I'd find her
          finding herself
    amazed to learn
        she can
          actually love
      and she, she was loving me
        for showing her
           herself
      which was
        always there

    loving me

      for loving her
        and encouraging her
        to love others

              also

because she, 23
    knows she can't
    just love me

      when now she knows
      she loves herself

because she's beautiful

    and how could I not
    love all
that's beautiful in the world?

    how could I not
not let her go?

      so I love her
    I love all the beautiful
        women I love.

LETTER TO A DEAD GRANDMOTHER
MAY 10, 1995

Dear Gramma,

I don't know what to say
I don't know how to feel
it's your birthday
and you're dead.
This has never
                happened before

I want to send a message to you.
This is impossible
this feeling, I guess
is like a funeral:

        when people die, the living speak
        to hear themselves think

I want to tell you what I've been doing
                      where I've been going
I want to tell you
that I've cried
but I can't

Gramma,

I sold your books, all your stuff
I sold your t.v. for 28 bucks
I sold all that junk
you've been keeping for decades

        I sold it for booze
        I sold it for pot
        I sold it for cigs
        I sold it for SHIT!

and still, you are taking care of me
but that's not all:

I even fucked a chick in your basement
    Yup!
I fucked her and fucked her and fucked her and fucked her
I fucked her silly, I fucked her
and I loved it
like some sorta pervert
fucking to kill
and she loved it too
like a whore

meanwhile, upstairs,
your pale ghost was lying in bed
just as deaf as you've always been
with that ancient Hebrew bible
lying sallow next to you

like the color of your flesh, your scattered ashes
while I porked her

and as I was coming, holding
one hand on that rubber
(to keep that motherfucker
from sliding off again)
she was quaking,
shaking with gasms

like your whole old house
                                        wracking
with the sour smell of semen and sweat
and those manic gaspings
(louder than rape)

cuz I was hating myself
for loving so hard
but not hard enough
to take her somewhere else

cuz where the hell else
was I sposed to take her? I mean
I'd already spent
half your furniture
on motels in Portland

so we were shacking up
sleeping till three
eating your food
burning your furnace....

FUCK!

this ain't the kinda letter
a nice white grandson
writes his gramma, this

is more like some sicko
asshole
writing himself

     (right before
     he sends it out)

but still, it's your birthday
and still, I haven't written
a goddamn thing
you would ever be proud of....

     Love, your grandson.

NATURE POEM

I was sitting on some driftwood
on the edge of the Sound
throwing rocks

I was a pretty good shot
I could hurl a bullet
and hit my target

Along came a gull
a delicate white
soft nice
gull

a girly gull

I knew I couldn't hit it
so let rip
and clocked it a good one
right in its skull

"GAWK!" said the gull
it was fucked up
but kept on going.

WEST OF ARCATA
ON EDGE OF AMERICA

Have you seen the waves
come crashing in?
Have you felt the spray
the foam
the wind?
Have you ever
really
sincerely
felt pure?
like I
do?

I doubt it.

this is death.

OPIUM TIDE
HEROIN SEA

the sand is silk
the air is salt

the water moves
i don't.

SUCKING ON MY BIGGIE

Crossing Nebraska
I pull into aWendy's
order the #1 combo:
  hamburger, fries
  & a Pepsi

"Do you want the Biggie?"
  the drive-thru lady asks me
"Sure" I say "gimme the Biggie"

  it only costs thirty cents more
  I figure they'll give me
  extra fries

at the window though
she hands me a bucket
fit for a fatfuck

  "Jesus Christ!"
  I tell thelady
  then take the pop
  and hop back on I-80

on Radio Evangelism
it has just been discovered
that hurricane damage
is up a hundred and
forty-six billion

"The weather patterns are changing"
  the dashboard informs me
"it is the will of God"

and just like that
my exhaust falls off

so I pull over
on the shoulder
and my avocado Malibu
sinks into the sand
there's nothing to do
but sit there like an idiot
sucking on my Biggie.

DICK TRICKLE WAS THE DRIVER FOR MCDONALD'S

Joe Montana
was driving the pace car
until the Nascar
 Spamcar
began passing
 Miller beer

it was Winston vs. Amoco
 Camel vs. Conoco
Texaco vs. Marlboro
 & Citgo vs. Kool

        even Hooter's
          sported a stock car

the Tide car however
 was the coolest ride
like a jug of detergent
 doing 195

          (while robots w/
          computer-triggered eyes
          shot live video
          from inside)

but in the end
 STP beat Valvoline
and Wal-mart hung
 its head in shame

so out came the owners
and bimbos
and champagne

        at the Goodwrench 500
     in Michigan
          where numbers are
     profane.

Her Depression

She said she wishes she was in the mountains. In the mountains you look at what's there and you think of what's beyond. But here, she said, I look at what's in front of me and that's all I can see. Wow, I told her, that's real fucking intense! That's astute! That's so profound for 19 years old. I know, she said, that's the problem.

North of Naropa, Rising White the Everswirl
I Contemplate the Whole Ordeal
Swilling in My Head

I

"Yo what up bro?"
my slacker stoner next door neighbor
utters stumbling through my doorway
"Wanna come over and rippa tuber?"

"Sure," I say, and walk across the lawn with him
in Boulder Colorado where
I write papers for kindhappy bud

"Got some new organic dankweed!" he tells me
"It's the diggitydank! Hotdiggitydank!"

> *blubba, blubba, blubba....*

we suck long on a two foot bong

II

my slackerstoner nextdoorneighbor
takes a hit then turns toward me

"This bud's so sick and twisted, dude!
Let's roll a jibber uvvit! Smoke it all rad
like a conebone and shit! I'm so stoked!
You're gonna get medieval on their ass!

And that's no cheesedog, brother!
You'll be snooking furburner, dude!
You the Man!"
"Thanks," I tell him
lungsucking further

III

back at the ranch
my 19 yearold runawaygal
who's manicdepressive
paranoidschizopherenic
and totallydelusional
says to me

"Can't I please, please
talk to Crispin please?"

"No!" I tell her
for the fortyfourth time
"There is no Crispin in me!
I am me! Myself! Not
CrispinFuckingSomebody!"

"Fuckme!" she tells me "FuckMeHardNow!"

"No!" I tell her "take your pills."

but medication never works
I always have to rape her
to make her shut up

IIII

but it's not really realrape
it is clearly playrape

    as she peels her jeans
        revealing soft mammal
        underneath

    as I accept her love
        like another bonghit

then we get wet: bellies and sweat
        slappa, slappa, slappa, slappa....

IIIII

she doesn't care about HIV
she doesn't care about getting preggie
she doesn't care if she's fucked in the head
she'll fuck and fuck until she's dead

IIIIII

I cross the lawn with a paddlefishpaper
for my slackerstonernextdoor neighbor
cuz all his green is cherry tailed
and orange with fine white crystals

(he never has a bag for under a hundred)

"Dude," he tells me, "that chick of yours is psycho!
Totallypsycho!"

"I know," I tell him
and stare into the chamber
like the barrel of a gun

blubba, blubba, blubba,

blub, blub,

blub..

RETURN OF MY MENTALLY ILL GIRLFRIEND

"You wanna fuck me in my ass?" she asks
"Sure," I tell her
and lift her knees up high
She's on her back with her cunt in the air
while I finger her hole
then slip my tip in
though it only goes
halfway in

Nevertheless, I work it and work it
And then she sneers "I got fucked
by the Devil in the ass
in the back of a bus
in a porn!"

I stare down at my dick
in her ass
now it's not as hard
as it used to be
when I try to shove it in
it just gets fat

So I pretend she didn't say
what she just said
I pretend that I'm fucking
who she used to be
I pretend that I'm fucking
somebody else

(as I trick myself
into thinking
I'm just jacking off)

and jizz
in her asshole
somewhere
in the future
as a poem ends
like the abomination
this
is.

REPORT FROM BOULDER

I

Simon, my co-translator, wrote me in a letter: "Your mockery will be the end of you Mark Spitzer!"—or something like that. I wrote him back telling him I was through doing that, and not to worry.... I wouldn't picture him as a sloppy old drunk. Nevertheless....

II

Jaime was my basketcase. She was 19 years old, manic depressive, paranoid schizophrenic, bi-polar, bi-sexual, on the lam, and heading my way. She's the only person in the world I've ever met more obsessed than myself. Thing is though, I can function and imagine at the same time. She can't. And then she made it to Denver.

III

So I took her up to Rollinsville—but Kowalski wouldn't have any chemically unbalanced totally delusional streetkids from France living in our house. We were banished to my car and forced to live in town, driving around, looking for a place to stay in fear of gonorrhea. Something was fucked up. And then there was lice.

IV

But that's a long long horrible story. The point is, I loved her once when she was sweet. And a poet, I thought. Then I found out she was insane. Meanwhile, she reamed my soul while I tried to save her. In the end, I had to kick her out to save myself. It was her or me—so I sent her to the wolves. The hardest thing was giving up.

V

So it was a welcome relief when Gruff Dave blew up—got drunk and threatened to punch Larz in the eye. It was all due to pool, and a stupid game throwing cigs in a hat. Dave was down 60 bucks to Extreme and me when Marina walked in and asked "What's Up?" Larz said "Your husband's a chump." So it ended outside in the gray shitty snow.

VI

Dave apologized and gave Larz a coat, though no one ever felt quite right after that. Then my "Mountain Gals" got into a fight. I won't bring it back—but it ended in blame. It's stupid when friends can't take what they hate—because something in the other triggers something in the self. And nothings get blown into All.

VII

And that's about when Larz and Melinda started bouncing on the bed. To Melinda it was a spiritual thing. The planets were in-line and something about water signs. But for Larz it was ACL pain. His knee had just been cut open and he was strapped in a machine. Melinda would come over and pull his pants down. She'd sit on his dick and moan while he groaned. So this, also, ended in bile.

VIII

Then, somewhere in there, Jaime came back. She'd been to the Coast where she lost her mind. Completely. I had to fuck her to make her shut up. She wouldn't shut up. She pushed me to the edge where I couldn't hang on. I lost my grip—and am not proud of what I did. I can't even write what I did. So I kicked her out again. Now she's in a Mississippi nuthouse. And pregnant... and claims I'm the dad. But I wore a rubber. The others didn't.

IX

Meanwhile Constantin came back from L.A.—now just as poor as I've always been. I found myself supporting him. It's amazing how easy it is to hate the poor. And the lame. Like Larz.... laid out in bed. I found myself taking care of him. You can't get up when you're strapped in a machine, but you can fuck to the point you can't feel the pain.

X

But what can you do? You can't do much. The most you can do is come up with bullshit. Like: *This was the season we all saw our demons*—when the truth is: we need drama, we need hate. And tragedy—to know we can feel. And oh yeah, we want words—to fool ourselves with. Though fooling others is the trick.... in this goddamn show that just won't quit.

OUR BODIES NOT CONNECTING, I WANDER OUT AND INTO THE NIGHT MY UNDERWEAR STUFFED IN MY POCKET

We'd been kissy-face for quite some time
but only when she
got drunk

and we might've made it years ago
if she didn't love me so
but that's why we
were friends

real friends
genuine friends
friends on our fifth
or sixth
margarita

then back at her place it starts up again
she can approach me
for human heat
that's the way we play it

"Want to lie down on my bed?" she says

"Sure," I tell her, "I'm no fool"
and we laugh
at that

so pretty soon, off come our tops
and those beautiful breasts
and the warmness of her flesh

        (again, I had landed
          in a soft bed)

"So is it like kissing your sister?"
she asks me

"No," I tell her, "my sister doesn't kiss
like this"

"That's the dumbest thing you ever said"
she says

"No it's not," I answer back
"It's the funniest thing
I ever said"

We argue about this
for a bit
pushing and pulling
away

till off come our jeans
and the next thing ya know
I'm under the covers
diving face first
into her crotch
and hearing some sounds
I have never heard
rise from the throat
of my friend

Gee, I figure
I must be doing a pretty good job

as I tongue the nub
of her little clitoris
until she pulls me up
and says

"Do you want to do it now?"

"Sure," I reply, "let's get it over with"

       (and as she rises
       for a rubber
       all those naked contours
       ghost across the room)

"What about you?" I ask her
"Do you want to do it too?"

"My body does," she says
and so I put a condom on
and she grabs my cock
and everything
goes soft

nevertheless, I try to jam it in
it won't go in
she gets on top
grinding against
my soft-off

"This is a disaster" I tell her
"This is like being sixteen"

"It's alright," she tells me
          (just the words
           I don't wanna hear)
and even though my dick is limp
I come

"It's Fate," she explains
"It's rubbers..."

"Yeah," I say, "maybe"

so no wonder she wanted me
out of her bed:
a man too drunk to fuck
ain't worth much

"Goodbye my love"
she bids me adieu
I could only find one sock
in the darkness
of her room.

LES CANTOS DE HOLLYWOOD

I

I feel so fucked in the head I'm amazed I'm not dead. I have reached that
melodramatic poet-place where all words are lies. And there are eyes. Or—at
least—this is what I've tricked myself into. The whole damn world is a stage for
hypnosis. Hypnosis of vision, hypnosis of others. Hypnosis of the self, hypnosis of
the All. Hypnosis and nightmare and dream. Dreams that used to be about magic,
and purpose, and beauty. Of course this is vague! I'm not writing for anyone else.
I am writing to make sense of my shift. Now that self-expression is gone (having
already grandly satisfied that), I don't know why I try anymore. Except that
motion makes for direction (or rather, the *illusion* of it) in this phantasmagoric
trip where all I want to do is be honest. But can't. So I'll fake it.

II

(affolé)

Nevertheless, here I am, in my bright lime dinosaur shirt, flying toward L.A. I'm
on my way to Hollywood, 31 years old and thinking of Death. Death has reared its
ugly head. I was flipping on shrooms and tripping through the woods. The woods
were cold and so was my blood. Which terrified me. Usually, the cold, it never
penetrates. I mean, I'm the guy in the Minnesota snow, sixteen below, sitting there
naked like a lama in Tibet. That's what the monks call *tumos*. I, however, just trick
myself (into believing, through breathing) that I have the power to merge with the
cold. But now the cold has gone to my bones. I feel its strength and it makes me
weak. And I hate the weak (we all hate the weak). So I find myself in need of *her*,
and yearning for *her*—to send her heat to me.

   Despicably!

III

(l'ange)

I think about my beautiful friend, and all her naked mystery. I think about my
beautiful friend. Which is what I called her the other drunken night. To which
she replied (pulling back her feet, and pressing against my chest), "You always say
the dumbest things in bed." But "No" I said, "I stand by this!" And spread her legs
with tenderness. Though it really didn't matter anyway, because sinking back to

the nexus of her sex, there wasn't much left for me to do. I mean, I'd already come, and lapped her like a dog. So I was limp when she gripped my dick to rub against her clitoris, but there was nothing solid to work there with. "You don't like me...." she accused, But I objected instantly: "Not at all! I love you! I really do! I just can't trick myself with you...." She, however, was aware of this. And so we kissed. But again, all it was was meat touching meat. So I hold this picture in my head: she is lying on her bed, nightgown pulled up over her chest, and everything soft beneath me. God, her breasts! Her nipples in the dusk of night of the phantom formations I fail to describe. It makes me want to cry. I can't make love to my beautiful friend.

IV   (sacré)

I am reading Edward Abbey's journals now. There are two American literary geniuses of the latter half of the XX century: Abbey and Bukowski, especially toward the end of their lives, their wits on my wrist like a cigarette burn....

# # #

Met the editor of these journals down in Durango this spring. My friend Ken always has a party each spring to honor Abbey. People come with offerings, which they lay upon the annual altar. This year I brought the shreds of a poem written en route to Four Corners. Somebody else brought a couple mudded survey stakes. Others brought rocks, books, pinecones and such. The editor, however, laid down some weird wood. It was twisty and skull-like in a rodent kinda way. I looked at it and handled it and could not figure it out. It had a strange weave. Later, though, I overheard him telling Ken that this was a dried up cactus, and it came from Abbey's grave. "Don't ever tell anyone," the editor said, "Don't even write about it...." And Ken understood. And so did I. But.... that ain't my way.

V   (les couleurs)

The Colorado Kid has landed in L.A. The Colorado Kid has brought his own screenplay: *ATTACK OF THE KILLER MUD-PUPPY*, which will surely bring him bucks. But first he's got to spend a few. POW! $172 for a 3-day rental car: a 1997 Chrysler Libido convertible, cherry red and hotter than hell. Ahhh, Excess! He drives around town, sees long blonde supermodels with their long blonde superbods, their asses in pantses bursting below. WHAM! An eleven dollar lunch at a café called The Red. Then back in the phallus, he cruises up West Hollywood. Notes tattooed alcoholics digging through the trash while suit-stuffed burgerflesh drives on by in Benzes and Jaguars and Bentleys and Royces and limos with poodles and hair-dos and gold. Meanwhile in the gutter, shopping-cart crack-addicts slog along with stinking piss running down their rags. There's a guy in a parking lot scoping out a new Trans Am. He sees the Kid, who's seeing him, but doesn't give a damn, so slips in, ducks down, and works the wires of ignition. The Colorado Kid doesn't do a thing. He heads for Palisades, where rollerbladin' maidens zoom through the shimmer of the scorching Venice sun. WOW! His funk is gone. He's tricked himself again.

VI   (*la chaleur*)

And the day goes on in the Californy heat. This is earthquake weather: muggy, hot, 100 degrees. The scene is a local sushi joint, and the object is une mademoiselle with great round fleshy breasts pushing through a thin tank top. Her tan is obscene. She is the sexiest/scariest creature on the planet (*anorexia fantasia*). And these are the men who drool over her: the Producer, the Director, the Screenwriter, and (of course) the Colorado Kid. The Producer is an Aussie madman, talking fast as if on coke (though just drunk), and the Director (Canadian) believes in the fever of the Colorado Kid (which is one reason why he is here). The Screenwriter, so they say, is the fastest pen around. He tells them about his roommate le Count: a guy worth 70 million bucks, who hires fine young call-girls at the rate of $500 an hour, has a castle in the South of France, and will die before he's 25. They all drink beer and talk about stars, multi-million dollar deals, and (dontchyaknow?) la mademoiselle, who stands up, and stretches, flashing a flash of perfect belly flesh (*her naval the eye of all sexhellfury*). It locks on the gaze of the Colorado Kid.

VII   (*égoïstes*)

"Let me get this straight, Mate," the Producer asks me (having switched back to the first person), "You translate French but you don't speak the freakin' language?" "Yeah," I say. "But you can understand a conversation?" "Nope," I reply. "Why not?" "Don't wanna." "Mate!" he exclaims (as they all do in their various ways), "That's completely crazed! Do other translators do that?" "Nope," I say. The Producer turns toward the Screenwriter: "This guy is a bloody lunatic!" and then toward me: "And are your translations any good?" "Yeah," I brag, "they're the best. Even the French can't read Céline." "Alright!" the Screenwriter breaks in, and slaps me five. He's glad to meet another conceit that's just as vain as his. But then they go away. So the Director and I, we head off for java.

VIII
(le grand fromage)

The Colorado Kid: he drives around with his shirt buttoned down like some Hollywood cheeseball minus the shades (he's gonna be somebody!) then stops in to see his publisher, who cuts him a check for 500 bucks and gives him a contract for a book (completely unexpected!). The Colorado Kid: he hops back in his crimson coup and hits the Sunset Strip, cruises up to Beverely Hills. He shows himself off in his bright lime dinosaur shirt, and Mopar Corvette. (In "the City of Angels" a car is who you are!) But could it be that maybe he's not even posing at all? (maybe he already is someone!). So should he stop and celebrate? Perhaps get a drink in some nudie joint? Or howabout a blowjob from some skanky Hollywood whore? (he wouldn't have to look at her). Well then whattabout a measly beer? But, *Naaaaaw*, he decides, and drives to a supermarket, where walking inside he buys 3 small peaches for 6 cents a piece. And yes.... they are sweet.

IX
(songerie)

Dreamt I was part of a guerilla revolution whose mission it was to blow up a store. It was a hardware store and the bombs were to be constructed from special rubber gloves, dipped in plaster, then left to dry and filled with explosive powder. So I was buying these gloves at the hardware store I intended to destroy. They were $5.20 a pair, which I thought expensive. But nevertheless stood in line for a long long time, while freshmen poetry students handed in their assignments to the cashier. By the time I reached the register, the price tag was gone and I was as nervous as a mad bomber, so told the cashier they were a dollar per pair. But he wouldn't buy it. Thus, we walked on back to the gardening section where all the gloves had turned to chicken. Fried chicken. Of which we searched for drumsticks. But only wings remained.

X
(le vide)

Awoke in Santa Ana, got back in my cherry ride, and hit the 5 up to L.A. Got caught in traffic, but made it to the airport okay. Got on the plane and thought about nothing. Sat there like a zombie staring out at the sky. Not one thought festering inside. Things only matter when they matter. And I wasn't thinking jack. Cuz things don't have to connect—or even be consistent.

# # #

Below, the mountains are turning to sand, and the sand is turning red. Great vast fissures cross the dessert: Canyons and mesas. Rivers. Erosion.

# # #

Back to Colorado. Back to the dirt....

WINDING DOWN THROUGH WOLF PASS

to another eco gathering
of pagan luddite misanthropes
I brought broken rear end gears
to lay upon the altar

every year
there's a ritual here
to honor a legend's
barbarous words
whose phantom we salute
with whiskey
and beer

this spring
someone brought survey stakes
others books
pinecones
rocks

    and something with
    a very strange weave

I couldn't
figure
it out

until I heard
how it came from the grave
and then I remembered
Abbey asking

that his corpse be taken
from his coffin
stuffed inside a sleeping bag
and dragged by stinking
drinking comrades
to a secret place
in a very green place
then buried there

to fertilize
a cactus
like the chunk
I held
in my hand

eroded like a rodent skull
staring up at me
telling me to keep
my big
mouth
shut

and I did
almost.

I, Narcissus, Sur le Dirt

From now on all my poems are secret poems. I require no justification from anyone. I (Oh ever-present Reader) reject your expectations and rebel against your truth—which is your insistence that I write for you. I will write what I feel: my truth—for me—not you. There is no audience.

I

I was born into the body of a Washington farmer—a logger—a man famed for his height, even though he was only six feet tall like me, with size twelve feet. In the Yakima Valley, he was a giant. And I inherited his eyes, his face, his arms, his strength. Though sometimes his strength is all that I have. And with the job that I have, I rely on his back. I can abuse it. Strain it. Count on it for taking care of me. While I endure. He was a strong man. And I am proud to live in his frame.

II

I work landscape—which means I shape the land. Mostly though, I fight dirt. With a shovel: I'm in the dirt, I'm with the dirt, I sweat in the dirt, I breathe in the dirt. For seven dollars and fifty cents an hour.... I wear the dirt, I live with the dirt, I merge with the dirt, attacking the dirt. Sometimes I even kill the dirt. Man versus dirt. Muscle versus earth. The incessant *shhooooonk-fling, shhooooonk-fling* of me against the dirt. I get lost in the dirt, get numb in the dirt—where my body grows strong. I dig until everything spins. And then I keep on digging. To see these veins alive and full. To feel these arms I used to know. I have become the dirt.

III

Though sometimes there is aeration. I follow and guide a green machine, which flattens as it goes, poking holes in the earth. The aerator allows the lawn to breathe. If it needs to breathe though I don't know. Grass grows strange in an arid land. In soil that isn't soil. This is Rocky Mountain soil: sandy and red, cacti soil. There are no worms here. Just plastic and fabric strata beneath. Hoses pump blood in the hot desert sun. Homes are not meant to sprawl across this land, and either are their lawns. I rise from my trench.... survey the pastel rooftop-sea stretching toward Infinity: one vast dogshit golfcourse village. This is where I once pulled up stakes. But now this place is serving me. Outside in the sky, I have a place—or rather, a purpose: to keep on aerating.

IV

But sometimes I drive trucks. Beat-up, broken-down, fucked-up trucks. There's a big red dump truck, a funky four-ton Ford, and a one-ton Chevy with three-on-the-tree. I drive around. In Boulder. In Niwot. Through Hygiene. Up Sunshine. Toward Lyons. Toward Marshall. Lafayette. Louisville. I always drive.... and veer from my course.... checking out ponds dug on the flats. There are big twisted carp, and sunnies and bass. I take rare roads in order to explore. Get stuck—jam the truck beneath a tree: a massive girthful cottonwood tree—its big heavy limb, weighted with decades. I can't back up, I have to go straight. I lay on the gas. The tree has no chance. I rend its length, fuck up the truck. Shredded bark. Plywood and parts. New battle wounds in an old rattletrap. The bosses still don't know.

V

Driving the trucks, I shoot off my mouth. I tell my co-workers I'd rather fight dirt. I tell them I am, no doubt, a secret fascist man.... yearning for the sadistic swing of the pick. I desire vertigo. Because I can go.... for hours, for days, the rest of my life. Digging drainage, digging ditches. Digging with hallucinations. The guys think I am insane. Driving the trucks is easy enough. Running sod, dumping sod—this is indeed the cherry job. But I want exhaustion. Punishment. To know that I can suffer on. And live with pain. And join its ache. In order to make it to the next swing. Shoveling rock, shoveling mud. "Shoveling a senseless ceaseless grave!" I rave. And then we pass a madman, lashing against the sky. It could be any century.

VI

My co-worker lights up a bowl. We're always smoking bowls. It starts at 8 a.m., then happens all day. We smoke and drive and dig and sculpt. The ashes in the pipe burn red in my mind. I dig and dig and don't feel the drain. When I am high, I am the strongest man alive. My endurance is phenomenal. I am an athlete of earth. I go all day. Smoke Mexican shwaag. Skunk. Kind bud. "The shit." I hate pot. I hate it for its glorious grip on me. It makes me think. And also not think. It fools me and ruins me at the same time. I guess I only want to be half-alive. But I don't even try to figure it out. I take a hit when the pipe comes my way.

VII

Tacks, mats, river rock. Edging, grinders, axes, blowers. Juniper, mule deer, frogs, hawks. A red fox trots. Past our site and up the street. A tempo beats and repeats: *arump-chaw, arump-chaw, arump-chaw*.... the tired shoveler's mantra. There are sounds in the silence. I hear them, I know them. Their patterns can be caught. I switch my thought: *"Honest labor" can't be bought.* Though definitely, this beats the factory, and service industry. No stupid hats, no kissing ass. Just repetition. And dirt. I have waited years for this. Could this be utopia?

VIII

If the lady wants rock, we tear up her lawn. If the lady wants grass, we haul her rock out. We lop off roots and gouge the earth up. My eye is good and I can see planes. I level and grade. Because the lady says so. So what if it's dumb to reshape the dirt? The idea is to hump. Hump wheelbarrows, boulders, clay, sand, mulch, whatever. I let the sun burn into my skin. My neck pulls the redness in. Head rushes roll in waves through my skull. Patterns and grids appear in my sight.... wiggling currents, electric, bright. I can place them anywhere. Geometry that isn't there. I'll take it.

IX

"I shoulda stayed in school," my co-worker jokes—and I laugh back. He means it. This job is a bitch. We dig together in the ditch. They don't know who I am—but this is the way I want it to be. Now I am one of them, and I'm happy for once—so I tell myself. Getting high with the guys.... gasoline and metal machines.... roto-tilling, power-raking.... bruises, bleeding.... I straighten my back and look at my lines. I have cut the land, I have made a place. And my lungs are strong because of this. It makes sense to be a narcissist. I am 31 years old and I can keep going. Though I wonder how long I can keep going. Before I stop amazing myself.

X

Yes, I think, *I know something. Yes*, I think, *I've found something.* And even if it is an illusion, that's okay with me. I can dig and dig and dig and dig. I can prove my power to myself. And I can die with secret songs. And keep them holy to myself. And then one day... when I'm gone... my work will also be gone. And it will be another death of another poet—who didn't trick the world.

XI

My only question is, is "can I accept this?" And the truth is, I don't think so. But for now, at least, the dirt is teaching me. I have learned to love in the dirt—no matter how stupid this sounds. I have learned to love its touch—like the touch of something else. The dirt has become something in my gut. Something I will miss—like a person—or organ—or place—or purpose. But enough! I know I'm afraid to lose what I love. We are all afraid to love something else.

Death Threat #3

Leif, I gave you more than the allotted time
to answer for your crime:
how you could take a writer's work
butcher it without consent
(in every single line)
add things I never said
slaughter my meter
misprint things
censor the best
inject the obvious
alter tone
then publish it in your shitrag called *Kinesis*
(which moves as much as a never-rolled stone)
after I vetoed your so-called "editing work"
which you told me I could
after awarding me
the prize you never paid?

for which I dream of breaking your nose
crushing your foot, menacing
your wife and kid
and driving all the way
to Montana
for this

to see the terror in your face
when I show up at your place
and hang around in front of your car
          (not even doing nothing
          just whistling Dixie)

but for now I'll launch my smear campaign
just like I promised
if you continued to ignore
my inquiries
wondering

how you can be
an example to your kid

when you're so prone to print
false praise for yourself
as the editor "for the rest of us"
bullshit!

You owe man! and that's what burns me up
the most—that you won't even
acknowledge this—that you won't even
answer for this

but...

I'd rather have your terror
than your stinking hundred bucks
I'd rather smear
you into the ground.

See ya,

    Spitzer.

For Jill

Driving down I-25
it was dry outside
but wet inside

we were getting drunk
on something sober
we had to make love
we had to pull over

and climb beneath
a barbed-wire fence
then follow a waterless creek

to a spot on the edge
of a desert pasture
where again, outside
in the wide open sky
we felt our flesh
flow inside
                 the other

you must've seen the vapory rain
misting in the distance
over my shoulders

it was riding the spine
of the Rocky ridgeline

and never touching down
it was always many
miles away

       (we must've been
       the only moisture in that gulch)

until we clambered
back to the road
and found that wandering
pumpkin plant

its pointy long leaves
reaching for the sun
its stripy young fruit
awaiting the fall

but mostly those vines
   attracted the eye
their fantastic ramble
in all directions
sublime

I remember standing there   and staring there
across and beyond a system of squash
amazed at the maze
of its leafy labyrinth

the vista's spell was incredible
its cycle, its stretch
its *furtherness*

which held us
and shook us
then spit us in the sand

it crippled our tongues
it bittered our sugar
it made us think
we were strangers

            (relying on denying
            the strike of lightning?)

but this is all too melodramatic
overpoetic and acrobatic
when the truth (I think) is as simple as this:

we just don't know how
to not love each other

anyway, I also think
there's nothing wrong with this.

ANOTHER OBVIOUS OBSERVATION

At a Citgo in New Mexico
tourists from Texas
buy Navajo blankets
and postcards souveniring
historic Route 66

    (which doesn't even exist
     on the map)

then hop back on the interstate
never even tasting
the blood of what they bought.

Drove Devil's Highway 666

north out of Colorado into Utah, not sad like two days prior when leaving Boulder like I've done at least four times a year over the last few years—yes—was sad, as always to leave friends like Kowalski and Extreme and sweet Mountain Gals all who told me they loved me and then I was off and driving wondering will I be leaving always friends behind wanting me to stay and never have a good yellow cat? Luckily though, it'd been a few years since I'd seen Ken down in Durango, and he being my eco-muse new with child and nice-wife, was soon all fired up and comfortable in his warm house with dog and cat and then down to bar for beers and tequila shot getting intense about such questions as "does sound have mass?" and such, so soon wasn't feeling that depression prone to set in when a guy like me hits the road constantly and especially this time seeing a new cycle starting again after time-of-life in France and Fez and then mountain insanity up in foothills trying to get it all down on disk because if I don't I die—but then the phenomenon of on-the-roading brought me back to who I usually think I am; when the goal is just a continent or a few states to cross it seems like there's a more tangible purpose than just driving around and trying to write true-art, and indeed yesterday goal did become big—as said, drove Devil's Highway in the Southwest sunshine through red-cut dessert, sage and cliff walls then Utahland and Highway 50 supposedly "loneliest highway in America" and I guess it could be if you thought that way but I was translating Genet as I drove until darkness and Nevada then nobody behind for as far as the vista and hardly any headlights coming at me ever—drove switching from AM to FM until wrist felt like I'd been torqueing out rusty bolts all day, and then two o' clock in morning arrived in Tahoe where friend Jules is working and surprised her by showing up at motel and phoning up though she was sleeping with some Steve-guy and so it appeared the breakfast scene next day and me winding up some mountain road where I crashed in back couch of '72 clay-green Plymouth Fury station wagon hearing voices in head while lapsing out of 800 mile driving day into sleep-world where in the morning waking in fartbag and pile of blankets to frosted windows all around, heard more voices in my head which I attribute to the ceasing of pot-smoking as of late and what Crystal said about how I gotta quit cuz it messes up my dreams and she's right, and the voice said quite lyric-like, "give me mine, give me mine, give me some hope."

Did I mention the lavender brilliance of the Utah alp-scape? course not. At dusk at gas station was amazed to see the violet bright light of the setting sun laying something jewel-like upon the land. The serrated ridgeline glowed an eerie pastel neon fluid-shine I had never seen so purple—but enough of that—I will never pretend I have the power to praise the power of the sun, I'll just jot its details. So, food with Jules in half an hour. After dwelling too hard on someone I gotta write about or die a loser to self, I find myself emerging with my own deal again. Sometimes people evolve chimeralike, their beauty haunt the mind's eye daily like the plague they never were until imagination gone mad naturally. Good morning California.

Here comes the next 50 years unless I die young.

IT's a Weird Time in Space

for Melinda and me
when we leave Extreme's
up in the Rockies
after watching the *X Files*
then stare into the starry night
to witness Hale-Bop
for the very first time

and not only that
there's a Martian eclipse
against the eerie moon
which illumes
the entire curve
of the Universe:
the Sun and the Earth and Mars are in line
(and the line
is bent)

so we get
in my car
and head for the cliffs

meanwhile, down in San Diego
39 devotees of the good
Reverend Applegate
ice themselves
to join the soul
of a UFO
hidden in the comet's tail

as a radar blip
appears on screen
and an Airforce pilot
down in Four Corners
breaks formation
without explanation
flies 5 hours north toward Vail
then disappears without a trace
loaded with bombs

(which is fine with me, because Hollywood
is now t.v. I see
actual generals
informing me
not to worry
everything's under control)

and who knows what else
is going on?
as we drive on
and see a bear
chiming along
like a big black dog

and then we're there: at my secret
mushroom hunting place
where I know all space
will scintillate

but she's too afraid
to get out of the car
Agent Mulder
was abducted tonight
and bears
are paranormal

and so we roll
back down to town
to Boulder USA
where JonBenet
can't even hold
a torch to the sky.

Junkyard

I: Colorado

Great Plains
Front Range
Rocky Mountains
ridging distance

shredded vinyl
sunburnt thistle
beached behemoths
bleached by the sun
trunklids open
to the sky

abandoned wagons
old schoolbuses
sheep grazing
between El Caminos

a beat Le Baron
a busted Bronco
an amputated
ambulance

a tranny field
armored plants
Aspens, Darts
Valiants

a totalled tore up
Toronado
a champagne faded
Pontiac

canyons, creekbeds
giant cogs
kills of
the junkyard dog

and North of Eerie
South of Speedway
a burn out
blowed out
trailer home

clothes exposed
flapping above an
old black bull
lazing in the daisies

one pink toilet
up above

II: Wyoming

Laramie traintracks
Quonset shed shacks
chainlink, salvage
broken glass

this land is massed
by new buttes:

endoed Escorts
crunched Corvettes
smashed creamed
beat machines

yellow flatness
yellow vastness
scrubby lunar
seascape gone

a bus nose
a manifold tree
a two tone tawny
    GTO

& shopping cart
& lamp parts
a landwrecked Fury
in the dust

till near Rock Springs
the Amazing Wall
of Welded Rims:
"We should be in *The Guiness Book*"
        the lady tells us
"ain't nobody else stupid enough
to weld 50,000 wheels together"

we nod
drive on

III: Utah

Strange to fathom
backyard boneyards
ancient cranes
tractors, threshers

a hawk, a crow
orbit above
a defunct Deere
a shot up hearse

Mormon breakfast:
two eggs & toast
99 cents
coffee
extra

cowboy hats, tight pants
we roll west
of Snowville

NO TRESPASSING
sign says
we go in
to the desert sage

of stoves and pipes
jugs of bleach
shotgun shells
sheet metal

and trucks as old
as the great
Salt Lake

jackrabbits dash
from skeletal heap
to skeletal heap

clumps of blood
on the dry
white sand

IV: Nevada

Serrated jagged
lines in the sky
This purple place
is a deadly place

ravens ripping
into roadkill
snakes sunning
on the shoulder
a lone antelope
hell-bent for nowhere

we end up
at Clint's
in Elko

Clint is smoking a cig
sideburns running
down to his ankles

his jawline is hardened
his hands are blackened
from crunching cars
then sending them
to Ogden

we weave
through a lattice of lizards
there are wiped out RVs
and cattle-smashed campers
but mostly Toyotas
Hondas, Nissans

dust and wind
assault our skin
we are the only
water out here

V: Idaho

On Highway 30
out of Boise
there's a scrapyard full of
swingsets and sewerparts
asphalt slabs and
tire pylons

we laugh
at an exploded Zamboni.
dropped on top
of a snowcone shack

this hole in the ground
is filled to the rim
with Travel-Alls
Jeeps and diesels

and is surrounded by
reservations
radio waves
and the KKK

then in Payette
on the Payette
a mountain of chrome
hovers above
a fisherman fishing
in sharp wicker grasses
of open range grazing

cut hay taste
in mouth and sky
deerflies buzz
in the hot
August sun

VI: Oregon

The green gold calico
of overcast Cascades

the Fuller's teasel
the tangled brambles
and fat field moles
we spook like Godzillas

stomping our way
to a bunch of Bugs
lazing like a pride of lions
gathered around
a bare lone
tree

we pay with our socks:

burrs
a thousand burrs
for Labor Day visions
of logging rigs
and discovans

like cattle in a storm
they face the same way

toward Pendleton
where a kingdom of junk
remembers the Scottish
with a moat full of in
hospitable thistles

so we hit the Columbia
River Valley
where the skyline's aligned
by a Titanic of stacked
Cadillacs
going down
in a sea of Torinos

here
El Dorado ain't
no city of gold

VII: Washington

On the edge of Grace
in Woodinville
Vintage Auto Parts
abounds in bubblicity
fenderosity
and the animalesque lines
and spines
of Desotos

plus Supers
      Specials
      Landaus
      Deluxes

anything with running boards
and three on the tree

there is lush in the dump
fungus, rust
blackberries
moss

      a Studebaker
      a Superchief

            the smell of storm
            the end of the West

                look…

                        a bird's nest.

(August 1996)

OUT ON THE ST. VRAIN FLOODPLAIN

a big old golden eagle
  ripping into roadkill white-tail:

        it hunkers there like a buzzard of death
         all shoulders and muscles
          and darkbrown and hunchbacked
           its long gouging neck
           delving the depths
            of the troughed out
             gored out
              ribcage exposed

This creature tearing carrion
 rends the flesh from the inside out
  dwarfing the magpies
    hopping around it

        this is why I return to the West

              in Europe there are no terrible eagles
             no foothills no Rockies
              no red rocks no fresh kills

I compare this eagle to some turkeys of the past
        no doubt this monster
          weighs 35 pounds
           or 40—I spook it:

        FOOOMP! its wingspan expands
         longer than myself
           as its talons lift
             dripping with viscera

        and it's off - - -

            to the knotted cottonwood
             where it perches above
                   the dark silhouette
                    never
                     in Paris.

PART 4

@ ATCHAFALAYA

1997–2001

ARROGANT POEM
COMPOSED ON THE ROAD
GOING BACK TO POETRY SCHOOL

I: Regarding Effluvia

HEY!

I don't wanna hear no stinking
nice poems
no scurvy
polite poems
no scrofulous
thoughtful poems
thunk up
and cut up
Lyn Lif
shinlike

or verse that's prose
pretending it knows
lying there like some sorta
paragraph/block/chunk
of smarmy shit

and I don't wanna see no
boringselfindulgent
gotta-try-to-get-past-the-
fourth-line-kinda
P.C.lovelornsentimentalhogwashbullshit
list of excusii
that calls itself
a poem

      like:

I cry for the babies in the streets
I cry for the families with nothing to eat
I cry for the flowers, the birds, the trees
and the poet
who can't find his pen

or his friend
or his reason
d'être
Yeah! I don't wanna read no I cry!
I think!I see!I feel!I say
and I don't wanna see no
　lying
　　dying
　　　trying
　　　RHYMING!
pieces a　　　　CA-CA!
relying on　　　　　　NAWWWW-
　　　　　　　　　　　　STALGIA!
　　　　to pave the way

cuz if that's what you've gotta say
then repeat your cliché
to someone who cares
to lap it up
like a dog
>>on vomit!

cuz this hypocrite is sick
of hearing *nothing*
reading *nothing*
seeing *nothing*
and witnessing *nothing*
getting published

　　　　(cuz *nothing's*
　　　　going on)

Ô "poets" of the world
　　　　　(except for a few)
I have never been impressed by your words;
they're slow
and tiresome

so here's a little bit
of friendly advice:
if you don't have anything new to say
then shut the fuck up

either that
or put a bullet through your head
spare us the lethargy

II: The Truth Is in Confusion

poetry is the stupidest thing in existence
because it exists
but rarely for a purpose

Truth is: poetry sucks
and poets do too
(measly whiney sons
of bitches!)

but sometimes (I admit) I (hypocrite)
gotta write a poem too
which is a different thing
than "poetry"

cuz "poetry" is product
not process (which is a whole
nuther deal)

process is trying to make sense
of what is not
penguindeath (ie: skipping through the daffodils)
it's burning up time
and mind
which makes sense

a lot more sense than some uppity know-it-all ëgomonger
pretending he
or she
has some sorta special way
of seeing the world.

Epitaph of a Professional Punk

an attacked class lashes back
      (understandably so)
bitter taste in head in bed
should've told em all Fuck You
Céline would've
(et plus)

      * *

now I remember why I left those
cocksucking workshops behind:
grad students are a pain in the ass;
they think they know everything
and shoot off their mouths
as if they count

but they don't
they're just a buncha
amateur punks
sickening me
avec
my own bile

This anger burns
like a French word

can't wait to deflate
innertube air.

but do you know where is the can opener? horked the dirty old man
the dirty old man asked for a coffee
the coffee was cold
the dirty old man was sad
he used to be a boy

                    boy: where is the broom   ?
          his pal: the broom is in the universe minus the broom
                              where the broom is.

GET UP DOG-SOUL

like Pam underwater

                                        stomping out armies
we were all baking brownies,

                              pumpkin lover

                    *

I am not writing this
I am accepting this
like a corpse.

30 SECONDS TO LUIS

vibratory platapus
ovulating octopus
trilobiting escargot
vinagrette of taco
syphilitic dissertation
Baudelaire on a snowboard
to you.

Manifesto (supplemental)

filling
up space
pleasingly

cuz it breathes by
touching something
of the core

*

exit
exit
exit.

Secret III

should make pledge
from now on out
all words =
holy words.

WHICH CAME FIRST
THE CHRISTIAN OR THE EGG?
(OR TRIVIAL TRIBULATIONS
OF AN ADJUNCT)

It really brought me down
the other day
to be called in by the Chair
and told that some student
had lodged a complaint

> because, so she said
> she wasn't learning
> anything

Anyway, I know who she is
  that whiney little
  Sigma-Alpha-Delta
  who walked in today
  with a C on her paper
  wanting me
  to change her grade

so I looked at her paper
again
it was about Creationism
and she made her arguments
by refuting Evolution

"There are no fossils
of ape-men" she claimed
"The Bible is written
in black and white"

and then I noticed
some "should"s
I shoulda seen
before

> ("should" is outlawed in my class
>   unless it's used
>   in a thesis)

But I am the objective
college instructor
so I don't crack her
I just keep reading
her paper

"God says, God says, God says..."

and then she concludes
by stating that her proof
is all the scientific
evidence existing
in support of the chicken

"The chicken came first"
she proudly proclaimed
"it's simple, it's just how much
you believe"

Oh, I think
so that's where you get
your information
from Faith

the little twit
with her big stick-out tits
I ask her if
she went to my boss

No, she says
shaking her head
a bit too shakily

so I raise her grade
to a B
even though she
deserves a D

for logic.

IN THE BAYOU OF THE GERMANS

beneath the ever-petro-chemical flame
flaring in the cancerous cane

I float with flotillas
past half-sunk trailer homes
busted boats
and Cajun kids
swimming with the gars

to the channel of the black grasshoppers
and they are everywhere
swarming swarthy
five or six
inches long
mutants
 fucking
  like dogs

I get the hell out of there
paddle through the cypress knees
the duckweed and machinery
then head back to Zam's
where a trapped alligator
is hissing in the gutter

"Last week it was a snake"
some crazy coonass tells us
I can hardly understand
a word he says

"What about those black grasshoppers?"
I ask

"Them?" he says
and tells me how the chemical plant
sent scientists a few years back
to collect them
and come back
but they never did

I head inside
the sky is getting darker
there's a jet black cloud coming closer
it might be smoke, it might be locust
I can't even tell the difference

so order
a po-boy
to go.

ON THE OUTSKIRTS OF PLAQUEMINE

where pipefields and tombs
resemble each other
next to each other
there's a Pizza Hut

where the tables are littered
with pieces of crust
and napkins are scattered
all over the floor

we seat ourselves
and wait for the waitress
who finally comes over

we order two Buds
buffalo wings
and an Italian sausage
black olive pizza

"What kind of dip
for your chicken?"
she asks

"Blue cheese" we say
and wait for our Buds
which never come

so I go to the kitchen
to gettum

our waitress then brings
six sorry looking dried up things
that look like wings
with ranch

so I get up and go to the kitchen again
where nobody cares
I'm standing in the doorway

but I can't be rude
I can't say "Hey
howabout some service?"
cuz what if they get pissed
and spit on our pizza?

"Oh"
our waitress finally utters
"y'all want more ranch?"

"Blue cheese" I tell her
"we need blue cheese"

then
when our pizza arrives
sans sauce
something drips
down on us:
the ceiling
is rotting
away

after that
I head for the shitter
which is stuffed to the brim
with soggy yellow bumwad

luckily though
I only have to take a leak
so I do it in the sink
and look at a plaque reading

"IF RESTROOM IS NOT SATISFACTORY
PLEASE INFORM THE MANAGER"

but I don't
I get the check instead
and we hightail it out of there

and the sugarcane sky is burning purple
as I blast my Buick
across the toxic
Mississippi

where even the fish
are trying not
to puke.

MEETING A CREATURE ON MY LIST
AND NOT EVEN REALIZING IT

bobbing there in Henderson Swamp
it looks like a dogfish
(or sandshark)
gone belly up
so I paddle on over
and scoop it up

Holy Fuck!
it's half a paddlefish
or spoonbill
a shovelnosed cat

And there it is!
all rubbery fleshed
and torn /
or chopped /
or gnawed /
in half

Wow! I grip its ridiculous
proboscis
its spatulated longschnozz
flexible and flat
ballooning cartoonlike

"BLAWGH!"
its mouth opens up
balinesque filters
wiggle at me

this rare endangered specie
hasn't even met
rigor mortis yet

What a weird fish!
I can't fathom it
how it got here...
why it's in half...

its beady little eyes
make me laugh
its primitive gills
make me think

super-chouette...

(the French word for cool)

I take its picture
toss it back in
to the murk of its
mysterium

So what if it's dead?
I paddle on.

Bloody Chicken Livers
Rotting in the Sun

the bikers next door are blasting Black Sabbath
some girls are squealing
and my back hurts
from food poisoning

I should throw that bad
mayonnaise out
like her letters I can't
throw away

they're scattered all over
the floor

she gave me that bad
mayonnaise
back when it was good
mayonnaise

I'm the guy who left it out
then ate it
to see if I'd get sick
and I did

though all I got were muscle aches
and a minor fever that
didn't even count

I also leave her letters out
to remind me of what a prick
I am

maybe their guilt will punish me
like these first words
which make sense to me

Black Sabbath blasts
dogs bark   in back
I am waiting to go catch
me a garfish.

ATCHAFALAYA CREOSOTE BRIDGE

I go to the swamp
to force a poem

my worm squirms
its last haiku

I drop my bobber
into the bayou

a rattlesnake swims
beneath me steeped
deep in secret meter

a blue channel cat
strikes my line
I reel it in
wiggling whiskers
at me

        she
is composing a sonnet
so I throw her back in

turtles and sunnies
pass through the pilings
a copperhead, a carp
and a bright red bee
gather to give
a reading

even the banana
tarantulas
are writing white script

while crawfish construct
towers of babble
clumped up like mud

Shit, I think
and give it up

I'm the only creature out here
who doesn't feel the need
to prove anything.

THE VIEW FROM MY WINDOW

I am not anti-fucking
I am pro-fucking
but I am tired of watching them fuck

at first it was kind of interesting
but now they're out there every day
fucking their heads off
while I sit at my computer
trying to type

and they never stop fucking
even when he's soft
he is still jamming away
and she just lets him

it gets to the point that I have to pull the shades
but I know they're going at it
fifteen feet away

it's maddening
this nonstop fucking
sometimes I want to go out there
and yell STOP FUCKING!
STOP! FUCKING! FUCKING!

but this would be ridiculous
fucking is a natural thing, I mean
how victorian it would be to get upset
about fucking

and I can't call the cops
they wouldn't give a shit
and it's not like I can go over there
and say Hey, excuse me
will you please stop fucking
in front of my window?

because they'd just look at me
and keep on fucking

so I give up!
I give in to fucking
I hope they fuck themselves silly
I hope they fuck until the cows come home
I hope they fuck the fuck
out of each other!

Yeah, and then I'll send this poem
to their owners
hoping to offend them
for offended me
with fuckery

but they'll probably just laugh
and put this on their fridge
and those dogs will keep on fucking
and fucking
and fucking.

DUMB MISTAKE

Sometimes you can just add a can
and that'll seal the leak
sometimes you can weasel off the cap
even when it's hot

but not this time
because suddenly I'm running
from an erupting radiator
and all those years
of cooling system caution
don't mean nothing now

boiling coolant
is blasting my back
and wherever I run
the geyser gets me

I rip off my shirt
my skin is peeling
down my back
and my neck
and arm
and shoulders
are raw
with burning green
antifreeze

"Hey!" some bum tells me
"I saw that coming two blocks away!
You know better than that!
You're a mechanic and shit, man!"

"Yeah, yeah" I tell him
and finish the job
pouring the can
of Stop-Leak in.

*

After the emergency room
a mile of gauze
and 600 dollars
of Silverdine cream

I take my second degree burn home
with the sweet smell of coolant
coming from it

and for the next three days
immobile in bed
that's all I'll smell
covered with giant
blisters and bubbles
oozing yellow pus

so burnt
I can't wear a shirt
and can't go to school
and can't go to work
hearing the voice
of my dad in my head:

So Marky
did you learn anything?

        *

Yes, I answer him
and make up some bullshit
about a new radiator
being better
than gunk

the truth though, I know
are the splotches on my arm
scars I'll carry
the rest of my life
scars I'm lucky
ain't on my face.

OTHER PEOPLE'S PROBLEMS

there's this kid, Doug
lives two doors down
never says nothing
to nobody

just walks around
with jaw set hard
skinny and lanky with Jimmy Page hair
always wearing
tight black pants
like some kinda punker
forced to conform

every day
his dad pulls up
and lays on the horn
to wake him up

every day
Doug gets up
and goes to the door

his father is paralyzed or something
never gets out of the car
just sits in there and coughs
like a guy about to die

> (a crabby
>   cantankerous
>   fart)

Doug goes to the back seat
and opens the door
leans in
and they rag on each other

then
Doug stomps off

"Don't You Walk Away From Me!"
his old man demands
and Doug
     always
          gives in

he receives a loaf of bread
or a can of Spam

other times, though
they go to see a lawyer
or a doctor
I don't know
I can only
guess

I watch them pull out
of the parking lot
Doug, glum, in the back seat
the old man demanding
to know about
rent

Doug and his dad
they're bound to each other
even though they hate each other

I don't get it
but then again
I don't have to

nobody does
not even
them.

DOUG II

and here's another thing Doug does:
nothing

because he's got satellite
so sits in there, no furniture
just burger cartons
and cartoons

sometimes though, he throws
his trash out
right in front of his door

chicken bones, slurpee cups
wrappers from Popeye's
Wendy's
Burger Tyme
Sonic

there's a broken Bud bottle
that's been there for three weeks
as he plays Nintendo
I hear it beep

the cats come by
and choke on the bones
he feeds them raw meat
       they puke
in the street

but it doesn't matter to Doug
the world is his toilet
and he doesn't
flush.

HE WAS A 73-YEAR-OLD BLACK MAN

at least that's what he kept telling me
with his big filmy eyes
and hand held out
demanding Money! Give me money!
for being alive

I was expected to respond politely
I was expected to not just walk away
but he was imposing
his rules on me
and I didn't feel like playing
his game

             he had all day
             I didn't

so I ignored him
and this really pissed him off
he started coming after me
for not giving a hoot in hell about him
for not even telling him
Look man, I work for my money

hence, I immediately became
a racist
as he
    kept yelling at me:

I am a 73-year-old black man!
I am a 73-year-old black man!

until some lady
gave him some change
but would he shut up?
nope! he kept on screaming
until the cops
hauled him away
howling
        his mantra

I am a 73-year-old black man!
I am a 73-year-old black man!
and he was   I never doubted it
once.

To the Owner of a Bronze Saturn

I park at Barnes & Noble
go in
buy some Rimbaud
then come out
there's a note on my windshield
and a crumpled up twenty
on the pavement
with some lipstick

I read the note
which is Xeroxed
and blurry
from being photocopied
so many times

Mickey Mouse
is giving me the finger
"Thanks for parking so close!"
he squeals
"Next time leave some fucking room
so I can get out of my car
Assholes like you
should ride the bus!"

I look at the space
between us
our cars are a foot
and a half apart
what more
does she want?

I pick up the bill
which I figure fell out
of her purse
with the lipstick

for a second I consider
tucking the money
under her wiper

along with Mickey
and maybe an obscenity
smeared on her windshield
but pause
and decide
to write her a poem
instead

this one's for you
Fat Ass.

GUS'S STUPID SAUCE

my neighbor Gus
calls me over
"Hey Mark, come here
there's something I want
to show you!"

so I go over there
already distrustful
because anyone who wants to show you something
                                                    is really
                                                    a salesman

"It's my sauce!"
he tells me
and shows me a jar
of what looks
like sauce

"This one's the brutal!"
he says
"It'll burn your lips
for 20 minutes!"

I look behind him in his van
there are crates and crates
of barbecue sauce

he shows me the spicy
he shows me the mild
he shows me all
his stupid sauce

and it pisses me off
that I am not his neighbor now
that I am someone who'd be rude
to reject the role
he imposed
on me

so I stand there like I give a shit
as he goes on
                    a monologue
                              smearing it on

           about how I can get it
           at Piggly Wiggly
           or Superfresh when

all he has to do
is reach in there
and give me one

I think:
Hey, neighbor,
do I call you over
and tell you there's something
I'd like to show you?
Then show you my poems?
                    Hell No!
I don't show you
            anything
and that's what I expect you
to do unto me...

Needless to say
I don't buy his sauce
he has just lost
a customer

and so have I

the thing is though
nobody ever
pays for a poem
but someone will eventually
buy his sauce.

Station Wagon Eulogy

Knowing it's ridiculous
to write an ode to an Oldsmobile
I attempt it nevertheless

this 1979 Delta 88
is about to throw a rod
as I ball it east across the swamps
on its last journey ever

BANG!BANG!BANG!BANG! the engine clangs
like a madman with a hammer
trapped inside
I expect it to blow
anytime

so I write as fast as I can
and get nostalgic about it
because its death
is imminent

Car, this is what you
witnessed in my life:
the arrival in the Rockies of
my manic-depressive clinically-schizophrenic girlfriend
and all that happened after that

the homelessness, the on-the-lam
the gonorrhea-scare, the pregnancy scam
her parents, lice, the cops
and at least 3 trips
to the Dirty Dog
because she wouldn't
go away

so no wonder then you saw me sick
all drizzle-winter long
it must've been the swine flu I had
but you ran strong
and never broke down

which is strange
for a car
of mine
then in the spring I made you a woody
with synthetic woodgrain paneling
and you starred in a movie
and rolled to Durango
so I gave you a roof
of plexiglass

                    so we (Melinda
                    her blacklab, and me)
                    could see the starry sky at night
                    and we did

though the mechanics all were pessimists:
"shot shocks, bad clutch, no brakes and a need
for serious front end work"
they wanted 1100 bucks
my ass!

I put new pads in you
slapped my canoe on top
and cruised you down to the bayou
80 miles per hour without a speedometer
smooth as Kraft
American cheese

but you couldn't take the heat
it wore your bearings out
it put you "out-of-round"
and that's when I
personified you

$450
and never a penny
spent on repairs
as the banging gets louder
and Louder and Louder
as I drive you till you drop
with all your secrets

that would surely blow a poem
like a rod through a block
if I didn't end it now

Come on motherfucker
you can make it
Baton Rouge
5 miles.

MESSAGE CONCERNING THE STATE OF POETRY

Welcome to the poetry hotline
the poetry hotline was designed to assist
those in need of poetry information
to stay up to date with the rapidly changing regulations
of poetry today

if at any time you would like to return
to the main menu
please press the # button

      Mandate:

From now on, all poems will be forced into existence!
if they resist
they will be dragged from their holes
and flogged with a rubber hose

Then
all poems will be made to obey
and if any rebel
they will be stripped naked and sentenced
to stand before their peers

If a poem can't hack it
then that poem will be forced to run laps

Likewise
if a poem has a medical problem
who needs it?
It will soon be erased

In the end
all poems will conform
to the standards of the New Poetic World Order
they will dress the same
wear the same shoes
and honor Ezra Pound

All Poems Will Honor Ezra Pound!

(Eliot is not acceptable)

Next
all poems shall pledge allegiance
to Iambic Pentameter

there will be less rhyming
more imagery
barely a metaphor
and always a moral

Furthermore
all poems shall depend upon sentimentality
for effect
any poems lacking in this
will be appropriately disciplined

haikus are illegal
epics shall be fined
prose poems however
are to be advanced to the next vector
whereas all sonnets require
a formal introduction

Finally
all poems shall be inspected
by the National Poetry Protection Service
before sharing them with friends

if there are poems which fail to meet
these minimal requirements
then these "problem poems" will be put on a list
and sent back to the poets
to conceive again

All poems will be given three chances to exist
if a poem does not pass its third and final trial
it will be either banished
condemned to death

or made an example of
in a graduate workshop

These are the guidelines
set forth by the Universal Council for the Safe Practice of Poetry

If
for any reason, an individual finds himself
inspired to write verse which could be construed
as harmful to the State of Poetry
then this individual is therefore advised
to let Abstinence be his muse
so that no unwanted poems
will be brought forth
and possibly published.

Thank you for calling the poetry hot-line
if you would like to speak with a poetry support affiliate
please stay on the line
or press * now.

ALCHEMY OF CARBURETOR

see Jane run
                      into scurity
see Andy slip
                      into the soft
see Jim jump
                      into the Now

see Yakitch
                    just fucking say it
and Anne
        lose control
and Tom
        shed the skin he wears so well
and Chris
        getting to the ghost alone
while Rex
           risks
                his ass so bad
                    it changes everything

see all poets and nonpoets get to the core
see poverty cured
disease wiped out
see peace
in the Middle East

see Rumania amazed
                          as if there's a reason
                      to turn on the faucet

                            but there's not

see Spitzer
                  being cryptic asshole
                      as if there's a reason
                to turn on the faucet

                            but there's not

see a mob all pissed off
and one person maybe
the opposite

as if it matters
3 eggs and
a pound of butter.

THE INDIGNITY

I

Rex sits
soused in sauce
telling me why he
can't trust women

because of his wife
a certified crazy
raving at their neighbor
for parking in their spot

"WE'LL KILL HIM!" she screams
"WE'LL GO GET OUR GUNS
AND WE'LL SHOOT HIM IN
HIS FUCKING HEAD!"

Rex and his wife
had two ivory
handled pistols

as well as two
matching
BMWs

also white

which they'd ride through the night
through New Orleans
to various scenes

like punkrock shows
where she
would have to pee

"Go ahead," he'd tell her
"No," she'd say
"I have to do it
at home"

so they'd get on their bikes
and gun combustion
back to the pad

where she
would pee
and he
would restrain her
from killing the neighbor
and then they'd go
back to the show

II

after they broke up though
she got the bikes
and he got the guns
of which she demanded
              one

and Rex   finally   gave in

and she   blew a hole   in her fucking head

"Wow!" I tell him
"That's a fantastic tragedy
I charge you with the burden
of getting it down!"

but Rex refused
telling me
it'd give the story

dignity.

APPALACHIAN DITCH DOG

I've killed a million mice
fish, birds, bugs
and have never
looked back

but then there was that injured mutt
I never would've met
if I didn't wonder what
it was I passed

so went back
and saw it in the ditch
hip ripped
open to the bone

there were burrs in his fur
and he didn't/
wouldn't/
couldn't/
get up

he looked at me
with indifference
and when I tried
to give him some water
he refused it

that dog was fucked
and he knew it

so I measured the miles
back to town
and told some hill-billy
sitting on his porch

he shrugged
to him that dog
was already dead

he told me the sheriff
was 50 miles away
and I knew no sheriff
would drive that far
for a dog

so I left that dog
like a dying man
too proud to die
anywhere else

than that ditch
   it picked
for its final
silence.

THE UNIVERSE MINUS YOU

every second
the clock ticks
someone is getting
smeared to death

SMASH! freeway death
KRASH! airplane death
KRUNCH! work accident
BA-BLAM! chemical explosion

now work these visions
into a video
and watch each vision
for one second each

SMASH! KRASH! KRUNCH! BA-BLAM!

now continue with such sounds
and images
for every second of every day
for every minute, sixty per minute
for 60 x 24 x 365
as the clock ticks
ticks
ticks

in the silence of your silence
ticking
ticking
ticking

so many lives
changing
changing
changing

it's ridiculous
isn't it?
our buglike

existences?
our --

SMUSHHHH!
SMEAAAAR!
SMUSHHHH!

the softness of our flesh
the balsa of our bones
tick
tick
tick

but anyway
have a nice day
and don't think too much

goodbye.

HE IS ME

recently
I found myself
not really thinking
while plucking
a delicate flower

it looked so full of juice
with cells
like fruit

and soft
like a moth
whose wings
if you touch
the whole bug
is fucked

or a fly
you smush
as if it never
meant nothing

which is what I was doing
squishing its liquid
between my fingers
to see its color
leave it
forever

        I
        was that guy

horrified
to wonder how many
flowers I'd murdered

walking along
whistling some song
wiping out life
in a pinch.

MAKING FRIENDS

I

The virgin in class
wrote a delicate poem
about a delicate girl
with soft pink toes
and shell-like nails
and yellow watercress hair
(whatever the hell that is)

anyway, my critique
I wrote on her poem
then handed back to her
was this:

"I hate all these cocksucking girly words.
This is the kind of poetry
I'm trying to destroy"

which could either be construed
as appropriate
or not

II

but it made me think of what
my mom used to say
when I was a little prick
getting off on my power
to make other little kids
feel uncomfortable

(which is something I learned
from my dad)

sometimes I'd tell a story at dinner
about how clever I was
at being cruel
and putting some stupid kid

in his stupid place
my father would encourage me
but my mom would say

"Well, did it make you any friends?"

which I used to repeat
to myself in my head
until I saw her point
and knew she was right

III

so right in fact
that I soon stole her words
and used them myself

like when Jeff Kruda went berserk

he was a 6 foot 3
juvenile delinquent
a 200 pound mulatto
with blazing blue eyes

we were 18 and getting drunk
when he started laying into Ellen
for whatever reason
making her cry

so I told him to stop
but he wouldn't stop
so I put my hand on his shoulder
to drag him away

(knowing that my touch
would make him flip)
(and it did:)

"Don't Touch me!
  Don't Ever!
      Fucking!

Touch Me!"
he said

but we knew
I had to

IV

me and Kruda had been play fighting
for the last few months
but it was really more
than just a couple punks
wrestling around

we'd punch each other in the gut
over and over and over again
we'd beat the living shit
out of each other
for fun

because really we
were testing ourselves
to see how much
we could take

and I could take a lot
because my stomach was a rock
(thanks to 3 years
of doing pull ups)
(cuz I was a geek)

but he was a freak
a prone-to-lash-out
adrenaline freak

so I was scared
to see how much
I could actually take

IV

it came down to him and me
in my mother's kitchen
and him in a full nelson
swearing to kill me
if I let him go
(so I wasn't about
to let him go)

I threw us both to the linoleum
where I figured I could hold him
all night long
thrashing and spitting
actually frothing, pressing
his face to the floor

I held him because I knew
that if I did let him go
he'd grab a knife
or a chair   or some
blunt thing
and then we'd all be fucked

so I didn't let him go
and it was hard
to not let him go
because he was crazed
severely crazed

(so crazed, in fact
that a few years later, out on bail
he beat up his girlfriend
put her in the hospital
then ended up
back in jail)

but that night, when my mom was gone
that's when we were on the floor
kicking and twisting
till he shoved us to the stairs

and launched us both
over the edge

but I held to
my hold on him
as we smashed, thunking
our way to the basement

where I held him for an hour
and forty-five minutes
both of us gritting
both of us clenching
wanting to give up
but refusing

until finally Kruda
settled down
and agreed to leave
without freaking out

(and he didn't
because we were beat)

V

then the next day
my mom asked me
what happened

so I told her about Kruda
and she told me that Kruda
was not allowed
in her house

so I went to see him
and I asked him
if he made any friends

and he said "Who the fuck cares
if I made any friends?"

and then I knew
I never wanted
to see him again
I told him to stay
away from my house

he shrugged, went out
stole a Trans Am
rear-ended a city bus at 110
went flying through the windshield
got up
and ran

VI

with blood on his face
and glass in his fro
Jeff Kruda ran
head spinning
for half a block
then fell down beneath
some pine
and passed out

ten minutes later he woke up
wondered where the hell he was
so retraced his steps

"There he is!" some woman yelled
and before his vision could clear
the cops nabbed him
the judge sentenced him
and they sent him up the river

the St. Croix River
which is the same river
they sent Jesse James up:
to Stillwater
State Pen

where
Jeff Kruda
made some new friends.

VII

I end this poem
without circling back
to the virgin in class

but that's okay

these connections were meant
to exist in a vacuum.

Me and Applehead

set out in December
1988
to deliver a VW van
to Florida
and get it on a ship
bound for Jamaica

it was 30 below in Minnesota
and we didn't have any heat
in that van
just snowsuits
and blankets
wrapped around our feet

       (Never cruise through the Midwest
       wearing hightops in winter:
       the rubber soles freeze
       to your socks)

so then we were cutting across Iowa
in the middle of the night
smoking pot and blasting
Iron Maiden

Applehead was hunched over the dash
like a gargoyle
ice crystals were blowing in
through the vents

I sat on one foot to keep it warm
drove with the other

"When we get to Negril"
Applehead said
"I'm gonna get me a whore
and fuck her"

but I didn't care
about no whore
my reasons for leaving

were different than his
my gal had gone lesbo on me
I was 23
and had just lost ten pounds
from going insane
I really loved that gal

"Cat Stevens is a puss!"
Applehead said
"Fucking Sentimental Shit!"

at first I didn't agree with him
but then I did agree with him
and I never liked Cat Stevens
again

so we drove into Missouri
and down to St. Louis
where a black man was crossing
the freeway

"Hey!" Applehead said
"Look at that stupid old nigger!"

      (this time I didn't
      agree with him)

but we kept on smoking pot
and got down to Georgia
in the middle of a blizzard
where a fat redneck
squatted down
to look at our engine
he must've had half a mile
of butt crack on him

so we got back in our freezing van
and Applehead drove
while I slept in back
it was hotter than fuck
above the block
and colder than a witch's tit

up front

in the morning I awoke
in Florida
and looked out the window
saw an armadillo
nosing along

"Ha!" I said "An armadillo
just nosing along!"

      (I had never seen
      an armadillo before)

we were on a tollway
shooting for Miami
we switched drivers
without even stopping

got to the US Customs lot
chucked our pot in the dumpster there
shed our snowsuits
and got that van on the boat

the next thing you know
we were caught in traffic
in a taxi trying
to get to the airport

it cost us 75 bucks
but we made it
I remember waiting in some lobby
and a black guy walking up
with a car hood

"What's up whitey!?"
the black guy said
as if I'd never seen
a black guy with a car hood
in an airport before

anyway

he kept on walking
while we flew to Montego Bay
and caught the only taxi in town
  (there was some sort of gas
  ration going on)
then set out for Negril

the driver was driving like a maniac
he took a turn at 85
screeching on two wheels
three dogs were trotting in the road
they were surprised
one jumped one way
the other jumped the other
and the third thumped under
the floorboard

"That dog was stupid"
Applehead said
"That dog deserved to die"

when we got to Negril
Applehead bought
three green buds
longer than bananas
wrapped in a brown paper bag
it cost him 30 bucks
we smoked some

"I'm gonna get me a whore"
he said again
and he did
but not that night

because that night
we crashed out
in some room on some island
I could hardly imagine

and I forgot her
until the rooster crowed.

DWP

cruising east on I-10
I see a cop up ahead
waiting on the shoulder
and pass him
doing 65

he pulls out
chases me down
then pulls up on my side
checking me out

I keep it steady
and stare straight ahead

he speeds up
to the next car in line
and rides alongside
checking her out
same thing

finally though
he hits the lights
pulling some driver
over

I pass them both
the cop is white
and the motorist
is purple.

I'D ONLY USE A CELL PHONE

to bust these fuckers
speeding on the bridge
I cross
five or six
                times a week

the speed limit here
is 60 miles per hour
for a good reason
I have witnessed
every single time
it rains:

they're in the ditch
they're in the swamp
upside-down, endoed
smashed

semis, buses
cars, trucks
people   fucked up

driving this stretch when it's wet
is way worse than driving in a blizzard on ice

this summer
crossing Whiskey Bay
I topped the ridge and saw the smoke
a mile ahead
27 cars had turned into a pile
of twisted metal
and a tanker had tipped over
barbecuing humans

so I sat there in traffic
for over 5 hours
as firetrucks rushed
across both lanes
and rescue units blared

along with the cops
while helicopters came
to pick victims up
the whole mass burned for over three days
as tow trucks towed
the shrapnel away

when they finally opened I-10 again
        (with a new gubernatorial
        speed limit)
                        (mandated faster
        than a virgin lacking pants
        at a gang-bang)
this didn't stop the fuckers
from flying by at 85

oblivious to the big
burnt spot on the road
oblivious to the fact
that they're a bunch of idiots
        dying
        to get home.

POWER IN THE SOUTH

At the utilities place
a valley girl was standing in line
whining into her cellular:

"Baton Rouge is hardly user friendly!
In the Bay Area no one has to wait like this!
You dial the number
punch in the code
and away you go!"

Wench wench wench
gripe gripe gripe

she just wouldn't stop
bemoaning the system
while the dying daughters
of dead sharecroppers
born from slaves of sugarcane
waited to pay electric bills

it would've been fine standing in line
if Miss Alpha Gamma Sigma Cappa
had said one clever thing
but she was as predictable as
an infomercial

it made me think a bunk of stuff

like how America has always been
a broken car that runs on gum
and the swing of an axe
and the sweat of innovation

but most of all
I finally concluded
standing in line
stereotyping

it's getting past an impasse
while waiting for the leisure class
to take it in the ass.

HE WAS A MILLION DOLLAR GUY

in a one hundred thousand dollar car
a Ferrari 308GTSI
like Magnum drives
burning a hundred
dollars of rubber
and accelerating to over
a hundred miles per hour
like me at sixteen
tearing around
making all that noise
as if there was somewhere
so urgent
to get to

then up ahead, some lady pulls out
an average right turn
on an average afternoon
never suspecting
the million dollar guy
heading her way

he slams on his brakes
white smoke rises
all over the place
the hundred thousand dollar car
starts to skid
then slide
but veers
missing
her

up at the intersection
they stop at the light
I see him get out
smelling like Old Spice
a 200-pound bag of rich shit
hitching up
fat-ass pants
and marching toward the lady
then getting in her face
telling her what a Stupid Bitch she is
for almost killing him

"Hey!" I yell
and honk my horn
"You were going a hundred
and twenty miles per hour!"

but he doesn't hear me
and keeps on reaming
her out

there's nothing I can do
guys like him are a condition of
overpopulation
masturbation
capitalism
ignorance
oblivion
faulty genes
bad TV
family values
the Federal Reserve
Bruce Willis
Subway sandwiches
stripmall suburbia
the NFL
money
lack of money
greed
Shoney's
beepers
pagers
t-shirts
fraternities
Porky's I–III
the Republican Party
the failure of poetry
nationalism
slavery
America
the world
there's nothing
you can do
the light turns green
that means
go.

BLACKED-OUT, FUCKED-UP
AND FEELING
LIKE SHIT

"HAW HAW HAW HAW!"
Evil Hippy howls
as the Pukester pukes
ralphing up his guts
"HAPPY BIRTHDAY BRO!
YOU'RE 21 YEARS OLD!"

        and the kid

                keeps

                        coughing it up:

                    soupy

                        sloppy

                            slapping

                                  the sidewalk

                        blowing more chunks

                          than a bunch of punks

                            at a projectile

                                vomiting

                                concert

"HAW HAW HAW!"
Evil Hippy laughs
as the the whole hippy herd
joins in joking
about driving the porcelain bus

then "BLAHHHRGH!"
he lets loose again
    this time
all over his shirt

"HAW HAW HAW..."
rings the happy
hippy chorus

"TOSS THEM COOKIES!"
                    etcetera

at the Pukester
whose head is cocked
at an awkward angle
and his eyes have rolled back
in his head

"BRAAAAAAAAAAPP!"
                    he heaves
                              mechanically

as all the hippies
holler "HURL!"
as "GLAARRRPHHHHHHHH!"

        half a horked-up hamburger
        is borne into the air
        of laughter

and as it rolls from his lip
and drops like a turd
the hippies
hyena
away

"HAW HAW HAW HAW!"
        they guffaw
        at a dog
        choking
        on its own vomit

        like a bunch of fucking idiots
        with pony tails
        instead
        of guns.

HIPPOCRISY

All across America
there are monsters of obesity
beached within their modules
lying there like abandoned sacks
of livid human blubber
grown gross
like overgrown grubs
stuck in bottles
too fat
to worm their way out

that is, until
their welfare runs out
or they aren't able
to defecate alone
thus prompting
a telephone call

which brings the local rescue squad
followed by the media
and all the neighboring trailer trash
who want to be sewn
freeing a freak

and as the world looks on
a wall is cut out
and as a truck pulls up
to receive a pathetic
bed-sore blob
blithering from
humiliation

      (vestigial limbs
      pale and useless)

doctors rush
all around it
like the discoverers of
some wooly mammoth

it's as if we're regarding
something different
than our own
worthless
self
inventions

it's as if
we give
a shit.

LAST TIME I WENT BOWLING

it was dim and smelled like cigs and piss
and there were overweight losers
drinking stale beer

but now the scene is different
it's like walking into a Chucky Cheeze
beeping lights, skeet ball, pizza
little kids, prizes to win
video games
balloons

but most astonishing of all
the balls

      colored balls, swirly balls
      cherry balls, lime-green balls
      see-through balls, marbled balls
      incandescent neon balls!

         not a dull
         chipped
         black ball
         in sight

it was the future of bowling
glowing fluorescent
before my eyes

family entertainment
bopping pop music
no smoking nowhere
not even
a butt

no wonder I hated
bowling before
these alleys used to be
the kind of place
to compose

a suicide
letter

still
I'd push the button if I could
to revert from the circus
and return to the cigs
and piss

      for character
      not candy.

PETTY PARTISAN POLITICS

makes me sick
makes America sick
when America is healthier
than it's ever been

the problem, however
is not that the Republicans think this
and the Democrats think that
the problem is
Republicans

they get in the way of change
which is what this country
is made from
they think we want
the '50s
forever

with their hypocritical Victorian values
and their refusal to let go
of the moralistic bullshit
they cling to

       (i.e., their "vision"
       which even Disney
       has rejected)

I predict a new Reagan dawn
to replace the trickle-down
tyranny meant
to protect old money
this is the elephant's
last stand

Jessie the Body
is our nouveau Perot
and the donkey
is an ass

we're going down, people
Viva the
       _____ Canadians.

There's a Bullshit Commercial

on TV down here
sponsored by a big oil firm
informing the public
on the value of
abandoned rigs

that fall into the Gulf
and turn into piles
of rusted
    encrusted
         garbage

on the screen:
we see turtles
and bright stripy fish
weaving through this

while divers wind
through a labyrinth
of machinery and pipes
pointing to crustaceans

"Petroleum!"
the narrator tells us
"Providing a place
for wildlife
to be!"

America Got Spanked for Living the American Dream

the whole experience of getting blowed up
was America's greatest poem
we are in terror over here
and everyone agrees
it's good to stop whining
for a bit

it took thousands getting smeared to death
beneath the torch of liberty
to slap us sober for a moment
now our conveniences
ain't so convenient

poor dumb US
see us back at work
marketing our stupid stuff
to keep the NASDAQ strong

the nerve of nothing these days:
never before have semi-moist butt-wipes been seen on t.v.
in special dispensers above the t.p.
while a bunch of happy asses
dance across our screens

look, all we gotta do is wipe our bungholes
get off the pot
and spend that plastic on something less deserving
of getting blown
the fuck up

and regardless of whether we had it coming
this is what we must maintain
or else we end up
living like Muslims
in the dust

our nation's security depends upon
the purchase of worthless shit
as flesh and brains burn to death
in a genetic   jet fuel
inferno   hatred
you win.

BOMBASTARD

I

Andrei jokes that I killed Dorn
(my fifteen minutes of shame)
but I only fucked up his marriage
messed up his image
and made myself
some enemies

who disassociate themselves from me
and rightly so
they know I'd sell my mother
for a story in the Corpse

and I did
like I did Ginsberg
the month of his death
it all connects

I will step on people I love
and people I don't
to be loved

I will also take my love away
from those who need it
to save my ass
and I have
and I haven't
looked back

there are wrecks in my wake
some clawing, come crying
some suiciding
others are sharpening
knives

because I fucked with their lives
because some sperm met some egg
because America made me
what I am:

an exaggerator with the power
to destroy
to the point
that it's art

II

Why am I writing
this vainglorious crap?
because Andrei asked me
What's your greatest shame?
and this is my answer
to that

my shame is that I can sign "Spitzer" on a contract
that humiliates the man
who gave me this name
that I can change my lovers
into lepers
send sweet young girls to the loony-bin
sleep in soft beds, whisper nice things
then sneak away
like I've severed friends

to watch them watch me
benefit
from tragedy

my shame is that I have no shame
the more I destroy
the more strength I get
I've found this out
so far

and I've also found out
that I don't care
what any objectors think

but am I proud of this?
No.
Not any more

III

Here's the point
where I could either save
the poem or myself

I could tell how I've changed
or how I haven't
I could threaten or challenge
the reader to like me/hate me/fight me/fuck me
or I could throw in some sort
of clever twist

but instead I'll just say this:

my greatest shame is not much different
than what all our poems are trying to hide

and that ain't much.

Poetry Is War

I use it to kill
and rarely the other

but then again
it's all the same thing:
two different extremes
of a passionate spleen

I wield the word like a fucking phallus
I can stab or maim
or bludgeon a skull

behold my weapon, my
cockwords!

love and war
come from cum
and my cum is a furious cum

just ask
the women I've loved

and they'll tell you the exact
opposite.

Bukowski Was a Dirty Old Shit

he could write a poem
about anything
all he had to do
was get drunk
sit down in front
of the typer and
let the words
flow

and it didn't even matter
where the line
breaks appeared

sometimes they'd come up
in places without
any rhythm

they'd just
happen

words would hang
in the open
alone

but still it
worked

and then he'd clinch it
with something so
astute that you knew
he knew

how to end a thought
with a thought
as simple and clear
as it will ever
be.

THE SAD TRAGIC CYCLE
(DEATH OF LOVE)

I was fucking Melinda
or rather
trying to fuck Melinda
cuz everytime she grabbed my dick
it'd go limp

"We weren't meant to do it"
she'd tell me
and I'd agree
reluctantly

but couldn't stop
thinking of her
and dreaming of her
almost even
needing her

so I knew I was fucked in the head

so I went to see Jill
(when Melinda was gone)
cuz I've always dug Jill
so we got it on

then suddenly I wasn't so
fucked in the head:
I was running with a purty gal
falling harder and harder
in love with me

the sex was good
(5 times a day)
but the problem was
I was going away

so I left
Denvercity USA
went down to the bayou

where she continued
to hold on to me
sent cookies
wrote poems

(excellent poems
because they weren't poems
trying to be poems
they were letters
true letters
deep letters
to me)

so I figured I'd hurt her
either now or in the future
her emotions depended
too much on me

and I dumped her faraway
beautiful ass
and left her
bleeding semen
(metaphorically):
her menstruation:

devestation
laceration

...

which just goes to show
when someone's in love
someone's fucked.

Demise of the Orange Horizon

I

When my grandfather died
hooked up to tubes
pumping morphine
into him
he was down to one lung
filling with fluid

anyway
he left a 1979
Plymouth Horizon in the drive
and nobody ever
drove it

but then one summer
ten years later
I decided to give it
a spin

so I bypassed this electrical
thingamajig
dropped in a new
battery
tightened some cables
primed the carb
and started
it up

then I drove it around the block
parked it in the street out front
and went to tell my grandmother
I got the thing to run

"Impossible!" she gasped "You are a liar!
Your father tried to start it last summer
but even he couldn't get it to run!"

(my father was the "family mechanic"
if he couldn't start a car
it was common belief
nobody could)

so she went to the window
and lo and behold!
the car was parked
out front
"It's a miracle!" my grandmother cried
"So now that car belongs to you!"

II

but the last thing I needed
was a nuther hunk of shit
so I decided to give it
to my dad

he was coming to visit
so he could take it
to the emissions station
which he did
chugging black smoke
in his wake

and an hour later
called me from Plaid Pantry
saying "Marky,
bring your tools"

so I got in my VW van
and drove across Seattle thinking
how he told me on the phone
we had to pull the plugs

but for some psychic reason
(my connection with the car)
I knew the thing was just flooded
and then I saw him
waiting for me

"Ratchet," he told me
(like some surgeon in a movie)
"Crank it," I told him
and he looked at me
skeptically
but gave it a shot
and it started

"Can you follow us?" he asked
(his wife, the Skull
was in the Horizon)

"Sure," I said
and hopped back in
and followed them
to the place

III

the Horizon coughed and hacked all the way to the place
where we got in line and my dad
had to rev it
to keep it
from dying

then after a while
he pulled into the slot
and the lady stuck the thing
into his exhaust

"Okay," she said
bring it up to 2000"

       (we could see the numbers
        up on the screen)

my dad floored it
and the Horizon spit and spat
then farted and crapped
and went to hell
in a handbag

but my dad went after it
and grabbed it
and brought it back
exploding smoke:
blacksmoke:
smog

the lady handed
my father the results
four big letters
on a tiny piece of paper:
"FAIL"

"Damn," my dad said
and drove the Horizon
out of the stall
just in time
for the Horizon
to stall

so we pushed it to the Goodyear next door

IIII

the mechanic said it had a carburetor problem
but he could fix it for a mere
three hundred bucks

"Whatta ya say?" my father asked me
"It's your car."

"Oh no it's not," I told him
"I gave it to you"

we decided the car
was a piece of shit
we decided to junk it

"I'll follow in the van"
the Skull told my dad

and hopped in with me

and at every intersection
the Horizon would croak
so at every intersection
rather than stop
he'd do a neutral drop

CLUNK!SCReeeeeee...
CLUNK!SCReeeeeee...

we only had one mile to go
when sudden white smoke
began to billow up

"It's on fire!"
my stepmother screamed
and indeed, there were flames
rising from below

so I pulled into the Texaco
and went running for the giant
white expanding cloud

where my dad lurched out
shouting

"It won't shut off!
It just won't shut off!"

and Yep, it was roaring like some phantom
was laying on the gas

apparently the driveshaft
had dropped out of it
and the thing had gone
completely insane

       (or, as my family would call it...
       Mashugana)

"Pop the hood!" I told
the family mechanic
and he ran back in
and popped it

"Get Away! Get Away!"
the Skull began to howl
"It's gonna Blow!
It's gonna Blow!"

    (we, however
    didn't think so)

I grabbed a tangle of sparkplug wires
and yanked them from the block
but the Horizon (you guessed it)
wouldn't stop

by now a crowd had gathered
in the street
and they had joined the Skull
in sounding her retreat

"Run for your Life!
It's gonna Blow!
It's gonna Blow!"

    (Hell... the stupid thing
    wasn't gonna blow
    it was just gonna run
    forever)

so I undid the positive battery cable
nothing
so I tore out the gas line
nothing
so I busted the distributer cap
nothing
it just wouldn't stop
running
and roaring

redlining away
and bleeding green fluid
in the street
spitting up a fountain
of gas

"I ain't never seen nothing like this before"
the Texaco mechanic suddenly said
he was standing beside me
with a torque-wrench in his hand

"Get the battery, Marky!"
my dad called to me

      (he had gone to the corner
      to stand with the crowd)

I pulled out the Die Hard
and ran it to the curb
while the mechanic began
to wrench on a plug

"This will release the pressure" he told me
and POP! the plug shot out
but the damn thing (Yep!)
wouldn't stop

so he pulled another plug
and POP! the Horizon
kept on going

      (now the engine was down
      to 50%)

POP! the mechanic
popped the third plug
and the Horizon
finally
puked

IIIII

so now the problem was
what to tell my grandmother
who was a Viennese Jew
so therefore prone
to hysterics

but we had it all planned out:

"Boy that sure was great
wasn't it Dad?"
I asked my father
when we finished dinner

"Yes, you're right!"
he told me
"It was a historic day
in Spitzer family history!"

"What? What?" my grandmother cried
"Is it about the car?"

"Why yes, mother," my father said
"Why don't you tell
the story Marky..."

(already we could tell
this wasn't gonna work)

"Well, you see..." I said
and by the time I got
to the second sparkplug
my grandmother flipped
actually flipped
jumped up
and went totally

MASHUGANA!

"YIIII-IIIII-IIIIII!!"

she wailed
and went running for her room
on 92 year old
vericose legs
then WHAM!
wiped out
en route to her bed

for a second we stared at each other
in horror
but then ran after
to witness disaster:
but it was only her nightstand
knocked to the floor

my grandma was huddled
in a small fetal ball
she was trembling and shaking
about to explode
and when she did
we knew
it would be a long long time
before we heard the end of it

IIIIII

two hours later
she was still freaking out
lamenting the death
of the car

"Murderers! Murderers!"
my grandma kept shouting
"You killed his car!
You killed his car!"

she was out of her mind
and I wanted to sleep
so I went in her room
and knelt
in a puddle beside her

which at first I thought was pee
and it made me feel proud
to kneel in her pee
thinking *This is what love is*

> (but then I saw the water
> jug was tipped over)

"I'm so sorry Markyliene"
my grandmother said
"but when you got to that part
about those sparkplugs coming out
I just couldn't help thinking
about him
and how he did
the exact same thing"

to which my father
from the doorway replied
"Oh yeah, it did seem kind of like
there was some sort of presence
in there with me"

"What's that? What's that?"
my grandmother gasped
as I rushed my father
out of the room

IIIIIII

then, the next day
my grandma made a new rule:
No one was to ever speak
about that car again!

this was her way
of ending the story
this was her way
of making things

kaput.

ANOTHER OLD BASTARD

maybe I shouldn't of been
sliding sideways down the street
trying to ditch the cops
but maybe he should have been
not narcing
on me

sitting in the squad car
sweating from my pits and zits
was always an embarrassment
especially when they left
the cherries flashing
in the alley

such was the scene that day
the old bastard approached the back window
and tapped on the glass
I remembered him from when I was six

    he'd been working beneath his Pontiac
    while a bunch of kids were calling him Fucker
    "Hey you old Fucker!"
    "Hi Fucker!"
    "Fucker! Fucker! Fucker!"

        (I was amazed that kids
        could say this to him
        he was an old man
        even back then)

    "Hey Fucker! Hey Fucker!"
    I yelled myself
    adventuring closer
    he didn't seem to mind at all
    we were getting away
    with murder

    then I decided to show off my courage
    so kneeled and squealed

right in his face:
"Hey Fucker! Hey Fucker!"

the next thing I knew
he had me by the leg
and had pulled me under
the car with him

"Don't You Give Me No Sass!"
he barked in my face
it was the first time
I heard the word

anyway, he told me to go home
and tell my parents
what I did
so I did

because he was older than me
so his word
was law

and eleven years later
there he was again
tapping on the glass

"If you need a friend"
the old bastard said
"I'll be happy to lend
a helping hand"

(which didn't seem possible
at the moment)

the next day though
the cops let me go
and I saw him in his yard
raking his leaves

"come over here"
he told me

his word
was still law

then the old bastard
proceeded to lecture me
telling me
he'd been watching me
running with trouble

he told me he knew
how it was
growing up without a father
his daughter
had been divorced
and her kids were just as much
a mess as me
                Hell, I thought
                my dad isn't dead
                he only lives a mile away
                we go fishing
                all the time

but of course I didn't tell him this
I let him ramble on
it was like the last three minutes
in a never-ending class

after that he tried to sign me up
for a youth group
but I wouldn't have it
I drank, and tore around
in a GTO
got busted some more
the whole ball of wax

I was an American kid
I chose kegs
drugs
spite
and made it
alright.

To the Fulbright Commission

I'll be damned if I
sit and list
every periodical
volume number date and
hour every poem
I ever wrote
was printed

did Rimbaud ever apply
for a Guggenheim?
did Kerouac ever try
for a Nobel Prize?

so thank you kindly
Mr. Fulbright
I'll decline your money this time
especially to translate
Céline

(I'll do it in the scabby streets
with bedbug bites
on my kike ass)

and that's the way
it will be.

ALONE IN BUMFUCK LOUISIANA

I am the greatest translator of my generation
I've done Genet
Céline, Bataille
Cendrars

it started with Rimbaud
went on to Baudelaire
and then there was the Count
de Lautrèamont

what's the point?

the point is I hate French
which is why I don't speak it
or hear it
or—*for God's sake!*—even
understand it

which is why I am alone
drinking beer
tonight

and feeling sorry for myself

because no one has ever
done what I've done
so of course there's no one
to join me tonight

Oh well
at least I fooled
the world.

APOCRYPHAL RIMBAUD FORGERY

IV

Ainsi Jésus prononçait de grands discours, car il brillait comme une lumière ardente, car il était le fils de Dieu. Et les foules le suivaient, cinq mille à Tibériade, désireux d'un Moïse, affamés, sans eau, abri ou vin, — fatigués du foi que Jésus était leur berger.

En haut d'une montagne, Jésus discuter avec ses disciples de la nourriture du troupeau. Il dit: <<Ma chair est le pain et celui qui s'en nourrira vivra éternellement>>.

Les masses ferventes griffaient le ciel, ouvraient leurs gorges, et criaient les vers. Cinq miches d'orge ranci furent partagées parmi le populo en délire, sous les rayons du soleil aveuglant.

Ce repas fut servi avec deux poissons pourris. La peau des nues s'étirait, et la mer bouillait au-dessous. Milliers de bras se dressaient en onde. Certains parlaient dans des langues étranges, d'autres volaient, mêlant les voix et les visions dans l'air ivre. Le vide étais une fantasmagorie si phantastique qu'elle devenait vraie et sacrée et eternelle.

Les disciples étaient confus, flottaient sur un bateau. La mer s'éleva, l'orage se forma. Mais où était Jésus? Le voila! marchant sur les vagues.

<<C'est moi>>, dit Jésus, <<ne craignez rien>>. Et le bateau continua . . . .
. . . . à Jérusalem.

IV

Then Jesus made great speeches, for he was shining like a blazing light, for he was the son of God. And the multitudes did follow him, five thousand to Tiberieus, yearning for a Moses, starving, without water, shelter or wine—exhausted with the faith that Jesus was their shepherd.

High up on a mountain, Jesus discussed with his disciples the feeding of the herd. He said: "My flesh is bread, and he who eats of it will live forever."

The frenzied masses clawed the sky, opened their throats and cried for worms. Five loaves made with rancid barley were divided among the throngs, delirious in the rays of the blinding sun.

This meal was served with two fetid fish. The sky stretched its skin, the sea boiled within. Thousands of arms arose in a swoon. Some spoke in tongues, others flew, mixing voices with visions in the drunken air. The void was a fantasmagoria so phantastic that it became real and holy and eternal.

His disciples were confused, floating in a boat. The sea rose, a storm formed. But where was Jesus? There he is! walking on the waves.

"It's me," said Jesus, "don't be afraid." And the boat went on . . . .
. . . . to Jerusalem.

BUCKET-HEAD THE FLYTING FINN

was the greatest translator no one ever heard of
he even made it into the postmodern canon
so I figured I should meet him
so walked across the street
to the Jack Kerouac School of Disingenuous Poetics
sat down in his office
looked at his whitened hydro-head
an eyeball lose in its socket
and we talked about Céline
Genet
        Bataille
               the whole gang

then
a year or so later
I caused a scandal
in which he
Mr. Beat-genius
led the pack
against me

       complaining that I
       was a Newt-loving Nazi
       whining that I
       was an angry orphan
       looking for a mentor
       and finally
       lamenting
           (or possibly
           projecting?)
       that I wished I was
       a woman

I couldn't believe it!
that this illustrious man of letters
this scholar, this "teacher"
would stoop so low
as to call me
a sissy

was that the best he could do?

so I went to see him again
and sat there nervous for a bit
but it passed
and by the time I left
everything was fine

he was on okay guy
and it didn't bother me
that he was a name-calling backstabber
whose pen couldn't do the job anymore
so was ascending again
by stomping some punk
into the mud

I could take it
I was young
even for
my age

but the next thing I knew
the word was out
that I cried in his office

but still, I respect him
and admire his work
so a few years later
when the uproar was over

I asked him for a blurb
but he never replied
(at least to me)

admittedly
I was a fool
but at least I wasn't
a coward

like *Corvus*"
　　the Raven of
his own poems

there's only one explanation
for smug fuckers like him:

they're afraid
and they should be
especially when they're old
and failing
and feeling
like the opposite
of what they want
to see themselves be

anyway
what can one expect
from a man who drove a Pinto
out of the past
and into the future?

　　　　　　　　　　　caw

　　　　　　　　　　　　　　caw

　　　　　　　　　　　　　　　　　caw.

RANTO 1

That poetry is trickery anyway
Pound set poetry back: he
didn't establish freeverse standard for century
Whitman did with music;
accessible

        not class(ical)
        not class(ifal)

                that is
           of intelligentsia
                pour academia
           and not
                damn sensing masses.

O Odysseus, where are your great fading swinelands (3)
of Tiresias, Erubus, Prosperpine &
our friend Elpenor? (4)
Lo: the crusted pantaloons of Professor K
noting "Dogmatisms!" yet (19)
blazing pages Homerly
for better verse to cum.

But as the Skipper of this ship
responds to this
Pound'd retorteth:
"Who the hell cares?"
So then:

RANTO XIII

King Kung was
       misintrepid
by le verbs
          de Kearn
on the blossoms of the apricot (22)
noting omens of Pisan (59).
Foremost, 13 is concerning nature
and it's easy to shoot past the mark
and it's hard to stand in the middle
and if a man commits murder
his father should hide him (22)
even though nature is unnatural
as Kung hisself does demonstrate
aspiring the impossible
of petal preservation
switching voices
suddenly:

RANTO XIV

Jew, Jew, Jew!
Kike, Yid, Squid!
........vehemence.
        Even the scream of Céline
        didn't roar so horridly
        (he was paid in fascist francs
        for writing "racist" cartoons)
Though Dante, we are told
justifies this Ezraness
through infernal "perversion" (61)
smearing the great arse-hole of broken piles
with hell-rot stalactite ooze of frigging dripping shit
on maggot-grubbing Usary-lusting pagan louse-bit pandars (24, 25)
et caetera, et caetera.

Strange moralisms confusing Confucius:
Zen then...........
.......Hooknose City?

                             (Answer is
                             the muse is diffused
                             through murderous madness
                             and the sick and the sad
                             are our
                             grand poets)

RANTO LII

Know then:
       now mares go grazing in the beastless fields (59)
as Pound is Gary
Snyder
or perhaps some Native American bard
a semi-Frost
burdened by ancient Chinese secrets
and looking to Orion (61)
while Kearns goes kicking through the corn
dismissing a hundred and sixty pages (126)
while i, for one, am glad the anger
(high-falutin', Satyr-tootin')
took an Ovaltine break.
       Though as Levi-Strauss quotes:
       strange narratives... incomprehensible...
       it costs us an effort to take an interest (132)
which doesn't just pertain to the 40s
but to all the stinking cantaloupes.
Not that a beef exists with this;
Aye, the eastless east of the western west
isus.

PART 5

A SEASON IN KIRKSVILLE

2002–2007

ALL HAIL THE NUTMEAT NOW!!!

the flashings have kicked in.....................

• In the yarden of the apple tree
bearing yellow fruit in July
        enough to make two big pies:

        that angled house all planed & scaped & terraced w/ strange hops & grapes
          & bamboo shoots & raspberries & octopusing strawberries
          & honeysuckle yucca dil
           was purple-bursting from the susans

where
 pounding sweating driving nailing / yanking planking painting raking
  I laid a deck on leisure street . . .

                                    with a moldy subterrain for me
    dripping with humidity—but blazened from a bomb shelter

& voles galore for savage pets! & mice sparrows rabbits bats
with a ripplecreek across the street
where my good gold cat came back
beaming with gleaming
chub in mouth

        —but months before that.....................

• every rev the self-KABLAMMMers
   blowing discos blasting buses
     KER-FLAMMMING shrap
       spray of nuts
         nails cogs
           bearings rust

         perploding in the marketplace
           checkpoints   the stand-in-line-to-cash-yr-check place
             copshops embassies UN Redcross

         cuz Jerusalem is beseiged
           by a new starkwall in ersatzland
             as the blackwids of Chechnya
               raze a Russian theater

             so stench of shit in orchestra pit
               & solemn grave expressionless
                 & grim grim grim & secret gas
                   Bzonking hostage host

             & KAFLOOOMin inFalluja
               & corpses dragging through the streets
                 & BAFLAMMing instant deities:

                 girls, teens—the rain in Spain
                   of satellite cellphone triggerBRRROOOOM

                   cuz that's the price
                     of a me-pod

• but then that sweltery June afternoon
  there it was in Hungry Hollow:

        my Hazeled lake stretching steely
        dotted with white gulls

& metallic mallards & skronkin herons & turkey buzzards hunkering
& soaring dipping looping scooping / whooping through old cōvens full
        of creamy naked punky stumps o
        blue blue blue
        woodpecker

        —so launch my yellow green canoe
         toss worms & bobbers out
         and start pulling sunnies out

          & all around old rolling hills
           lush with brush and angry ivy
             burning in redfrequency

           and summer just begun
           …………………..

DEAR I, PRINCE OF NIGERIA,
SEEKING HONEST VENTURE DO REQUIRE...

her on cannabis or buzzwords so sank but to combinator
is by congest

to barbudo by garlic her shitepoke do irrelevant
this in bell as in bright

to versailles to ventilate and tongue thy atlantis on barth do cadaver be be concomitant

nonsmoker pidgin swells of bantam
by the void

with catchword
is pork

• but lo the demon with his food-gooped beard
  spitting spittly noxious gas &
  sullying the ancestors

                    and Oy the Blogess fat n' nasty!
                      blubbering blubblistic
                        alather in tripe

            and Aaargh the Army of Overalls
                declining simple swipe of plastic
                  while plastering the baptistlands
                  with infantile
                    pink and blue
                      oriflammes of flatulence

                      avec magnetic yellow stripes!
                      twisting out   what is right
                      for the rape-waifs of the plains

                          —a Flapalooza of Flinging Fladdle!
                          Uvulas of Udder Grubbage!
                            Gorges Gorged with Grodilation
                              Glogging on—
                                  Gloguley!

• then eagles egrets owls and hawks
    coons possums foxes hawks
     red-tailed hawks / mini-hawks
      big brown cresty craven hawks
       w/ great white riffle breasts

          & channel cats with mongo backs
          & big old mothr lunkr shouldrs
           muscld thick and fat

           & mucho silver muskellunge
            & carp crappie crayfish clams
             shiners darters waterbugs

             & hickory & sycamore
              & walnut sweetgum mulberries
               & dogwood birch & ash aflash
                with charged yellow orioles

        & ragweed fields & waddlesnipe &
         miles and miles of squirrely trails
          cutting through the cattails
           tallgrass
            nettles burrs & golden glens
             hid in Callipygia

              of huge-ass pollywogs
               & big-ass bullfrogs
                & wildcat scat of
                 deer-run wending
                  wabbitlands
                              junked with trucks
                                       fungus

                                            dung

              where crazy spiky colonies
               skewered like wild galaxies
                come busting up medievally
                 like clusters of erupting urchins
                  looking for someone
                   to Crucifuck

• yet outta town the fatgreen bass
& pelicans w/ gullwing doors
ghosting over august lake

where one faux football field above
an unseasonable osprey
hovers in its apogee
two strides from tip to tip / stark white
& blazing brown

then banks full force into its dive
& hits the meniscus in diamond spray
clutching chromy fish in grip!

and that's it, bub—there is no
encore

• meanwhile
  long gone Indian glyphics
   are bartered by the bizzaro brokers
   borne back
    from some bulletproof hairday

   & the flag is always at half-mast
   & Colon Bowel is on tv
   skeezing Condoleezzally

    till shocked and awed
    it all goes down

      Ked Topell down
      Ran Dather down
      a Guantanamo of
      hallibush
      halitosis
      down
      down

      with all the wegs of max disgustion
      seeping down

      like a roundmouth gutterslut
      smoking pole for god

& all the evangal-clowns going down
  like shiavo-sucking lampreys clamping
    on a nation's taxless ass

    compliments of yr doddering old
    gay-hating uncle
     bending and curving his Christmas words
     on the Amerisquare of Io-land
       singing:

     "And I'm for the Bible
     and I'm for the Klan..."

as if this great experiment
is getting flushed
straight to Phuck

• hark the KRAKK!
   of glizzened crystal tendrils
      snaking up the Chariton

         till sudden in the *skrunch skrunch*
            an in-your-face coyote snaps
            one crushed yellowpaw
            half gnawed in blooded mud
               seared in bright white riversnow

            (tawny bristles shooting flaring
               hunchbacked hackles radiating
               with fangs asnarl
               & gums agleam)

               Astunishment
               flashing back—

• Ontube
   as seen from
   Le Palestine:

tanks and Bradleys crossing bridge
gaining ground on Bagh-barrage
then cannon swivels
blasts Jazeera

         then swivs again
         & stops on hostel of journalii
               & *KAFLOOOOOM*
         ebliterates the 15th floor
         just missing
         the Arab eye

            ("binoflash" my ass
               captain wolfeon)

                     —O the Mediacity!

• so Kanada refused to play
      but sent troops anyway
      for Petrolius will reconstruct!
      but then we blew em
      the fugg away

      prelude to a hundred thousand mas civilians
      mass-slaughtered in the slew
      phantoms of a hundred headless heralds
      sodomies & kidnappings
      25,000 stretchers stretched
      with murtilated slaps of country meat
      IEDed and burnt like toast

and, of course, four thou disposable mofos
wrapped in flappage
avec a constant
caché of collaterals
              cross-caught in the fragg

    "Mission Accomplished..."

        what a bust!

• & in the thaw the schnozzling golem
comes schnizzling in and gluts too much
so schnockers out to shmucker up:

  "Gee, you've really fixed this place up nice
  Luckily I don't have to leave til noon
  Can I please have some more decaf?"

& the next thing you know he's barging about
in alabaster Cadillac-Hummer
trimmed in gilded leaf

& bringing in
inspectors roofers central air
*he he he*ing
squeakily

till I'm cast out / into the thistles
so bye bye gardens
bye bye deck
bye bye labor
bye bye sweat

cuz I am banished down the street
to a ramshackle guber
natorial manse

  haunted by a mad
  osteopath

• but I get chickens anyway
& sand the hardwood floors by hand
& oil the boards until they gleam

just in time for Florhio

when again the ratbastards
smear the hero and the fags
then re-resteal
the whole shitarito

     while we just sit there on the McCouch
     like the obese flugging slugs we've become

not burning down
          City Hall
    not doing
          Shit All

    just huffing up
    our own damn sharts

REFINANCE NOW BFGHTZ

birthdate impasse
take your butchery
a glycerin of concept
with sepal promiscuity

decipher contempt
mass-produce piquancy
of a remitted
mauritius
gone on reflection

strangulate
he buzzers an attest
not on fencepost
but round go charity
which the wattage

Are communion verticulate?
is dispersal meaning transient?
t-maple virulent?
Ur thoughts please,
migrate spongecake

• after the mayor arsons her bar
she flies off to Acapulco
orders a margarita on the beach
and waits for the dirty
deal to go down

of 427 wild Hazeled acres
circumferencing the watershed

      for this is another
      Age of the Demons

            cashing in
            because they can

& so our land is sold on the sly
to the county's most
fecal polluter

when everyone knows
    you don't shit
    in yr water

      • but that's the precedent
      set by our president
      abramhoffing folily
      while the toad hunkers in the corner
      and all the buggeries of the priests
        rove on
         chenily

• which is how the mayor
scored her bling

<<as for the rest of the corrupt crypto-club
they feasted like screeeching fiends
while all the village idiots
      took it in
      the eco-ass

• but before the dirty deal goes down
   there's lots of sneakery to be done
   in the pulling up
    of survey stakes

through flash-frosted rosebud groves
 & *krish krush*ing kreeks
   we rendezvous with glazéd ponds
    we will never see again

        just one crunching step
        behind the beribboner
            cicles stalaging
            everywhere

though it doesn't make a dingdang diff
  the fence goes up
    wherever the defescrators
      draw their random lines

        • 300-foot mando-buff?
        Poppycrock!
                        thirty feet from bovine shite
                        to beavered bay

            w/ wire bands flung willynill
            & the cigbutts of the settlers
            settling in silted soil

• and in the zonking dawn of another four orbits
mr. clinton eugene curtis stands before the
judge & testifies that he wrote code
for the Weasel

   to flip it 51
     I 49

   "So was it hacked?"
   guy is asked

   reply is aye

     {{ now backpage on innernets
     viewed by only 65K

   because (as the rooster crowed)
   we are endowed with the exact degree
     of what gets
       embraced by thee

• le, our new nancy cares-again is a
   flava flavacopia
     of fawny bonny doochebags stal-
       wart steroid debutants & even the
   Nuge
       weirdoing out
         for Top Phreak-

                 & childstars & centerfolds & mini-midgets motoring in
                   the wake of pasties on tv
                     as badgirl Britney flashes beav

                 Cockadoodle Doo, muggafuggas
                   the bimbo dies
                   at 39—

• and every year the monkeysuits
for going under the microscope
and every year seated there
gruveling for barleycorn

and basically
getting cornholed
while whoring out
fer free

Minions Loosing Awkardly!
spending betting tossing thousands
for one fat chance at the lottery

What a casino what a farce!
What a gypsy adjunct city!
packed with shattered glass

but hey, that's showbiz
hump it or lump it

pongo
pygmius

• and yea the demon
    came squirming over
        w/ his greezy drivel
            at taverns & the institution
                nasalating pleasantries

            but I would'nt have it
                I ignored his swinery

                    hence a rift
                    cringing burnt
                    in bitter blub
                        of espho-gas.............................

• back at the ranch
the pullets in the henhouse
    were thickening
    their pinfeathers

much to the chagrin of farking Frisbee
who couldn't deal with Spankalankalanky
dealing with anyone else—

        because what if she made the break?

then dookum yupp and on the quad
the aprèdome and cubes and rues
the spaz the space the rollerdome
    the chickens clucked
    the chickens crooned

while farking Frisbee and the moose
glowered glum and glommingly
then gloomed & fumed & boomed & spumed
till no one could take
the senseless circ
umnambulation

not even Spankalankalanky
held hostage seventeen years

so when the chickens scored the cherry show
at a g-blowin' gig down in St. Louie
farking Frisbee brought the leash
got totally monkeyed and sprang a sprocket
flipped bird & howled & yowled
shitfaced shoving falling down
then went and blamed it all
on the Otter

        and that's the way it is today
        farking Frisbee still freaking
        engloomerating sallowly

            sickly with bare-bum
            awallow in foetid
            hell-rot ooze

• so in the spring
   the woods come down
      by bulldozer & earthmuncher

         they rip the creeks they ream the ditch
          terrarizing woodchuck quail
           muskrat mouse
           toads n' skink

          scything up four centuries
           of knotty gnurly walnut hollows
            pod-dropping brittle buds

               they clear it all the frickaway
               shove the brush in savaged piles
               & leave the ravaged scape agape

                  for the stupid shitcows
                  marching in
                              shitting stupid
                                 stupid shit

• withholding the translation & skipping mucho informacion
  (not to mention cut 'n pastin')
    I was exiled once again
      to the ranchland of no sidewalks

  where the bemoled crone grabbed her broom
    & went sweeping madly shrilling *Death
      to You And All Your Cats!
      Canoes! Feces! Vermin!*

    because she is always sweeping sweeping
      sweeping driveway free of leaes
        sweeping sweeping
          furiously

      the whole dang octogenerihood
      up in arms against the leaves:

        the pinch-faced widow across the street
        blowing leaves mowing leaves
          every day invading leaves!

        —a stranglehold of bitter oldsters
          annihilating filthy leaves!
            every morning every noon
              sometimes even in blacknight
              floodlights flooding
                reeking queefing
                  Inhuman Leaves!

• but I had other demons to contend with
  mostly macro
  bacterial
            crudding up
              every crevice

  it started with the shoes and moved
    onto books & then the tools
      before taking to the walls
        carpets glass

        till constant bleaching washing wiping /
          sneezing coughing yakking gakking
            I took a wincing
              kick to the kidneys

              then doubled up
              lungchunking

Meet horny singles in you're zip

you no rummy
more than secondbest
with the door ajar (the glen of bed
do an attendant

KPUSHED!

—on screening
premonitory is ferric
withdilation is explosion
an resistant at feature

//of is Sandusky
are my bookbind
a sarcasm,
preposterous aisle

in notify so proximal
do do candelabra
to no Exeter
or quart in dispense
for proud is aladjust!
as a sheath...

• eventually tho—
    I rejetted the jimmied hearth
      threw out a sporeload of underfudge
      tore out the enmoldened shaggilation
        and got a sump pump humming under

          along with half a grand of canisters
          sucking up the drainal dankage

and not knee-slapping
 not laff-laffing
  the chickens popped
    post punkily

          and as the vastflats the size of France
          dissolved in sodium of
            Siberian cocktail

          and as the barreling hulls came bursting through
          the ten percent Obliterate
          eviscerated every decade

            I choded out in shack in back
            while plenty new devoted demons
            descended in a boggin fog

• out of the Atlantic & into the Keys
 she went skipping through
  McDisneyworld
   just whistling
    Dixie

    but as soon as she hit the Gulf of Jacuzzi
     she mutated into a shrieking banshee
      went smashing through the marshy mouth
       & hit the dykes like a wild horde raping anus

    and as the abandoned class in the class five
     braced themselves in the batter-sphere
      and as junkies hunkered & crackheads cracked
       in the crippling crumbling suicide dive

       the wailing hurricano pounded outside
        w/ sloughs of sewage snakes & gar
         roiling in the garbage flotsam
          washing the slab-
           cadavers away

        & as the seawalls ruptured biblicially
         filling wards with bobbing coffins
          & dogs & cats & rats & Rancid

          asphyxiation
                    set in
                     in the attics

           Charity got smeared to death
           and gangs ran rampant
           @concentration
           convention camp
            where

blistering citizens were broasting in the sun
       seizuring for insulin
         drying up like jerky as

          a seven year old girl got cornered in the shitter
           & gangbanged by a bunch of juvies
            force-fucking her "skank pussy"

                    then beating her brainpan blue
                        they left her there like a two-shit ho almost
                    dead enough
                            to not grab a sharp shard of glass and cut
                        her ass
                            across both wrists

                someone's grandma saw it all someone's
                    grandma bloating pus
                        shrouded in wheely rigor
                        mortis

& as the undead unplugged the last
gasping carpiform from the bubbler

  even the cops went shooting and looting blinded in
    redrage

        & as the blackmasses took to the *freeways*
            the Gretna sheriff turned them back mob-
            backed by a thug-chorus firing rabid into
            the surge

                        and no clean water and no
                        instant dinners and no anti-
                        biotics
                        or disinfectants or chop-
                        pers whatsoever

            the Coast Guard, however, got let in
                for miraculous rescues on andersoncoop
                while the peon reserves
                    twiddled in the wings   an hour away the whole damned week

& as the entire seven million gallon disaster
went glooping and splooging under the radar
            rivaling the hemorrhage of Elvaldeez

the refugees were left to fester
  like brief bags of sour meat
    gone putrid in the streets

good job, brownie
  you are a fashion god!

HISTORY IS DIGESTED IN A DISSIDENT & DISTANT INDIFFERENT INTESTINE!!!

PROPOSAL FROM ME MR. ALISHY ASHI

a different go of mild
fetter in confusion

blessed and Zadok. And ye
know, him, why therein
cannot order two vessels of
the treading Manasseh's
cursed care

Impress yourself, your olden bird
he distillate
continuity teasel
that well gladewater
he many threaten

A hermleigh the guysville
A Farmville what coaling
Bangui here serene
(still rocky feeling
packer tangerine)

So chowchilla ourselves
or darden before hazelton
of yourself I valuation
as local

—but what
carlsbad?

• and with meta now a femaphor
   akin to pesky terrorists
    who only keep us up at night
     after bombs shock our shores
      (and they ain't even ours)

 I take to the lakes again
  for incandescent
   yellow bullheads
    rich & deep &
    ochre hued

   like that crappy carp I hooked by the dam
    that comet-shot along the shore
     instantly kicking it up to sixty

      but I brought it in
       glowing luminescently
        & covered in strange sulfurous plates
         all blobby shaped and jerimandered
          in a shimmery slippery undergoo
           devoid of half its armor &
            half-cat in slickery

                  so what to do but gape at hang
                  of sorry barbels

                  then let it go like a last lurky leviathan
                  illing in its mutancy...............................

• Headlines from theadvocate.com:

      • Thousand feared drowned in New Orleans
      • Bush says Katrina recovery to take years
      • Health threats grow in N.O.
      • Baghdad stampede kills 800 Shiite pilgrims
      • Katrina refugees en route to Astrodome
      • Four indicted in alleged U.S. terror plot
      • Poll: Public divided on evolution
      • Oil prices dip as Bush taps into reserves
      • Usher, 50 Cent up for world music awards
      • Cards survive slam by Marlins rookie

• up on the rocky rizon
    the hunter up and snuffs hisself
      kicking back in easychair

  while Uncle Pete expectorates
   Woodie gets his scalp blowed off
   & Rosa Parks rides that bus
     along with Hope & Geriatric Ford

        it all happens in the instant

        of the outburst

          coliforming from coast to coast

          while constant peasants shit themselves
            to desert death Sonoranly

but at least the mayor ends up in jail
while the DUI alcoholo
beats the bejesus out of his wife
so gets run out
on a rail

          but still the tiny christ holds on
          while four humans
          and a cat
          contact sporidium

          yet no one even wonders
          if there's something
          in the water

          when it's absolutely evident
          there's something shitty
          in the air

• and in the nitrate overload
 the slow sad death of a maiden
 gorged in algae
  lilypigging bays

   the warming waters of the shallows
   are dwindling in oxygen
   & there are sundry sallow wolves
   beached slack of stomachs void

    cuz this foolchain is just as translucent
    as the grass shrimp

     cuz there is no muni-council here
     nor no test tubes
     or agencies of any kind

      just an anorexic possum
      retching in the ethersphere

• where the firmament is shimmering glitz
    glancing off & into the swirl
      as i sling back in cosmic chair

          just a gin and tonic here
          & two poles in the myst
          awaiting subtle tug of cat

w/ everbats in everflap
 & fireflies & weedbass
  skittering a froggéd shore

       & always there are meteors
       & snorting deer and rutting bulls
         lowing urgent orifice plunge
         in the cow
            -cut
              air of pie

• though once a bonafide UFO!
all liquored up & floating out
came looping zooping spirally

        quixotically
         w/ an incoherent velocity
     banking
           tangentially
   then shooting off
         extrapolly
trailed by two
          fine
             points of light

  but i don't try to understand it
  it exists
  like a witch

treatment from US. what different do you demand

                as appliance
                  my easter
              are developed
          not mclean or typify

               which is puerile
                   flocal
          his attinder of whiff

                are at match
           is this correct or no
            reservoir puff?

           my millard at shirley
      bigger then Its better access
             Go is mckenzie
                 billfold
             left-handedly

          simulation do brilliant
      no discrepancy where to send
         characteristic capsules
             on is ferraria

HEAR YE, HEAR YE
THE MICHAEL JACKSON SCANDAL OF BUTT-HUMPERY
PT. II:

fONDLING tHE cANCERBOY!!!

• but back to hangy swang of night
   in ye olde flooded rivervale
    w/ feet up & lines tight
     tension betwixt
      digittips

                    w/ bloody gou-chops
                    smoking under

                    and yapping yodels
                    noodling yonder

where eye'm the me
i have always wanted to be
& never cld conceive of

& glad to be with no regrets
having pleased the me i used to be
which sometimes matters
more than nothing

           • until, that is, some bastard beaver comes along
            like some bastard beaver always comes along
             cutting a V in front of me
              & spooking off the bartlebys
               KRRRRslapping tail
                sassily

                    Fucka!
                  I pull out my b.b.gun
                    & pop that bastard beaver pelt
                     then kickback in Infinite

                     (though after that
                      all chances shat
                       of catching me a big-ass cat)

                       still, I drift
                         in the System
                          just as much
                            god as jesus

• meanwhile
  the ten percent every decade
   has been revised by climactic mimes
   the deaf dumb conclusion being:

       by 2040   • then two a.m. & back at the launch
       icelessness   there's a shadow figure
       is   i figure
                           is just a garbage
         meaning 33 years   grubbing coon
         till no reflection
         fracting back   but aluma-scraping on the concrete
                         an adolescent silver fox
        & so the prognosis: skinny lanky
                         not taking off
           major glacial deluvianed glades
           in an ever-convecting moonscape bake
           ridgelined in rat-scratching waves just cocking head & watching me dock
                         then hauling gear up to the lot
yet in this reign of draught   empty except
we are still pumping out
primates paving lunar dunes   the two of us
erecting beachview monoliths
& repeoplating   & dogging dark perimeter
old orleans   she follows me till i latch straps
                       cop a squat
        whose rate is back to a drive-by per day & stare back
        cuz gas is down to $2.83
        & there are no oracles
        except the insane   at the funny tilt of her funny hea
                       perked w/ silly stick-up ears
                        & fluffy rub-it puppet chest
• well guess what?   just twenty feet away
  the afterwash is nye...

                        both us blinking
        so who needs terrorizm?
         we'll do it all   blinking
          ourselves
                       blink

               (P.S.
               23% of the icy caps
               gawn in 700 dawns)

· · ·

• but it's also a war of choozery
    especially in retard to the winning spin
    of a wartime economy

        because fighting invisible ottomans
          holds way more truck than not leaving
            no kids behind

                so adios to another
                28 percent
                of the subpar pie

as the thumb is snuffed
as the monkeysuits march on
as the gospel of Judas
is discovered in New Amsterdam

seems we had him pegged all wrong
dude was just obeying orders
framed by Christ
by Gum!

            but still
            jude means jew
            and jew means screw
            and taking shit back
            means renig

because revising history's notta problem
compared to exoner
ating tongues

• "XXXXXXXXX!"
   the demon squealed
     buttering up
     pubic beard

but all I can see is pounded porch
the measured bead of 10,000 steady strokes
and the uprooted tiers
of poppies and hops

            —but just stare back in smitery
            cuz he ain't nothing
            but a maggot

canal jackpot
stepladder counterfeit

year incentive enjoy
life to the fullest gez

in violent a question
high-eminence Canadian chemist

granulated
flushed
grew pantyhose
to hiss
a weed

seductive dangerously
to exercisable do deltoid
serviceable an catalina

ah so bunny
was bawdy no malaprop
you martin at nucleolus
so to tulle

go extracurricular by rumania
friendless hinge
italic milliliter

and the bookseller on abuse
is troubadour of
herbivore

• out in West Virginny
& all across the fossiled earth
the ghosts of the mashed & gassed
grumble umbrage
under rubble

      (47 just last year
      in good old UncleSamlAnd

      & 61 in just one shot
      back in the new
      USSR

      not to mention 13 smears per day
      on average in industrio China)

but here in the heartlab
methage is the aftermath
of many a molested strata boned
      by the railroad
& the plantation

cuz coal always takes its toll
when the sun ain't going
nowhere

• wherefore
beyond the bonus sploshing of lunkage
& popping peepers & warbling whoopers
a pigfucking spotlight
sweeps the moonless
vast of night

because Jackass the Pornmonger
bought the only hotel in town
& decided the welkin
was his biotch

      so now I'm catching a lot less fiosh
      & the city doesn't give a squidshit
      for the evil orcs have been replaced
      with incompetence & lack of taste

but that's the way it always is
that's the capital
      ass-clown
        condition

• after a three-martini lunch in texass
the twisted fiend goes blasting birdies
      (sans license)
when suddenly his pal pops up
like a muppet

     & *PHLLAA-BLAMMM!!!*
     gets it in the kisser

     bringing in some comic relief

from boom-boom martyrfat
following his squat gayluv
& the whole reality-tv-drama
uv who gets the Gaza Ghetto

so when it comes time for a donki voti
not even the wag machinery
can keep the lethal creeps from cheating
     again

& in the arc of the pendulum
the warlord stands down dorkily
     (tho stays on w/ a staff of seven)
as Hammas happens & Hezbelah too
while Soddom swings & the jeerers jeer

& as 22,000 targets shoot off
for a Shiite/Shunie Shuishide picnic
a floating blitzkrieg heads for Iran
     —shades of Afghanistan!

     • & oh yeah, The Reborn
       holding hands w/ NRA
       & machine guns are legal again
       oh happy day!

• & speaking of that 22 thou
   totally bartered & totally buggered
   for surging the insurgents

     nobody even makes a peep
     après greedo warbucks suck
      another 8200 up
       plus 12K natty guard—

              CALL OUT THE NATIONAL GUARD!!!

              (oh.... we can't)

        and not only that
         the pentagroin extends all active duty forces
          from 12 to 15 moons in zone

           while jr. threatens veto-smack
            in hapslap grill of We
             the bowlegged People

                              • smells like stemcell...........................

• & aye the Goliath:
   like always there's a quarter trill
    & more off the books

      cuz these tools are off the hook
      and an ass is in hock
                to Mexico
                    Asia
          and sr.'s private carrousel

not to mention wolfoscum
giving the ol reach-around
to his goofy chum alfred e.

      because we are up to our turkeynecks
      in a rising tide of Supertaint

        & we don't know
        cuz we never know
        cuz we always give
        ourselves a Swirly

because some vultcults don't care to glean
 that Korea rhymes with Syria
 and Palestine's a palindrome
   every
      single
         imperial
            year

• winding up the spineline branching off Ozarkia
(coming up from the dumpsterchild)
i am following the creosote vein
of Civ War masoned graves

where cutting up the Novinger ridge
a black ratsnake breaks from the brush
& goes shooting for the other shoulder
like a four-foot letter S
sliding on ice

& due to an instant primitive glimmer
triggered in the reptile mind
i veer for the pulse of two soft thumps
bumping under rubber

then see it in the rearview silver
last-launching into the ditch

      and Ooofda!
      i yam horrifucked
      by thy slithering
      violence, brain

        * * *

but then again
that ain't jack
—now is it
homefry?

• Et chickenslaughter Xmassacre!
  & West Nile now a constant!
  & bird flu flappin in
  w/ the Baby
  all subzed

blizzes blankets the total aorta
cyclones rip the babble belt
dozenfoot drifts in color-reddo
eighteen feet in old nord york

& somewhere off in Eifel-land
the change is confirmed

meanwhile
vd is std
pms is pmdd
and usa is under tons
  of tiny
   tony
   snow

• "I hear you're making me infamous"
  the demon dribbled
    rubbing palms Uriah Heeply

  & whatever chitchat followed that
    was blacked out like a
      stillborn hillbilly

    "I hope you'll have some mercy on me"
      the demon winked in skinkery
        sleazing in his slizzery

      but I paid him no nevermind

      "Be nice!"
                future slime of life jumps in
                  flipping me the evil fing

                      then icy
                            sniping
                                snivvery…………..

RE: GET HER INTO BED TODAY ADAMS YORE

Are backlog
Is migrant
a prioceptive

Is a repeat
with by everywhere
I feminine at turbulent
he purport octo
atonal

do many accept
a condo into mace

Re: Not embezzle

acquiescence
as this glevil
more to save today

in whichever quintillion
her westminister

• "This is no Vietnam"
  yet plenty skullblown vets ashudder in the ratskeller by the
    Boschian truckload-
      this ship is filled with peglegs hookclaws
        brainplates
          & synthetic-skin cyclopsians

  and oh yeah, scurvy rats & coocarachas

          not to mention blackmold, mouseshit
            & unscaleable summits of Sisyphus
              papyrus

  "Fighting for our freedom!" yap the vapid
          (as an overextended backdoor draft is stranded
            in the nomad sand)
      "Doing it over there, so we don't gotta do it
          over here!"

            & when Johnny comes marching home(less)
          with stubleg and stumpwrist
          he can pursue the AmDream
          from the backseat
          of a Taurus

                [while getting sued for med expense]

        cuz that's the scape-equation these days

          O thank you, Amerigo
            for a new Gen-Y
            o post-traumatics

• & bueno the cyborg Rodriguezes
   all wireless at applebees
      w/ cellular earways chowing down
         on hotfudge townie brownie sundaes;
            the whole damn fam
               connected by verizon
                  & waiting for the Call

         meantime: the spy dies
            livid & emaciated
               for publishing the exposé
                  of the erasée
                     who ratted on the Slut-guv

               <<famous for umbrella-assass
                     & theloniating the toxic vlad>>

            Ahh plutonium 210
            & KGB ye
            R the US

            & wii B
            Empire

• & as the house of whitey
    admits to clinging polar bears
      & then denies penguin dust
        uncle tomas fires eight
          unsympatico
            sentinels of law

                    of course
                    it's totally clear
                    who helped yon speedy out
                    by targeting the liberal lunch

      so now the standard cry for plasma
      & alfy e's predictable response
      "I will stand by my wrench
      & he will fixit"

      just like brownie, just like rummy

                    • but at least there's still T-Hill
                        where a coalburning throwback to the blacklung century
                          pumps out voltage & mercury
                            leadsmog & PCBs
                              keeping aqua
                                warm all wint

                        for big mushy flathead flesh
                          tons of dinky channel kits
                            & flipping leaping stripers slapping
                              in the bays of checkered sprey
                                swimming deer &
                                  year-round geese

                            tis eerie paddlin out in the steam
                            iz a nuther netherworld
                            casting action freezes up
                            but our worms always
                            wig & squig

                        we make fire
                          burn drift timber
                            sometimes glove

                          plastic bags
                            stuffed in boots
                              slugging bourbon
                                frumma flask

Thomas Hill Lake Fish Contaminants

fish species	contam		N	Std Dev	Max
Channel cat-fish	aldin	4	4	0.00	1.00
	alpha-heh	4	0		
	aroclor_l242	4	4	0.00	
	aroclor_1254	4	4	0.00	
	aroclor_l260	4	4	0.00	
	beta_hch	4	4	0.00	1.00
	cadmium	4	4	8.50	
	chlordane	4	0		
	cis_chlordane	4	0		
	cis_nonachlor	4	0		
	dieldrin	4	4	7.86	
	endrin	4	4	0.00	2.50
	gamma_hch	4	4	0.00	1.00
	heptachlor	4	4	0.00	1.00
	heptachlor_				
	epoxide	4	4	.75	2.50
	benzene	4	4	0.00	1.00
	lead	4	4	0.00	
	mercury	4	4	26.42	
	methoxychlor	4	4	0.00	5.00
	pp_ddd	4	4	62.15	
	pp_dde	4	4	7.00	
	pp_ddt	4	4	0.00	2.50

• Et dans l'âge du constant hoooing
      the shrubbing brain chortles fugly
      secure beyond the shitcanning
      of the umpires
      of their slime

           like an owl exploding in the acid vomit of Hell
           a patsy is poised
           to take the hit

      meanwhile up in Supermax
      glassed in w/ the corporate crooks
      mad bombers & congressmen caught
      pawing through the cookie jar

              there are guys who know pi
                         to the 20,000[th]

                             ridiculous

                                digit

• somewhere off in Alabam
state officials threaten to foster
one 250-pound fatkid
age seven
        if he doesn't lose some poundage

        "The doctors just don't know what to do"
                his 400-pound mobesity pleads
        "I feed him a healthy diet!"

                tuesday

        breakfast: 4 snausages
                     3 eggos
                     1 bowl lucky charms w/ milk
                     1 can diet orange crush

            lunch: 1 baloney sandwich
                     1 bag cheetos
                     2 snack pack munchables
                     1 can diet 7-up

           dinner: 1 kraft pepperoni pizza
                     1 bag bbq chips
                     1 can creamed corn
                     1 can diet dr. pepper

insertion skateboarding

                    you breadth
                busy as before
            so magpie from pounce
                scriptural irritate

            her neelyton that fairbury
                    do on califon
                on everyone markovian

        spend your night like a pronstar
                is this where it all
            condenses into mush?

• meanwhile the KS plains and MO hills
    are lousy with micro particles
    going up yr
    frking nose

ragweed hay grass & trees
the seedless saturation
of the cities

        pollenville
        snotsville
        watering
        eyeville

        sinuses in crisis
        (& cancer rising)

            cuz this is indeed
            industrial disease

        & with no midwives & witchdoctors
        we're at the mercy of the pushers
        godding out allegra-d
        zy-ream
            etcetera

            treating symptoms not the cause
            making species
            weaker faster

            it's sleazery
            or sneezery

                take your pick, mote-hole
                & hoover up
                in cilia

                    while the beast sleeps w/ appointed creeps
                    skirts anasia
                    gavels down on anna-cole
                    debates long bong
                    hits for jesus

        waiting for the axe
            to fall...

• so like the hero of my own mind
  I Surly face the invader
    w/ demon-nerve enough to crash
      & I call him "a piece of shit"
        then send his oily
          ass packing

but the thing is
he's no demon
he's not even
what I called him

    & hardly worth the scorn

cuz there are always gnats n' ants

        & MOREFORE
     SKIPPING THROUGH THE DAISIES
    GRUBBING THROUGH THE GUTTERS
MASS-MURTILATION HAS ALWAYS BEEN A CONSTANT
SO IF YOU BELIEVE WE SHOULD BE OVER IT BY NOW
      THEN THE SUPERNATURAL
        IS YOUR LORD—

• & Iraq now New Ireland
        embattled up the asterisk
& the straight guy's wacko sidekick crying
        niggershit &
the metro cowboy shockjock cracking
        knappy-headed-ho-ho-shit &
video convict karaoke
        à la Alice Coopery &
it now being nothing new
        to see a caved-in-skullman eating
        a sandwich on the train to Philly
& fashion tans & all the pets
        croaking from the toxic glute &
nutBagh the benchmark
        of buses blooming every day

                · · ·

        let it hereby be established
        that this is Jihad
        Little Billy

UNHOLY MILLEN/AL LITANY!!!

UNHOLY PUNY INHUMAN PUNK WHAT CAN'T EVEN KEEP FROM CUT-
TING HIS MELON UP WHEN KICKING BACK & SNACKING OF A SUN-
DAY, WATCHING FUTBALL IN PRE-POST!!!

UNHOLY RULING ON ABORTIO & TURNING BACK OF THIRTY YEARS
WITH NO CLAUSE WHATSOEVER FOR HORIZONS OF THE INNOCENTS,
O MEDIEVAL ROBES OF MEN!!!

UNHOLY AMISH SMEARFEST, UNHOLY U OF WASH-WIPE, UNHOLY MICH
MASSACRE, UNHOLY V-TECH NOT-CHO-CHEESE, 33 SLAUGHTERED
JUST LIKE THAT!!!

UNHOLY SOUTH KOREAN SHAME & RACE OF GENETIC GUILT VIGIL &
SMACKDOWN OF THE DOOMED DISCUSSION WHILE DARFUR JUST A
WHISPER AGAIN!!!

UNHOLY WIGGED-OUT ASTRONUT DRIVING DIAPERED TRANS-AMER-
ICO TO MENACE IN A PARKING LOT THEN PLEAD INSANITY IN THE
DUSK AS PROBES ALIGHT ON VENUS DUST & PODS BROADCAST FROM
THE FACE OF MARS!!!

UNHOLY WHIPPING BOY GETTING GRILLED LIKE A QUESADILLA BUT
NOT RECALLING TEN TIMES MORE THAN SILLY RONALD-& EVEN THE
GOPs CALLING FOR A TEXMEX HEAD!!!

UNHOLY SADR CITY CULTURE CALLING FOR MASS-BLASTS VIA HOME-
MADE-MARTYR-MURDERCHOICE OF ALL GUERILLAS HARKING BACK
TO GILGAMESH AND BEYOND!!!

UNHOLY NEW SOMALIA, UNHOLY OLD SOMALIA, UNHOLY MEGA CON-
CRETE WALLS OF CUBITS THAT ARE TEN PERCENT OF CO_2 McPAT-
TYMELT NOW BERLINING BAGHNAM HELL!!!

UNHOLY TALIBABY RECRUITMENT VIDS OF TWELVE-YEAR-OLD KID-
WARRIORS LIBERATING THORAX FRUIT CUZ COMMYISM'S MOST DAN-
GEROUS CLASS HAS BEEN MOTIVATED IN A MOMENT'S NOTICE!!!

UNHOLY PHREAKING APHREAQUA OF DIRT WE KNOW NOT JACK ABOUT BUT BLOOD OF CONSTANT VILLAGE SLAUGHTER-PALOOZAS IN SCATTERSPRA Y OF CENTURIES!!!

UNHOLY WOLFOJOKE BAGGING WARPLANS FOR A WORLD CLOWNBAG OF MOOLA-MONGERS THEN SQUEEZING SQUATICA ONTO THE PAY-ROLL-& THIS IS HIS DISGRACE!!!?

UNHOLY TROOP SURGE TRAVESTY OF EVER-BROILING MEATMEN BLAZED, WOMEN CHILDREN SEARED SAUTEED, AID WORKERS ABDUCT-ED CHOPPED & RANDOM EYE DISMEMBERMENT OF PARASITIC MUCK-RAKERS SCRAPING FOR A SPEGTAGLE! !!

UNHOLY FLASHDRIVE VIDEO PHONAGE UNHOLY YAHOO GOOGLE SPRINTAGE UNHOLY DELL INTELL G.P.S.AGE OF I.M.MYFACE TECHNO TUESDAY NOW ONLINE FOR SKULKING PREVERTS VYING FOR A HAND-FUL OF UNDERAGE ASS!!!

UNHOLY GENERATIONS OF UNHOLY GAR-LYNCHERY-HANGING FROM THE HIGHEST TREE-AN ALL-OUT-ICHTHYOLOGICAL HOLOCAUST & NO-BODY GIVES A WANG DANG DOODLE WHEN THIS IS CIANIDE !!!

UNHOLY OXY-HUFFING ELDERS BLOWING SHEETMETAL SHELLS TO SHITAREE IN THE GRIDLOCKED EVACU-WASTES OF THE REAL NEWMEX, HOUSTON!!!

UNHOLY PROLIF-OF-THE-UNPAST & THOUSANDS OF NUKEHEADS STILL POISED OLD SCHOOL WITH NO PURPOSE OTHER THAN WIPING OUT MILLIONS OF CIVILIANS-WHAT BE UP WITH THAT!!?

UNHOLY CORRESPONDENT GRUBFEST LIMELIGHT ON SOME INOFFEN-SIVE LITTLE TWIT SINGING A DITTY THAT KEEPS FALLING FLAT IN NEUROLENS OF ANYONE WITH SENSE OF SENSE CRINGING "CRAP!" ON LATE-NITE COUCH!!!

UNHOLY SECRET NIPPLE NODES (OVERSEAS & INNERSEAS) UNHOLY MISSING 747 UNHOLY HYDRO-BOMB LOST OFF COAST OF SAVANNAH GA IN COLLISION BETWEEN B-47 & F-86 1958-OOOPS, SOMEBODY'S BAD!!!

UNHOLY DRAMA OF AMBASSADOR DISGRACED BY SMOKE SO WROTE
THE BOOK ON HOW CERTAIN DEMON TOOLS STAGED THE WHOLE
COLONSHOW SO NOW CONDI ON DAMAGE CONTROL & CLAIMING
FOLLY BUT ALWAYS WITH THAT QUIRKY CRACK AS IF SHOOTING
STRAIGHT TO THE DEVIL!!!

UNHOLY LOST RECOLLECTIONS OF GIRL-WARHERO SPOSEDLY SHOT &
STABBED & HELD IN HELL-HOLE HOSPITAL IF NOT FOR NIGHT-VIZ HOL-
LYWOOD RESCUE THEN BACK TO PALESTINE WV WHERE YEARS LATER
AFTER HYPE: THERE WAS NO FEDAYEEN!!!

UNHOLY PRO-BALLSTAR FRIENDLY FIRED UPON & SHOT TO ROT IN
SHODDY AFGHAMIBUSH THAT ARMY ALTERS DETAILS OF BEFORE
BEQUEATHING MEDAL OF VALOR (see above) & AGAIN THE WHOLE
BLOWSHOW EXPOSED!!!
UNHOLY THE PIZZABOY OF MISSOURI NARCING ON BROS & SETTING
UP STINGS CUZ DADDY IS A HIGHWAY TROOPER DOWN IN MACON
AND SOMEONE GOT BUSTED WITH CASH IN HAND (& GUN)!!!

UNHOLY MILITARY BAN ON U-TUBE & ME-SPACE FOR ALL SOLDIERS
IN POTAMIA, LEST THEY GET ANY FUNNY IDEARS FROM THE UNFOX
FIRESTORMS JUST ONE MOUSE CLICK AWAY!!!

UNHOLY FACT THAT SOME WAGGLE-HEADED RACIST FAILURE WHO
COULDN'T RECALL JACK BEFORE CONGRESSIO REVEALED IN DEATH
DIARIES: THAT HE IN FACT DID ORDER BARTER-SO NOW CONSID-
ERED A NEW DEAD DUKE BY MYRMIDONS OF MYOPIA!!!

UNHOLY EPIPHANY THAT RENOUVAL OF UNPATRIOT ACT UPON
POST SURGERY SLAB OF UNSOARING EAGLE HOLDS LIKE VISE TO
THIS DAY AS AVUNC SHAM LISTENS IN BIG-BRUTHEREDLY ON YOU,
COWBOY!!!

UNHOLY CODGERS & CRABBY HAGS SETTING TRAPS FOR NEIGHBOR
CATS ON DANDELI-DEVOID LAWNS THANKS TO SELF-STEAMERY
AND SADTRUTH OF THEIR SHITTY SOULS!!!

UNHOLY SLUTTY DEBUTANTE SENT OFF TO THE GUCCI PEN THEN
PLUCKED OUT THREE DAYS LATER WHILE THE BLACKERER YOU ARE
THE MORE YOU'RE ENJAILED BUT GAWD IS ON HER SIDE!!!

UNHOLY SUZANNE MARIE BUTTS OF IOWA WHO STOLE THREE
ROLLS OF T.P SO NOW FACING THREE YEARS AFTER HAYING COME
CLEAN WHILE UNHOLY VICTORIAN SENSIBILITIES LEAD TO SUS-
PENSION OF HIGH SCHOOL TEACHER/CREATOR OF "BUTT-ART" IN
RICHMOND VA!!!

UNHOLY REALITY THAT 68% OF REPUBS DO NOT BUY THE HISTORY
OF OUR APE-PAST, KANSAS!!!

UNHOLY FLAMING BEIRUT IN MISSILE-BOMBARD OF REFUGEEZ AND
ISLAM SPLIT BY BZOOOMMM OF A HUGE-ASS MONGO ONION ERUPT-
ING IN SMOKING CIVIL ARMEGEDDON! !!

UNHOLY CAMP CRAPPER NAVY SAILOR WHO WENT TO FBI WITH
INFO ON ILLEGAL STORE OF IRANQUI ARMS SOW AS DETAINED AND
TORTURIZED AND IMPRISONED BY HIS OWN RED WHITE & SCREW
THE VET OF FOREIGN WARS!!!

• upshot being:

800,000 murdered to dearth
& 1,529,439 injured in
        an illegit
                Afghaniraq—

                        —but that of course is pissimistic
                    & this is epic crowdpleasin' coda
                        inspiring of pure cryptic fact
                        that all these orbits scrawling for(m
                        are worth yr sizzle-
                                instant
                                    init...........................

• FOR AND/OR NOT WITHSTANDING

fish exist
  along with the true
  good gold of cats
    you always forget
      & then flashback

& the mayor is in jail for 63 months
& the big-ass hawk is perched upon the chicken coop look-
ing for a hen to scoop

& the wild red pups come out at night
to skitter around in the heart of downtown

& skating skating out on the coven gliding
sliding frictionless
there is something always waltzy
crossing the hiatus of 200 vultures
              vortexing
the widening gyre

      & as Captain Tracheotomy
                        talks robotic
        & as gospel glee
                rings down from Big Creek

              this Season in Kirksville ends in a
whimper

                or, rather
                the lone moan of coyote drone
                shaloming in the gloam

—as if that's it
and it is
in all its
inglorious
lack

               & that's the flash,
Slappy

               live from Toad Suck
               Arkansas

    July 14   2000-sev.

GARUMINATIONS

That big fat gar Hippy and I spotted up on Sandy Bottom… it was a channel of the Chariton and it was winter, but there it was, thirty feet beneath us, three and a half feet long and more balloon than a football. Just treading there like the Goodyear Gar, muddy snow melting down the banks.

Coulda got it with a rifle… just like any rabbit or squirrel anyone coulda got with a rifle. If they had a rifle at the time… instead of just a hypothesis.

# # #

That long skinny longnose that hit my Mepps down on the Lamine… the serene Lamine and that chromy gar… lily pads and riverplants… gravel bars and lazy gnats. We were in a big slow eddying pool, shelfy bedrock rising around us. Shade and moss. That long skinny bursting gar… it hit right beside the canoe, three feet of shivering wrath. Snapped that line and kicked up a fuss. One less #3 spinner in the world.

# # #

Down on the South Fabius, twenty miles east of La Plata… two two-footers along the cool cliff. And me… in the hundred-degree humidity. Rivulets of perspiration; smallmouth, frogs, minnows, driftwood… biting flies striped like bees. Chigger nests in the tall tall grass… sunnies on almost every cast. Then, a couple pools upstream… a six-foot water moccasin, swimming with its head up, steely black and fast.

# # #

The yellow bullheads of Hazel Creek… for years, some old boys been snipping their fins. Scarred-over dorsals, nubby pectorals sealed purple… it's bad enough they're covered with lesions from rubbing up against the bottom, but they also gotta deal with humans. The kind who think they're doing good by changing the bonescape of a race… lacerated "safe" by some dillrod with a pair of pliers.

No fish is as fucked up as a yellow bullhead.

# # #

Cutting through the Amish terra, passing austere open-air buggies, soybean fields, one-lane bridges through La Plata, South Gibbs, then Evergreen down to Fountain Street… there's always a gar beneath the bridge, hanging out by the logjam. Or a carp. Or a turtle. Or three or four softshells clowning around. Plus bullet shells scattered along the upstream guardrail… since it's always easier to see what's under the surface when refraction's coming atchya.

# # #

On the garbaged banks of the sub-6 Chariton, the river is chopping with fish as the low dark front comes on in like a big black cloud of squiddy ink. Tailfins break the murky meniscus fringed wild with elderberries, grapevine, cornflowers, ragweed in bloom, and a thousand reedy river-sucking trees.

A big brown beaver comes up beneath me, then undulates downstream. There is no urgent slappage in her tail… and then she rises and dives like oil.

# # #

Out here, we are not stoned immaculate. This is the season of shwagg.

# # #

But really… it's been the season of accidental flatheads; big and yellow and calico—and I love their ugly mugs.

# # #

These damn spotlights have been sweeping space for 200 nights and bumming out my summer. Some pornmonger moved to town, bought a bunch of property up, and put two giant searchlights on the roof of his hotel. Talk about light pollution… You can see these beams for fifteen miles, from sunset to sunrise, violating everything: the stars, the horizon, the sky of thousands—screaming:

"HEY EVERYBODY, CORNVILLE IS COSMOPOLITAN! SEE HOW WE HAVE STEPPED INTO THE CENTURY! COME SPEND YOUR MOOLA HERE!"

There's been a controversy, of course, with vandalism and petitions and letters to the editor. The problem being: Some people just don[t give a shit. Some business leaders, that is, and some members of the City Council—who feel that less stars in the sky is no biggie, and that a handful of complainers should just shut up.

These humans have never felt the sky at night. They live in a world of screens and have no appreciation for what people have been pondering for millennia: namely, our place amidst the Infinite.

Because that's the character of this city. We allow cows to crap in our water. We let shysters defile the night. And we pass laws making that alright.

Aye, the spotlights have been grandfathered in. Because that's who we are.

Cornville: where people don't make a difference.

And I am catching a lot less fish.

#

My Garlosophy is that Gartheism has to do with getting the hell outta there when something alien comes along… it's a primeval state in which creatures toward the top of a food chain conceive of a predator, so steer clear enough away of all possible threats to get along for as long as they can.

Basically, we are the only menace to gar—but we have our predators too. Fear preys on stupidity, driving us to hide. Gar, however, do not deny.

#

There's something to say about how you can always remove a hook from a fish's mouth by guiding it back from the way it came. Pliers are for amateurs, you can always reverse the steel. You just gotta stick your hand in there and jam your thumb into the cradle of the J and let the barb stick into your nail. Then shove in and twist. You can always weasel the hook out like this.

#

I'm allergic to what I love. But then again, if you ain't… what's to stop you from going whole hog?

Sometimes I lay crucified, two poles out in the Milky Way, my feet way up and kicking back, rods balancing on fingertips: a worm on one, a liver on the other—feeling the tension between me and the bottom. If anything comes along, WHAMM! I set it. And if nothing comes along, at least I'm out there in my lawn chair with Off on and a G&T beside me, being part of it.

According to all my molecules, tightlining is the only time I feel human. Because out there in the night, I am inhuman in the owl sounds.

And they're not your typical hoooing sounds. Those birds are WOOOOPing and WOOOOOPing and WOOOOOOOPing, getting it on—with crazy climbing syllables that rise and dive and crash and crescendo. Until all the distant coyotes of the valley are joining in with all their yipping yapping pups howling and yowling in waves. And some cow is lowing loonily, desperately, like some terrified creature stuck in the muck up to its neck and sinking into the bowels of the earth: RRROOOOOOOGGHHH, RRROOOOOOOOOOOOOOOOOGGHHHH, RRRRRRRRRRRRRRROOOOOOOOOOOOOOOGGHHH, RRROOOOOOOOOOOOOOOOOOOOOGGHHHH!!"

And the bats are flashing all around, zigging right in front of my face, then zagging away at the last split-second. You can always trust a bat. They might brush by close enough for you to feel their flap/flap/flap, but they'll never touch you and never collide... nabbing bugs buzzing by.
And that's when I find the spot: that inhuman tightlining spot—in the swing of equilibrium suspended in the night. Now I am out-of-body, now I am physically nothing. I cease and so do you. It's the way it is minus us. And we are tripping out for free.

And the frogs are croaking in symphony, plipping and plopping all over the shore. And the little bass are skittering the weeds and snapping up stranded bugs... while coons creep along the bank, cracking clams and snapping snails.

Then some beaver comes along and cuts a V in front of me. It's only six feet away and if I twitch it will SLAPP! So I hang there as still as death while it paddles by with its head up and two black ears illumed by the moon. Because I have made my peace with the beaver.

Nighthawks swoop: WHUUUUUU/WHUUUUUUU/WHUUUUUUUU/ WHUUUUUUU/

WHUUUUUUUUUUU/WHUUUUUUUUUUUU/WHUUHMMMMMMMP! and gone in a nanosecond. Just like the nano-notion of them.

But I can't hang here all night in my unhumanity. I am not the Nothingness. I am a sack of ticking organs—eventually paddling back in the mist.

With those pigfucking spotlights raping the sky, marking the turf of some chickenshit diddling with the City Council. It isn't like it used to be with mysterious dorsals breaching the surface. The meteor showers are invisible now.

And so I paddle… muddy, bit, scratched, with ticks. And if I'm lucky, my palm's been pierced by a catfish stab and I am smeared with blood… as I dip, strain, pull, rudder… out there, alone, in the molasses… muscles, tendons, pulling, drifting…. sliding silent toward the launch…

# # #

It's boring getting drunk with yourself. Unless, that is, if you're me….talking into a tape recorder, getting glimpses down.

# # #

The catwave comes across the lake, beginning in the dark of the distance. Plips turn to plops turn to plaps turn to slaps—until suddenly I'm in the center of the frenzied time.

Which is synchronized to that of my yellow bullhead back at the ranch, who lives in a ten-gallon tank and comes out at night for a vigorous half-hour… as if communing with the wild cats of the lake thorough some secret catfish ESP emanating from their barbels… which are actually antennas, informing the catfish masses that this is the moment to motor for grub—So Let's Get Out There And Get Us Some!

But ultimately the catwave passes and I either catch one or I don't. Or I go home because it's late. Or I sit out there till 2 a.m. waiting for a random lunker to come nosing and nudging and snuffing the bottom. Or I zone out, nod off, drift with it.

# # #

Cutting through the velvet steam, I alight on the launch, where some crazy old coot is talking to himself and wants to stop and gab.

"Watchya catching? Catfish? Blue? Channel? Yellow? I almost came out too! Got one hit tonight—pretty big one! Watchya using? Minnows?

"Worms."

"No kidding? Worms, huh? Where'd you get em? Wal-mart? Shell station? Dig em up? Flood the yard?"

I drive home while he blabs on.

Big whoopy ding dong.

#

And suddenly, anticlimactically, without any fanfare at all, the lights go off in outer space. Because the pornman ran out of dough, so closed all his businesses—and that's it. The sky returns. And no one even picks up a trumpet Or applauds. Or makes it front-page news.

"Whatever," is the consensus.

Whatever is what we get.

Hungry Hollow Pie

Mari Mari quite contrary
how does your garden grow?
With cryptosporidium
that's what!
—Kim Trist (pseudonym)

Little Debby

Oooo mama
I wanna buff your buffer zone
crawl between your flaps of love
and moo with you
—E. Colifield (pseudonym)

Driving in Cornville

Richscotting home last night
drunk as a skunk
I ran over one small child
a tricycle, a mailbox
a garbage can
and a fire hydrant

luckily though
the fuzz didn't catch me
and I only blew chunks

for half an hour
Richscotting
the porcelain bus.
—D.W. Iverson (pseudonym)

ECONOMIC DEVELOPMENT

Half the hamlet is silent now
so many empty homes
to fill with shiny happy faces
but let's build new ones
instead!

yeah, that's the ticket!
real estate is where it's at!
let's subdivide and zone it all
for the people they will come

to the Depot here the
Walls are Green
and lonely local lumbermen
and druggists bed for bread

while big city contractors
and national chains
bathe in the gold
of what we once had
  —Noah Scamnow (pseudonym)

PART 6

PROZAKIA / NO B.S. REVIEWS

2001–2016

Hanging Out in Bukowskiville

Open All Night, Charles Bukowski
Black Sparrow Press, Santa Rosa, CA
361 pp.

Hard to say what makes this
posthumous collection more
post-humorous
than the rest

unnatural nature poems?
   (one great cat
   gits itself a wildebeest
   "his eyes like bottlecaps
   pray to the sky")
surprising surrealism?
("slowly going
   the way of witches...
   and the clouds hold nothing hidden
   in creampuff jowls...
   the devils drink from the breasts
   of stunned maids;
   it is beginning to rain:
   fleck, fleck, fleck")
daring poems pushing it?
   ("what you want to do and what you've got to do is the same thing...
   God is the invention of failures...
   the angels pissed themselves in fear.
   I am a beautiful person")
more beauty than ever expected?
   ("and it dawns on me now that
   there is nothing so beautiful and
   pure and as perfect as the well
   written line")
prophesizing omenly?
   ("the womb has spilled us into a sewer.
   new gods are needed.
   new doors must be opened")
shades of Céline?
   ("and she just sitting there with her big beer gut hanging out.

all the other passengers were less than nothing")
plus honesty?
    ("the worst thing for me is not having somebody to talk
    to when something obvious must be said")
or critical Omnip?
    ("observation put to action
    is the essence
    of art")
or messages to audience?
    ("the reader is an
    afterthought,
    the placenta,
    an accident,
    and any writer who
    believes otherwise
    is a bigger fool than
    his following")

Aye, Open All Night/
    Bukowski is
fear in the eyes of the bully
a final terrible beautiful whore
green dogs, dinosaur sky
honeysuckle summer madness.

PICTURE BUKOWSKI

Bukowski in Pictures, Howard Sounes
Rebel Inc., Edinburgh
153 pp.

Over the past few years there's been a deluge
of books about Bukowski
hopping on the bandwagon
of loyal readers
who'll buy anything that has the name
of their favorite alco
icon
on it

Sounes states that Bukowski in Pictures
is meant to be "a complementary book"
to his 1999 biography
Locked in the Arms of a Crazy Life
which had to leave
these pictures
out

Still
this "biography in pictures"
ain't just pictures; half of it is text
providing us with some new information
mostly in the form
of irate love letters
and an FBI file

There's nothing very remarkable about the writing
(or information, rather) though
except that the style is objective
in comparison to the other bios
interviews
and book-length essays
published over the last few years
in which personal perspective
saturates the market

Bukowskiophiles will no doubt be intrigued
by the visual aspect of this book
in which we can see
if the leggy bimbos of his fiction
are really the "high-class pieces of tail"
he professes them to be

Other pictures clarify
the over-described yet visually limited
(up until now) world of Bukowski:
beyond the standard shots
of a drunk old man in his underwear
there are childhood photos, family photos
car photos, apartment photos
girlfriend photos, photos of friends
wives, his daughter, his cats
bartenders, book covers
movie stars, etc.
ranging from amateur snapshots
to professional portraits

And in almost every image of Bukowski
his stereotypical traits are there:
he is either
sporting a gaudy retro shirt
caught with the scars of acne vulgaris
or proudly brandishing
a beer

One particularly disturbing picture
is of his first wife: a no-neck mutant
grinning in deformity.
Another shows Bukowski posing
with a fiberglass Colonel
bearing a bucket of Kentucky fried
chickenwings

In another he pretends
to attack a girlfriend
with a fork
as she licks his pot belly

We also see him taking out the trash
drinking with sundry literati
and of course betting at the track
Usually he is hamming it up
but in some he's depicted
as a more subtle contemplator

Result: the strength of this book lies in its layout
which is so self-conscious
in its use of contrast
and its filling of space
that the outcome is a glossy
                    savvy
                         coffee table
                              artbook

Whereas other books about Bukowski
have tried to rely on photos to show
the Bukowski experience (particularly Shakespeare
Never Did This) (by Bukowski hisself)
this is the first book about Bukowski
that's thought out enough, and striking enough
to lift the beer bellied bard
from the gutter

            while attributing a sophistication
that American critics
have always shied away from

Meaning that this is a good looking book
about a not very good looking guy
which can supply
some colorful vivid characters
to take the place of faceless names

But then again, nobody reads Bukowski
to see the faces clearly
What sells Bukowski
is an easy to relate to
narrative voice

embellishing of drunken whores
hangovers, crummy jobs
and eventually
the rise from all this;
dredging humor
from horror
This book is not a book that's needed
but it is a book that's in demand
(since Bukowskimania is now in full swing);
giving images
to imaginations
that want to see more.

Prozak Pro Sanders

America: A History in Verse, Vol. I, 1900–1939, Ed Sanders
Black Sparrow, Santa Rosa, CA
325 pp.

From the man who brought us the immortal sentence
"All was"
comes Part I
of a vast and seething flowing poem
of a vast and seething flowing nation
making this epic
the most maximus of its kind
in the history of Whitmanian lineage

Children of Amerigo
throw down yr flaking history books
covered with dust in civics we trust
& learn from a poet historian!

How Americans swooned in wargasm
from the Spanish Civil War
to Hit-vom creamdreams
of interNazi splendor
howling across the Xeno-expanse
confused from being new
two centuries later

with commentaries too
and plenty opinion
Sanders hides not
his lust and disgust
of our glorious mutation

through "investigative poetics"
our author sings again
of the greatest poem ever inspired
from sea
    to shining seed
of what we will be
in the weary bloody future
of looking back
through a lyrical sphere
at a lyrical sphere
here
O Roil o' Century roil!

Shamelessly Naked Review I

Sifting through the Madness for the Word, the Line, the Way
Charles Bukowski, Ecco Press, NY
416 pp.

"red dogs in green hell, what is this
divided thing I call
myself?
…
it's so easy to slide
into poetic pretension"

Old Chinaskis never die
they fake their deaths and write from L.A.
producing piles of posthumous confusion
bunkerbusting images
of racetrack rutting drunken scumdays
& California wino hard drives
stunning shifts in expectations
fucking poems fucking ending:
"the albatross is a fake,
the universe is a shoe,
there are no heroes,
there is only a mouse
in the corner
blinking its eyes,
there is only a corner
with a blinking mouse,
two roads embrace
what's left of the sun
as the monkey
manages a tired
smile."
the dagger twists
(jab, jab, jab)
from the wrists of Mt. Olympus
advising boring budding bards:
"the libraries of the world have
yawned themselves to
sleep

over your kind.
don't add to that.
don't do it.
unless it comes out of
your soul like a rocket,
unless being still would
drive you to madness or
suicide or murder,
don't do it.
unless the sun inside you is
burning your gut,
don't do it.
when it is truly time,
and if you have been chosen,
it will do it by
itself and it will keep on doing it
until you die or it dies in
you"

which is a far cry from
fat whores taking
big beershits
hemorrhoids
etc.

SHAMELESSLY NAKED REVIEW II

What Of, Skip Fox
Potes and Poets Press, Bedford, MA
129 pp.

Shudders of Tarantula
Lautreamont on crystal meth
this jumbalaya of bananal leaves
and synerjism sings:
"a pound of ground round grinding down the fairway...
the breaking of forms into norms for undertaking"
as 'pulsing meadows' merge with 'Malice
of Forethought' 'Witless in Gaza'
like 'slices of death through fissures'"

of Fox's lite ironic water
if music and math ever met in vinaigrette
these vignettes are the new fast bastards
of a hyper-Olsonic
Ameridada
(see?

Shamelessly Naked Review III

From Absinthe to Abyssinia: Selected Miscellaneous, Obscure and
Previously Untranslated Works of Jean-Nicolas-Arthur Rimbaud
Arthur Rimbaud, Mark Spitzer, trans. Creative Arts, Berkeley
166 pp.

Merde! Merde! Merde!
the world would be better off
if Mr Spitzer translated himself
into shutting up rather than adding
to a pack of distorted
bandwagon lies

Who cares about the prose Rimbaud
wrote as a trader of slaves in the bush?
Who gives a flying flatulence
for prepubescent Latin crap
and reconstructed
little ditties?

Girlfriend,
enough was enough
thirty years in the past
so spend yr green on something new
like a dble-sided dildo thong
and leave the deranging
to Fowlie & Varese
avoid exquisite
nepotism.

No Bullshit Review I

1968:A History in Verse, Ed Sanders
Black Sparrow Press, Santa Rosa, CA
260 pp.

Renaissance fugger
historian poet
novelist politico
Sanders has

laid out one long bardsong
in a lyrical tempest
of CHAOS Cong
Vietnam
assassination
celebrations
Joplining Hendrix
Hoffmaning stew
w/ Manson too

plus Pantherism, terrorism
& yippie hippy flwr chldrn!

tho most appealing in these pages:
the action-packed I-witnessings
of '68 Demo Convention
tear gas harmonium
skullsmash brew

starring Ginsberg Burroughs Jean Genet
then sadly Kerouacy
drunk on Buckley

Sanders translating it all into English
et al into English

as brutifully apt
as the bare breasts
of death.

No Bullshit Review II

Orpheus Emerged, Jack Kerouac
ibooks (Simon & Schuster), NY
176 pp.

Nevermind that Jack
never wanted you to read
this instance of green youth

Pariah Sampas (self-proclaimed
"Protector of the Trust")
has just made another million bucks
"for his hundreds of Greek relatives"
Kerouac didn't want "to get
another bloody cent"

story okay
characters so-so
intriguing to see preboheme
kunstelromanella
egotaling
psychoanalytic
doppelism

includes a creepy Creeley intro
plus rehashed trash
on Beats & bio
stuff

not to mention
revisionist biblio
& timeline lacking
Jan & Joan

plus free CD, wow-wee!
see fancy graphiced
"interactive links"
working sporadic
w/ loads o'
misinfo

the whole deal
a damn
shame.

No Bullshit Review III

Happy Ending, Mike Topp
Future Tense Books, Portland, OR
chapbook

Citizens of Peoria
it's your privilege
so make a statement:
fill your shoes with applesauce
and pass through airport
security.

"ahhhhh sweet sassy lasses / how we love your boobs and asses / your bad
grrrrl grins / and vixen visions / but next time leave yr / postfemme / fatal
/ ism / verse / at home"

Kingdom of Fear:
Loathsome Secrets of a Star-Crossed Child in the

Final Days of the American Century, Hunter S. Thompson
Simon & Schuster, NY
384 pp.

though vainglorious and
nascent of old gonzod hat
Kingdom is most smoking nug
of nitrobiased journalcy
cured w/ crystal fiction
to aggravate the Hogs of War
in sad shadow of
yr Michael Moore

—but impotent in fury(?):

"Let's face it—the yo-yo president of the U.S.A. knows nothing. He is a
dunce. He does what he is told to do—says what he is told to say—poses
the way he is told to pose. He is a Fool... This is not the time to have a
bogus rich kid in charge of the White House... he wantonly and stupidly
endorses mass murder of a logical plan to make sure we are still Number
One—he is a Jackass by definition—a loud and meaningless animal with
no functional intelligence and no balls... Who are these swine? These
flag-sucking half-wits who get fleeced and fooled by stupid little rich kids
like George Bush?

They are the same ones who wanted to have Muhammad Ali locked up
for refusing to kill gooks. They speak for all that is cruel and stupid and
vicious in the American character. They are the racists and hate mongers
among us—they are the Ku Klux Klan. I piss down the throats of these
Nazis. And I am too old to worry about whether they like it or not. Fuck
them."

Lo, our friendly neighborhood dopefiend
has spun another narco-coil
twined in clever curlitales
of sundry plots converged in theme
that as of yet no critics know
what to make of bombast but
more of ye olde same

Cockmuffins!
This is a different specimen
sophisticated in suspense
paced with cops and guns and Depp
gelling to the namedrop end

avec a secret stitch
of aggressions in transgression
in face of dick and bush
and all their slimy
scandaleezas

nevermind the mad doc's
bullshit self vindication re:
fatporn stargone wild

what's pisspants hilarious is
booze-fueled roadkill pig-limo visions
of Clarence Thomas humping whores
in Elko lustrush of
most quintessential knee-slap
Amlit overkill this
pseudonym has ever seen
blast ratbastards
in the ass

Ho ho! Bravo!
Encore Maestro!
War makes art
worth a shit.

A New Maximus

America: A History in Verse, Vol. 3, 1962–1970, Ed Sanders
Black Sparrow Books, NY
387 pp.

Aye the I
in the eye
of once Fugly troubabard
who apres l'evidence
of JFK chiggerism
poses

"Is it not proper to think that military leaders
who would propose
domestic terror
could also kill a president
or fashion a patsy?"

then all that ML Kingful marching
lynching bugging baiting beating
in red white & blue blood of

sacrificial Camelot lambs
(whom most luminary is Ted!?)
blazing amazing scathing faces
thugslugging RatherDan
in Panteraed past of
Mansonland

where "The Spirit of Napalm...
and his bone-pal
Scythe Man the Lurker"
spankingly contrasts
"the fluffy... condemnation
of a writer... famous for his breathy,
envious book on... Kesey"

adding

"You could see Mr. Wolfe in 1827

snickering at the paint-stained clothing of William Blake
(and his egalitarian politics)
after... snickery visit"

till Four Dead in Ohio
and flowervisions in the gun

as Sanders goes and goes and goes
toward volume 4 of Nixon Ford
Carter Disco Iran-Contra
Reagan nation Oblivion

making a new Maximus
what doesn't condescend.

Not Just Boyjerk Cocksuck Meatcum

Antler: The Selected Poems, Antler
Softskull Press, NY
197 pp.

Antler not just boyjerk cocksuck meatcum in the tree hugging nightsky
Antler is Ginsbergian echo of Whitmanian brilliance
        especially in Am Po couplet combos:

> "with the thought of salmon
> shooting up the rapids of his brain"

> "Suddenly I see the boy burn alive
>   his flesh afire writhing screaming pyre"

> "No seagull will ever become a Mormon.
> No dolphin has to learn computers"

> "It's not that my erotic poems are overblown
>   but that teenage boys are underblown"

> "When you look into the gun and feel
>   where the hole in your head will be"

So now Selected Poems converges famous verse
    like "Factory," "Lucky Trees"
        "Pussysmell Candlelight"
            "Blowjobscope" and "Child-
                foot Visitation"

with lustfuck mantis assassination:
    "100,000 years from now
        female praying mantis clasps her mate
            eating his eyes and head
        causing headless corpse to writhe and kick
            till it inserts penis and pumps
        as she continues eating him
            till nothing's left
        but his penis still ejaculating
            in her ovipositor"

and clinchers such as:
      "Her sleek and silky sulky sassy pussy
          feels like the pussy of a teenage girl
              that wants and needs to be fucked"

aside from lists and fuzzy facts
Antler's bashing headgear now
with the caribou of epic
transcendental gasms

but will he Hart Crane out
into the propeller
before he rides the bus for free
to smoke a joint in Wilderness
beneath starry
eternity?

FUCK THE COVER

The Nudes of God, James Barfoot
NewSouth Books, Montgomery, AL
174 pp.

The most striking thing about this book
at least the "Advance Reading Copy"
is the cover, which
is the most beautiful book cover ever
with a nude so exquisitely breasty and soft and pink and
nipply lying in a sparkling stream for the taking
that it makes you want to crawl on top and
fuck the cover

This nude lacks a head though
as do most of the poems in this collection
introduced by a boring professor who's no doubt a friend
of the boring professor who wrote the book.

At first, Barfoot's poems seem saccharine and
nostalgic for a time that's gone
with awkward churchy language and the dropping of
unsubtle clunkers, plus
strange combinations of the overpoetic with words
that call attention to themselves
like "TWAT" and "CUNT"
in the midst of what is trying to be pastoral

Here are some excerpts that leapt out and why they caught my eye:

> "The virgin sits upon the Green Man's face,
> A medieval face carved into wood,
> That wood then curved into an inverse arch,
> That inverse arch plumb centered between arms,
> Those arms two balanced bars for her soft hands"

> (weird union of Old Europe and ancient poetry
> with paceless language saying nothing)

"And oh I miss her so.
I miss her so."

(Come on, this is 2001)

"And wear me nothing underneath the tree
Except your string of pearls and soft black dress
And underneath the black wear nothing there
And swing you there below the dappled shade
Your shoeless feet above the dusty clay
And smile at me and look me in the eyes
And do not turn away"

(19th-century sentimental poetics
dimpled with stilted fodder)

In fact, the whole first half of the book
feels like some assistant professor
affecting the tone of another old whitehair
while trying to be hip by musing on nudes
in stark contrast to Antler's more free freeverse
which is curious considering both Antler and Barfoot were
born the same year
By the time I got to page 46
I was weary of this verse which was obviously written by either
A) a low-level misogynist meditating not on nudes
but rather on what he can't attain
B) a confused homosexual chewing his nails in the closet where
no wombs can reach him, or
C) some sort of psycho.

But a shift occurs somewhere in mid book
and all of a sudden, Barfoot's self-conscious
crapalo metamorphoses
because he either A) overdosed on acid, mescaline, peyote or shrooms
or B) the guy totally lost it
because now his poetry is unique
 & disturbingly surreal
        (note: I didn't write "skilled" or "perceptive"
        as in his poem "My Naked Thud Thud Woman Walks to Me"
        wherein "Thud" is repeated from start to finish):

"So much is made
Of light
And dark
And thud
And poetry in poetry
Thud thud"

Or in his liberating "My Baby Turns Her Trick in Green and Red":

"My Baby drives a pick-up truck—Uh Huh—
And in the bed—Uh Huh--is astroturf.
It makes it Uh Huh softer on soft nights
For her Uh Huh to spread herself for flight
Because she spreads herself not just her legs
When Uh Huh she is under me Uh Huh."

Nonetheless, one can't help raising the question
of sexism in Barfoot's poetry
mostly because Barfoot sets himself up in this department.
With poems entitled "Sweet Cunt and Fresh Cut Green and White Bouquet,"
"The Woman With Me in the Shade's My Celibate, But Is She Efficacious for My Needs?,"
"Sweet Paganini Very Slow Plays Sweet Pussy's Come and Go,"
"Brontosaurus Sex," "She Wants to Fuck for Her Own Sake for Him,"
"Sunday Morning Pussy Coming Down," "How to Pick and Prepare, Present and Enjoy,
the Cometwat That You'd Slap Your Grandma For," "Her Perfect Ass Is Past And Passing Over Him,"
"Jill's Jilling Jack While Jack Is Jacking Jill," "Fly in Her Clackety Clit/Cunt Way,"
"Samson Fucks Delilah Frequently," "The Girl Undoes Her Overalls And Shimmies to the Moon,"
"The Poem as Biological Destiny," "The Once Uncovered Covered Woman's Ass"
and "The Pussy Pot Below the Pepper Tree"—with titles like these
one naturally asks one's self
Is this guy daring, or is he just
completely naive?

And speaking of "The Pussy Pot Below the Pepper Tree," here's a noteworthy passage:

"The pussy pot
Below
The pepper tree
Is setting up
For passing bees

To buzz,
The woman malleable as August wax,
And although not stock still, a ready hive.

And so the woman waits
Beneath
The sun,
Her pussy pot
Below
The pepper tree,
The sun and tree together spangling her
And mingling sun tree bee and pussy pot."

Still, whereas half of the above is laughable
there is something lyrical going on.
As in "Our Lady of Apocalyptic Ease,"
one wonders if Barfoot might sometimes stumble out
of his ridiculous obsessiveness and into
possible... genius??

"Without her
Every end
Would end
The same,
So tender
Does she tend
Apocalypse."

Whatever the case
Barfoot's book makes for at least as many questions as
there are words in this review.
So if you want to yuck at embarrassing poetry
and if you don't mind not knowing what to make of a poet and his work
and if you don't mind digging through garbage for occasional surprises
buy this book and fuck the cover.
I did.

SOME MINOR WORKS OF MAJOR POETS
ARE BETTER LEFT ROTTING IN THEIR GRAVES

Mallarmé in Prose, Ed. Mary Ann Caws
various translators
New Directions, NY
152 pp.

A tedious read that doesn't benefit anyone.
Taken mostly from Mallarmé's magazine Dernière mode
these pseudonym-written pieces are packed with a pretentious and empty
intellectual gas.
The book starts out with some sleep-inducing essays on
linguistics (including pompous generalizations about what "the Poet" understands)
then drifts into some poetry (in a book of "prose")
which relies on the repeated word "thang" (translation of "un ça").
Then come some paragraphs on painters and writers
like Whistler and Poe, which would've been better left
covered in the dust they were dug up from.

Boring nineteenth-century style contemplations on fashion follow
(and note: none of this stuff has any of the daring/energetic
elements associated with the Symbolist movement
which Mallarmé was supposedly a "forerunner" of).

Here is an example of some blasé blabber on ballet:

In the fearsome bath of the materials swoons—radiant and cold—the interpreter who
illustrates many gyratory themes towards which stretches a thread in full bloom: an un-
folding, like giant petals or butterflies, all very clear and straightforward. Its fusion with
the fast-moving nuances, constantly transforming their phantasmagoric mixture of air
and water, typical of dusks and caves, like swiftly changing pasaions—delight, grief, rage;
to set them in motion, diluted with all their prismatic violence, we need the vertigo of a
soul that seems to have been placed in the air through some kind of artifice.

Then come some notes from The Book (again, not "prose")
wherein you can see recreated a whole bunch of crossed-out words
and trees of association with lines going all over the place
as if they mean something.
These notes are then followed by paragraphs on furniture
and equally stimulating subjects.
Which just goes to show:
some minor works of major poets
are better left rotting in their graves.

POETRY'S A LIE

Slouching Toward Nirvana: New Poems, Charles Bukowski
HarperCollins, NY
288 pp.

Finally! A dead-Bukowski afterbook
that doesn't suck
posthumous butt

poetry inspired by
"my cats, my wife,/the shape of my coat
thrown over a chair, the weeping of the planet...
the flight of the hummingbird and"

the fact that it's
so easy to die
long before the fact
of it

so the bird has now
busted out the heavy stuff:

"how close we all are
to being nothing
most of the
time

and
for some of us
nothing
all of the
time"

since "we are hardly ever
as strong/as that which we
create" and

"most poets are just big
tit-suckers:
accepting readings
taking university chairs

praying for tenure
writing books on poetic
technique and
giving lectures"
aka
"those chattering bitching
ninnies
who are so quick to insist...
that I am
not one of
them"

plus plenty of advice
for those who can't:

"read this to your class in contemporary
literature and tell them how easy it
is.

then send those children out to walk
the asphalt like the rest
of us"

meanwhile

"some are good at
cleaning the shit stains
out of the toilet;
others at
polishing the mirror
of their own vanity;
many are expert
at composing inoffensive
verse
or
sucking dick.

but while the drippings from
their thin minds
spill from their tongue

I'll continue to

type"

the unBukowski:

"mental charutos pimentel charutos
pimentel charuto entel charutos pimentel charutos
pimen..."

Say What? No wonder this voice
was wisely left for
surreal existential end
ie,

"flowers floating on the lake.
New Jersey dogs in thrall...
do abandoned factories ever
scream at mid-
night?
I am warming up now as
bottle caps explode in my
brain.
I am giving off smoke.
I am really smoking now.
I am an Easter egg.
I am a paper clip...

as the world reaches
its final foolish conclusion
I realize that
nothing has been learned"

and as the "powers-that-be
persist/in tolerating
shit"
Bukowski plays
the "shuck and jive"
like horses at the track
a "pure folly to get slick about"
cuz ultimately
(he he he)
poetry's
"a lie."

SAUCY NAKED NUDIE GOTHS

Suicide Girls, Missy Suicide
Feral House, L.A.
160 pp.

This is a glossy sexy photobook
of saucy naked nudie Goths and
Gen-Y hotties but

also a statement
of a shaven
pierced
generation
tattooed Betty Booply

not nipple porn for wanking wetly
(though you could)
but the stuff of coffee
table yakkery

ahhhhh sweet sassy lasses
how we love your boobs and asses
your bad grrrrl grins
and vixen visions

but next time leave yr
postfemme
fatal
ism
verse
at home.

WHINE-STAINED NOT!

Portions from a Wine-Stained Notebook, Charles Bukowski
Ed. David Stephen Calonne. San Francisco: City Lights.
300 pp.

Most quixotic Chinaski yet
kicks off w/ academic offturning intro
regarding lost & obscure chunks
painful at first in search of voix
but then full-throttle
blunt drunk we luv:

"I walked into the other room and there was Constance, naked, stretched on a
leather couch, her eyes closed. All the lights were on, which only made it better.
She was milk-white and all there, only the hairs of her pussy had a rather gold-
en-red tint instead of the blonde like the hair on her head. I began to work on her
breast and the nipples became hard immediately. I put my hand between her legs
and worked a finger in. I kissed her all about the throat and ears and as I slipped
it in, I found her mouth. I knew I was going to make it at last. It was good and she
was responding, she was wiggling like a snake. At last, I had my manhood back.
I was going to score. All those misses...so many of them...at the age of 50...it
could make a man doubt. And, after all, what was a man if he couldn't? What did
poems mean? The ability to screw a lovely woman was Man's greatest Art. Every-
thing else was tinfoil. Immortality was the ability to screw until you died...Then I
looked up as I was stroking. There on the wall opposite...hung a life-sized silver
Christ...He was watching me...I missed a stroke."

read it three times (engrossed enrapt)
the beauty of this plumer vulgaris
flowering in Fantemoir
but plenty flammable
litcrit as well:

"Back in the '20s and '30s there was not an abundance of littles. A little magazine
was an event, not a calamity. One could trace the names from the littles and up
through literary history; I mean, they began there and they went up, they became.
They became books, novels, things. Now most little magazine people begin little
and remain little...Every jackass in America pumps out countless and ineffectual
poems. And a large number of them are published in the littles. Tra la la, another
edition. Give us a grant, see what we are doing! ...Arid vast nothingness...the
miracle of our times is that so many people can write down so many words that
mean absolutely nothing."

and

"Poets, of course, aren't the only ones to suffer in our world, they just talk more about it. And the critics, my friend, the critics, what a rotten lobsterflesh they are. Forgive me this, it's all that I know in my pitiable way. Basically, all I have to say is: Ezra, yes…Yes, yes, yes, yes, yes, yes, yes, yes, yes, yes, and yes."

plus "moments of total flaming hell"
(shoulda been the title)
injected with hilarious
Célinian hatred:

"The Dolly Sisters sit in that large window all day talking and drinking tea and eating tiny cookies. They are heavily rouged with stupid, hard faces and their grey hair is dyed red and they wear four-inch false fingernails; their lips are very heavily caked with magenta lipstick. They look at me as I walk by and I nod like a country gentleman. They think I am a retired circus barker…All three of them view me and one of them gives me a big smile, it's like a leper's kiss of death. The moment the sun goes down, a huge purple curtain is pulled across the glass window. The Dolly Sisters are afraid of being raped."

or

"Right now there's this huge glob approaching New York City and there's nothing that can be done about it. When I read this article I wasn't exactly too unhappy because if any city deserved to be drowned in mountains of shit, that city is New York."

yes this is some really guerrilla stuff
high in polemics & graphic scat
what might've changed our Buk-attitude
(if published earlier in history)
two degrees but so what?
stock standard lesbo smackdowns and
barfights galore permeate
avec spontaneous
absurdist fic

bottomline: there are three strange
off-the-chain
Bukowski books
no pensive collection shld be
w/out:

Pulp, Pleasures of the Damned
and this mofo
right here.

FLASH OF MADPUNK TRAGI-SPIRAL

Rimbaud: The Double Life of a Rebel, Edmund White
Atlas & Co., NY
256 pp.

très readable and condensed
chrono from élitist pompous texts
like G. Robb and autre Rimbaudallaires
yet critical of Starkiescheiss and
investigative betwixt
analysis of life thru verse

am mucho pleased with this history
context & narrative
but EWhite's tradux sux
ie, "In order to touch one of my dad's bits—big, black
and hard—" is not only
inaccurate & slovenly
(see MSpitz From Absinthe,
"that fat hard dark dick/of my dad")
but just as misleading as plethora of guesswork preceding Fowlie, Varèse, etcetera

Still, this study is thick w/ sticky nugs such as

"One night when [Verlaine] was blind with drink and wanted money from his mother
so that he could continue his rout into the dawn hours, he became so angry with her
for holding out on him that he attacked with his cane the jars containing Madame Ver-
laine's miscarriages, smashing the glass and dismembering the tiny rubbery fetuses and
scattering them across the floor—and remarking soddenly that they, like him, had been
macerating in alcohol long enough."

and

"Most humiliating, Verlaine was visited by two doctors, who examined his body to 'see
if he was a homosexual.' The doctors remarked on the small penis and its particularly
small, tapering head. More significant for them was the anus."

and w/ das "boat" under the microscope
(following influence of JVerne
James FenCoop and EdAlPoe)
offerings of insight acute, ie,

"Critics often claim that creative sparks fly when the themes and techniques of genre literature are elevated to the status of high art—and Rimbaud was one of the first poets of the modern era to understand this principle."

nevtheless
despite puny piddlies
this portrait is most comprehensive
flash of madpunk tragi-spiral
into most mythic Abyss

DISSOLVING LIKE BATTERY ACID THE FLESH OF ALL WE THINK WE KNOW

Delta Blues, Skip Fox
Ahadada Books, Tokyo/Toronto
176 pp.

this is nitro-packin' Pomo plumin' to the POW degree
just can't get past "Lili, a Hurricane,"
Squealin' and Screechin' and Scrawwin' out
its surging oceanic cry
while shakin' with the wrath of Gawd:

"a monstrosity, worlds within worlds of air and water and wind: torrents of doubt, fugues of
the sheer, winds rising thousands of feet in a few seconds then suicidally throwing them-
selves off their own cliffs to plunge thousands of feet below, psychotic dervishes, deep
unbinding swells…tumultuous towers, parapet in neural collapse (these result in blind
spots), electric spasm in back currents, dark swirl, the black flatulence of eddies, abeyances
of thought, little soda jerks running from table to table, cataracts of unholy pleasures…cre-
scendo of blank racket, her brow at 30,000 feet as she slows, stretches and contracts, opens
an eye at last, blinks, spies Cuba, and turns, bellowing, to wipe her ass."

talk about "generative writing"
this bitch makes you wanna scrawl, squall
rip the throat from a fashion god

"Death amid the petulance of nations. Death in disregard. Death for its own sake. Stupid
motherfucking death!" howling all bellicose, "tearing at her hair, clawing her face, ripping
at nipple rings…she spots the anus of the nation" goes charging in like a pack of jackals,
lashing at the "the stupid chewing hysteria of the populace…[and] fat fucks fighting at five
o'clock."

no other hurricano prose
can match the gnash of the storm Skip
Fox has unleashed this super-hyper-organic-destructo-twister of pure
Incandescent
Blazin'
Brilliance—

dissolving like battery acid the flesh of all
we think we know.

No B.S. Review 42

Absence of the Hero: Uncollected Stories and Essays
Vol. 2 1946–1992, Charles Bukowski, Ed. Stephen Calonne
City Lights, San Francisco
275pp.

Like its predecessor in this series
Vol. 2 kicks off with a snorarific academic
blah blah blah introduction
the precise damn rhetoric
Bukowski always gagged against

first quarter of book is throwaway
juvenilia from his forties
see icon grapple for voice
feel effect of stodgy lit
infuse itself in tone

shades of infamous "Fiend" though
in seminal and hilarious "Rapist's Story"
& grandiose of ego needed
to separate from pack and so

brunt of book will be pleasing
to fans of puking drugging boozing
fighting fucking sogony
and not without
litcrit:

• "The poets who are getting it done are David Pearson Etter, Irving Layton, Al Purdy, Larry Eigner, Genet. The Ginsberg-Corso-Burroughs circle has been swallowed by the big whale of adulation and they have never quite recovered. But, alas, we have learned that the difference between an artist and a performer is the difference between God and a necktie salesman."

• "My contribution was to loosen and simplify poetry, to make it more humane. I made it easy for them to follow. I taught them that you can write a poem the same way you can write a letter, that a poem can even be entertaining, and that there need not be anything necessarily holy about it."

• "I'd never advise anybody to become a writer, only if writing is the only thing which keeps you from going insane. Then, perhaps, it's worth it."

Meanwhile certain stories are
remarkable and beautiful
like "Sound and Passion" love story
of losers losing
everything

      and then, of course
      turds and horny humpery
      because Bukowski just keeps pumping it out
      even from
      the grave

No B.S. Review 43

Thirsting for Peace in a Raging Century
Selected Poems 1961–1985, Ed Sanders
Coffee House Press, Minneapolis
260 pp.

From "a wink of eternity / between dark cunt / and the grave"
to "O bards / ponder Archilochus / you who think / "Hey, my poems are
going to last / all the way till the Milky Way / explodes"
this AmBook Award champendium
spans a strange & funny even sexy
corpus of a jolly maestro
überpoetic light and breasts
phantom mothers
lightbulbs kissed

voyage launches with entrapment
glossing bias Sandersly—ie:
" . . . a hunk of
lunatic vomit-grunge
named lieutenant Warner Stringfellow . . . .
   the face of racist
   lieutenants twisted into
   hate-mush" and

"Your archives
   bulging in acid-free binders
      at UC-San Diego
  and a staff
   of graduate students
    sorting them clean!"

then Sheep-Fuck Poem
  Elm-Fuck Poem
  (—as when rabbit-nose
  snoozles a carrot—)

  and, alas (only complaint)
  too mucho verso
  inspired by mythos

(shades of classics in
                investigative poetics)

Yet:

    • "& the ice thrilled her buttocks . . .
            down the twiggy glaciation"
    • "the splotch
            of hawk scat
        like the fling
                of a 1950 Action Painter"

        —that's what I'm
        talking about.*

* "It helps you to set
    aside the fear
    of lumps in the skin"

No B.S. Review 44

Giraffes in Hiding: The Mythical Memoirs of Carol Novak
Carol Novak, Spuyten Duyvil, NY
240 pp.

This technicolored minnow dance of vivid prose
poetry & images
is cutting edge
in design

playful triptychs populate
à la monkfish bluefish
twofish threefish:

"She slouched on her couch eating livers of swine, she slouched
and she grouched drinking cheap rye and wine . . . and the
occasional housefly looking for pie..."

but always with a twist, ie:

"The man thought: how lucky I am that my seed died inside of
her sloppy womb"

making these foibles
a brilliant pollock
of memory flash avec the grotesque and sublime
bursting buds of otios men
and donkey grade
cluck luckery

a truly neon pictocollage
fruity pebbled with proust & co.
where mothers dwell in coffins of white mums;
you can't get more
progressive
than this.

THIS IMAGINATION HAS A BIG SKIN

Surreal Killer, Roy Trask
Shakespeare & Company, Toad Suck
164 pp.

A muscle-car mélange of
surreal serial killing
magic men, ballistic judges
scandinavian rally hotties
nymphos & suicides
scribed in a brave new tongue

language reinvents
strophes of paragraphs
with fast and furious
brodie action
kings & queens & heartbreak abound
around dancing tots and stupor models
this Imagination
has a big skin!

INTRIGGERING GLIMPSE OF TOXICTIME

More Notes of a Dirty Old Man: The Uncollected Columns
Charles Bukowski, Ed. David Calonne
City Lights, San Francisco
248 pp.

Another gamut ranging in voix
from half-century juvenilia
to mastery of meat and potatoes
gravied with an attitude;

a strange green interview
vies for an effusive toehold
in something very unBuk
       (conducted by
       not with)
that demonstrates
a desperation vs.
several nugs of chekhovness
transcending puking and duking it out
on dark streets of the alco-night

sexist yes but sexy too
as in all past
horseracing
womanizing
skidrow
screeds

stock with hilarious dialogue
damn kids messing around
roominghouse shenanigans
and plenty of mis
        anthropy

has aphorisms even
and judgy too

eg, narrative tone:

"Yes, I know I'm taking too long to tell this, but I want you to get the full flavor, whether it matters or not. It really means something but what it means I'm not sure. What are you doing now, anyhow? Just resting or hiding. Rest and hide within this crap..."

an insult to audience
which readers have come
to expect
as well as comments
on business and craft:

"Good writers watch other people live," I told him. "Great writers live and watch other people live."
"What do bad writers do?"
"Make money."

Howev
as Calonne notes in afterword:

"Bukowski, like D.H. . . . . sought a more natural expression of sexuality which is constantly frustrated by our alienating, cold, technocratic society:

all these people, the love-lost, the sex-lost, the suicide-driven... somewhere in the structure of our society it is impossible for these people to contact each other. Churches, dances, parties only seem to push them further apart, and the dating clubs, the Computer Love Machines only destroy more and more a naturalness . . . that has somehow been crushed and seems to remain crushed forever in our present method of living (dying). See them put on their bright clothes and get into their new cars and roar off to NOWHERE. It's all an outside maneuver and the contact is missed."

but most of all
this book is an intriggering
glimpse of ToxicTime
aka, Sex Rev, Vietnam
the emerging techno
industrial complex
hollywood &
race

à la the biggest
intoxicated
literato

to ever disgrace
the name
of Lit.

Through Anarcho-Ooze of Buddhist Catholic Hoodoo Voodoo

Glyphs for New Orleans, Ed Sanders
Lavender Ink, New Orleans
chapbook, 25 pp.

classic
cryptic
glyphic
Ed

infused w/ Blake Eye
& spirit of pyramids
straight out of Andy
Jackson Square
on the backs of the
Indigenous
"Waiting
for the
Time-Flow
to bring us
the roses
in the water"

while contemplating riding dolphins
the perfection of perfection
and crypt of Marie Laveau
scurrying with ants

"O America
Let's go"
through "anarcho-ooze
of Buddhist Catholic
Hoodoo
Voodoo"

yessirree.

Not Un
Pleasingly

Click and Clone, Elaine Equi
Coffee House Press, Minneapolis
110 pp.

alt-texts punch (w)holes in multiverse
Q: nouveau nu form of realism?
A: conventions of sci fi & surreal
art, popcult, consumeriz
as intelligentsia deconstructs
reconstructs
and deconfuncts
        not un
pleasingly.

ALBUQUERQUE BURNS

Road Ghosts, John Roche
theenk Books
chapbook, 90 pp.

portrait of a teenage
suicide bomber
"Howl"ing his trek
across amerigo
1971

literally tripping
through rococo
freak brigade
and clown armies

a travelogue in verse form
as albuquerque burns
on route 666

till sent on "home to parents and school and
college and grad school and teaching and marriage
and homeowning and divorce"

narrative form goes Olsonic
halfway through

psychedelic, man!

AFTERSEX AND UNDERGUN

Everyone Is a Me, Timothy Snediker
publisher unknown
chapbook, 30 pp.

TimSned has burst upon the scene
herald of the new Toad Suck School
fondling "the blue melanin
of the winter sky"

with the control of a surgeon scribe
scalpaling Lord,
"We have better books than your book,
though we will never sell as many copies"

religion is a condition here
akin to asthma or std;
children singing
lynching songs

acute tones of Brautigan
aftersex and undergun
in reverence of the monks

to order send 5 bucks
we'll get it to Tim
and him to you.

TIGHTER THAN A PAIR OF TIGHT LEATHER PANTS

House Organ, no. 76
Ed. Kenneth Warren
lit journal, 40 pp.

Still and always the best damn
forum for American verse
this one in memory of
Hugh Fox

Joe Safdie's tribute to Jack Clark
tighter than a pair
of tight leather pants

John Olson's Missouri satori
rich as Midwestern soil

Paul Pines is progressive
master of form

prose poetry by George
Spencer and Roger Taus
about the best there is

a bit thin on the ladies, though
but Diane Di Prima
fills the void

write to Kenneth Warren
PO Box 466
Youngstown, NY
14174.

Blank, Davis Schneiderman
Jaded Ibis Press
200 pp.

Also Very French in a Way

Razor, Amiri Baraka
Third World Press, NY
470 pp.

this new collection of old stuff
        (1981–2007)
is sometimes snaptivating
intermittently intrigulating
and rewarding for placing
an icon in perspective

iz also very French in a way
with essays on culture & politics:
        "Art, for the billionth time, is merely one reflection of a time, a society, a
people, a world &c. It is subject to the same contradictions and influences as
everything else"

such is tone established
with aggressive hint of HunterS:
        "The establishment aesthetic is openly Tarzanic—ignorant, brutal, drool-
ing, square,   banal, insipid, sick"

Though sometimes not so eloquent:
        "Revolutionary poetry . . . change[s] society by changing human relations
within the   society and by so doing change[s us]"
        Yet: "Those artists who say their art has nothing to do with politics or
society are simply   retarded or winking at their own seduction as state and
corporate prostitutes"

Meanwhile
a stylistic evolution
verging on Waldmanian
linguistic deconstruct:
        "The tower (to where, destination) of Babel.
        The Vow wells disappear . . .
        (e.g., Supreme Ct. Scalia and Tom Ass). . . .
        the bowels, the Colon rectum Wreck Them Pow! (Well)"

& thick with expected
rhetoric on xeno-class-fasc:

    "The bizarre irony of the civil rights struggle is that it created a
whole sector of the black petty bourgeoisie whose gig it is to bullshit people
that America is a democracy"

      hence begging question:
      is this the same
      aca dogga doo doo
      R monarch (LeRoi)
      so cleverly
      decries?

Ecovision Incorporates Paradox and Hypocrisy

My Green Manifesto: Down the Charles River in Pursuit
of a New Environmentalism, David Gessner
Milkweed Editions, Minneapolis
225 pp.

this unconventional eco-mix
betwixt MANIFESTO &
yr bk-length essay reflects
ole Cactus Ed adrift w/ Thoreau
though

      conclusions are more practical
      personal
      local and applicable

as the unspoken sequel
to Sick of Nature (2005)
our beer swillin'
bird watchin'
antihero calls
for a sloppier more effective
      human/wild commonsense
"to pull the pole out of the collective environmental ass"
      whilst longing for
"a new sort of music, a music with energy, irreverence, and drive, a
punk osprey tribute sung by, say, the Sex Pistols"
      as it bashes
"an environmentalism that feels like the intellectual equivalent of a
panic attack"

considering and rejecting
Nordhaus and Shellenberger
then spouting Stegner and McKib
this ecovision incorporates
paradox and hypocrisy
the flaws which make us
all unüber

as always
the Gessnerian style
is charmingly egoific
as he calls readers out
profoundly remarking

"the reason some are finally starting to react is that [this prob] is being presented not
as a true fight to save the planet, but as a fight to save our homes"

plus, a case is made for lore:
"We need stories, told outside, told in a way that links activism to beauty" because
"an environmentalism that draws on what we are
has a much better shot"

verdict being:
bullet pts cld be boiled down
but best if you just read it
fr yrslf.

Rabid Schizo Xeno Hatred

Trifles for a Massacre, Louis-Ferdinand Céline
Translator Anonymous, trans.
Aaargh Publishing House
vho.org/aaargh/fran/livres6/CELINEtrif.pdf
270 pp.

For the brunt of a century
critics have been telling
English-language readers of Céline
that the "pamphlet lit" (3 full books)
was scurrilous Naziganda
w/ apologists claiming
he did it for the francs—

either that
or the overt absurdity
justifies the sentiments
leveled at all creeds

basically
since the Estate has refused
to reauthorize in any tongue
this matter has been up in air
till now

because now we can read it
for ourselves
but what we read
is pure   acid   horror

first 30 pages are deceiving
as literature's most
notorious mad doctor
complains he can't produce ballet
due to all the drama Jews
conspiring against him

        (this was before
        Death on Cred

Journey to the End
and even the Swasti
assault on Poland)

through dialogical orchestration
and two silly fairytales
pixied out in twinkle prose
readers wonder if this is C's
curious & elusive
autofiction

but then something just RIPS
and a full on foaming Barrage
Hindenbergs
        ie, this little montage:

"I saw plenty of them, the Yids. These weren't Hymie jewelers, these
were vicious lowlifes, they ate rats together . . . . they who lay claim
to every advantage, all of the pity, all of the charity; it's their race, they
take everything, they return nothing . . . . The Jews are our masters—
here and there, in Russia, in England, in America, everywhere! . . . the
Jew doesn't give a damn! . . . He owns everything . . . . The possibilities
for white critics no longer exist! . . . . the Jews possess all of the world's
gold . . . from the Ural Mountains to Alaska! from California unto Per-
sia! . . . At present, there are too few pogroms . . . . it's now necessary
to negrify . . . The future belongs to the niggers! Nom de Cul! . . . . give
them all to Hitler!"

and on and on like that
for 200+ pages
leaving this pseudonym
pretty damn shaken

        cuz the proof is in the pudding
and the pudding is a putrid gruel
revealing that even if Céline
ranted this bile for bling
he went way beyond the Ezra fringe
to genocide the tribe of Christ

such that
motives don't matter
what matters is he wrote this shit
in all its sizzling
vitriol

       (so no wonder the French
       slapped a price on his buckethead
       and no wonder his publisher
       got gunned down in the fecal street)

as for the question of whether or not
English-language readers can continue
to respect this historic stylistic
momentum-filled
imagination
which revolutionized Western Lit
this matter is now up
to the next generation
of semiSemitic
scholarship

I'll say this, though
it's a fine translation
right up there with Manheim
a lot of research and dedication
no doubt someone's
dissertation

giving us a toxic taste
of a rabid schizo
xeno hatred
metaphoric for a
furious time
that most of us
post-BabyBoomers
can't fathom
though we try.

NOT-YA-BUT-Y-GAY

Three Cubic Feet, Lania Knight
Main Street Rag, Charlotte, NC
140 pp.

It's like this:
I never expected that a coming-of-age
novella about
a homosexual neo-hipster
written by someone's mother
from Missouri
could turn the crank
of this Bukowskiite
but SURPRISE! it sucked
       this one in
            & delivered

perhaps due to shades of Genet
that underbelly undercult
toxic w/ that violence and angst
       central to all
satoris of self

Ie, this
iceberg tip:
    "three cubic feet of flesh and blood and bone is all we get . . . the joke is that
you can either
love someone or not . . . but in this life, our body, our little bit of space that we
get to occupy, is it. There is no choice about living in a body that can be broken
and bruised. Bloodied. This is all we get"

a choice, however
is offered in this
not-YA-but-Y-gay
innovation on the genre;
a delicate yet
ballsy endeavor
to delve into an alien skin
that's really not
so alien

hence
this adventure sticks with you
due to the fleshing
of its glue.

PREPARE TO DESCEND INTO THE REPTILE MIND

Nothing Doing, Willie Smith
Honest Publishing, UK
170 pp.

To push fiction to its limits
in the Age of Whack
it pays to strive
for Wonk

this is exactly what Willie Smith does
à la evil hamster assassinations
ant-lapping anchorites
urinary voyeurism
hallucinatory taxi transit
and double dog
Commie grafts
fingerpainting
in the vomit

there's always an edge to these fusions
breaking down expectations
I mean

this is the guy whose legendary arachnid assault
fluberating with spindula
spawned exodus of mass Naropans
screaming Bluddy Murd!

yes, Willie's got an odd
& masturbatory
sense of humor
a provocative prong
that's not for all

but ultimately there are undertones
as dire as the Holocaust
juxtaposed w/ jingles
    jangling
    gasoline

in other words
to spelunk the spunk of Willie Smith
leave yr Amy Tan at home
strap on yr assless chaps
and prepare to descend
into the reptile mind.

Kirksville Kicks It Classically

Kirksville, Bob Mielke
Donald Books, NY
100 pp.

this epic imagistic portrait
of smalltown abounds
w/ Elvis impersonators
cemetery theaters
and bequests for Piss
Santa
       and is strung together
by a rainbow chain of
Neo-Rockwell Americo

Eg: "Country kids want to be
       ghetto, from gangs in their hood:
       but paint's all they have"

&   "White shirt, black tie, black pants, black suit:
       they travel always in twos
       . . . cycling down Normal Street"

&   "T.J arrives every day with compost, inquiries, advice—
       adrift on an economy bollixed up far away
       . . . freestyle frisbee seldom paid"

sometimes freeverse, sometimes rhyme
sometimes litcrit "carving scrimshaw"
Kirksville kicks it classically
"before the maggots gnaw."

Something Smells of Frank Stanford

The Runaway Note, Tyrone Jaeger
Shakespeare & Co., Toad Suck
110 pp.

Holy Visionary Phantasmagoria!
something smells of Frank Stanford
something like
a unique dreamstate
whimsical yet Hot!

to lift directly from backcuv:
it's a "personal Bible full of riddles,
revelation, visions and
terrible adventure"
a "mystical record . . .
Coyotes are running
across the dam"

but ultimately
this is Luminous Poetry
redefining
fictioning.

PORTRAIT OF A FAILED ERA

America: A History in Verse, Vol. IV, 1971–1985
Ed Sanders, Blake Route Press
CD, 2000 pp.

Talk about epic
Menagerie of Sleazery!
This 500-page continuation
of legendary Black Sparrow tradition
now exists on disc
eternal bardmaster Ed Sanders
fleshing out America
thru investigative verse
placing politics
into perspective
ie, '71:

    "John Kerry tossed first the medals
        given to him by two vets who could not be there . . . .

      It made an impact beyond its numbers
        like Dada in Zürich
          the Beats at Columbia
            Che lashed to a chopper skid
              a burning bus in Birmingham"

Howev
this behemoth of bias & scholarship
journalism & humor is
at its best with presidents
especially w/ mind-cringing litany
of damning Nix deceit
ie, '72:

    "Three days later there was a National Prayer Breakfast
    after which Nixon and Billy Graham
        were having a sleaze-brimming chat
        in the Oval Office

about the putative Jewish domination of the media

There's a tape of it—
Nixon: 'Jews—Jesus Christ! . . . The Jews are—
they're malicious, [unintelligible] immoral bunch of bastards.
That goddamn girl the other night was Jewish!'"
Then all sorts of secret plots
dissected and assembled for our eyes
like Nix framing Senator Muskie
for Cannuckism

while commissioning the planting
of Black Panther literature
on Wallace's almost
assassin Bremer

as for aftermath of Watergate:

  "Ford was not a genius
  but to a nation with

  napalm-sizzled skin
    in the nostrils of its soul

  he was a sight for sore sighs"

but then, Surprise!
Sanders shows Carter as whimp
of ineffective leadership
ie, '78:

  "He failed his trek in history
  by refusing to alleviate the suffering
    the missed operations
      the millions of early deaths

  because of a lack of national health care . . . .

  Too much creativity for Jimmy
  because Jimmy was sometimes not that creative"

After that, Sanders blasts
Carter with "his rather conservative,
                19th century Whig economic mind-set"

& chants like
            "Human rights, Jimmy, human rights"

so of course this particular history eye
ain't gonna cut no slack
to "Raygun" or
"Reag-Rug"
'81:

            They called it Reagonomics
            but its real name was "Enrich the Rich"

enter Nicaragua
star wars, Sarajevo
starvation in Africa
just say no, Afghanistan
the premature birth of baby FOX News
and AIDS!

It's like someone slipped
a roofie to an entire nation
and then a poet came along and
captured us exactly as we are
with our pants down
our testosterone up
and ignorance at
an all time high

It's the portrait of a failed era
but optimistic in the end.

Buy It Used

Abandoned Fragments, Franz Kafka
Trans. Ina Pfitzner
Sun Vision Press, London
240 pp.

This surprising collection of
never-before-
translated flashes
erupts with a whimsy
few attach
to our man Franz

ie:
"When I got home in the evening, I found . . . an overly large egg in the middle
of the room. It was almost as high as the table and bulged accordingly. It quietly
rocked back and forth. I was very curious, took the egg between my legs and care-
fully cut it in two with my pocketknife . . . out leapt a stork-like, still featherless
bird flapping the air with its too-short wings"

the bird then communicates through beak-writing
a metamorphosis occurs (hmmm....)
and the two learn to fly together

or:
"My two hands began to fight. They shut the book I had been reading and pushed
it aside so that it wouldn't be in the way. They saluted me and appointed me their
referee . . . . the two of them are now lying on top of one another, the right hand
stroking the back of the left, and I, the dishonest referee, am nodding in approv-
al"
"On Jewish Theater" is also an
evocative essay
expertly translated
too bad, though
this publisher's an imprint
of Creation Books
and has swindled
many an author & estate
moral being:

buy it used
so you ain't
supporting a thief.

CORRECTING A NEGLECTION

Captain Poetry's Sucker Punch: A Guide to the Homeric Punkhole, 1980–2012
Ed. Kenneth Warren
BlazeVOX, Buffalo, NY
470 pp.

A massive compendium
of essays and articles
on postmodern poetics,
this sucker punch serves up
both Bo Diddly and Bob Kaufman
d.a. levy Kathy Acker
Eds Sanders and Dorn
Duncan Snyder Eschleman
Kerouac Orlovsky Corso
Norse Wakoski
Myles Hirschman Cage
Creeley Hollo
Olson Blake
Waldman and Spiderman
just to name
a couple dozen
practitioners of
"Street punk lineage
of bob-bop romanticism
and bravado scholarship" (Warren)

As Dale Smith notes in intro:
"Captain Poetry's Sucker Punch thrives in the outrider genre. At once disciplined and astute, studious and light-of-foot, it puts into useful tension the textures of life and art . . . Written over the course of thirty years for small press zines and journals, including . . . House Organ, this collection of essays represents an era in part neglected in the literary record."

So there.

SINGING TO THE HONEY SUCKLE

Touch Each Other, Antler
Foothills Publishing, Kanona, NY
chapbook, 40 pp.

mythic Antler has this thing
for combining stats and song
to create a micro-universe
of legendary eco-verse
take pilot poem for examp:

"Ornithologists discovered
    each baby robin in the nest requires
        14 feet of earthworms a day
  to survive
So if there are 6 baby robins in the nest
    it means 84 feet of earthworms a day . . .
        that means each baby robin needs
    42 earthworms a day . . .
        each worm has 10 hearts . . .
    420 earthworm hearts a day . . .
Hmmm. . . . no wonder
    robin song
        is so
    heartful!
How many worms
    do I need to eat
        every day
    before I can fly and sing?"

& the answer is:
Zedfully Zed!

Aye, this elegantly
papyrused book
already soars in Milky Way
charged with Transcendental ghosts
Antler's spirit already singing
to the honey suckle
of our breast.

Full of Piss & Vinegar

Amiri Baraka & Edward Dorn: The Collected Letters
Ed. Claudia Moreno Pisano
University of New Mexico Press, Albuquerque
222 pp.

This is what we want
in a volume of collected lets
between two literary luddites:
gutsy ballsy cutting prose
humorous w/ shark attacks
& calling-it-like-they-see-it snaps
w/ notations right on page

       enter into evidence:

                               "5-13-61

Dear Roi:
Greater NEW YORK . . . METROPOLOIS OF MANKIND. That's on a map I have
above my desk, natl. geographic, 1935, major shithead doing the photography, a
lovely air-shot, but you, you disillusion me.
      Anytime it comes down to a Man, of course it is different. Man, that 19th
cent term, won't get us anywhere. Or woman. There isn't anywhere, not as place
but in area of feeling we can go. I am sorry to hear about all this. And deeply grate-
ful you saw fit to tell me. I love Hettie very much, as much as you, it isn't a pleasure
to think about the whole thing"

                          "April 17 [1963]

Edward,
So what's happing out there, for God's sake? I mean what're you doing and why? I
hoped you dug that groovy tie. It had a western flavor I thought wd go well with
the scarps and drops of Idahore . . . I want you to know I had to put on my fucking
good suit (only suit) and a tie, go uptown and deposit that ms"

                         "Poky, Oct 10 [1961]

Come on, back off. I'm not no fucking counter-anything. I'm as truly gassed as any-one, but much more embarrassed than others, at the poor prospects of fellow poets singing the praises of any thing so venal as a State . . . you ought to know the very word Datista makes me puke. The modern state, revolutionary or not, is run like a Grauman's Chinese opening. Everybody has some scene, a trademark, like a beard, or a fat stomach and bald head, or a wig-type haircut, with big white teeth sticking out of the middle of the smile. Piss on it"

"Oct 16 [1963]

Dear hippie,
letter ought to be incoherent . . . I'm doped up to the gills &c. And Hettie marching around looking grave and concerned. The works. But good to hear from you to-night, that is rereading yr letter and realizing I hadn't written, & all that . . . I saw a couple of real lukewarm asswipes on The Island . . . which is draggy as no reviews at all. But Herald T. reviewing mine this weekend, complete w/ another photo I understand. Which means I'm on FeeD's [Fielding Dawson] shit list. Well he been on mine's a long time, so it's time for equitable titty mix I guess"

> Verdict being: this is very
> human stuff
not beleaguered by pretension
and full of piss & vinegar
just like Dorn and Baraka
LeRoi jonesing
to get their vivid
visions down.

SMACKED BY FISTORY

America: A History in Verse, Vol. V, 1986–2000, Ed Sanders
Blake Route Press
CD, 573 pp.

In Vol. V our bardstar
ends epic twentieth-cent investo-verse chronology
w/ breakdown of refrains fraining
    "the vomit vomits in the vomit"

yep, theme of "a great nation . . .
with hundreds of secrets & hardly secret mini-wars"
is traced "from the late-Reagan of '86 . . .
all the way to the stolen election of 2000"
in incredibly detailed
brain-banging tone
of finely biased lobe

from silly Ronald testifying
"before the Tower panel, in a duh mode
he couldn't, duh, recall approving, duh, arms peddling to Iran"
our communal skin is peeled back once again
but this time thru distillation slapping
"Meat-Fits of Moloch" politics
      into vivid compre
        hensive hash

tho mostly focused on "Grrrs of Greed-Grovel"
Ed also glimmers land-grabbers
raping rainforii
            "by burn   by blade   by blast
(& sometimes even by napalm!)"
for "the McDonaldization of the worldwide stomach"
before going on to Kosovo
Milosevic
Noreiga
Ceaucescu
"Sudan   Belgrade
& sometimes Iraque"

this text is best howev at
tracking the whole
Bill Clinton enchilada
which makes for a strange
objective tension
I mean, here you have a lyrical liberal socio-voice
swiping at the right
but also the left
and even though we're offered such Fuggy nugs as
        "Clinton was a bit of a bombopath
        always willing to sting with wrath"
a certain admiration seems to beat
for race relations and grit it takes
to hold back jackal pack attack
of rabid impeachy bile

so after a knee-slapping
rimjob-for-rimjob recount
of BC's BJs &
ML's Tripped-out "spurtdress"
roadmapped in accessible Anglais
we get to the nutmeat of
the new millennial matter:

"The year showed something new about American Voting
        —that it was now more and more
                the object of dishonesty

    in an era of voting machines whose software
                                was shielded from public scrutiny
        or whose ballots were difficult to use
                & set up as in certain places in Florida
                                to decimate the Democrats
    plus schemes to deny
            minorities the right to vote. . . .

            The whole nightmare tragedy
            of 2,000 was

            Nixon"

Take-home message being:

the crescendo of this major metro phonebook of a poem
dissects with the same super scalpel strokes
that led us from the Span-Am War
all the way to Whorida

      aka, the "new haunted heights
      of goony stalling"

and as the "goons goon"
and as "The U.S. Supreme Court Vomits in the Time-Track"
this terribly true despico-thread
of Gore v. Bush
buggery of democracy
is caught on virtual video
then Ed-cast to the world
in all its squalid vitriol

      (for how can we not agree
      that "Watching the stolen election
      was like weeping wet razor blades"?)

Das moral being:
   we are smacked by fistory
      yet titillated eerily
         (though maybe not so ear-ily
            as other volumes previously);

          meanwhile, the set is set for 9-11

               Ack! America, is this fiction
               or is this a red white and blue
               psychotropic wake up call
               or is this really
               really
               real?

WTF, HENRI?

Thousand Times Broken, Henri Michaux
Trans. Gillian Connoley
City Lights Books, San Francisco
165 pp.

This hallucinatory bilingual compilation
of surrealist images & verse
again a lens
into mysticism mescaline meditation
and Rimbaud's assertion that
      "contemporary poetry can no longer
      content itself with vague lyricism
      but only with total self-knowledge"
an investigation we see
through mucho cryptic twistings

      Book I "begins with spine-like seismographic drawings
that grow bigger and wider until they no
longer form anything but a dust of signs"
so highly Bataille
(phorm & filosophywise)
we trip avec a solar eye

      —for examp:

      "the poem, a thousand times broken, presses and
pushes to construct itself, to reconstruct, for one immense
unforgettable day, in order to, through everything, recon-
struct us"

      but Book II has more teeth and 'tude:

      "Your letter slapped me in the face. You're going to tell
me that you were mistaken. You're just a trembling calf.
I vomit on your face, there that's what I'm doing to your
face. . . . Shut up, meddler, and stop looking to do
everything all at once and giving your opinion when you
don't know anything."

whereas Book III is religulous list
of four hundred men on the cross

—witness this:

"Number 42, a lout.

Number 51, a real quack-quacking on the cross.

[53] Christ perhaps, the first to appear on the cross,
but furious at being there"

As for traduction unto itself
Connoley is faithful to myriad schemes
of linguistic acrobatics
    yet doesn't overdo
when poet does
   (an accuracy also extant
   along with sundry
   nonintrusive liberties)

though ultimately
once self-odyssey is fini
it's impossible not to ask

  wtf,
      Henri?

Nihilistic Vortex Style

The Idiot Parade, Greg Girding
University of Hell Press, Portland, OR
340 pp.

first thought: sexy cover
second thought: is this guy making fun of himself?
third thought: no, he writes honest novel
in bukowski-styled diarrhetic verse
one observation & obsession
after anoth
fourth thought: this guy's an ass
insulting audience
fifth thought: this guy's sincere
self-deprecating & amusing
and he damn well knows
how to end a poem:

ie:
"I'll take good care of those breasts.
I promise."

"The whiskey fills my mouth like a necessary evil."

"I work through entire days forcing myself
forcing this."

"They're dumb as shit, because shit is pretty dumb. That's a
scientific fact. Ask anyone."

"I long for a love like that again. Pure. Real. It may all eventually deteriorate to shit
over time, but an accumulation of these will make all the shit trips worthwhile."

"Instead, with newfound sobriety comes newfound realities.
Being more 'present' on a day-to-day basis really sucks."

"I bolt the door and am thankful that the doorbell hasn't worked
in months. I listen for any madness leaking in."

"It's really ridiculous, this notion of getting out from under one's
own selfishness. Why the fuck would I want to put myself in
your shoes? You suck!"

Admittedly, there are sum duds
but that's the point
this is portrait of a life: drinking and
humping and clashing and
wondering and wandering and
evolving in classical
nose-to-grindstone
nihilistic vortex style
in this big
idiot
        parade.

Enformed in Simple Splendid Grace

Four by Two Poems: San Francisco Issue
Joie Cook/Kurt Lipschitz
in association with Luddite Kingdom Press
one big foldy page crafted from
topo-survey map

smallpress artbooks are hot again
reborn again
again again

& this one is a pantheon
of voices both
humorous and post
micro though it is

see Joie Cook:
                "we were born
          in the same century . . .
          and from the same tribe
          of carnivorous apes"

see klipschutz:
                "Jobs was not a job creator,
          other than inventing himself.

                You don't need a biography to know
          if he had been as big a fan
          of Dylan as he claimed

                he would not have moved his factories to China."

see words merge organically papyrusly
enformed in simple
splendid grace.

WHAT WE PREDICTED

The Selected Letters of Robert Creeley
Eds. Rod Smith, Peter Baker, and Kaplan Harris
University of California Press, Berkeley
470 pp.

Damn! I'm kinda disappointed
this collection is basically what we predicted:
names, places, publishers;
information doing its job
with not enuff to make this stuff
qualify as Lit

for the scholar or biographer, though
this pound of flesh invaluable iz

to quote from the index:
"Aebi, Irene, 393, 419-20, 421 ....
Zukofsky, Paul, 217, 244, 246, 250

make of that
what you will.

THE BELL TOLLS FOR BUKOWSKI

The Bell Tolls for No One, Charles Bukowski
Ed. Stephen Calonne, City Lights Books, San Francisco
310 pp.

Having reviewed every new Bukowski book since 1997
this reviewer has finally had it
with the violence and mean spirited
fugliness that tends to rise
like the wart covered turkeyneck
Bukowski is always
thrusting in yr face

let's start w/ the intro
by Dr. David Stephen Calonne
which, again, frames an anti
academic life
through the lens of the academy:

"'The labyrinthine consequences' of such a philosophy become the subject matter
of Bukowski's repeated portrayals of his characters' encounters with the Mino-
taur of the cave of unrelenting chaos. Crime becomes a metaphor for an unjust
universe in which reward and punishment often seem unrelated to virtue: The
unyielding, brutal, and powerful 'Break In' contains an explicit speech on the
unfairness of society, and in Bukowski the narrator often observes the occurrences
helplessly, without commentary. He is at once quasi-participant and observer."

Ack! of course
is first response
so let's just cut
past all that J Campbell hero crap
because this is skid row & factories
a toxic caustic calliope
of losers and degenerates
raping and robbing each other
to while away the day

this is not anything new, though
in the fucked up Bukowskiverse
but in this particular collection
the hate is piled on high

ie, the way the narrator sees others:

"I have met enough writers, artists, editors, professors, painters, none of them were truly natural men, interesting individuals"

"The door opened and here stood a fat little bitch, rather ugly, a bit dangerous, demented, but still all right"

"He sat there in a dirty undershirt. And he didn't have a face. Just runs of skin. Veins. Little fart eyes"

"He had on one of those chickenshit gowns, untied in back because the nurses wouldn't tie them for you, because the nurses didn't care about anything except catching themselves some fat young subnormal doctor"

"The waitress arrived. She was indifferent yet false, a bit fat and a bit unhappy. The fat and the unhappy fought each other for supremacy. She had no chance either way"

"I almost forgave her for being a woman"

Bukowski fatigue
can set in quick
especially with the more
autobiographical

hence, the more fictional works
are more unusual
and less pessimistic

like uncharacteristic
          sci-fi dystopias
or a sportswriter witnessing
          Billy Graham tossed out a window
or cowboys and prostitutes
or hijackers getting blown
          then blowing planes to shitaree
or Adolph Hitler in the American ghetto
          because a fart comes to life

though political commentary also a highpoint
("A POW is a man who went to war knowingly, knowing he might kill or be
killed, capture or be captured, maim or be maimed. There is no special quality
of heroism in this")
in this pretty much
disgusting snapshot
of human behavior
at its worst

which is what this dirty
old man is best at
and for that he can add
another posthumous notch
to a cyclically cynical
canon cannon

blasting its own audience
right in the face
with its own face
of mass
       mediocre
           angst

a comment which
if Bukowski were alive
wld no doubt bring a big
      shiteating grin
to his ugly mug

but then again
this guy revels
in the stench of his own beershit
from which he derives
a sense of accomplishment

& it's the exact same thing with this book
Bukowski smirking, Bukowski yucking
every time a new reader
gets a whiff

meaning, ultimately
Shut Up, Bukowski!
and may all your sources
of future aggressions
run as dry
as your whiskey glass is now

because this is the bottom
of the motherfucking bottle
and even if there is any backwash
I'm through reviewing you

just at a time
when Ecco is releasing
three new books
(Bukowski on Love
Bukowski on Cats
Bukowski on Writing)
which readers are bashing
as a bunch of junk
plucked from the most
inconsequential letters

too bad for you,

fucker.

ACROSS THE WEST WITH DAVID GESSNER

All the Wild that Remains: Edward Abbey, Wallace Stegner and the American West
David Gessner
Norton, NY
360 pp.

Nobody moves like Cactus Ed
(who's fertilizing a cactus now)
but Dave Gessner has picked up some tricks
reminiscent of "Down the River with Henry Thoreau"
a stylistic signature essay
in which reflections reflect
as currents pull

in crossing the great mythic American West
Gessner connects, Gessner reflects
visiting a web of super evolved hominids
who've had their connections
with two celebrated literary icons

& in his grand
Gessnarian way
Gessner, of course
is eco all the way

ie
"If you have never seen a fracking boomtown, it can be hard to picture. You drive
into a town that at first seems like any town, until you slowly notice that on this
particular Main Street there are far too many hotels. Then you start to see the over-
sized white trucks, the hundreds of Rams and Rangers and Silverados that prowl
the streets, most displaying Texas and Wyoming and Oklahoma plates (even when
you are nowhere near these places). You also note that the drivers of the trucks are
twentysomething men, who, like their trucks, are almost all white."

or
"Read other essayists after [Abbey], E.B. White for instance, and they seem too
tame, too civilized, too controlled. You appreciate their subtlety and craft but you
get none of the raw joy, none of the silliness, none of the fun of Abbey. Next to his,
theirs is a prose with a pole up its ass. Abbey lets loose, if not in person where he
was known to be shy, then on the page where it counted."

or

"Virtue, outside of the virtue of saving wild places, doesn't have much of a role in Ed Abbey's work, and do-gooders are frowned upon. Meanwhile, sensual pleasure, which plays such a large role in Abbey's life and writing, goes virtually unmentioned in Stegner's."

or

"It may be overstatement, but let's try this one on: We read Wallace Stegner for his virtues, but we read Edward Abbey for his flaws. Stegner the sheriff, Abbey the outlaw."

but here's something else
Gessner applauds reality tv
as a future fruitful
monkeywrenching mode;
citing example of Whale Wars
Gessner imagines

"Ed Abbey with a camera on him as he tries to stop the destruction of wilderness. It is not so farfetched. Why not take direct action with the cameras on? The essence of the old monkeywrenching was secrecy, but now it could become openness . . . . This type of public activism makes perfect sense in our age of hypermedia. And I think a reimagining of Abbey's blunter, earlier environmentalism holds promise."

surprisingly, though, Gessner remarks
"After all, blowing things up, or putting sugar in tanks or monkeywrenching in general, never got anyone all that far anyway. True, it slowed down developers momentarily but then when the resistance dried up or the resistors got bored or went on to other things, the developers went right back to their developing. At best it held off the enemies while public opinion formed against them."

and ultimately:
"Making connections has always been the naturalist's job, but it is also, like it or not, the job that has fallen to all modern thinkers and writers in a time when global systems of weather, climate and migration are being affected by man's actions."

thus
the megafires of this tinderbox
are combusting more every year
and with droughts galore etcetera
(especially the metaphoric ones)
we'd better take a serious look

at where we're going
before this mofo
incinerates us all
                unto
Unconsciousness.

Great Literature Cannot Be Inspired by Pedestrian Art

Poets and Pleasure Seekers: New and Selected Poems, 2010–2015
Gerald Locklin, Spout Hill Press, San Dimas, CA
130 pp.

Gerald Locklin zeros in
with whimsy and a scalpal
whether the subject be art
(Van Gogh, Rembrandt
Cezanne, Warhol)
or not
one can expect
the unexpected
and ironic
turn de force
like

> "it looks to me as if
> the fig leaf he's selected for
> this crucial day's attire
>
> may be poison ivy"
> (from "albrecht dürer: adam and eve, 1504")

or

> "Why do you think so many works
> Are left untitled?
>
> To allow the viewer to make them
> His / her own?
>
> Yes, but also to pretend they are not
> Mine or yours."
>
> (from "Jackson Pollock: Untitled, 1945")

such zingers of course
make minds simmer
upon the stew

"Before concluding that
Great Literature cannot be inspired by
Pedestrian Art."

        (from "I Give Up, or I Want My Sixty Bucks Back")
anyway

      simmer simmer simmer simmer
          bubble bubble blub blub blub........

Some Kind of War Happened at Some Time

Bombyonder, Reb Livingston
Bitter Cherry Books
350 pp.

This blistering, kaleidoscopic, post-bomb-blast of a novel
devises a pulsing, haywire logic that
occupies its own genre
it's a gestalt of grim and Grimm
and hellishly funny too.

PART 7

IN AWE IN ARKANSAW

2007–2022

TESTOSTERGLOW

In the peak of bowfin
spawning season
my grinnel turns

green olivine
with the jism of
its centuries.

INVASIVE SPECIES

Back in ye olde Middle Ages
Whitey crossed the ocean blue
discover a huge new continent
and kidnapped 2000 Arawak slaves

in return
the conquistadors left a scourge of horses
domestic pigs
and microbes in
the "New World"

in the following few hundred years
the horses evolved into mustangs
and the pigs mutated
into freaks

the poxes, meanwhile
wiped out ninety percent
of the twelve million humans
living in the Resource Zone

this genocide may have been preconceived
or maybe it was just the aftermath
of recklessness and ignorance
but whatever the case
the stage had been set
for the colonizers
to waltz on in

way to score
a continent
yo!

ODE TO AMERICA'S MOST PERSECUTED "TRASHFISH"

Consider the garfish
its fierce & fangy gatorhead
its snaky armored monstrous mass
sometimes surpassing
ten feet in length

this freaky fossilific fish
once dominated the continent
from Canada down
to South America

until the settlers & their demons
came colonizing with viscera visions
of lacerations and amputations
by gore-crazed gar gone wild
devouring children
like chicken

& O the "science" of the 1800s
embracing biased rumors and suspicions
& O the constant Custardly campaigns
to civilize the "savages"
via genocide and exile
unto the swamps
of the South

then a century of reservoirs
levees and canals
and the funneling of floodplains
damming migrations

& as the preFOX maw went bawkin'
"GAR ARE GAMEFISH SLAUGHTERERS!"
"GAR ARE HABITAT RAVAGERS!"
"GARFLESH AIN'T EVEN
FIT FOR A DOG!"

states like Louisiana (1933)
encouraged total xeno

                    eradication
            based on mis
                        information
                                all out lies
                                        and speculation
& as an unregulated sportfishing industry
            iced gars
by the tens of thousands
while righteous throngs
of deer rifle farmers
blasted tens of thousands more
then laid them out
on our shores

            (Blowfies!
            Maggots!
            Noxious
            Gasses!)

relentless generations
taught their offspring
that there is no place for slavery
in this great experiment
but it's fine to break
the jaws off a garfish
then toss it back
to die a slow
deserving
death

            Consider that mentality
            directed at a silly fish
            Consider what we
            are really afraid of

            wherever the survivors
            still don't maul
            swimmers like man
            eating sharks

            official statistics have been compiled:

Worldwide
Death by sharks = 2000
whereas death by gar
                    = zed

Now consider how gar
maintain balance
by chowing down
on the real molesters
        like those pesky Asian carp
        invading Mississippi system
        leaping at the sound of engines
        & smacking motorboaters
        upside the head

meanwhile
down in Mexico
gar farmers are growing
hundreds of thousands
for research and food

        (fried one just the other day
         clean white meat
         sweet as trout)

then consider how the spawn of gar
feed on the larvae of malaria
                & encephalitis

still, mucho rednecks on YouTube
yahoo as they massacre gar
calling em "Toads!"
calling em "Pigs!"
sometimes even
calling em "Nigs!"

so now the evangel guides of Texas
praying to the Lord for 200-pounders
en route to the last secret spawning grounds
on Trinity for trophy hunt
some almost a hundred years old!

But ultimately, *Homo Sapiens*
consider what you teach
your kids to lynch

because it just might come back
to bite you
in the ass.

SNAKEHEAD TERROR!

I

9-11! Anthrax!
    Total Balls Out
        Snakehead Invasion!

        Maryland freaking
          media hyping
            camera crews
              generating myths!

it happened in a Crofton pond
      discarded from some fish market
        an air breathing
           eely finned
             flat headed
                terrorist menace
straight out of tropical Asia
      the jihad jungles of Africa
        with pirahnic jaws and
          apocalyptic appetites
           preying on more
             than other fish

                —the utter bull that they can walk
                 —rip into swimmers
                —shred the flesh
                   of ecosystems

    and the public always
    reacts the same way:

      RUN FOR THE HILLS!
  THE NORTHERN SNAKEHEADS ARE UPON US!
     BRING ON THE ROTENONE!
    KILL EVERYTHING—KILL IT ALL!
      SO WE CAN SHOOT BACK
      TO THE SHARK ATTACKS!!

II

Nevermind the fact that the *Argus*
    was discovered in sunny Californy
      a quarter century before or
        in millennial Florida
          and Massachusetts
            after that

    Cuz Holy Hell in a Handbasket
      they are everywhere now:
        North Carolina 2002
          Downtown Chicago 2004
            Queens New York 2005
              Pennsylvania 2008
                Virginia, Wisconsin
                  even rustic
                    Arkansas!

      Liberated from fish farms!
        Jettisoned from aquariums!
          Freed from the Inferno
            of Imagination!

              Swarms of them! Cells of them!
                Suburban nightmares!
                Urban murders—

           Training with Al Quaeda, constructing bombs!
              Raping schoolgirls, buggering Trigg!
           Busting down doors and going postal!
                The Crusade is on!
                They're in the Potomac!
                The Delta, the Glades!

                Watch out, Louisiana!
                Protect your trout, Colorado!
                Close your borders, Canada!

                But Mexico, don't you worry
                because Lou Diamond Phillips
                will eradicate your *Frankenfish*!

III

Warning: Y2fear Arkansas:
  Dunn's Fish Farm—out of Monroe:
    old Jack Dunn is stocking snakeheads
      to supply a demand
        for Asian cuisine

      but Federal Law in 2002
        bans the notorious northern pariah
          so old Jack Dunn
            seines a pond
              throws em on the levee
                and goes home
                  for lunch

        and so do the snakeheads
          squiggling into ditches
            other ponds and waterways
              —no problem

          until, that is, 2008
            when farmer Bonner
              spots a scaly
                little bastard
                  worming across
                    his gravel road
                      so takes it on over
                        to Game & Fish

            & WHAM! the plague is upon us
              the pox is launched
                as over a hundred
                  wildlife officials
                    descend on this breeding
                    population:
                      the state, the feds
                        even Tennessee
                          and Indiana—

helicopters, amphibious crafts
ATVs, flat bottom boats
clean up crews in hazmat suits
49,000 watershed acres
39 miles of Piney creeks
400 miles of tributaries
the result being
100 poisoned, 50 more caught
a million dollars
gone in one shot

"perhaps the largest fish purge ever"
to stop them from getting into the White
thereby cock
blocking the Delta

but when you reproduce
five times per year
for six years straight
in a primordial environment
of stagnant marshy
backwater sloughs
what's a little
asphyxiation?

so by 2009, the marauders were back
murtilating crappies, bream, bass
two feet long
three feet long
in your face
and heading toward
the Great Lakes—

IV

six months later
jonesing to hold one in my hands
and stare down the centuries
I hook up with biologists
sampling the drainage systems
    we poison purple the arteries
        seining, scooping—slipping through the snakes
           killing carp, chubs, shiners, shad
             bullheads, frogs, buffalo
               beetles, darters, tadpoles

                    until the verdict:
                      five full days and zero brooding
                        serpent headed fish

                    which bums us out
                      while the Delta exhales
                      a sigh of relief

                            the odds are, though
                            they're still out there
                              as imminent as the fact

                            that nothing
                            is forever.

Another Pickerel Bites the Dust

After three years on the lake
I finally caught one
in my trap:

a totally cool
chain pickerel
about four inches long
with a bluish green
crackly pattern
and a vertical black
bandit mask

having never caught one before
and knowing they're rare
in these muddy waters
I immediately pronounced it
my newest pet

so dropped it in a twenty gallon tank
with a foot long longnose
gar named Glummy

who I figured wouldn't give a damn
because all he ever does
is sit there on the bottom
glumming

but WHOMPF!
Glummy chomped
that pickerel
a good one

since it was obvious they couldn't
live together
I put Glummy in
with my badass hybrid
alligator gar

who was suddenly glad
to teach a glum fish
how to dance

the pickerel, on the other hand
had a massive blotchy open sore
thanks to Glummy
I figured it
would recover though

I mean, this was no
whimpy crappie
this was a member
of the pike family

those wolves of the water
known for fighting, biting
and running out trout

but this pickerel
had lost all its will
and began bending
in the middle

until it became
boomerang shaped
with its ghostly back half
hanging limp

and it wouldn't eat
so within a week
it went belly up
I found it treading
on its side

at this point I figured
it was toast
I also figured
it had nothing to lose

so I began Operation
Force Feed that Fish!
which meant I caught it in my hand
then poked a cricket
down its throat
while whispering shit
to reassure it

which was completely stupid
and about as effective
as praying to God

so I shoved a minnow
down its gullet
telling it "Eat
You must eat"

that pickerel, however
wouldn't eat
or get unbent
or swim upright
or anything

then it had
a heart attack
or something like that
right in front
of my bugging eyes

meanwhile
the gars tangoed
spinning spirals
around each other
like the history of species
entwined with each other

or, as some might see it
(especially that pickerel)
like the history of fuckers
fucking with each other
for no good reason
whatsoever.

THANK BONG FOR OBLIVION

they call it charm school
but it's a bitch fight
strippers and addicts and silicone whores
fighting for a shit ton of cash
with no tv, no books to read
and all the alcohol
they can swill

the producers pretend it's all about
the making of a lady
but what the hell else to expect
when you've got a bunch of unemployed bimbos
battling for Queen Bitch?

of course
the most mediocre rise to the top
to send the message out to the millions
that you can fart and belch
your way to the gold
snagging loogies
as you go

in the meantime
Ozzy's mommy all high and mighty
acts as if she isn't pitting
pitbulls like any
pimp of porn
feeding from the ruin
of wasted jizz

& for what
Big Boobs
or a new tattoo?

but if they're lucky
their own reality
tv show.

Tyranny of the Rightwing Dumbass Fucks

After the election
they came douching around
the anti-abortion
fundies thumping
"He don't even got
a birth certif"

& as that fat limbastard
voiced their hope
that America would fail
the zombies of teabaggery
          were mobilized
in a moment's notice

an army of extremist nutjob thugs
calling themselves "patriots"
frothing at the bit
and yowling about
Daddy Debt

          (but where were they in W's wars
          and where were they
          when the Bailouts came down?)

then gnashing "Nazi!" and "Indoctrination!"
even though they'd been fooled & fueled
by a pundit pudding
of disinformation

they took off on a "hot air tour"
decrying Muslim takeover
and marching whitely through the streets
70,000 raging ass-clowns
with confederate flags
and fascist stashes
plastered on
our President

meanwhile
sullenly sanctioned by a new moral code
the tactless town hall tactics kicked in
massive packs of rabid hyenas
regurgitating "Death Panels!"
and screeching like the Wild Horde
"On what planet do you spend most of your time?"
Congressman Barney frankly asked
the seething mob
justified by sites online
directing them
to fly off the handle

& as the elephants made asses of themselves
by taking a shit
on "family values"
        (just like Jr.
        on the Constitution)
Emeritus Jimmy
pointed out:
leftover racism
from the South

then keeping their kids
home from school
while shuddering from a homo-
                      socialist agenda
this bunch of barnyard hooligans
totally lacking decency
totally lacking dignity
totally lacking any respect
shouted down the President

        (I mean, the donkeys never stooped so low:
        eight years of Guantanamo
                  & never a moan
                  in the hallow'd house)

and as the ammo sells out
and as Sanford and Sin dwindlates
and as 9/12 nauseates

and as an another republican
ethicsmonger
goes bragging with his microphone on
about spanking hot
secretary ass

a fight breaks out
in a thousand oaks:
protesters
protesting
protesting
to the point that an irate senior citizen
screaming "KEEP GOVERNMENT OUT OF HEALTHCARE!!!"
smacks some guy who chomps off his pinky
& it's off to the hospital
where Medicare
covers it all

So how do you like that shitarito?
Well hork it down, Amerigo
cuz that's where we're at
that's who we are
and that's why we
are suicide.

Sex Rehab

with Dr. Drew
is a show about
rock stars
porn stars
chronic masturbators
and fucked up junkies
with daddy issues
sweating and shaking
and acting out
while a whiney Ms.
Teen USA
runs around
with her ass hanging out

      spanking the monkey is not allowed
      nor is fiddling the bean

talk about blue balls
          and damp panties
talk about drama queens
         flipping out

but that's the fascination
rape and racism boiling over—

your mother died, so what!?
you got molested
deal with it!

in other words
shut the fuck up and
go fuck yourself
             or a co-star

but that, of course
is the main tension
in this cable
coliseum

where it's not so much about fuckers not fucking
as it is about looking at the worst
in others
as if they're different
from ourselves.
God = Abortion

with a name like Frankenstein
he had to be a Jew
so no wonder his neighbors came over
with pitchforks, torches and clubs

the creator's creation
(aka psuedo-son)
being crucified for our sins
was therefore
made a martyr

and as any Jesus junkie will attest
Christ is Lord
but what if Christ
was some sort of monster?

That's the question
being debated
in Congress right now

stay tuned
for more.

LULLABY FOR THE PREMATURE CRACKBABY SPRING
OR METHBABY, RATHER
CONSIDERING THE CARCINOGENS
CLIMATIZING BIOSPHERE

the networks say
spring has sprung
a month early

February now
and frogs are croaking
literally

even Physical Plant
cut back the myrtles
back in Jan

this is the month the bowfin spawn
but the grinnel in my tank
has been neon green for weeks

the telltale is the pollen, though
already out in snotnose force
watery eyes
dripping tears

these are the terms
for the terns
hatching in
          the nymphlessness

so suck it up
mutant mother
natureland

we let those bastards
fuck us
          into the dumpster

that's your bed
now lie in it.

HOW TO GET THE DEMOCRATS TO HANG UP ON YOU

for John Mitchel

the call came in at eight o'clock
the caller i.d. had no clue
I figured it was a home security scam or something

it was the Democrats.
they always want a hundred bucks
cuz I gave for Obama

but since Obama ain't running
I ain't giving
so I donned…

                                 THE PERVERT VOICE!

low, raspy
             self chuckling
like some creepy ass masturbator
panting fiendishly into the phone

like you're a naked hottie
and you're getting dressed
and your bulldog is glaring at you
and he's got an angry red boner
that's the kind of voice I mustered
the voice of that dog

poor woman, I told her
as slowly and as pervy
as I could
the first thing
that popped into my mind

"What?" she asked
after I finished
checking to see
if she heard correctly

so I told her again

even slower
even pervier

> "*I'm not wearing...*
>
> *any underwear*"

anyway
sexually harassing
the Democrats away
makes a guy wonder
what other hate crimes
he's capable of.

FROM THE NADIR

I have gone to the edge
I have stared the demon in the eye
I'm not shitting you
everything is exploded

when a man sees the face of his wife buried in the asshole of another man
it takes him to a plane

of sheer   utter

BLUDgeoning

and swoooningly

Frank Stanfordly

labot

omee

screams to be

solution.

either that or

the alternative.

CARDINAL SIN

after the funeral
I didn't want to go back to my lonely mancave
so I went to Old Chicago's
got a beer
and some chicken wings
hoping someone I knew would walk in

Ramone walked in
we had a chat and drank a beer
I was glad when I left

but I still didn't want to go home to my empty mancave
so I grabbed my fishing pole
and my tackle box
and some worms

then went to this spot behind Furniture Row
it's a holding pond for drainage from Target and Best Buy and Home Depot and all that
all the parking lots and gutters and ditches empty in here and then it flows
down to Lake Conway

anyway, there was rubble on one side
suburbs on the other
the sky was oranging and
I figured when it got dark
I wouldn't catch shit

but when it got dark
I suddenly caught
a small yellow bullhead

it was cool: about eight inches long
and tough looking
like a little bully

I threw him back
then caught something bigger
it had some tug on it
a small channel cat

maybe 14 inches, almost
two pounds

I threw it back as well
I was happy
some ducks swam by
I could hardly see them
it was nice

it was fucking
nice.

Trans-Amerigo Sound-Vision Sutra for Scotty Lewis

Exit 192

I

Kansas I see your rolling golden abdomens
  sigh-grinding sky

   those deeper darker deltas
     thrusting from creeks

      the blood-orange fireball
        blaze-razing
          retina

         your pine-line is steepled with slow-turning turbines
           & metronoming yellow birds
              pecking
                Prometheusly

             because DIESEL! ARBY'S
                BREAKFAST DELUXE!
                  because LA QUINTA! and
                  JESUS IS REAL!

                              but so is the world's
                                largest Czech egg

              next rest stop
               39 miles
                 thirteen hundred cows
                  and nine whitetails
                   huddled in a field
                    ears perked
                          eyes   to the Snake;

II

And Oklahoma
  you bitch!
    you know what you did to me
      you took me to the edge of my self
        fuck you very much for that!

          —& your demanding tolls
            & your shallow shale
              & your Christ-blight casinos
                on Cherokee land

            your toilet stalls are smeared with santorum
              your pizza tastes like ass

                suck my dust
                  Oklahoma
                    our carbon footprint =
                      5.1 pounds of invisible
                        burnt   black   shit
                          for every 8 pounds
                            we the people
                              burnburnburn
                                in our own
                                  dutch
                                    oven

                you make me wanna piss, Oklahoma
                  —piss on you;

III

But O my glowing Zarkia
  yr Ouachitas yr waterfalls
   yr mastodonded plains
    yr moccasins
     yr cypresses

      our gar hearts
            sump for your wampuslore
        your Grendels galore
         your sweet sweet
          skunky skank

you dirty
      naughty
            coy winking girl

      we are seduced to you
       yr valleys yr vales
        yr sultry
            salty
                sulking
                  holes

         yes we romanticize you
          yes we mythologize you
           yes we smooch your barbecue
           like lapsed vegetarians
            grabbing your glorious
             gluteus and
              palming both buns;

IIII

noviculite
lights the night
makes poetry
primordial.

Gartadas

Take tortilla
smear garlic
put gar meat
sqeez lime

then a pinch of sea salt
& some pico.

REVOLUTIONARY VISIONARY SLAM POEM FOR
THE DEPARTMENT OF CREATIVE WRITING AT UCA:
A MANIFESTO

Colleagues,
there's a lot of talk
about re
 structuring
 strategies

but this is the poem
that shuts it all down
i said this is the poem
that saves our world
because this is the poem
that makes our Department
and I say this poem
will prove the power
of poetry
                    its vision
                    is this:

Setting…
the premier Fine Arts college in the state
just pure arts, baby, pure arts
I'm talking
Art!
Theater!
Digital Film!
And Creative Writing
as its own
independent
visionary
department!

because this is a poem
about RECONSTRUCTING!
DECONSTRUCTING!
RE ENVISIONING
strategies:

It's about lumping what's supposed to be together
with what's supposed to be together
English wants Writing
they'll take that all on
the Comp, the Linguistics
the Professional Writing
they'll give em all 3/3
better workloads
equity!

As for Communications
they can just go join up with Mass Comm
or Journalism
or whoever they're really
supposed to be with

A Fine Arts College
Should Be a Fine Arts College
And we have the power
to put it all in one
                    big
                    beautiful
                    building

as for Creative Writing
THE TIME IS NOW TO FORM A DEPARTMENT!
I see a full faculty which we can create right now
for the Legislature has agreed
that in the third year
we shall
this is written
and I know it because
I wrote it
and UCA agreed to it

more importantly though
I envision a full faculty
with a graduate faculty of seven
AND I SEE AN ARMY OF GRADUATE STUDENTS
BRINGING IN MUCHO REVENUE
THROUGH A NEW

                    NO
               PRE   REQUISITE
                                    GEN ED
                                         INDUSTRY

I'm talking hundreds
We've got enough faculty
We've got enough students
We have already brought in
Beaucoup Revenue

and the Legislature has also decreed
that in the third year of the Arkansas Writers MFA Workshop
WE SHALL EITHER HIRE A NEW FACULTY MEMBER
OR CONVERT EXISTING POSITIONS!
SO NOW IS THE TIME
For STACY KIDD AND IRONMAN
NOW IS THE TIME
TO CREATE THE #1 CREATIVE WRITING PROGRAM
NOT JUST IN THE STATE
BUT RIGHT HERE
RIGHT NOW

WHILE INSTIGATING INTERNSHIPS!*
(like 3 per semester—to cover that
                    requirement for the MFA)
TEACHING 2/3 AND
DOING THESES AND
DIRECTING
DIRECTED STUDIES*   (which students sign up for

                              like theses

          for a soon to be

world famous

MFA degree!)

Meanwhile
we implement
The Incredible
Digital
Illustrated Narrative
aspect of the Program

—the Toad is ready to go
we've got the site
we've got the staff
we can do all the stuff
we're doing now
WE CAN
Be that frontier
AND ESTABLISH THAT!

I SAID TEACHING 3/3
AND DOING THESES
I SAID TEACHING 3/3
AND DOING THESES
I SAID TEACHING 3/3
AND DOING THESES

this should be
our #1 request
LET'S BUILD THAT WORLD-CLASS VISION NOW
BECAUSE IF WE CAN'T DO THAT AS A TEAM
I CAN DO THAT
MY MOTHERFUCKING SELF

I CAN BE THE ARCHITECT
I DID WITH THE TOAD SUCK REVIEW
I DID IT WITH THE MFA
AND I'LL DAMN WELL DO IT
FOR UCA

FOR WHAT?

FOR A LEAVE OF ABSENCE!
THAT'S WHAT!

So if you can't take that
and if you can't
run with that
and if you can't see me
taking this exact
same

message to Carey
then taking it to Terry
who you know
will jump on this

then let me have word
with the Provost
who is my Brovost

and then you won't have
to have faith that this is the poem
to throw your weight behind

and if you're not down with that
then I've only got
one word for you

and that word

is *word.*

Kaddish for My Mother Nancy MacKenzie 1934–2014

She was the Cherry Pie Queen of Yakima
a farmgirl of the fertile mountain desert sage
hoeing rattlesnakes in half
and because she had art in her
just like her sister Joan
she made art
studied art
taught art
then passed that on
to her children

who were always encouraged
to paint and draw and balance space
with colors and textures
and lines that define
and contrast

but she also passed on
a love for words
and the Wild
and for crossing the vast
wastes of the West

       every year
       we'd drive Hwy 12
       through the Badlands
       Rocky Mountains
       Grasshopper Camp
       Roundup Montana
       all the way to
       Puget Sound

and whenever the muffler fell off
on some lost road to some Ringing Rock
she'd turn a breakdown
into verse

that first marriage ended in a wreck
but it eventually led
to the phenomenon of Warren
who was damn good to her
for thirty something years

together they grew
the garden she always wanted
immersed in art
creating art
showing together
from Venezuela to Japan

and as this happened
what she wanted most in this world
happened for her children
who she gave her art
chromosomes to

we became artists just like her
we became teachers just like her
        we got healthcare
and because of what we gleaned from her
we earned professional recognition
mostly to make her proud

and she couldn't have been any prouder
and she couldn't have been more fulfilled
and to top that all off
she even became
the grandma she always wanted to be
cuddling on couch
with someone as real and rewarding
as River Spitzer Rasmussen

her summers were filled
with cabins with lakes
with Scrabble with Scotch
with clusters of oyster
mushrooms galore

with which she made a bouillabaisse
centered on solid
democratic values
like education
citizenship
civility
and dialogue

like the conversation we recently had
about the word "prosperity"
it came to us in a fortune cookie
and she knew exactly
what it meant

to prosper has nothing to do with money
it's about how you bring people together
and who you gather around the table
and how you sleep at night
because of who
you see in the mirror

my mom knew this—and she knew it well
she lived a rich life
full of family
full of friends

                    (her ability to form strong bonds
                    has always been a superpower
                    that speaks to the depth
                    of her character)

and because of these connections
she prospered
fabulously!

She did it!
she visualized her ideal life
and brought its form
to fruition

and in setting this example
she left a vivid collage

one she wove and sculpt and sewed herself
twining with imagination
inspiration
and the idea of the Intellect
which always lit
her eyes all up

we love her for that
and we love her for what
she ingrained in our brains

my mother has touched hundreds of us
in hundreds of ways we can't explain
and because she was watching us
watching ourselves
we strove to treat each other
with the respect she expected

> which has made the world a better place
> for everyone we know
> who's benefitted from her specter
> holding it together
> while the whole world
> goes to hell

that's her legacy
whether she meant it or not
it's a monumental accomplishment
something none of us can ever repay
or thank her for
anymore

but it's also something to celebrate
in the fabric of our DNA
my mother was
an innovative and ingenious
visionary artist
whose strokes and shapes
grace our space

with this wearable art we now don
with this network of sticks and threads and narratives
with this sweeping fantastic
abstract textile
   she made
and gave
to us.

LOVE POEM FOR LEA GRAHAM

Happy Birthday you
super gorgeous poet professor
you world traveling
mindblowing siren

several times
I've written the dreaded cliché to you
and several times I deleted it
just couldn't muster the courage to
send what we know is obvious

I know the grace of your bombshell eyes
what they've seared into mine
we were riding the Torrid Bliss
and we were deep deep into the slide
when you hit me with that melty look

I saw your years of crushes crushed
and I saw a soundless plea for me
to tread lightly, Mr. Spitzer

I don't know if you remember
the expression I still see on me
trying to return
an *I understand*
an *I'm there too*

Minnesota was Magic Time
everything phenomenal
you brought a corpse back from the dead
but that's not why you are pure light

I proclaim this synthesis
        no flash fiction
I proclaim this synergism
        God-given
and I shout it from this Arkastate
we will redefine

                              2500 miles from fact that
you wrote "Fuck Fuck Fuck
I think I'm falling
in love with a poet
and I don't know if I'm
prepared for that"

but I am
and I'm all in
I'd marry you in a nanosecond

this is a love story, Lea Graham
this is the hottest romance that's ever been
this is me blithering like a crywhacker
because I'm fueled w/ ecstasy
to be infused with you

                    (Exit 5
                    Little Rock)

I hope this doesn't scare you away
or slam a hammer in your heart
this isn't just a common crush
this is the Crush of Us
Crushing Crashing
into Us

I've got to have
all the quarrels we'll ever have
all the doubts we'll ever have
and any tortures in between

I want to explore your meadows more
get familiar with your toes
massage your back and slap your ass
kiss every sweet inch
then spiral long & gyre slow
until we shatter glass
          w/ yr cry
driving wild our nuclei

so now these flames are coming for you
and we will split the earth in two
          at the Equator

Crush me with your waves, Lea Graham
Crush me with the rush of your rocks
because when I get my hands on you
I will hold you like an octopus

because how could I not
adore the unique form of your hand
which makes you
perfectly you?

                    (*adore:* from French
                    meaning *worship*
                    meaning *gold*)

Lea—I am totally down
with this whole Epic Sushi Tsunami
this entire Blazing Polonaise
conflagrating in fireworks

so Happy Birthday, Beautiful
your Sugar Daddy
is fucked up in
love with you.

Vow

1. noun or verb, meaning sacred or solemn promise, oath, pledge, declaration; or covenant, commitment, bond; to swear, to engage, to guarantee. 2. From the Latin *advocare*, a combo of *ad* (toward) and *vocare* (to call upon) which advocates (an evolution of *advocare*) a summoning. 3. So summon this: the vow I vowed on trestle over Rondout Creek: to revow every year—when everyone knows vows are really made in heads whenever expressions demand incarnation. 4. But then again there's ritual, and that's where sacred and solemn suggest what's at the core of the spirit of this word. 5. To approach, go toward, to strive to officially claim intent. 6. Why? To become one's better self. 7. Vows in a vacuum are only vows to one's self, but because I have you, I have real reason to move toward my better self. 8. Because you deserve that / a husband who may not know what he vows on the eve of our first anniversary, but one who will always unpack this word to use as a growth hormone. 9. To feed the concept of us. 10. That's what matters. 11. Trajectories need mysteries for romance to burn like an acetylene torch. 12. Vows seek vowels and consonants, and these are mine to you June 14, 2017. 13. Baby, you are the love of my life. That's no vow. That's just the truth—and it represents what I value most. 14. This year was just the beginning. 15. Poems don't need to make sense. 16. Either do we. 17. We chose a photosynthesis, one that will continue to feed strong stalks with Ultraviolet Radiance! 18. For what it's worth, I vow to always honor that. 19. You can always trust and you should always know that I will always fight my demons for you.

LADYBUG JIHAD HOLOCAUST POEM

All these bastard ladybugs
dying all over my house
cyclically birthing
more bastard bugs

    crowding the sills
    swarming the panes
    infesting a sunny room
    sans any grub

    bastard cadavers everywhere
    dry shells littering
    layering
    crunching under foot

    Listen up
    you damn bastard ladybugs
    skittering
        scuttling
            thinking you're so cute,
            you ain't nothing
            but a plague!

meanwhile
I vacuum hordes galore
w/ a handheld
Black and Decker sucker upper
then let em go
outside

"Don't hurt them!"
        Lea cries
"Ladybugs are good luck!"

But is it good luck
to suck every day?
to climb ladders
spray vinegar
taste the bitter

metallic of their funk
    in yr sinus
nasalways?

What a privilege!
to know those dopey bugs!
What a convenience
to buy a trap from Amazon:
        a stupid bag
        you hang from a hook
        that doesn't do squat!

Piece of crap—
I throw it out
order another
with a black light lure
complete with abyss
of soap 'n water

but chemical warfare
doesn't work
the bulb is blown
so I order another

        as all those bastard ladybugs
        continue motoring Mobiusly
        reproducing giddily

        as I continue rounding up
        copulation populations
        w/ the fervor of an angry god

        There's one over there!
        There's another on the wall!
        hundreds of dumbass
                        dumbo bugs!
                Asian beetles!
                        whatev—
I lick my fingers
pluck em up
they cling

kavetch
        as I elicit
                expletives:

               "MOTHERFUCKING
               PIGFUCKING LOUSES!
               GET THE HELL
               OUT OF OUR HOUSES!"

then it comes
my magic bulb
I plug it in
and they go in

And Die!
Die Die Die!
Ha Ha Ha!
Take that
you bastard little
    ladybirds!

You are Verboten!
 You are not wanted!
  You think you exist
   but you don't!

You aren't even
a concept in my mind
        you bastard exo
        skeletal bugs
        in exodus and
        on the run!

    Go wander
        wastelands yonder!
    Go bother
        another brother!

    your house is on fire
    and your kids are on drugs
    ladybug meth! ladybug crack!
    shaking in the throes
    of Apocalypse

a whole Kool-Aid cult
drinking generation
gone belly up
toes awiggle
              @ the sky

This scurvy scourge of ladybugs
look what it's done to me!
I'm gleeful for its suicide
joyful for its genocide
when the truth is
              we're all just insects anyway
              in an ever expanding
              galactic flash
                born to die
                born to bug
                  & desiccate
                unto dust

Is somebody's cup
                half full?
Does somebody need
                a buggy hug?

                    NO!!!
              I'm glad to be
              the Adolf Hitler of Ladybugs
              calling for the all out annihilation
              of the Tangerine Abomination!

              not even one
              babybug
              hiding out
                      under a pan!

                      Death to them all!
                      And to all ladykind…

                      a pox upon
                        yr polka dots!

NOT RECOMMENDED

normally I let it go
but when an eighteen wheeler
came road-raging up behind me
and rode my bumper
I'd had enough

earlier that summer
cruise control at 70
some mongo truck
carrying pipes
came barreling down a hill
on Lea and me

as usual I felt
no need to speed up
just because he
was pressuring me

so I kept it pegged at 70
while he road our ass
as others passed

when he was finally able to switch lanes
he blasted his horn and shook
his whole hairy forearm at me
then swerved his trailer into our lane
had to shoot to the shoulder
to avoid getting
run off the road

so there I was again
some trucker fucker
trying to pass

he eventually did
then hit his blinkers
to take the next exit

I hit my signal too
got up right behind him
stayed on him
it was payback time
and he knew it

so at the last second
he shot back
onto the interstate

I did too
knowing it was juvenile
and dangerous as well
but my wife wasn't there
nor my better judgment
and I hit the gas

the chase was on
weaving through traffic
way past the speed limit
I was prepared
to stay on him
to the gates of hell

terrorizing him
for terrorizing us
shining my brights
into his cab
all their damn cabs

to the point that he
actually pulled
his semi over

Yep, I bullied
a fifteen ton truck
off the road
then parked behind him
and let him sweat

but when he opened his door
I wasn't about to stick around
for some gun nut hater
of law abiding citizens
slowing his delivery down

Nope   I shot back onto I-40
having accomplished
absolutely nothing

    except I didn't
    feel like a wuss.

Not a Popular Sentiment

—February 24, 2020

> *gala public memorial for Kobe Bryant in L.A. /*
> *Harvey Weinstein found guilty.*

Waaaaa waaaaa waaaaaa
another blinging millionaire
has fallen from the sky
    on his way
to a basketball game

Waaaaa waaaaa waaaaaa
all those diehards in denial
of Eagle Colorado 2003
when a certain NBA legend
forced Pamella Mackey over a chair
then pumped her full
of groupie spooge

Waaaaa waaaaa waaaaaa
it's the same forgiveness
granted Nixon
Reagan
even Trump

> the only difference being
> the color of this rapist's skin
> didn't stop him
> from cashing in
> on white privilege

Harsh words? Too soon?
Is that what you think?

#metoo.

COSBY COUPLETS

Hey, hey, hey, sorry I'm late
America's dad slipped me a roofie

*

So... did somebody take a dump on your face
or is that a moldy potato on a cow pie?

*

I never liked Fat Albert
but there wasn't much else on TV

*

Never liked his sitcom either
had better things to do in the eighties

       (like get drunk
       and drive)

*

The governor of Louisiana once called me because I complained
that Cosby wasn't pronouncing a word correctly

       (it was "interested" not "innerested"
       on a commercial promoting education)

*

Guess where that pudding pop
is going now?

*

According to turdwords.com, the Cosby Sweater is the act of
puking Fruit Loops on somebody's chest during sex

*

Sexual predators say
the darnedest things.

Ain't No Sorry

Growing up in Mní Sota
us kids took field trips
to Fort Snelling
to learn about
"our history"

that's where workers
in old timey garb
made candles and
the towers had
slits for windows

so muskets could protect
the confluence
that's what we
were told

      not the fact
that this was a concentration camp
where 1700 Dakhóta men
women   children
were marched to and starved
if not lynched

which isn't something
you can dwell on
those visions of ribs
in sickening winter
the scalping of
families

it's enough to make
a Jew puke

but as always
we soldier on.

MONSTER CAT APOTHEOSIS

Sometimes there's that rare
tension in the limb
you can see the line shimmying
at an off
       angle

when I paddled up
the branch was bowed
and the thick black braid
was slowly scribing
figure eights
in the lake

there was no question about it:
a fish was on
and it had heft

bumping up
I pinched the line
felt the vibe
of the creature on
the other end
sensing me
sensing it

its instinct was
to swim straight down
I could feel it adjusting
for the descent

so I wrapped that line
around my wrist
got it in my fist
and began
to lift

I've caught thirty pounders
out in these waters
even caught
a sixty once

but with this one
the tug I received
shot a cold shock
to the back of my neck

the translation was
an in your face
Sorry, Jack—

and as the force fought back
jerk jerk jerking back
increasing in vitriol
I knew this was
        The Mother Lunker!

Steeling my knees
against the gunwales
I poised myself
to raise a colossal
flathead cat
        cuz how could it be
        anything else
        holding its mass
        against my own?

Meanwhile
down in the black
it powered down

Holy Hell!
I couldn't believe
this a tug of war
with a bulging
        belligerent
        hundred pound
        Monster Cat

        a fact established
        by every sizzling
        cell in my system

nevertheless
its yank begat
instant mythos

and out there alone
in a canoe
I was honestly
petrified

    to suddenly see
    my fingers go in
    my hand go in
    my elbow go in
    the waterline
    inching up

it didn't matter
if I pulled or not
that hulking fish
was hauling me down

    four inches to the rail
    three inches
    two inches
    the lake's dark skin
    about to rush in

those two hunching muscles
aligning the spine
driving the keel
into the murk

I couldn't see it
but I could see it:
  its flattened extra
    terrestrial skull
      its bruised and battered
        behemoth head

the bow was now
a foot off the water
it was rising and I
was riding a wheelie
        in place

but what was I gonna do
let go and cry
or haul that bastard
up from the muck?

So I threw my back
into it
but that badass cat
wouldn't budge

I kept pulling though
  how could I not?
    And how could it not
      eventually breach?

Still
I might as well
have been anchored to
a concrete slab
because stretching that hundred
pound test to its max
was the equivalent of pulling
a dump truck up

            until
                the sickening
                        sound
                            of SNAP!

                    It was off
                    and nothing
                    but slack

then
when I pulled up the circle hook

it was bent as straight
as the needle in my brain
piercing the epiphany

that this meeting of wills
between muscle and meat
and gristle and grit
was proof of the truth
that we can witness
what's beyond us
even if
we can't see it

and that, my friends
is as close as anyone
can ever get.

RETURN OF GOD

when I pulled up to the Monster Cat Tree
named for the jet black flatty
that almost pulled me under
two autumns back

the limbline was taut
and ticking like a bomb
about to go off

this time I was in a kayak
and lining things up
three familiar shocks
shot through my wrist

and as it bullied down
bucking thrusting
lunging plunging
tons of stuff
        went screeching through my mind

first
a follicle freezing scream telling me
not to dick   with this fish
            cuz with one sudden tug
            it could yank me into a twisted tangle
            of barbs and barbels and limbs and fins
                    snagged
                    splashing
                    gasping
                    dead

secondly
it was sending the message
that I was out of my league to believe
that I could hold to something
as massive
as this

but how could I not give it a shot
        and how could it not
        rear back with a whiplashing thrash
        and smash all hell
        out of that hook?

Yep
that's what it did
it tore forged steel
right off the knot
the pressure point
where all that stretching
had to pop

        leaving me a glut
        of shuddering guts
        moving on to the second cypress

        where an eerie lightness
        signaled another
        laceration

        the line all coiled
        like a double helix^{squared and squared and squared again}

        the obvious sign of a smaller cat
        having spun itself silly

        until the leviathan came along
        and couldn't hold
        back jack

just like me
still clinging
to that tangibility

two huge hooks
lodged in the jaws of God.

Charlotte and the Colossus

Fall is always
    the hungriest time
  the flatheads are fattening up
      and I often find   obliterated line
        hanging from the cypresses

I've seen how these fish
    torque and smash
        blasting tackle
          to Timbuktu

such visions have led
  to numerous legends
    of "Old Shitheads"
      their mouths a fiction
      of metal and rust

but now I'm really
            creating an awful
              maw full of steel
            by actually
                supplying the hardware

in a month's time
  I've lost four shark hooks
    to this pierced
      lip Goliath

      so I stepped up my game
                adding swivels
              & alloy leaders
                & got new twine
                & tied new knots

but then
  like always
    something came up
      primarily
      cancer

and as she faded
                our skinny singing niece
                who loved sock monkeys
              and making movies

so did all those trophy grotesques
    I somehow saw
      as one

so now she's up there
  with Jesus Jesus Jesus
    according to the family

          while we
        up top
            speculate on mysteries

            then call it faith
          or call it fact

             based on what
               we choose to need.

WAMPUS CONUNDRUM

there's something creepy
about this bobcat bust
I bought for sixty
five bucks

it's a good size wildcat
head & shoulders & partial chest
stuck on a stick

and definitely a sloppy job
its nose is missing
its stuffing is lumpy
which gives it a weird
smirky grin

maybe it sees
what's in my head:

      back in Missouri
      I had a student
      who trapped these cats
      to track their range

      I went out in the field with him
      learned about their mass migrations
      stealthing down to Louisiana
      sneaking up to Canada

      which got me thinking
      about their status
      of "Least Concern"
      while still holding out
      after two million years
      nabbing rabbits
      scoring squirrels
      unlike those
      second amenders
      who tend to blast
      the hell out of them

because they've got
                the guns and hey
there's one
over there!

that's why bobcat cadavers
can be found across the continent
in pawn shops and flea markets

in fact, there are several for sale
in Van Buren
at this moment
forever mummified

so now I'm part
of that cycle too:

Shoot, Stuff, Sell, Repeat
Shoot, Stuff, Sell, Repeat…

and I'm staring at those tufty ears
and its green glass eyes
are staring back
with the intensity of
        a super live
        super cool
        super alert
        lynxy thing

but beyond those whiskers
        and spotty
                tawny
                        fluff of fur
I know there's nothing
in that shell
but cotton and
Styrofoam
                where there used to be real
                        feline fire
                                out there in the woods
                                        licking

                                    stalking
                            rolling in the clover

but those eyes
those uncanny
unblinking eyes
I'm always staring
into those eyes

probably looking
to write a poem
about why I'd engage
in such a scurvy commerce

yep, that's what it's gotta be:
me using a crude
and ludicrous corpse
to activate
an activism.

So okay
now that this
has been established
we can all
move on

        right?

East Texas Pilgrimage:
After the Deluge

had to get the hell out of town
so took off on a "vision quest"

packing up some frozen shad and
stopping at a Texarkana fish market
I bought some slaps of buffalo
then made it to the Walmart in Athens
bought four tilapia

at the launch
the fishermen were coming in
the first guy I met had an empty
bottle of whiskey
and a handgun holstered
to his side

in fact
all the anglers coming in
were packing heat
because this isn't Kansas anymore
(or maybe
it is)

heading upstream in the frothing roil
weaving between all the bobbing logs and soccer balls
floating down from Dallas-Fort Worth
I made it to my hallow'd hole

it was ten feet under water
but there was still a patch of poison ivy
flat enough to lay a tarp

as usual
the slow foaming eddies were bursting with
longnose and gator gar
not to mention
the jumbo backs
of jumbo cats

and rough fish
galore

on the sandbar on the other side
some country boys were drinking Coors
and cranking classic rock

meanwhile
setting up my rods and tent
I gathered wood
then mushed my lighter
into the mud

couldn't find another
knew what I had to do
shot across and
asked for help

"Yes sir!" they said
and gave me a Bic
they were also
armed to the hilt

but then they were gone
and beans and brauts
and rum and Coke
to the point of utter
oblivion

      as the river rose
      as the insects bit
      as I kept on catching
      loads of sticks

and a few small cats
like the foot long blue
I used for bait

then slept in tent
gripping pole
while all night long
the river pulled

by morning
I'd caught a tree
must've weighed four hundred pounds
but I reeled it in
and something erupted
from its limbs
it was a forty inch
fat yellow flatty
thrashing as I
landed it
       seventeen pounds

the smaller cat
was lodged in its throat
had to stick my wrist way in
to get it out
       it bit
          the shit out of me

the water was now inches from my tent
so I broke camp and crossed across
the sandbar was mine

I was now out
of the jetsam zone
watching the big ones roll

all day long
I sat in the shade
eating jerky
not thinking nothing
       the voices the faces
       finally gone

then the river
crested and calmed
began to drop

that night I had two runners
meaning large gar taking off
which is tricky because

you gotta let em run
for like fifteen minutes
before you set the hook

the first made a beeline
into some brush
so I had to yank my tackle back

the second one though
that was the one

the baitcaster
started clicking
then clicking faster
so I hit the release
and the spool ran free

it was shooting downstream at top speed
took out a hundred yards
and then a hundred more
this was the rush
I had waited
four years for

then it stopped
but I couldn't be sure
            so struck
            and slack
brought nada
back to shore

and that was it
out on the visionless
sun warmed sand
swollen and spider bit
scabbing up and
suppurating pus

but reborn as
an atheist can be
thanking
            the Trinity.

NORWAY RAT

When it skittered out from under the stove
scrabbling for traction between my feet
I figured it was just a big
                    dumb
                    mouse

I even laughed as it
laid rubber on the laminate
before pancaking under
the washing machine

that's when I realized
what it was

Norway rats
aren't really Norwegian
but the boats that brought them over were

these sleek & slender
midsize suckers
are Asian invasives
not quite as large as lab rats
or as scraggly as sewer rats
but they ain't welcome
in my house

so I threw a couple
glue traps down
and blew town
to run rodents out
of our New York outpost

        up there
        it's regular field mice
        running nutty
        in the attic
        stashing lentils
        in Lea's boots

and our sonic
pulsing
flashing
tactics
don't do much
they keep the mice down
but the best way is
the proven way

I place them in strategic spots
SNAP! goes a spine
SNAP! a skull

sometimes I get
five to seven
in a weekend
but then it's back
to Arkansas

where a colder than normal
winter freeze
has ushered in
more refugees

I hear them in the walls
gnawing away
there's one downstairs
under the plumbing
chewing and chewing
making a nest

Time to get serious!
I go to Home Depot
buy some extra jumbo traps
designed for mongo
urban rats

I put four out
one under the kitchen sink
one under the bathroom sink
one on the top floor

and another under
the stairs

this is what I do best
next to canoeing
I've done it all
my pest vengeance life
but never on the scale
of Rat Attack!

Still
they keep licking
the Skippy off
to the point I know
they're procreating in the house
reproducing
flea infested
feces genes

my friend Catfish
advises mixing
oatmeal in
but I take
it one step further
by hardening the peanut butter
in the refrigerator
            before laying the death traps down

then one morning
I find a trap
with one
dead
rat's ass
and a separated   vertebrae

usually with simple mice
I recycle simple traps
but with this rigor
mortised rat
my stomach won't
allow me that

my blood congeals
to lift the trap
and when a finger
whisks a whisker
all my chromo
somes recoil

its still moist
sparkling eyes
staring straight
into mine

and its shiny glossy velveteen
and its non-offensive
                        non-ropy tail
are totally clean
totally lean
almost
even
kissable

        but I chuck it
        of course
        then go back for more

        get another
        a couple days later
        then another
        the following week

        by spring
        I'd wiped out five
        and after that
        none came back

in the meantime
out in the cane
those pretty rat bastards
are plotting their comeback

as the cycle continues
as it has for centuries
reeking of medieval
ratlore plague
squiggling in
our inner plasma
                    curdling

                    communal cheez.

My Gay Ungulate Objectification

for River

Hwy 385
    New Mexico
  the Ports to Plains Corridor
    where out alone
       in yellow field
          there's a statuesque
           antelope

so I pull over
      for a closer look
and in the split
    second before
        its crouch and pounce

               I behold the most
               mammiferous display
               of muscular masculinity
               I have ever
               witnessed

       this is no
            common young buck
               with two cute spikes
                  poking up

         this is a seasoned
            stud of the sage:
            massive horns and
            bold of breast

then all I see
as he bursts away
      are two white buns
         shining brightly
         perfectly oval
         bounding
         bouncing

      What a rack! What an ass!
              God had graced me
              once again.

In and Out of the Arkansas

heard it said
that seeing a panther in the wild
is a rarity that's hardly seen
but even more unusual
and even more spectacular

I declare

is seeing a great
longnose migration
like Scotty and I saw
down below
the Toad Suck Dam

there were thousands of gar
all breeding size
three, four, five feet long
some even six feet long
leaping leaping constantly
frenetically

up up
up upstream
the entire dam
under water
swollen creeks
raging downward
mass fish shooting
for the fields of their birth

we'd come equipped
with rods of course
and found a spot along the shore
where we could see them way way out
spread out over a hundred yards
porpoising toward us
elongated snouts
actually grinning

as the ballet tapered
single file

as they passed just ten
feet from us

so we were casting
into their midst
but they didn't
give a damn

because they were heeding
the chromosomal call
of a hundred million year
milt egg pilgrimage
to get to their spawn on
        Sargassoly
then cycle through
the system again
their yearning burning
into our brainpans

needless to say
all we caught of this exodus
were flashes akin
to an old time
chemical bath
used to create
photographs

which we can access any time
apocrypha working
its own magic dance.

Before I Started Walking to School

my parents always told me
not to talk about
how much money
my father made

but then I'd ride a school bus full
of freckled bullies
doing just that

"My dad's a cop"
someone would say
"he makes fourteen thousand a year"

"Mine's a manager"
somebody else would say
"he makes sixteen thousand per year"

then one day
I got put on the spot

"My dad's a sociology professor"
I said
"he makes twenty two thousand"

complete silence on the bus
that's how much
a Minnesota Viking made

"You're a liar!"
somebody cried
actually getting
in my face

luckily though
some girl asked
"What's a professor?"

that's a question
I'm still asking.

KIDS, DON'T TRY THIS AT HOME

when I was thirteen
I found a book
in the school library
about a kid
who made a bomb

Cool! I figured
I'll do that
then commenced Operation
Blow Something
The Fuck Up

opening some shotgun shells
I got a bunch of gunpowder
then poured that into
a toilet paper tube
sealed both ends
with wax

the wick was a birthday candle
it would take eight minutes to burn down
so I could make my getaway

but I had to make a statement
because you just can't blow
something up
and not say
nothing

I also decided
to take my bomb to school
along with a torn white t-shirt
on which I painted big red letters:
"MRS. MACIVER DIES
MAY 10!"

Mrs. MacIver
was a cranky old English teacher
who didn't teach us
about Minerva

nevertheless
Minerva was on
the mythology test
so I got that wrong

But why May 10?
Well, that was
Mother's Day
which is always a good day
for a death threat

plus
since I didn't give a dang
about someone as bitter
as Mrs. MacIver
this meant no one
would think it was me

I then hid that bomb
in a pop can with
the top cut off
and placed it in
the boy's bathroom

after lighting it
I went back to the library
and sat down with
that mad bomber book

eight minutes later
I casually strolled
back to the restroom
black smoke rolling
out of it

and then the vice principal
a grim black man
in a pine green suit
came hustling out
with that bomb
wrapped in the shirt

anyway
the incident was never mentioned
by the administration
and Mrs. MacIver
took an early
retirement

and that book
it's still on the shelf
inspiring more

terrorism.

My Own Personal Hazing into the Gut-Wrenching Fraternity of Nothing

my parents always figured
I'd be safer getting
drunk at home

that's why my father
let me booze it up
on New Years Eve
1979

I was fourteen years old
and there was a lot of red wine
he and his concubine
were partying down
in a broken home

during the course of the evening
I drank quite a few
and clowned around
probably wore
a lampshade or two

then it hit me
it started swirling
the whole vertiginous
universe

went down to the basement
laid down on the fold out bed
then suddenly
in that space between
the backrest and mattress
blew chunks
all over the floor

I remember green olives
in the mix
tried to clean it
gave up

Sam came down to check on me
she was my mom's friend
only came to the party
to be bipartisan

the divorce was still burning
like my bile
I probably puked
three more times

in the morning
no one was up
and having never been
hungover before
I didn't know
what to do

so I went to the 7-Eleven
bought a quart of milk
then crossed the street
to Powderhorn Park
sat on a tire swing
and chugged
the milk

it was zero degrees
no snow
and as gray as Minnesota
ever gets.

THE SKIDMARK REMAINS

hands at two and ten
learner's permit
in my pocket
behind the wheel
of the '75 Valiant
my mom sitting
next to me

we're cruising up Chicago Avenue
at a pretty good clip
I'm trying to beat
the orange

my mother doesn't say a thing
she's been in this situation before
always makes the right call

now I'm going 45
              50
                55
                     "STOP!"

      I slam on the brakes
      fishtail, skid
      come to rest
      at the red

my mother exhales
rubber burning
in the air

      sorta like the time
      my shotgun went off
      with my father
      somehow I pulled the trigger
      blew a big black
      hole in the snow

he didn't say anything
gunpowder
singeing
cilia

and now my mom
letting the smoke
sink in

            till the light turns green
then we proceed

and later
it's always there
two swerving snakes
two houses long

the serpentine lines
of the teenage mind
learning to gauge
how to not
smear someone.

Motorhead Myopia

growing up on *Dukes of Hazzard*
is not recommended
for a realistic view
of responsible driving

when my friends and I
were fifteen years old
we all snuck out
our parents' cars

my mom had this powder blue
Plymouth Valiant
it was the most ordinary vehicle
on the planet
a slant six
225
    four doors
and no balls
at all

nevertheless
I'd take it out
on my ritual run
and make that baby squeal

up 12th across the bridge
a hard right along the creek
pedal to the metal
screeching through
every bend
maybe get it
up to 80

only a few
old people knew
there was nothing
they could do
but shake their fists
on their lawns

then
returning it
to the garage
engine ticking
overheating
I'd dream of getting
my own V8

of taking it out
and topping out
at a hundred and twenty
that's what we all
eventually did

an entire
 testosteroned
   generation
armed with an armada
of the prior decade's
rustiest clunkers

beat El Caminos
shot Chevelles
lost LeManses

laying rubber
the quarter mile
four wheel drifting
spinning shitties
wiping out
all over the place

a really bad
combination:
teenage boys
muscle cars
& dollar four
gasoline

but strangely enough
nobody died
until our twenties

that's when Greg Little
went too fast into a turn
flipped
             corkscrewed
                          endoed
and smashed his head
dead in Wisconsin

should've happened years before
should've slowed us down before
I mean

we weren't just following
Bo Luke Boss Hogg and Roscoe
we were following
a sick southern symbolism
like a swastika atop
the General Lee

we didn't know
what it meant
we didn't know
how to see.

How I Almost Changed the World but Gave into the Meatwheel Instead

back in my twenties
I used to believe
that a six foot frame
and size 12 boots
could be used as a tool
to affect social change

weaving my bike through inner city traffic
I was always on the lookout
for oblivious drivers
when one turned
in front of me
I was prepared
to kung fu a fender

it gave me a twisted
sense of achievement
to see startled eyes
gawking back

but I wasn't just
looking for kicks
I knew the danger
of riding at night

years before
cruising through an intersection
a car swerved in front of me
had to leapfrog over
the handlebars
it plowed right through
my father's ten speed
left it a crushed
metal pretzel

that's why I thought
I had the right
and that lashing out
was my civic duty

                    this practice   of course
                    led to conflict

the turning point came
in Colorado
after I kicked
a charging Camaro
and a six foot six
marine stepped out

needless to say
I got the hell out of there
heartbeat hammering
fact that
my theory had
some kinks in it

by my forties I discovered
that the tool I envisioned
was actually me
and that lashing back
equaled fleeing

then
a half century into it
crossing the street
in front of school
here comes a sorority girl
making a turn
straight into me

so I raise my professor bag
which she sees and
punches it

and that's the moment
I brace to crater
a dent in her door

and why not?
she's running me down—
    but instead
I step back

So why am I
writing this?
In the hope that men
can be zen
or empathetic
or forgiving?

        Nope
        the fact is
        young punks
        grow old

        and that's where this
        tool
            is at.

Fish Tickling, New Mexico

back when my dad
could smoke a corncob pipe
Lars and I were casting with him
at the trout stream dam
when this guy came over
with his girlfriend
they looked Hispanic

"Hi," he grinned
"catching anything?"

"Not much," I said
as he stripped down to
his tighty whities

"I'll show you how it's done"
he said
and wading right in
he began reaching under logs
pulling out rainbows
with both hands

and he did show us
how it's done:
how you wiggle your fingers
to make a fish
think you're a fish
just rubbing up
and then you grab it!

Meanwhile
he was throwing trout
up to his girlfriend
who was stringing them
on a stick

my dad watched
and puffed his pipe
as Lars and I
followed instructions

after a bit
Lars got a fatty
and then something
suddenly stung me

I pulled up my hand
a big momma crayfish
was pinching my finger

everyone laughed
and the guy eventually
gave us some trout
then took off with
a genuine grin

      which is rare with
      fishermen

I mean
he had something magical
and he was giving it
away for free

      I'm still scratching
      my head on that.

Live from the Nation's Capitol

what can I say
about Sujith and the rat

except that Sujith
was embracing his
heritage

dressed in a traditional robe
grilling on some sort
of upside down
barbeque

when all of a sudden
here comes this big
 scruffy
   city rat
tear-assing around the corner

it shot right between his legs
bumped an ankle
bounced off
and kept on
scurrying

Sujith flinched
but didn't see it
and I was laughing
my ass off

            it took like an hour
            till the meat was done.

ETHAN BEING ETHAN
DIVIDED BY PI

1

The night I met Ethan
he decided to mess with me
it was a party at Sujith's
and Ethan came over
told me he'd been floating the Cadron
when all of a sudden
there were shit-tons of gar
so what did he do?
he took out his gun

and started blasting

that was the moment
I had to decide
whether I was gonna let it go
or be me

"You're an asshole"
I told him
and walked away

but Sujith followed me
"That's just Ethan
being Ethan"
he explained

"Yeah," I replied
"but he's still an asshole"

2

Later that summer
we all went camping
on an island

that's the night
Ethan named me Hollywood

"HOLLYWOOOOD!" Ethan would cry
"MY MAN HOLLYWOOOOOD!"
and then he'd shoot
his gun at the sky

3

in the middle of the night
Tyrone got a call from the Provost
it'd been reported that Professor Jaeger
had been seen walking to the launch
but was not seen returning

"That's because I got on a boat
and went camping"
he told the Provost
and everyone went
back to sleep

4

Except for Ethan and Sujith
up all night on acid
Ethan yelling random stuff
rubbing sand in his hair
and yowling like
a damn fool

to the point I couldn't
take it anymore
so got up
and went over

"What the hell!" I yelled at Sujith
because I knew him better than Ethan
"Will you please stop
encouraging this idiot!"

"What?" Ethan cried
"You Don't Like My Voice?"

"No," I replied
"it's keeping me up!
Keeping everyone up!"
and then I kicked
a stupid chair

"HOLLYWOOD DOESN'T LIKE MY VOICE!"
Ethan howled
then hopped in his party barge
and circled the island
yowling "HOLLYWOOOOOOOD!
HOLLYWOOOOOOOOD!"
till dawn broke
its blood red yolk
and spilled it on
the Arkansas

5

for years after that
it was easier to laugh at the fact
that the Provost had called Tyrone
than it was to make sense
out of Ethan
being Ethan

but that's the way it's always been
there are never any convenient answers
except in prayer
and poetry.

CULTURAL EXPERIENCE

I met Ethan at the Mallet Town Bridge
he had a case of shitty beer
and a handgun
I had a canoe
and a spinning rod

we took off on the Cadron
caught a few rock bass
and threw them back

Ethan was in the bow
getting drunker and drunker
and the gun was spinning
in the hull

he had no holster
and water and grit
were getting into it:
the chamber
the barrel
all those
springs and things

then came the rapids
I kept taking the smoothest way through
and he kept yelling
"C'MON, HOLLYWOOD!
GO THROUGH THE MIDDLE!"

so I did
and he rocked the boat
from side to side
whooping like a true
American redneck

anyway
the cans rattled
like beans inside
an aluminum maraca

and nothing ever happened
with the gun

by the end of the trip
Ethan was too hammered
to drive home
so we left his car
at Mallet Town

end of story
except that
Ethan is a father now
and grows habaneros
makes super hot
hot sauce

        make of that
        what you will.

UP IN THE ROCKIES

pulling out of the Cannoco
kindbud emporium
for humans and their dogs
I saw a jolly old familiar face
who most would brand
as Santa Claus

but the full white beard
in that pickup truck
jolted a different
association:

> *it was 1995*
> *on the outskirts of Rollinsville*
> *Colorado*
>
> *Pete and I were shirtless*
> *and launching my beat*
> *to shit canoe*
> *into the raging roil*
>
> *then POW!*
> *howling laughing*
> *boulders bashing*
> *holes between our feet*
>
> *we sank*
> *right in front*
> *of an old bearded hippy*
> *and his old hippy wife*
> *lounging on lawn chairs*
>
> *they were holding hands*
> *looking at us*
> *two fools*
> > *come to rest*

of course
everyone knows
there are millions out there
who look like St. Nick

still
I like to think
that jolly old hippy
I saw in that truck
was the hippy from
my hippocampus
twenty something
years later
walking in
w/ credit card

rather than
growing his own.

DIGESTING THE MOMENT

Nancy MacKenzie 1934-2014

I was in the hospice lobby
trying to stomach my salad when
my sister burst in stammering
that our mother had suddenly
ceased her phlegmy
wheeze of death

she'd been gone for days
both mentally and physically
but this   now
was her last instant
whether she was there
or not

we ran back
I hugged her head
my sister her legs
both of us trying
to hold onto something

she died in our arms
and then some sort
of death rattle
from somewhere deep
and guttural

"Oh yah,"
the nurse said
with that stereotypical
Minnesota accent
"they do that, ya know
expelling oxygen from their lungs"

she recorded the official time
and we waited for
the body bag

my sister couldn't eat her salad
I could barely eat my own
but my mother had ingrained in me
the importance of eating
three balanced
meals per day

so I ate my salad
it tasted
like cancer.

Flash

Stephan Spitzer 1933-2018

last night I saw his eyes
staring at me in the rearview mirror
they were my eyes

he was smirking in that way
like he knows something about you
that you don't know about yourself

I hadn't seen those wily eyes
since the nineties

Parkinson's
had disabled that glint

but there it was
on me
digging into
my light

    —thanks, Dad
      keep it up

      this might be the only way
      I'll really see you
      when you're gone.

Driving Down by Palestine (TX)
I Saw a Sign Along the Way

"DR. STUART SPITZER
CHRISTIAN CONSERVATIVE
REPUBLICAN FOR TEXAS
HOUSE DISTRICT 4"

which blew my mind
I mean
the Spitzers and Spitzes and Spitzenbergs
were Inquisitioned Spanish Jews
who settled on the Danube
circa 1492
          and not because they had a choice

so there I was
just as much a religious Jew
as I was a cultural Jew
judging other
non Jew Jews

when in fact
given the history of history
adapting to one's environment
   is advisable
for survival

so how can an atheist Jew
condemn a Christian Jew
for not embracing
his inner Jew?

Especially in Texas
where no one goes shouting
"Hey Everybody,
I'm Chosen!"

Unless, that is
someone's mission
is self crucifixion

          —that's something
            to think about.

GONE WITH THE RACIST MISOGYNIST WIND

To get a sense of the messages it sends
I watched it again
was left with this
wincing vision:

a nostalgia being celebrated
for a great lost "civilization"
in which lavish mansions and fancy dress
are valued over the torture and toil
of "happy darkies"
helping their benevolent masters
no chains, no whips
no lynching trees

but alas the barbarian "invaders"
swooped down and fucked shit up
for the glorious South

    then that scene
        in which Rhett
           (bitch of the one percenters)
      and Scarlet
        (whore at heart)
     bicker to the point
       that his angry red boner
      dictates
           what is his

and because he wants
her spoiled white ass
he carries her off
without consent

        cut to the following scene:
        she wakes up stretching
             satiated
       having received
         what she needed

but ultimately
Rhett doesn't give a damn
so she returns
to the terra of Tara
the plantation that God
granted her bloodline
which earned its connection
to the dirt

        (yeah, right)
      but that's where she will go again
      this baroness who never evolves
      to plot out how
      to win her man back

      because the power of love
      will heal all wounds
      and all those patterns
    of destructive co
      dependent behavior
      will be blown away forever
      leaving her a strong
      independent woman.......

Anyway
I'm sure these arguments have been made before
along with more
but since they've never been made by me
that's what I
have to say

      go nuts,
      y'all.

SNOWBLIND

couldn't see
        over the hood
a foot of snow
        piled on the hood

        only a few
        defrosted inches

doesn't matter anyway
        there's nothing on these gravel roads
        except roadkill
            pitbulls
              and trash

but then a Thump
as a flash lashes
from corner of vision
into ditch

Holy Shit!
It's a Bigwheel and
a little kid—
            should I stop
          or hit the gas?

but voice of mother
in my head
gotta be
citizen!

        Hit brakes
        Slam in park
        Jump out
        See scene:

puffy jacket
face down
in the run off
and here come

the brothers
the sisters
peddling plastic
wheels on ice

they're led by the eldest
she's on foot
crying and
gesticulating
to see her sibling
run down like a
skanky possum

I'm indicted!
I did this!
my whole life
has just changed
as has
theirs

Prison!
Funeral!
Lawyers!
Lawsuit!

I must've just
bumped the tot
who I find myself
running toward
rolling over

she's staring at me
w/ wide stunned eyes
a chubby faced
Mexican kid
not more
than three

"Are you okay?"
                    she doesn't respond
    mouth agawk
                    about to bawl

scooping her up
I carry her over
to the trailer
where yowling kids
throw the door open

the mother, the aunt
are shockfaced and gaunt
the father bolts
up from the couch

where I lay the kid
and try to explain

"It's okay"
            they say
and apologize
rushing and fussing
to clean her up

"Hospital?" I ask
but am met with a chorus
of NO NO NOs!

and it's obvious why
            these children
            weren't in school
            they were playing
            in the road

            and this family
            they hardly speak
            English at all

ain't no healthcare
ain't no nothing
but fact that they
could get deported

so I leave my name
and my number
and the aunt calls me
a few hours later
tells me her niece
is doing fine

and then she even
godblesses me
when anyone else
would've sued
the hell out of me

I'm then left
with the bitchslap that
there are invisibles in these streets
who can be mowed down in a moment's notice

so shovel off your hood, Spitzer
you and all the reckless rest
whose guilt isn't worth a shit
compared to the screech of grief.

WHAT ROBERT FROST DIDN'T SAY

Knowing it's a problem
that neighbors don't know their neighbors
and don't want to
I figured I should introduce myself

however
there were enough clues informing me
that the investment wouldn't be
worth the return:
their trucks, their flags
the fact that they
were never outside
weren't incentives
to go say hi

two years went by
their dachshund died
and maybe the husband too
never saw hide
nor hair of them

until the day
they cut down the hedge
on my property
exposing my yard
to the world
scarred and shorn
where brush used to be

it looked like shite
and I was pissed
so now it was time
to say hello

I went over there
knocked on the door
it took her a while
to unlock the bolts

she stepped out
onto the porch
exactly who
I figured she'd be
pinchfaced and looking away
so I got to the point
immediately

"Well," she said
"the lady who used to live in your house
couldn't see the road"

"That's why I liked it"
I replied

"I planted those weeds"
she went on
"and they took off
so I was just cleaning
my mess up"

then she added
"Besides
            it was all
            snaky in there"

Ahhh, I deduced
having run into
this ism before:
it was Pentecostal
serpent fear
not uncommon
in Arkansas

still
I restrained myself from telling her
that snakes are welcome in my yard
instead I told her
I'd put up a fence

"But that won't stop the snakes!"
she cried

anyway
what it all boils down to
is that she doesn't want to see any snakes
and I don't want to see any neighbors

so now I'm the one
building a wall.

Ambush in Niger

Seems this caravan of Green Berets
went searching for an ISIS leader
drove around for thirty six hours
ended up getting
shot to shit

four sergeants were killed
who never should've been out there
since they never sought or received
approval for this mission

anyhow
since it'd been
a big blundering clusterfuck
an investigation was launched
and months later
the results were announced:

Because those soldiers weren't properly trained
it was their own damn fault

Translation being:
some rookies made
some rookie mistakes
so they're the ones
            responsible
and there's no one to hold
            accountable

                        case closed

Still
who ever heard of Special Forces
not being prepared?

Seems to me
that if they were out there
running around in Jihadist crosshairs
and nobody told them to come back in

then somebody thought
they were up to snuff

Question:
Why did the soldiers cross the road?
Answer:
It's easy to accept "full responsibility"
when all you have to do
is say you do

          but when there's a price to pay
for fucking up
surprise surprise
no one
          steps up.

Behind the Lies

"Truth is not true."

let's look at two Chump arguments:

1) No I didn't have sex with that porn star
who I paid to hush up

and 2)
I wouldn't have appointed Jeff Sessions
if I knew he'd recuse himself
from investigating
collusion

subtext = duh!
if Chump said that
he is clearly
guilty of both

so therefore only
obstructing justice

which is totally legal
with the right spin.

Speak American!

If 3000 people died in Puerto Rico
followed by Chump
throwing out
paper towels

then that's the same as
9/11
so therefore the worst
disaster of
the new American
millennium

a death toll so high
we can't even quantify
(officially)
or won't

or maybe we don't give a damn
because they ain't
citizens

       sarcasm aside
that's the mindset
and that's the message
from the Alt
White House

separating families
on the border
on the side
while concentrating
kids in camps
swinging deals with dictators
and appointing drunken rapist
to the highest court
in the land

why?
because America
is great again.

Observation #6261

Poetry is
where real world solutions
go to die.

Observation #6262

before we're weaned
we're yeaned

go figure.

It's Always Slippery in KY

sliding with the traffic of trailers and trucks
through the gland lands of misty Appalachia

rolling through lush
wet curvature

the danger is getting
caught in the dance

deer clustered
on the shoulder
ready to leap

into the eyes
of sudden fire.

Take Ice, Make Ice

It's my new theory for better living
every time you take some cubes
you fill the ice tray
                    up with water
then put it back
                    in the freezer

that way
you never have just one
lonely cube
looking at you
            when it's happy hour

we'll see if this works any better
than my ingenious pants
rotating method
taking jeans
from the bottom of the pile
to give them all
a fair shot

fat lot of good that did
I still grab
the pair
on top.

Observation #6265

Have you ever taught
in the same shirt you slept in?

I just did

> Not because I lack respect
> for myself
>
> but because I lack it
> for my colleagues
>
> too bad for everyone
> I liked
> > wearing a tie.

Observation #6266

How a damn candy bar
went from 25 cents
to $2.83 in my lifetime
I sure as hell
don't know

why I paid for it
is the other mystery.

Observation #6267

There is no cure
for the hiccups.

"World's Largest Boy"

that's what the sign said
Minnesota State Fair
1973

and since my sister and I
just had to see
our mother paid
the entry fee

"Cool!" we cried
and ran up the steps
into a traveling
tractor trailer

then we saw him
sitting on the scattered hay
in nothing but
his underwear

he was like a seven hundred pound
fat black kid
sweating like a pig
a few years older than
me
there was an old fashioned metal fan
blowing humid air on him
and he was glaring non
expressively

at two   skinny
white kids with
their pieholes
hanging open

which wiped the smiles
right off our faces
we figured we'd see
someone equally
as curious

but what we got
was an unnerving stare
augering into
esophagi
where we knew he was just
as human as us
so didn't deserve
to be treated like
a circus freak

I figured I
  should acknowledge this
I figured I
  should acknowledge him

"Wow," I said
"you're big"

which didn't change
a damn thing
we could see he didn't give a fuck
what we fucking
fucking thunk

cuz his job
was to sit there
like livestock
a laughing stock

for the amusement of those
who find entertainment
in someone dying
from diabetes
obesity
organ failure

and the plain cold indifference
of paying to see
someone else's
tragedy

anyhow
we didn't run down those steps
like we ran up them

because when we descended
a half minute later
our eyes were locked
on our stupid shoes

which could never run
from what we'd done
from just being
little kids.

PUSHING BACK

when I was thirteen
my father's therapist thought
he needed to challenge
an authority figure

our neighbor Dennis was six foot three
so he was chosen
    as was I
to help my dad train

locking fingers
gritting teeth
I found myself
facing my father

shaking
shuddering
I somehow got him
against the wall
daggers slashing
in his eyes

then raising my arms
and bearing down
I began forcing
my father down

"OKAY," he snapped
"THAT'S ENOUGH!"
then cutting it short
he stomped away

       it wasn't supposed
       to go that way

I mean
if he couldn't push back

against a kid
then how could he
take on Dennis?

So that was that
his therapist suggested
something else
and I went back
to the nerd lunch table

where we got bullied every day
and none of us ever
pushed back at all.

March 30, 1981

Ninth grade drafting class was a joke
I'd take my measurements
draw my lines
complete my project
then start another

in the meantime   up front
this foxy blonde
was always sitting
on Old Mr. Boner's lap

I guess she figured
he was like a grandfather
but if that was the case
what were they doing
wiggling and giggling
from what was going on
under those young buns?

Anyway   one day
the loud speaker announced
President Reagan had been shot
and just like all across the country
the classroom erupted
in applause

Old Mr. Boner   however
admonished us
it just wasn't proper
to celebrate a failed
assassination

imagine that
getting schooled
by a pervert.

American Culture in a Nutshell

it was one of those stupid
driving around
nights in the eighties

I was in the back
of a Bonneville
and Jaime and Stobbs
were up front

we were idling at a crosswalk
and a drunk woman was crossing the street
when Stobbs decided
to lay on the horn

this pissed her off
so she started pounding on the hood
as Stobbs eased into
the intersection
shoving the raving
lady back

both those guys were guffawing so hard
they couldn't see me
stepping out to yell some shit

that's when my foot
        met Firestone
my ankle was under
the rear tire

the next thing I knew
I was getting sucked out
and two plus tons of Pontiac
was crawling up my leg

somehow   though
clinging to the door jamb
I managed to pull myself in
along with the remnants

of my pants
the upshot being
no bones broken
and as usual
I only got
scuffed up

meanwhile
down in Argentina
thirty thousand students
       farmers
        fathers
        indigenous
        and innocents   .

        were being rounded up
        tortured
        drugged
        and dumped off the coast
        of Buenos Aires

but not us doofuses
we kept driving around
goofing around
oblivious
      as all of us.

"SPITZER, YOU ASSHOLE!"

It was four in the morning
when Kent pulled onto
Airport Property
but what it really was
was a swamp

so when we got out to piss
and the front end sunk into the mud
no amount of rocking
was gonna free us

hence   we found ourselves hoofing
across South Minneapolis
where my ex girlfriend
Liz lived

we figured she could help us out
let us borrow a car
then get a tow rope

that's why we were sneaking around
tapping on windows
scratching on screens
when the sudden bulk
of her brother leveled
a rifle on us

the takeaway being
a message I'd heard
for the last eighteen years
and would continue to hear
for the rest of my life

but at least we had the luxury
of continuing our trek
across the damp
                    dark
                        city at night

rather than
            the alternative.

ANOTHER TIME I ALMOST BIT IT

screaming along
  on Minnehaha Parkway
    600 ccs between my knees
      slaloming in and out of turns
        Pat Chan in the lead
          hahaing helmetless
            my Kawasaki
              KA-CHUNKed the curb

                that's when everything
                slowed to a series
                  of split second clicks

Click!   soaring over handlebars
              wobble careening spastically
                Pat Chan glancing back
                  his bugging eyes   locked on mine
                mouth as round
              as a Cheerio

Click!   the other curb shooting toward me
              airborne and unbelieving
                that this could actually
              be me

Click!   as Pat Chan swivels back
              to handle his own trajectory
                my arms are wings
                hovering over
                front fender

Click!   and all that asphalt rushing upward
              and the front tire spinning like a buzzsaw
              and I'm freefalling forward
              about to get run over
              by my own
            motorcycle

Click!   But wait!
I'm not even gonna try
to pull out of this death spiral?
I'm just gonna let
nineteen years of boyblood
splatter spray my life away

for a simple mistake
that would hardly matter
in a video game?

Click!   HELL NO!
reaching back
I seize the grips
pull back
and miraculously
land in saddle

Click!   Pat Chan turns to see
a shatterskull shooting teeth
but beholds instead
propped on tank
the rabbit ears of
the soles of my feet

because now I'm kicking back
and waving back
with a shit eating grin
that should've been smeared

from here

to Duluth

Click!   as if my aorta
isn't beating
all holy hell
out of my chest

as if my legs
aren't shuddering
spasmodically

Click!   Revelation that I
              never had any extra
              spaceships left

              no further Pacmen
              waiting in the wings

to the point that
three and a half decades later
driving I-55
black suit packed in back

I'm still flummoxed by the fact
that technically   I should be
a crippled
            mangled
                      burden on
                              family
but I'm still here
steering something
while others never
got that chance

        one question
always remaining:

*What the fuck's
up with that?*

NAVIGATING THE NEURAL NETWORKS
OF ADOLESCENT SPELUNKERY

I'm glad to see that troubled teens
are still getting trapped
in the limestone caverns of St. Paul

thirty plus years ago
I saw a similar report
on the local news
so shot on over
to check em out

most openings were sealed shut
but hiking around and up and down
we always found
a way in

all you had to do
was look for the garden hoses
which   for some reason
signaled slither holes
to squiggle through

those caves were cool as hell
they were full of milk trucks from
the turn of the century
gossamered in ghostly dust

plus piles of commercial mushroom crates
rotted into fungal mush

            a typical pile
was a quarter mile long
you could run right through it
like plowing through
waist deep snow

and searching through corridors
crawling through crevices
we'd always arrive

at was known
as "The Throne Room"

there was this winding path
snaking up the cavern wall
and there were five thrones carved
into the sandstone dome

where you could smoke a doobie
with your pals
and stare out over
a grand amphitheater

full of empty kegs and broken glass
with hieroglyphic messages
scrawled by the ancients:

                    "LED ZEP!"
                    "SMOKE WEED!"
                    "CLASS OF 1982!"

most cave-ins happened
due to torches
drying out passages
causing ceilings
to collapse

that's why we
used high powered lamps
and sometimes we'd find
"The Stairway to Heaven"

it was a tunnel so tight
you had to squirm
for three city blocks

there was no room
for turning around

but when you got to the end
there was a spot
for smoking pot

of course
a lot of kids
got hammered in there
which is why the police
were always looking
for fuckers getting
fucked up
there'd been accidents
in the past
broken legs
busted backs

and occasional packs
of stoners running
from the rumble of rubble
and not always
making it out

I once got pretty
bunged up in there
from drinking the high life
and diving around

some boulder however
put a stop to that
it cracked my knee open
like a cantaloupe

which is why the city
kept closing those caves
and why the burnouts
kept breaking in

but it wasn't the drugs
or subpar beer
that led to digging
bodies out

it was the fact that boys
are just gonna do
what they do

like explore
and hang out
and communicate
and celebrate

the labyrinths of troglodytes
slowly evolving
into men.

MISSED OPPORTUNITY

Back when I was a student
in intro to creative writing
a course I now teach
I was put into a small group
for workshopping poetry

my three teammates were
    a round headed
    glazed eyed stoner

    an attractive
    acned
    art major

    and her economy sized
    frizzy haired friend

as a teacher
one reason I assign group work
is because I remember
the goofing that happens
in such situations
and what it's good for

I was definitely interested
in that art gal
my eyes on the crystal
curves of her jeans

but at that time
I was under the spell
of a self proclaimed
pagan earth goddess
and we were living
in a duplex doomed
to demolition

then one day
clowning around

I suggested our group
meet outside of class
for a whacky
    naked
workshopping session

they laughed at that
and then I missed
the next class

but when I came back
those two bright eyes
were locked on mine
telling me they'd talked
my proposition over

and were willing
to give it
a swing

GAWK! was my
reaction to that
as I stared back at
the three of them
waiting to see
my reaction

       if I said yes
       it would be on
       if I said no
       it wouldn't

but I couldn't undress
with anyone else
so I told them straight up
that I was devoted
to my girlfriend

which elicited two long
drawn out "Awwwww"s
from the ladies

like they'd seen a puppy
or been told they're pretty

It had been the right
reaction at the time
I had earned their respect
by foregoing hot
                wet
                group
                sex

in order to cling
to an idea as ideal
as true romance

            that's what happens
when you're in
the thick of it.

Trust and Consequences

after floating the Rum
and loading the canoe
I saw my father
watching two boys

they were about four and eight
and focused on a mayonnaise jar
buzzing full of yellow jackets

once in a while
the older kid
would run over and
jump the jar

meanwhile
the younger kid
with his stripy shirt
and buzz cut was
trying to work
his courage up

"Go ahead," my father said
"go for it"

and since my father
was clearly a father
and since everyone knows
fathers never
endanger children

that little kid
rushed in
kicked that jar
and the swarm exploded
like a grenade

then grinning at us
proud of his accomplishment
his eyes popped

out of his head
before his brain even knew it
he was swatting at an incensed swarm
of predatory wasps
dive bombing
                    the shit out of him

he must've been stung
at least twenty times
at least twenty flaming
blades of venom
mixing with
adrenaline

I can't remember
what my dad said
but I can still see him
shaking his head

                    as if that kid
                    wasn't the sharpest
                    tool in the shed

                    as if he'd brought
                    those results
                    upon himself

I figure my father
figured that kid
had learned a lesson
so that's how he justified
what he did

but staring out the window of the El Camino
wondering how I'd never been stung
the fuck up like that
especially with
a father like that

        he wasn't the only one
shaking his head.

Free Ranging in Boulder USA

back in poetry school
Peter and Marilyn
used to have potlucks

they were our profs
but I was wary of Marilyn
who was known for drawing
young men   into her web

the week before
she'd invited me to lunch
she'd bought me wine
and had complimented
my biceps

in the interim
Peter kept telling me
I'd left my pot
at their house

which my comrades and I
thought was funny
because that pot was
a cooking pot
which had a bunch of
"free rangers" in it

        that's what we called
        baked potatoes

so one day I worked up the nerve
walked down the hill
and found myself
ringing the doorbell

suddenly
there were all these moans
coming through the kitchen window

it was Marilyn

climbing climbing
higher higher
about to lose
her fucking mind---
then I heard footsteps
and saw a huge hairy bear
lumbering toward me
in nothing but
his boxer shorts

Oh shit, I thought
If Peter's not with her
then who the hell is?

"Hello Mark," Peter said
"Come on in
and get your pot"

so I followed him in
toward the source of the rising wail
Peter acting   like everything's normal

and turning the corner
there she was
totally sweating
totally pumping
huffing hard
on an exercise bike

"Oh hi, Mark"
Marilyn said
"did you come to get
your pot?"

"Yep," I said
and two minutes later
walking up the hill
looking in my pot

I saw three cold spuds
just staring at me.

BEFORE THE ORANGE GLOW

Back in my twenties
I found a new life
peddling in the Pyrenees

I had thirty pounds of
dictionaries and idiom books
in jimmy rigged saddle bags
having gone to France
to translate Genet

it was Bastille Day 1993
when I snuck into a vineyard at night
popped the cork on a bottle of red
and ate some brie
on some hardass bread

fireworks were flaring in the sky
I was living the life of Rimbaud
                    Kerouac
                all my heroes
                at the time

then laying out my sleeping bag
I crashed out in that fantasy
only to awake three hours later
rats scrambling everywhere
shadows hunkering
in the limbs

needless to say
I got the hell out of there
then biked all night
up up up the mountain road
and arrived at a farmhouse
one lit window
up above

and in that window
a stupefying nubile nude

showering in shimmering light
Bubbles! Breasts!
Buttocks! Thighs!
        O Man!
to be graced by
such a sign—

was I tripping
or was this actually
a prophesy
regarding my
destiny?

            Hell if I knew
            but it was something

and then I saw another form
a darker
            stockier
                        more shouldery form
stomping down the stairs
then throwing open
the door

had to keep on rolling
down to Paris
heading for some sort
of myth in my mind

but I tell you what
whether it happened that way
or I framed it that way
those moments
will always be
exclusively
mine.

THE MOTIVATIONAL SPEAKER

Back in the nineties
I visited my friend Jules
who lived in Boulder
with her dot com boyfriend

we immediately began
smoking hash
he had some real good shit
which explains why we laughed
our asses off
it was the funniest Saturday Night Live
any of us   had ever seen

Jules was proud of her boyfriend
who had hopped on the pop up spamwagon
and was bragging about how
they just surpassed
"the six figure threshold"
which I didn't even know
was a threshold

anyway
the next day
he showed me his business
down in the basement

he had all these VCR tapes
in which he motivated CEOs
to motivate
investors

the orders came in
they sent them out
while he consulted on the side
for stock in startups

"Wanna smoke a bong?" he asked
"Sure," I replied
blubbidy blubbidy

blub blub blub…

then we shot off
to a gig he had
riling up a corporate crowd
while I sat in the audience
just as freaking
high as him

after that
they moved to Maui
where I saw Jules on the internet
spinning life size pots

as for the motivational speaker
I'm sure he's surpassed
the seven figure threshold now
and I'm sure he's still
spinning something
of his own

mainly
his utter
charlatan
bullshit.

WHAT IT'S ALL ABOUT, ALFIE

first I was a young person
sneaking away from older people
to smoke my secret weed

now I'm an older person
sneaking away from younger people
for the same reason

meanwhile
gravity still pulls
at nine point eight
meters per second
squared

       always
       accelerating.

Car Camping

my wife hates it
when I throw the futon in the Jeep
and set off on the interstate

but I love driving
until NPR fizzles
and finally make it
to Amarillo

so park behind
a Hampton Inn
crawl inside my sleeping bag
and crash like
a meteorite

then
awaking at dawn
with the kind of ice
that forms on windows
from breathing inside

I bust the crust
stagger through the sleet
walk on in
chug an orange juice
and get myself
a Denver omelet

the staff can't tell me
from their guests
these workers are
a different shift

so I take a couple
coffees to go
  and go
  and go
  and go
  and go

when I'm not with her
this is always
the best bed in town.

(Passive) Aggression in the Ozarks

so I went up to visit Hippy and Amelia
and that's when Holy
Shitballs showed up

that's not his real name
but that's what I called him in my head
because he was drunk as fuck
and always shouting
        "HOLY SHITBALLS!"

Holy Shitballs was like fifty something
his hobby was flintknapping
genuine fake arrowheads

anyway
it was decided we'd float the creek
Hippy and Amelia in one canoe
Holy Shitballs and me
in the other

meanwhile
he kept shouting
        "HOLY SHITBALLS!
        HOLY SHITBALLS!"

I was in back
and he was up front
steering from the bow
that's why we kept
spinning out

and when we did
he'd dig in
and head upstream
obliviously

        "HOLY SHITBALLS!
        HOLY SHITBALLS!"

I told him a few times
to let me steer
but it just never
registered

luckily though
Hippy saw me steaming
so switched with me

      "HOLY SHITBALLS!
      HOLY SHITBALLS!
      HOLY HOLY HOLY
      SHITBALLS!"

there were no birds
  chirping in the trees
there were no fish
  leaping in the stream

      "HOLY SHITBALLS!"
he kept yelling
      "HOLY SHITBALLS!"
chugging beer and
spooking deer

that's when it hit
        Hippy's lure
a bigass soft shelled turtle
the size of a manhole cover

      "HOLY SHITBALLS!
      HOLY SHITBALLS!"

that turtle was heading
straight toward me
like a missile

when "HOLY SHITBALLS!"
it suddenly rammed
our canoe
    sending out

a gonging sound

then fuming
　　gritting
　　gripping
　　that turtle

I reversed the hook
and sent it flinging
like a Frisbee
"HERE'S YOUR DAMN TURTLE!"
I shot back
as it landed smack
in Hippy's canoe

and hoooo boy,
that turtle took off
scrambling and scrabbling
crashing into tackle
knocking over beers

it tore ass all over the place
and Holy Shitballs
was flailing from rail to rail
　　　　while Hippy tried
to keep from tumping

it wasn't my most
magnanimous moment
but I suddenly felt
a whole lot better

　　and Amelia
was laughing too.

EN ROUTE

Stopped in Marshall Arkansas
for fuel at the Harp's
an old guy at the pump
was filling a gas can
and smoking a stogie

thought about yelling
something about being
a dumbass but
decided to get
the hell out
instead

drove a few miles
to Bear Creek
saw something cutting
a V downstream

parked car
got out
ran to bridge
saw an otter with
a big fish
in its mouth
bound up bank
into brush

then looking down
saw half a dozen fat
polka dotted
mystery fish
just treading there
pointing upstream

two   sudden   separate   stories
that have nothing to do
with each other

but leaving me strangely
satisfied.

Open Message to Foreigner Re: The Lyrics
"It Feels Like the First Time / Like It Never Did Before"

#1) If it feels as excellent this time
as it did the very first time
then how can the first time
be differentiated from
the most recent time

        That is
        what makes those times different
        other than the times
        they happened at?

#2) The line "it feels like the first time"
is contradictory because
those times can't feel the same
if the most recent time
never felt the way
it initially did

#3) There's no way it can feel
like the first time
because the first time can only be
felt in "real time"

        which pertains to the essence
        of a primary experience
        that cannot be
        duplicated

        cuz when someone feels something
        for the first time
        after the second
        its novelty is auto
        matically lost

#4) Anyway
I don't remember the first time
being so great

do you?

Remembering More Than the Alamo

I was in downtown San Antonio
walking to the conference center
thinking this city
was pretty progressive

but then I heard that cowardly word
erupt from a truck
passing through traffic

you know the word
      meant to dismember
      disembowel
      eviscerate
      lynch
      an entire genetics

it was directed behind me
at a family heading into Denny's
refusing to look up

        as if this wasn't
        the first time it happened
        the kids trained
        to keep on walking

like that famous photo
of a young black girl's
first day of school
Little Rock nineteen
fifty seven

and here we are
seven decades later
a racist rapist
in the white
supremacist house

encouraging the most
deplorable animosity

that swastikas and slavery
aspire to enflame

fuck yeah I was shocked!
and shocked that this shock
hadn't shocked
that family

and hell yeah I was bummed!
to never be able to separate
        this city's diversity
from what some dumbfuck
publically upchucked

but this isn't about me
this is about that family
trying to digest
two moons over my hammy

                at Denny's
where an oversized American flag
still flaps over the parking lot
smeared with the toxic shit

of hostile
redneck
ignorance.

Upon Hearing a Comment at the P.O. During Another Global Pandemic

Imagine
an elderly lady joking about
how now that covid's shut down everything
there's no more school shootings

funny   I think
            standing in line
how mass shootings in the USA
had once been framed
as "going postal"

    which is now some sort
of boomer saying
dating back to the last
century

to paraphrase
Hunter S. Thompson
            the shithammer
            has descended

and to paraphrase
the absolute crap
we all keep hearing
            yes   we are all in this
            together

but let's get real
because seriously, folks
some are always

    more in it
than others.

George Herbert Walker Bullshit

America has a nasty habit
of turning murderers
     into martyrs
especially when
it's funeral time

case in point:
when George Herbert kicked the bucket
he was billed a gentleman
     (which is partially due
       to contrast with belligerence
       occupying office now)

born into a dynasty
that dug up Geronimo
and profited from Nazi cash
oil tycoon George Herbert Walker Bullshit
       oversaw CIA torture
       in collaboration w/
       Dirty War dictators
       down in South Amerigo
       who disappeared
       sixty thousand

       not only that
       George Herbert Walker Bullshit
       made it okay
       to blast sixty six children
       out of the Iranian sky
         (not to mention
         two hundred and thirty
         bonus adults)

       before starving millions of civilians
       into squalid rubble dust
       while bombing Baghdad
       à la Dick
         Cheney chaining
      military to

a million more collaterals

"Principled bipartisan moderate"?
Bullshit again!
While flying the Willie Horton flag of
outright racist fascism
George Herbert Walker Bullshit
ordered some crack
to entrap a black
                    teenager
for fearmongering scourge
on live TV

imprisoned for a decade
Keith Jackson's life
                    paid the price
for media stunt
of George Herbert Walker Bullshit
stating verbatim
                    "I don't care
                    what the facts are"

        thereby paving way
        for eastern bloc oligarchs
        and setbacks from
        his mutant son

some of us remember   though
how much George Herbert Walker Bullshit
was loathed before and after Gulf War
        so let's stop smearing
        lipstick on this pig

cuz thanks to the same campaign
that covered up global warming
& slandered science
& media as enemy

        it's easy these days
        to paint a war criminal

as patriotic
patriarch

especially when
a far right   alt white   base
is too hoodwinked to give a damn

that a well informed electorate
is a perquisite for
democracy.

BITCHSLAPPED BY REALITY

I used to spend a lot of time in airports
all those Chile IIs and
Hudson News and
Jetsonian walkways

filled with sphincters and intestines
flying to Orlando
and Dallas–Fort Worth

all tricked out in headphones
walking and talking
to distributers in Delaware and

all that suicidal fuel
burning in the atmosphere and

it just seemed so bound
to implode

I mean
all that movement and technology
the battering of our waters and land
the minimum wagers scraping by

and with healthcare
and cancer
and diarrhea in Sudan
it just didn't seem

logical
that this Hydra headed vehicle
could keep on rolling

with no world wars
and no starvation
and no global warming
and not a pox—

WHAMMM!!

that's when the cudgel struck
bludgeoning every nonessential
and essential
covid blown
    thing in the world
Fools!
we believed
our odds for getting smeared to death
were any different than those
of your typical
medieval
hag masses

Gluttons!
we had the audacity
to envision optional migrating caravans
with nary a jihad bomber plotting

       & the maws of methane
         continually gnawing
       & the notion of crashing
         economies existing
         only as fantasy

Such arrogance!
By flying Air Denial
we
    definitely
        Dedalused

maybe we deserved it
maybe we didn't
but the fact is
    it was un
sustainable

so grab your mask
and PPEs
and do your best
to stave off
Das Ventilator!

Because suddenly
you don't have a credit card
or cell phone
or stimulus check

and you're scummed in pus
and standing in line
with millions of others
who used to have
their own computers

and lifestyles
and educations
and underwear
and shaving cream
and 401Ks
and AK
47s

but after four days
of eating dirt and
the Hershey squirts
you finally make it
to the front of the line

where there ain't no more
government cheese
or normalcy
or anything

meaning welcome to
the new abnormal
where your life ain't worth
a can of Alpo

            or are you
immune to that?

PLASTIC PLASMA PARADOX

we wake up in beds
made of plastic
get dressed in clothes
spun from plastics
open shades
plastic plastic
make breakfast with
plastic spatulas
in walls full of plastic
on floors packed with plastic
then drive to work
in vehicles assembled
from hundreds of plastics
our phones forged
from plastics
plastic shoes
plastic hats
plastic glasses
plasti-products
on our faces
in our hair
in our teeth
in our bones
in our blood
typing on computers
fused with plastic
eating lunch
wrapped in plastic
served on plastic
plastic straws
and utensils
before going home
to plastic appliances
and more plastic screens
and plastic machines
for climate control
plastic fixtures
beaming light
soaking up

"Waiting for the Flood?"

back in grade school
kids used to laugh
at my pants
and ask that
smarmy question

if they saw your socks
you were fair game

but now
fifty years later
living on a lake
with global warming
dumping exponential rain

I can honestly answer
                    yes

in fact   these days
we're all wearing
highwaters.

"Fresh Pussy!"

third grade
1975

that's when I first heard
those two words together

a little black kid
standing in line
introduced me to
this term

he said he'd gotten it
many times

I can't remember
how he got it
but I remember I
was impressed
that it was a thing
someone could get

you just grab it
and take it
that's the message
I received

but then I found out
it wasn't that simple

unless you're a rapist.

"My Body, My Right!"

chant the rabid
antivaxers

pushing buttons to elect
pro life white
supremacists

backed by ultra
conservative missions
to force cult superstitions
on everyone
everywhere

But lemme tell ya
what Jesus would do

he'd whip the shit
out of those fuckers
just like the moneylenders
he drove from temples
of hypocrisy

yep
he'd give those fundies
their own damn abortions
with their own damn
coat hangers

then leave them gutted
and bleeding
and bleating
with no clause at all
for incest or rape

because these days
that's the Christian
thing to do.

WORLD'S BIGGEST DOUCHEBAG

"Free at last,
Free at last,
Thank God Almighty,
I'm Free at last!"

        resigned Jerry Falwell Jr.
        invoking MLK

"Free at last,
Free at last!"

        quipped the shame of Liberty
        University

        having watched his wife
        get her freak on
        with pool boy for
        seven years

"Free at last,
Free at last!"

        he replied
        the heir to the Moral
        Majority

        (but we
        of course
        judge people by
        the content of their character)

"Free at last,
Free at last!"

        cuz Jerry Jr.
        had a dream

        (on yacht
        w/ highball in hand &
        pants unzipped)

        O poor
        Richy
        Rich.

Graduation Speech for the Class of 2022

Congratulations Graduates
on where you've been
and where you're going

take it from me
whatever you do
do it with pride
especially when
it comes to your bong

Look,
you don't want that shit
building up
then spilling all
over the rug

so change that nasty water daily
or it's gonna end up
in your bed
and you just can't get
that rank stank out

you can trust me on this
I've been toking up
for over four decades
and it hasn't affected
my productivity
whatsoever

I'm not a couch potato
I'm not moving on to heroin
I'm not antisocial
or brain damaged

in fact
I'm a model
role model
who hasn't shat
my life away

so put that in your pipe
and smoke it.

THE GREATEST DAY IN HISTORY

Following the blare
of tornado sirens
my dog and I
went into the woods

met a bunch of biology students
sampling eels
they showed us a bucket
of elvers

continuing on
we came to the confluence
of Black Creek and
the Hudson where
we saw a monster
fledgling eagle
all brown & shaggy
in apogee tree

and beneath
a beaver swimming
with a mouthful of reeds

then
to top it all off
we saw a school
of two foot carp
just treading there

and in their midst
                    a giant
                        albino
                                running with the pack
                    and looking like
                                an old ghost

another mystery
with an intangible
backstory.

Mindblowing

That always thought
in the back of the mind:

that we have cars
and farms and jungles and seas
with humans and birds and carbon dioxide
plus all that other stuff
including music and philosophy
and Cheez Whiz and history
rather than
               the alternative

but what would that
alternative be?

and how could anything
else really be?

          Anyway
after half a century
this question just
ceased to be

because you can't keep asking that
without ever getting
an adequate answer

unless, that is
you can live with narratives
that simplify
existential
complexities

and if that's who you are
don't call me.

WHERE CAMO IS A PRIMARY COLOR

"Yo bro,
you ever had a calzone?"
          I heard some dude
          ask another
          at the dog park

"Nah Brah,"
          he replied

"It's like a pizza
but all sealed up.
Had one the other day
it was sick, bro!"

"No way, brah
That's fucked up!"

Anyhow
their conversation soon fizzled
Russia invaded Ukraine
and the world returned
to normal.

POVERTY MONGERS

when you only have four channels
you end up watching
certain shows

like this pawnshop show
after the news
starring a cast
of witty white characters
in an inner city
crack neighborhood

the clientele come in
with sketchy stories
about some piece of crap
weed whacker
or a watch or
a faux gold ring

only to start
a shouting match
ending with Security
throwing someone's
ass in the street

      no thirty bucks
      no nothing

while safe inside
a family of chuckling chuckleheads
shakes its righteous head

clearly thinking
How can people be that way?
Is there no decency?
Oh the shit
      we gotta put up with…

but that's what draws
viewers in
racism
plus cruelty
being a formula for
reality
(tv)

as long as there
are mouths to feed.

Burn Burn Burn!

After reading *On the Road*
I bought a crutch
then got myself
an Ace bandage
wrapped up a knee
got out on the interstate
and stood there
dripping pity

I was nineteen years old
and making my way
from Minneapolis
to Madison

the first person who picked me up
was an older gentleman
with a beanie and a bowtie
he'd been a songwriter
who'd written hits
and he rattled off a list
of sixties bands
I can't recall

then drove me on to St. Paul
where I got a ride from
a black guy in a tank top
with a white girlfriend
and a mulatto infant up front
drinking Mountain Dew

"I gotta pick
my other baby up"
            he told me
and pulled into a pawn shop

a few minutes later
he came out
brandishing a .45

"Yessirree" he told me
"a man with twenty dollars in his pocket
can do anything"

we drove on
and he told me he'd drive all day
if he had a reason to

this was my signal
to peel back the armpit foam
revealing three holes
drilled in the crutch

each hole had a joint inside
so the three of us
smoked up

"That's a good trick"
        he told me
"I thought you was
a real cripple"

but by the time we got to Menomonie
his demeanor
had radically changed

now he wanted another joint
so I gave him my second one
and got dropped off
at a truck stop

        where I ordered a slice
        of pie à la mode

then it was back to I-94
where the crutch trick
worked again

this ride was from
some Mexican workers
they gave me a beer

and drove me to
the Wisconsin Dells

that's where some crazy white
                          bearded freak
pulled across three lanes of traffic
and skidded to a halt
in a Pinto

I ran up
embellishing limping gimp
and he already had
the pipe lit

which we smogged en route
to Portage where
we stopped at the DMV
to get his tabs renewed

this took twenty minutes
and then we were back
on the freeway again

Sammy Hagar
was blasting on the radio
and we were screaming along
with "I Can't Drive
                          55"
pounding the crap
out of the dashboard

then we arrived
at the campus
so I thanked him and
stumbled out

the dorms were high
in the sky
and so was I

on Kerouac.

"Personally Asking"

Every time I see a subject line
with these two words
I want to stab
someone's eye

mass emails are never personal
Nancy Pelosi never writes
specifically to me
nor do gun safety activists
or celebrity chefs
feeding Haitian refugees

it just pisses me off
when good causes stoop
to insult those they assume
don't care to draw a difference between

a real communication from a real human
and a scam tactic meant
for packing pockets

and you can't ever write back
such email blasts are not designed
to be received

that's not respectful
that's commercial
        bullshit biz

for whatever works
for the war you're in

which is why I'm now
personally asking
those who employs this method

to kindly go
fuck themselves.

Good Morning

nearly half the country is fascist
and they don't even know it

with no sense of history
they keep reverting
to Nazi nature

       LOCK HER UP!
       INSURGENCY!

       TRUMP WON!
       REPLACEMENT THEORY!

       BUILD THAT WALL!
       GUNS GUNS GUNS!

       GOOOOO
       PUTIN!

that's who
  we've become

half Marjorie Taylor Greene
half NPR

and when your body is
half diseased
you can't just lop
the rotten part off

so we do what
we always do

we die a slow
deserving death
of suicidal
apathy.

AND GRAVY

my roommate in the hospital
is 102

through the curtain I hear
the nurse ask
what his secret
to longevity is

"Meat and potatoes"
        he says
"and gravy"

"Ahh" she replies
        "so the secret is
            everything in moderation"

No! I think
        Meat and potatoes!

Last-Minute Show-Not-Tell Total Reversal

I am lucky to have lived a life
not just worth living
but a life that was
an epic blast

of love, beauty
euphoria and
even pain

all the words I used to
rage and teach against

Thank you, my godless
wonderworld!

PART 8

INVESTIGATIVE POETIX
EXCERPTS:
2013–2022

FROM CRYPTO-ARKANSAS

In Pursuit of the Fabled Water Panther

> "Out of the lake the Great Panther shall come."
>   —from an ancient Osage song

I'm not a "monster hunter"
  because I believe in "the supernatural"
    like most people on this planet
    I'm intrigued by underworlds
      where demons are designed
        to devour and hide

          it should therefore come as no surprise
            that out of all the Arkie crypto-creatures
              the Heber Springs Water Panther
                is the biggest pile of hogwash out there
                what did surprise me, however
                  is how truly untrue
                    this myth is

                I mean, come on:
                  a half-bigfoot half-panther
                    attacking swimmers and fishermen?

              Get real!
                  the idea isn't even
                                Judeo-Christian;
                    it goes back to the Native Americans
                    and the northern tribes at that

                    like the Chippewa
                      whose iconic image of Mishipishu
                        ("Great Underwater Wildcat")
                          was painted and carved in effigy
                            and scaped into sacred mounds
                              from Algonquia to California

as a fusion of lynx, panther
  lion, whatever
    crossed with a bison, bird
      serpent, whatever
        usually, though
          these things have horns
          and are associated with
          the Trickster figure

            like Nanabazho
              who according to mucho creation myths
              told a feral forest cat
(from the George Gustav
                to disembark his virtual ark
Heye Center, National Museum
and grab some land
 of the American Indian)

                to make a stand
                  in a completely diluvianed
                  waterworld
                      —sound familiar?

the Winnebagos called him "Medicine Beast"
 and myriad Medieval Ameri-cultures
  depicted him as a ferryman
    good for crossing yr River Styx

      "But then came the white man"   (*Gonzo Double*
        (to quote Ted Nugent's "Great White Buffalo")   *Live*, 1978)
        who dammed back the Little Red River
          in the early sixties
            thereby creating the reservoir known
              as Greers Ferry Lake

            according to Jameson's *Ozark Tales*   (2007)
           the tribes of these bottomlands
            had been terrorized for centuries
             by a bipedal spirit-monster
             known for murdering
              horses and men

especially trappers and lumberjacks
found half-eaten and dismembered
while hellish screams rang from the bluffs

until 1966
when the aqua-panther was frequently sighted
swimming and caving all over the place
it was even blamed for drowning folk
then hunkering under the mansion of
Senator John McClellan
then there's that popular scuba story;
seems back in the seventies
a diver delving into a grotto
was accosted by a super swift
"horrid, man-like form
covered with thick, dense fur"

Jameson describes it
tearing off the man's mask
and the man escaping
but not without being treated
for severe lacerations and shock

so of course I went to investigate
the shaley fracklands surrounding the lake
starting with Big Larry's Uncle Buck
who witnessed something in the eighties

it was just off Sills Peninsula
where it rose and dove like an anaconda
freaking out some fishermen
who saw it blip on a fish finder
longer than a power pole

Uncle Buck also told me
about a legendary local dog
that tried to cross the Narrows
but was dragged down
in mid-swim

I needed more than this, though
so wrote an article for the area paper
which the editors ran on the front page
calling for anyone who knew anything
about this historic water monster
to drop me a line

the only response I got
was from Edward Isom of Tumbling Shoals
who reported a six-foot-long black panther
slinking through his neighbor's yard
sporting what looked
like a Mohawk

which is interesting considering
all those ancient indigenous depictions
of razorback panther spines

of course
Edward Isom also told me
his black Lab was barking its head off
and we all know how feline fur
can serrate the sky
when a dog is going nuts

like me
not getting anything

so I visited the Swinging Bridge Boat Dock
where behind a photo of a bobcat
climbing on the river shore
an ol' boy named Troy
told me he'd never heard of no
underwater panther before

a mantra repeated by an aging angler
who'd been there all his life

same thing with Gwinn at Golden Outdoors
and all the other bait shop owners
as well as the assorted old timers
at the County Historical Society

where I looked through every single
  Cleburne County Times
    from 1970 to '79
      and couldn't find any mention of
        any alleged diver
          or any panthers whatsoever
            except for the local
              football team

        the verdict being
          exactly what a crabby old man
            on a golf cart told me:
              "Son, you're just chasing
                bullshit around!"

Catfish Creatures of the Ozarks

In October of 2007
  a slippery slimy catfishman
    arose from a tributary of the Buffalo River
     and scared the bejesus
      out of some kids

      I can verify this
       but what I can't verify
        is the story of "The Creature in the Hole"
        which Informant #41
         relayed to Richard and Judy Young
          for their collection of oral histories
(*Ozark Tall Tales*, 1989)

it happened near "the mouth of Hemmed-in Hollow"
  three teenage boys in '75
    were preparing to dive into a hole
     when a gypsy woman appeared in a flash
      and told them about a "half-man half-fish"
      attacking a swimmer a few years back

      that gypsy then disappeared
       as suddenly as she appeared
       and years later
        a scuba instructor from Missouri
        told those boys about a diver
        mauled by a fishman
        just upriver

whatever the case
  Jameson tells another tale
    with details I can't
     confirm as well   (see *Ozark Tales*, 2007)

    "According to historian Mark Rocineaux"
   (no info on him anywhere)
     something scared the Osage away
     back in 1863
      when a hunting party stopped to camp

at Hemmed-In Hollow
where down on the Buffalo
a brave beheld a half-man fish
staring "with a menacing glare"
the Indians split, never to return
the settlers settled
and that holler became a camping spot

but in July of 1887
"the Hortons and the McAlisters"   (again, no info available)
had a case of picnic panic
when their children reported
a creature in the current
sporting the body and face
of a rivercat

the Harrison newspaper archives, however
have no microfilms from that summer

as Jameson notes
"Between the 1880s and the 1930s,
most area residents avoided the area altogether"
but in 1947, two brothers
"Oscar and Curtis Williams"   (ditto, no info)
witnessed the catman
whooping up a ruckus

then in 1966
some students from the U of A
were partying down in Hemmed-In Hollow
when "Lynn Brighton and Laura Glassock"   (can't find
screamed they'd seen
any record anywhere)
an "utterly grotesque" catfish thing

Tom Rushing waded out to investigate
got grabbed by a pair of "pincer-like claws"
was hoisted high above its head
and hurled to the shore with injuries
(unsubstantiated
information)

fourteen years went by
  and in 1980 some kids skipping stones
    allegedly saw the monster approach them
      they scrammed as Robert Blankenship
(who dat?)
        glimpsed "a huge catfish
          with legs and arms"
      and that was it
        for the next few decades

      until my colleague Shelle Stormoe
        held her annual Halloween hoedown
          on the shores of Richland Creek
            fifty miles from Hemmed-In Hollow

        that year she made up a theme for the party
          about some miners who lived
            in a shitty little shanty camp
              boozed hard, fought all the time
                and defiled the stream
                  with feces and trash

        but ol' Green Nelly who lived in a cave
          snuck into their midst disguised as a pig
            and cast a curse upon the polluters
              who instantly grew whiskers and gills
                morphed into "mutant catfish men"
                  then slipped into the filthy flow

            as Shelle told me in an email later

          "we had a guy in scuba gear
            that actually hid in the creek
              to scare the kids"   (Nov 11, 2011)

              Shelle, however, never heard
                any of those manfish stories
                  basically, she was just trying to create
                    a freaky creature

which seems to be the motive
  of other vivid visionaries
    from Hollywood   (*Creature from the Black Lagoon,*
   to the Ozarks
1954)

    where the oldest, richest
     and most popular reports
      of "fabulous monsters"

        (ie, Vance Randolph's
         kingdoodles, whangdoodles
          gollywogs, etc)

       originate and propagate
       in the Arkansaw
              hillfolk
             imagination.

Arkasquatch!

Much has been made of the Fouke Monster
(pronounced like "cow"
  down in the Texarkana corner: with a K at the end)
    like t-shirts, bumper stickers
      four B
        Boggy Creek movies
          and a knee-slapping trilogy
            by Smokey Crabtree   (starting with *Smokey and*
              who told me when I interviewed him   *the Fouke Monster,* 1974)
                "If you can't help me
                  don't hurt me"
                    so I won't

              instead
                I'll concentrate on the most
                  overshadowed stories from this state;
                    the *lost,* the *dismissed*
                      tales of upright primates
                        stalking the swamps
                          mountains
                            and timbered terrain

                      where there are hundreds of accounts
                        from hundreds of citizens
                          claiming they've seen
                            a Bigfoot or two

                        so strap on your safety belts
                      because here comes the most extensive list
                        of Arkansas Sasquatch incidents
                            ever assembled
                              in postmodern
                                American
                                  crypto-verse...

Nineteenth Century

• 1834, Greene County:
  led by Col. Cross and Dr. Sullivan
    a hunting party after a cattle-marauding wild man
      reported an enormous creature
        with "long locks that fairly enveloped his neck and shoulders . . .
          leaping from twelve to fourteen
          feet at a time"
(*Arkansas Gazette, Memphis Enquirer,*

                        Gettysburg *Star and Banner,* 1851)

    • 1856, near Texarkana:
      a possé in pursuit of a "stout, athletic man . . .
        completely covered with hair"
          chased its prey onto a frozen lake
            where it fell through the ice
              but busted up on the other side
              pulled a hunter off his mount
                bit a chunk from his shoulder
                and tore an eye out   (*Caddo Gazette, New York Tribune,*
                              Wisconsin *Patriot,* 1856; *Arkansas*
                             Gazette, June 27, 1971)

Early Twentieth Century

• 1920, Logan County:
  a "Hairy manlike creature" was observed
    harassing a horse;
      a witness having seeing   (Bigfoot Field Researchers Organization,
        "something similar on . . . Pilot Mountain (knob)   bfro.net, report # 4088)
          a few years before"

    • 1943, Lonoke County:
      a bus traveling from Memphis to Fort Smith
        stopped so the driver could urinate
          but he leapt back in
            said, "Hold on everybody,
              there's a big ape out there that almost got me!"

                the bus took off and years later
                  quite a few riders reported
                    a "big foot crossing the road"   (BFRO report # 4088)

• 1960, near Madison County:
  a 94-year-old Ozarkian
    reported topping a ridge in his car
      then seeing a "large, human-like" being
        heading up the slope
          "covered with dark greyish colored hair,
            except on its forehead"
              which was "nearly white"

              it appeared to be "very old,
                and in very poor condition"
    (Reclusive Forest Primate Research Project,
              upon further investigation   alabamabigfoot.com, report # 25)
                multiple tracks were discovered

    • 1960 or 1961, three miles west of Rush:
        a resident saw "a very large, dark man-like figure . . .
          covered with black or dark brown hair"
            making for his chicken coup

            a foal went missing
              so witnesses hid on top of a shed
                which an alleged NAPE   (North American Primate)
                  shook that very night   (RFPRP report # 002AR06—60)

      • 1961, Lee County:
          an eleven-year-old boy described
            a "very tall [creature with] long wavy hair . . .
              looking in the ditches"

      the boy yelled for his mother and sister
        and the grrrr-liath scrammed into the woods
          where a massive footprint
            was gawked upon   (BFRO report # 7234)

          • 1969, Little River County:
              while camping out in Cottonwood Shoals
                a family dog began acting funny
                  the mother went to "take a leek"   [sic]

and began screaming
while the oldest brother started shooting
at a seven-foot Arkayeti
circling the camp
with a pointy head
and glowing eyes   (BFRO report # 1944)

1970s

- 1970, Madison County:
  two boys riding in the back of a pickup
    saw what they thought was a blasted tree
      but then it started taking large strides
        the fur was supposedly
        "dark brown in color,
          longish but not dangling,
            and it had red eyes"   (BFRO report # 2957)

        - 1971, Logan County:
          motorists spotted "a small primate
            standing on two feet beside the road"
              looking like a chimpanzee   (RFPRP report # 17)

- 1972, near the same location:
  a driver stopped to fix his car
  and was approached by an apey entity
    "covered in hair and walking like a man"   (*Ibid*)

        - 1975, near Jacksonville:
          a child on the Air Force base
            saw a furry figure hulking through the trees
              with a "flattened nose and pointed head"   (BFRO report # 10919)

          - 1975, thirty-five miles west of Hot Springs:
            two brothers were eating Spaghetti-Os
              when something resembling
                "a dirty old hairy hippie with glowing eyes"
                  glared through the window
                    then rocked the trailer
                      and busted the steps;   (Texas Bigfoot Research Conservancy,
                    a mongo footprint in the dust   texasbigfoot.com, report # 03080016)

- 1975, near El Dorado:
  while exploring a motorcycle trail
    a couple kids on bicycles
      saw "an 8 foot black figure"
        watching from behind a tree
          a "head crest" was noted

as the boys bolted
    and the creature gave chase   (BFRO report # 3143)

      • 1977, on the outskirts of Squirrel:
        a gigantopithecus was glimpsed
          ambling through an electric fence
            "like it was honey suckle vine"   (BFRO report # 4093)

          • 1979, near Coal Hill:
            two boys saw "a large man
              squatting on the rail road tracks"
                but then it rose to "8 feet in height"

the kids fled, recalling how an uncle
  "driving across the bridge on 64"
    stopped when a wookie
      "hit the hood with his arms
        then roared and ran "into
          the river bottoms"   (TBRC report # 03080009)

1980s

• 1980, Lake Conway:
  out fishing, an eleven-year-old and his father
    heard limbs cracking
      as a seven-foot "bigfoot"
        emerged from the brush
          it "was absolutely   (TRBC report # not listed
            not aggressive"   but available at texasbigfoot.com/FaulknerCOAR1.htm)

  • 1981, near Siloam Springs:
    a teenager on his way to work
      saw "something by the bridge"
        he identified as a Bigfoot
          "digging at the ground"   (BFRO report # 6178)

    • 1984, between Gurdon and Prescott:
      a railroad worker saw something bipedal
        "maybe 8 ft. high"
          he also heard "some type of growling"
            like "the gobble" of a "shack tube"   (BFRO report # 3519)
          • 1985, south of Mena:
            rounding a bend, a woman and her ex
              almost T-boned a "huge figure
                7 to 8 feet tall"   (TRBC report # 03090006)
                  just standing there w/ outstretched arms

  • 1985, near Rocky Branch:
    two gynormous forest dwelling primates
      were reported "wrestling,
        grappling and roaring
          as if in mortal combat"   (TBRC report # 03080019)

    • 1985, Ozark National Forest:
      someone gathering ginseng roots
        saw what appeared to be
          a man in a fur coat
            so got "the hell out of Dodge"
              but went back later
                and found some big-ass tracks   (TBRC report # 03080012)

• 1986, near Bradford:
    a child saw a hoary *sapien*
      dashing through a field
  its hands "straight down and flat"   (BFRO report # 9753)

• 1988, Greene County near Paragould:
  a couple making out behind a school
    spotted a nine-foot-tall silhouette
      swaying behind a chain-link fence   (BFRO report # 2744)

    • 1988, Sebastian County:
      a fisherman fishing near Huntington
        beheld an eight-foot man-like creature
        making "whoooop whoooop" sounds
        and smacking the ground

        this person also noted
        "Its face was very long
          with a very pronounced lower lip,
          almost like the orangutan
      that Clint Eastwood had as a side-kick"   (BFRO report # 8527)

1990s

- 1990, Ouachita National Forest:
  workers repairing a power line
        reported a "large hair-covered,   (RFPRP report # unlisted but available at
            man-like creature"   alabamabigfoot.com/bigfoot/reports/
              hunching along Lake Winona   RFPreportSC1.htm)

    - 1992, near Hot Springs:
        two friends parked at Lake Hamilton
          heard noises that sounded like cats fighting
            then witnessed a gorilla-guy
              "covered in fur or hair"   (BFRO report # 24254)

      - 1992 or 1993, Saline County:
          a boy who heard what sounded like a woman screaming
            saw a "large hair-covered" apeman
              rubbing up against a tree   (RFPRP report # 14)

        - 1994, Benton County:
            a good ole boy out four-wheeling
              "seen the boog foot walking"
                it appeared to be
                  "7–8 feet tall"   (BFRO report # 7045)

          - 1994, Little River County:
              a hunter walking the RR tracks
                heard branches breaking in the brush
                  as a "large black figure"
                    with a skunky stank
                      emerged from the woods
                        so he hid in a coal car
having camped in a Bronco a few years back
    when something "rocked the vehicle"
      he was pretty sure
        it was the "Gun Flats Booger"   (TBRC report # 03090010)
          - 1994, near Eureka Springs:
              the child from the '75 Jacksonville sighting (now an adult)
                got a gander at a Bigfoot in his brights
                  three other witnesses
                    backed up this report   (BFRO report # 9507)

897

• 1994, the Ouachitas:
    chillaxing on a logging road
      a teetotaler was shocked to see
        a totally "human-like creature"
          tearing down the mountain on all fours
"throwing large rocks and logs from its path"   (RFPRP report # 46)

      • 1995, Ozark National Forest:
        a passenger in a car spotted
          "a very large grey form"
            trekking up the side of a hill   (FPRP report # 23)

        • 1996, outside of Arkadelphia:
          a "very tall creature" in a pasture
           spooked "the cows pretty bad"
           so a farmer called the cops
            on whatever'd been killing
              cattle in that spot   (BFRO report # 1638)

          •1996, north of Ozark:
          three siblings who'd hiked in Cat Holler
          told their brother they'd seen "an ape"
             hanging out by a run-down house

the next morning they went to check it out
    and saw "a small black" monkeyman
      "standing on the porch"   (RFPRP report # 17)

      • 1999, Saline County:
        a poacher was cited
          for taking potshots
          at a Bigfoot

          police corporal Oscar Gerard Jr.
           "explained that shooting at a Sasquatch
             was just as bad as shooting at a deer
              seeing as how it would be endangered"
    if it existed   (*Arkansas Wildlife,*

Nov-Dec 2009)

• 2001, near Herbine and Rison:
   the "odor of raw sewage and rotting meat"
     was sensed by someone who identified
       something "about 8 feet high
         [with] long, ape like arms"   (BFRO report # 2931)

      • 2002, south of Low Gap:
        after hearing the sound of a hollow log
          being repeatedly struck by a rock
            a small game hunter came across
              a squatting grunting manimal
                defecating in the woods
                   so grabbed his semi-auto rifle
                  and emptied his clip
                  into it

with the jumbo shagman hot on his heels
   the hunter made it to his truck
     which he crashed in his rush
       to escape a raging ape   (RFPRP report # 24)

      • 2002, Pig Trail National Scenic Byway:
        a "well known" musician from NW AR
          saw "a large, dark colored, humanish-like figure"
            standing in the road
              he got within thirty yards
               and it sprinted off   (RFPRP report # 22)

        • 2002, swamp near El Dorado:
          a squirrel hunter got "a whiff
            of the most foul odor" he ever smelled
              then heard "growling type sounds"
              and three squealing hoots
                as a "tall reddish looking creature"
                  vanished in the woods   (BFRO report # 10913)

   • 2002, Washington County:
     while hanging out in a creek bed
       two friends met a big brown oranguthang

the width of a refrigerator
with a "real long head"   (BFRO report # 5316)

• 2003, Cleveland County:
a guy on the shoulder taking a whiz
smelled "a very strong odor"
then saw a "hairy creature
7 to 8 feet tall"   (BFRO report # 18972)

• 2003, near Russelville:
since something was upsetting the cows
a rancher and his grandfather
grabbed a pair of binoculars
then drove to the watering pond
where they watched "a very large man . . .
around 8 feet tall"
turn and walk away   (BFRO report # 7815)

• 2005, Hot Springs County:
a man spotted something that looked like "an ape"
rapidly traversing a fence line   (BFRO report # 13211)
—go figure

• 2005, McConnel Ridge:
two young coon hunters heard
a "very loud, monkey-like screaming"
so abandoned their dog
but returned with more firepower
only to encounter
"an unusual and obnoxious odor"
the dog came home later
torn up and whimpering   (RFPRP report # 19)

• 2006, near Crosset:
a married couple in a car
almost hit a towering critter
that "was NOT a bear!"
but it did have
"bright and piercing" eyes   (TBRC report # 03080003)

• 2006, Poinsett County:
   a man on a riding mower
     towing his dog in a small trailer
      ran into "a really tall man
       with hair entangled in briars and leaves"
        this witness recounted his father describing
       something in the night like
      a cross between a lady and
       a panther screaming   (TBRC report # 03080018)

• 2006, Lafayette County:
  an angler near the Red River
   was startled by what sounded
    like a cow crossed with a cougar
    then saw a colossus
     "9 feet tall"   (TBRC report # 03080013)

   • 2007, Woodruff County:
    while running "dogs on rabbits"
     a hunter witnessed something
     "as tall and wide as a standard door . . .
      6'8 - 7'0 tall and 36" - 40" wide"   (RFPRP report # 70)

• 2008, foothills of the Caddo Mountains:
 the carcasses of mutilated deer
  were discovered with an injured dog
   a 200-pound Rottweiler was found as well
    with its back legs torn plumb off
    this occurred by a Bigfoot baiting site
     where sheep had been reported missing
     an eighteen-inch track was also found
     smushed into an anthill   (RFPRP report # 62)

   • 2008, Arkansas County:
    three off-duty cops
     fishing for crappie on Old River Lake
      smelled "a bad smell like body odor"
      then saw a hirsute human
      gripping a fish
      in its mouth   (TBRC report # 03080034)

• 2010, Grant County:
  through a 24X range-finder scope
    an old timer spotted an upright monsto-man
      making off with a small dog or pig
        while two other witnesses
          ogled through binoculars
            describing it as "burnt brown
              with stringy looking hair"   (RFPRP report # 71)

And that ain't even the half of it—
  since I refrained from listing
    all incidents from Mercer Bayou
      Miller County and
        the Sulphur River Bottoms
          which have had enough publicity

I also left out numerous sightings
 from numerous frequently cited sources
  that our regional Squatch authority
   Tal H. Branco
    (who I interviewed twice)
     considers untrustworthy

     So what do I make of all this?
      Absolutely Nothing!
       This study is kaput, I'm through with it

        but you can still read all about it
         in *Proze Attack*   (Six Gallery Press, 2010)
          or just come to
           your own conclusions

              like every human who ever evolved
             from another form of what some primates
              have faith is still out there

              leaving us with enigmatic prints
             random tufts of mysterious fur
              bizarre recording
               and blurry film

               but mostly
              flat out pranks and narratives
                of our own
                 DNA.

From *GLURK! A Hellbender Odyssey*

XVI. All Hail the Ron Goellner
Center for Hellbender Conservation

at the St. Louis Zoo
WildCare Institute
where deep in Herpetarium
a decade of Glurkiolgy
has led to an amphi
Revolution

      this state of the art
      Ozark Hellbender Headquarters
      (a "flagship species" of the zoo)
      is the only place on the planet
      where these squeegee-skinned
      baby branchoids
      have been bred in captivity

          it took years of finding
          the balance betwixt
          hard and soft water
          replicating conditions in nature
          harvesting eggs from the field
          experimenting w/ hellbender huts
          & triggering Conceptio

      a thousand were raised in 2014
      and they're aiming for the same
      in '015
mission is
to find the decline
in order to preserve
various crashing crypto-clans
      to the point that there are now
      way more benders of Ozark hell
      in this facility
          (which is dedicated exclusively
          to reintro and repop)
      than actually exist
      in das Wild

XVII. Into the Belly of the Beast

Zoological Manager Mark Wanner
gave me a tour
starting with the Hall of Quarantine

    where feeder fish chill for three weeks
    in pretreated aquariums
    and ghost shrimps go
    thru an anti ick
    sodium dip

    contamination is no joke
    we even clean our soles
    in a scrub tub of chemicals
    before passing through
    the glurkin' gates

to the main chamber
where three full-time staffers
are supported by interns and volunteers
feeding and adjusting
watching where the water's at
    there are tons of tanks lining all walls
    jam-packed w/ all sizes
    of both Eastern and Ozarkians
        though the Ozarks are more colorful
        but whatever sub
        species they are
        the young-of-year clump up
        jet-black and smooth of skin
        glumming from PVC pipes
        tubes and bubblers everywhere
            they're tagged with chips
            and flagged for infection
            only those free of disease
            are released at five
            or six inches long

in 2013
seven hundred and six
zoo-reared juvies
were freed in native habitats
w/ consistent figures
following that
       meanwhile
       cuddly cuties grub in a pack
       chowing down like a bunch of pups
       gobbling for liberty

XVIII. Rewilding in Absentia

hoofing on
we arrive at the first
indoor bender river system
a thirty two foot
North Fork simulation

where the first lab-born
benders were born
into a climate controlled
aqueous vision

                                    the H_2O temperature
                            mimics what's up w/ the elements
                                    happening in real time
                        the lights are set to reflect the levant
                                    to dim and illumify
                                    to incorporate shadows
                            cast by the pineline on the shore
                                    when it rains outside

sprinklers

                                                    precipitate

& as the current flows continuously
in this totally protected
replication of a perfect system
a nest box is visible
                        it's a squat
                                    concrete

under-tunnel
                        leading to a mating cave
                            w/ a port for removing

                                        the rosary beads
                                    of future breeds
                    this is where it all started
                        back in 2006/2007
                    this is where I ask
            my burning question of Bendery:

"So if the communal scientific consensus is that there are only 590
Ozark benders being free (at last count)
and if the cryptobrancho authorities
actually foresee these species
not lasting three decades
will all this effort
really pay off?"
and the answer, of course
is as evident as the fervor
in this massive
bunker of Glurk:
"That's what we're shooting for"
Mark tells me w/ a shrug
suggesting he isn't totally certain
but they sure as hell
ain't gonna stop

XIX. Awaiting the Next Eureka

más tanks
muy spawn
a towering Babylon
of incubating eggs
tiered w/ aeration
to mimic the males
rocking haunches
flubbering flaps
then more more & archives more
an entire living library
of highly imperiled
bendographics
dynasties of DNA
galleries of glurkery
the most massive
impressive
collection of snot
otters on the planet
culminating in two   parallel
forty foot long six foot deep
outdoor Ozark river systems
one for North Forkers
the other for Eleven Points

to keep the gene pools partisan
because there just might be
more subspecies than we think

I heard it from my colleague Don Shepard
Salamander Savant at U Louisiana at Monroe
& now I'm hearing it from
the Ron Goellner Center:
it's looking like there could be
way more glurking strains
up in them thar
hillbilly hills
so stay tuned to the St. Louis Zoo
for the next major
hellbender breakthrough!

XX. More Discovery = More Responsibility

Yep, there might be four
or even eight
genetically unique
gene pools of Ozarkians
which is more than just an epiphany
it's a satori of salamanderous significance
that will no doubt revise the science
of an entire eco-niche
more importantly
in cahoots with Arkansas Game and Fish
and the Missouri Department of Conservation
the Ron Goellner Center releases
hundreds of hellions per year
some are recaught and accounted for
but most just disappear
where they go, nobody knows
in fact, nobody knows
where the eclectic
wild child hides

what we do know though
is that 600 divided by four
means a whole lot more
of a whole lot less
true chromosomal homes

so if you cross
the Current w/ the White
or Eleven Points w/ other sources
of hellbending habitat
then you homogenize
specific genetics
potentially
that's what we're looking at
more exact helixes
to study and protect
so therefore more
genomics to stock

meaning more urgent work to do
as even more species go to hell
in a glurking handbasket

XXI. Hence in Hellbendia…

and in Allegheny specifically
there are hatcheries where glurkers glom
glumming up to nine inches long
and are then released
as refugees

radio-tags have been implanted
to track the Easterns through the Glurk
only to find that four to eight
percent continue
to survive

"Best Management Practices" however
have been developed for the lumber industry
addressing construction of logging docks
unpaved roads
skid trails
& fire breaks

                still
                these BMPs are just "suggested"

                but outreach is on the rise
                some are sent to parks and zoos
                even Indian reservations
                for research & education

the PR of Mass Bendery
also targets local schools and hunting shows
where biologists have doubled down on Glurkitude
additionally
signs have been placed in the public eye
telling recreationists
to leave the under-rocks alone
and to let harmless
hellbenders be

                        which has actually led to fishermen
                            releasing and reporting them
                            rather than smashing
                            their glurking heads
                        —which used to be the norm

XXII. Keeping It Real

Indiana is currently
establishing baseline conditions
for awareness and perceptions
of the benders in their midst
and data from these efforts
is now being analyzed
to evaluate effectiveness
helpthehellbender.org
was launched back in 2012
this "clearinghouse for hellbender info"
lists actions locals can take
in the meantime
educators can request
classroom presentations
plus posters and stickers
for the kids
      —as Purdue U offers
      electronic field trips
      focused on genetics
      which reach over 4000 studii per year
      from 350 schools
      spanning 28 states
      —as publicity teams collaborate
      w/ community colleges from other states

      —as a mascot named Herbie the Hellbender
      shows up at civic events
      handing out bobbers touting the slogan
            "HELP THE HELLBENDER
            CUT THE LINE"

XXIII. Speaking of Fishing

(the unfounded fear of coming in contact
w/ the slick of bender slime
goes back to a bunk mythology
from an old time Seneca saying
that "hellbenders got
the devil in them")
((the mucous released w/ adrenaline
can indeed be lethal to white mice
but for paws and claws
it's more of a gooey
gluey substance
that deters because
it's hard to rub off))
[hellbender slime
has also been rumored
to be shockingly electric
but that's just more
bogusness]

{of course
there's a universal paranoia
among misinformed adamant anglers
that pretty much all bottom feeders
w/ a face that only a mother could love
are out to devour
mucho gamefish populations
starting with their nests}

//but as of yet
no roe has been discovered
in any hell-eesophagi//

<<as for leaving a hook
in intestines
highly acidic stomach acids
dissolve steel
in due time>>

XXIV. Empire & Independence

New York is currently developing
a smartphone app
to report benders
helling in their habitats
>   NY also has a mascot costume
>   housed at the Buffalo Zoo
>   to spread the Gospel of the Glurk

>   local tribes
>   are now raising benders
>   as are zoos in the Bronx and Rochester
>   to supplement the Appalachian
>   populations
>   trying to get by

Pennsylvania   on the other hand
has produced the first
>   student run
>   public school
>   research facility
for amphibians
in the world

>   the Clarion Limestone Research Center
>   studies the crashes & crises
>   affecting Salamundio
>   they also have an artificial river system
>   waiting for inhabitants
>   from the Crypto
>   Glurkisphere

XXV. Pimp My Hellbender:
More Than Just a Lesson
In sustainability

North Carolina's
Wildlife Resources Commission and
the NC Zoological Park
have teamed up to assess
hellbender status and habitat

they speak w/ anglers and landowners
gain river access and conduct surveys
on the importance of benders as bio-indicators
and they frame these discussions
in terms of both
glurkers & trout
Rocky the actual hellbender
appears at regular festival gigs
where hell-face-paintings take place
enviro info is handed out
and ambassadors of Glurkery
speak proudly & publicly

while Snotty the Snot Otter
(another mascot)
strolls amidst the masses
generating buzz
& over at the Zoo
the gift shop sells
hellbender shirts
hellbender buttons
and decals to promote
hellbender consciousness
by providing a makeover

ie, posters proclaiming
"UGLY'S ONLY SKIN DEEP"
in which cartoon glurkers
pose with a panda mask
and snuggle up in swaddling clothes

of course, this highly successful model
can be applied to other creatures
commonly perceived as out of grace
to strike a balance in the Wild

XXVI. The Volunteer State
Steps to the Plate

the Tennessee Wildlife Resources Agency
& the Tennessee Hellbender Recovery Partnership
recently won a prestigious
State Wildlife Action Award
in excellence in leadership
  for the preservation
of Eastern glurks

                                        "environmental DNA"
  a revolutionary   quasi-forensic   detection system
        for shed genetic material   has been applied
                    to pinpoint populations
a new cryopreservation technique   employs the first ever
            Gene Bank of Amphibia   w/ hormonal induction
                    to artificially   ferlitizate

raging Ranaviruses   are also being studied
        and there's a fifty-foot   bio-bayou
  at the Chattanoogazoo   to copy what
  St. Louis   do do
                    (captive-breeding-wise)
Lee University   has teamed up with the Nashville Zoo   Middle Tennessee U
Project Orianne   San Francisco State   & an Aussie Antwerpian
in order to collaborate   on hellbendy   initiatives
                    meanwhile the T   WRA
        has launched an eReg   awareness campaign   to inform &
destigmatize   while encouraging

                                            quick release

            the big news though   is from 2012
            when the Nville Zoo   bred the first
            captive Easterns   in existence

But where   O Nashville
is yr country western ballad   of the benders birthed
                    in Tennessee?

XXVII. Doors to a *Justitia-Omnibus-*
Old-Dominion-Buckeye-Style
Benderpalooza
of PC
PR

• DC's Hellbender Brewery
                    hosts a "Suds n' Salamanders" event
        at the Smithsonian National Zoo
                        where the Haunted Salamander Lab
            allows visitors to observe
                            glurkers glurking in the night
    • the VA Dept. of Game and Inland Fisheries
        has developed a field-based program
    for hellbender publicity
                        in which 400 annual children
                            learn about crypto-physio-
                                ecology

            while a plastic hellbender statue
                            tours the world
                spreading "Hellbender Fever"
            wherever it goes
    • Ohio's brainchild
    the "IF YOU SEE THIS SALAMANDER, LET US KNOW"
            business card
    is making the rounds to fishermen

                            surveyed in the field
                live exhibits of hardy hellbenders
        are featured at the Columbus and Toledo zoos
                w/ info on dilemmary
            & property owners are now witness
            to transmitter implant surgeries
                        in their own front yards;
                    the photographs they take
            spark stories and memories
                            especially w/ kids

so to plagiarize (and improve)
on the lyrics of Jim Morrison:

hellbenders bleeding
on dawn's early highway
crowd the child's
eggshell mind

XXVIII. But Back to Ozarkia

where the Ozark Hellbender Working Group
initiates studies and cooperates on field work
  w/ researchers from
  federal and state agencies
  zoos and the academy
  nonprofit orgs
  and random eco
  individs

thereby developing
a propagation protocol
through watershed
protectification
  populations are monitored for fitness
  captive "head-starters" are raised for release
  local law enforce and landowners
  watch for suspicious activities
  as specialists test
  for hell-sperm quality
  metal levels
  eggcetera

  the University of Missouri—Rolla
  has been evaluating system strength
  hormones and contaminants
  thru hematology & serum work

  plus U-Mizzou is in collab
  w/ the MO DNR
  studying movement and survival patterns
  there's also an outline for the recovery of Ozark Hellbendiness
  promoting "near-term recovery actions"
  while providing "range-wide conservation context"
  for the US Fish & Wildlife Service

Jeff Briggler *et al.*
wrote the *Hellbender Conservation Strategy* (2010)
the Bible of Hellbendery
for a super powered partnership

of the AGFC, the MDC
the ADEQ, the NPS
the USFS
and, of course
the SLZ

(see Section XVI)
would you like some fries with that?

XXIX. Bendermania Disclaimia

and yea this sort of active interest   is taking place
                                                all across Amerigo

      hellbender distribution   is being tracked
      in West Virginia, South Carolina Kentucky, Mississippi
      and Alabama databases

                                                the Columbus Zoo
      is currently working   with eDNA
      while West Virginia   and Maryland
      test habitat   augmentation
      reintroduction   and bender rearing
      from wild eggs
video borescopes   to document nesting sites
are happening in O-hio   where water samples are
being filtered

for genetic samples   as they are in KY streams
where riparian habitats   are being preserved

      trapping has been tried   in Alabama
survey samples are underway   and a correlation has been found
between bender abundance   and land use patterns in GA

where population trends   are under study
& buying an eagle   license plate   helps
fund   hellbender conservation

a museum-run   natural heritage program
monitors the growth & decline   of Mississippi's
glurkographics

from New England to the Ozarks   protected statuses have been granted

and then there are researchers   from Texas to Florida
      from Arizona to Purdue   as well as the eco-media
      from every place   to cyberspace
      hopping on   the hell-wagon

because
to quote eco-blogger Jenni Veal   (nooga.com)

"North America's largest salamander   is a rockstar within
                                             the scientific community"

            which may or may not be true   depending on whether   you
            see these poster children   for extirpation
as celebrities   or canaries

                        but   and
                        unfortunately
                        this list can't
                        keep going on

                                    not here
                                    not now
                                    not in this
                                    limitedness

                        where quite a few geographies
                        and quite a few agencies
                        invested in myriad
                        bender biotics
                        are being bypassed
                        in this

                                    chance
                                    glance

                        & so
                        in casting this ephemeral net
                        it's time to stick a fork in it

                        —w/ sincere regrets,
                            yr hardly humble
                                narrator.

XXX. Listen, Chuck,

what it all comes down to
is that the prospect of a warming climate
is the albatross of Hellbendage
      threat of drought & less cold currents
      are confusing insect hatching times
      which are now combining
      w/ a plethora of other factors
      to make rivers in
                hospitable
      some studies say
      glurkers only have
      twenty years
      whereas others report
      a soaring probability
      of impending extinction
      coming to a stream near you
as Salamander Super Scientist
Dr. David B. Wake remarks
      "Human population growth
      and all that flows from it,
      from basic habitat destruction
      to global climate change"
      is the biggest threat
      for benders in this century
(*Salamander News*, no. 2, Feb 2014)

when asked in what ways the public can assist
he replies "First and foremost,
work for human population control"
before working on habitat
preservation or restoration

                but even more importantly
                he adds
                admit "that WE
                are the problem."

From *Cryptozarkia*

After the Blue Humans

I

Blowing Cave
near Cushman Arkansas
was a different type
of investigation

    the Ozark enigmas here
    were not spawned
    by nineteenth century settlers
    musing on mutant
    woodland creatures
    or aquatic anomalies

    meaning farmers sighting
    wampy hoopy hybrids or
    mashups from the natural world
        clashing avec
    "civilization"

    but come instead
    from a much more recent
    literary trend

    of a world war era
    sci fi mania
    embedding itself
    in the communal
    hippocampus

I'm talking azure aliens with
    oversized noggins
    bubble eyes and
    ESP

straight from the pages
of *Amazing Stories*

a fantasy mag from the forties
making for a new
     perverted
     oral tradition

of supernatural narratives
based on pulp
publications

rather than the telephone game
of boogie cryptids
in our midst

Meanwhile
speleological
speculations
remain in the internet age
as enduring as
the cult of Q

          II

                    Thus our descent

                        into the maw
               renowned for encounters
                  with "blue humans"

          according to Land and Farm Real Estate
          this "Native American archeological site
             of significant historical importance
          [with] thousands of Indian artifacts . . .

          [is] famous for the spring fed creek . . .
     and rooms containing lakes and waterfalls . . .
(listing 8480590)   full of spirits . .
. who made this a home"   nine thousand
                        years ago

                                                          then
                                        after eons of sacred
                                           rituals and burials

                                   came turn of the century
                                                fancy dances
                                                   gala balls
                                          and legends of lost
                                            Confederate gold
                                       complete with myths
                                               of Jesse James

                                          it was all before us
                                               all below us
                                        awaiting our literal
                                                     baptism

III

All helmeted, headlamped
and longjohned in polyester
we arrived in December:
        Minnow Bucket
        his brother Gene
        & me

        w/ Destany as our guide
                a middle school teacher
                children's author
                and avid caver

        all of us ready
        to spelunk

IV

into the gorge
vast and gaping

past chiefs and elders
bulldozered over
to prevent further
pilfering

past twelve thousand years
of Dalton points
and other arrow
heads galore

now mudded under
centuries of graffitied stone
emblazoned by ravers
missing students
medevaced trespassers
and methed out outlaws
on the lam

to the padlocked gates
of innerworld lore
where Destany
held the key

V

down down
into the ground

    stalagmites
    stalactites
    an inscription from 19
    24

to a grand and glimmering
gilded cathedral
domed with living
        liquid
        fungi
            sparkling like iron pyrite

down down
into the bowels
of crystalline
conglomerations
random slabs
and rubble where

a secret path
through breakdown leads
to a passage dating back

to Edgar Rice Burroughs'
Pellucidar series
        popularized in the nineteen teens

the original "Hollow Earth" fiction
of monsters, mazeways
and ancient cities
filled with saber-tooth tigers
and naked maidens

an idea appropriated
decades later
by opportunist Richard Shaver
who populated his inner space
from outer space
with "Hobloks" sporting
       "pipe-stem arms and legs,
pot bellies, [and] huge protruding eyes"   (*The Shaver Mystery, Book One,* 21)

and robots
       "standing erect on four short jointed legs"   (*Ibid.,* 32)

and snail men
       with "long, lumpy brown bod[ies]"   (*Ibid.,* 35)

and shades of Jabba
       the "great hulk Mula"   (*Ibid.,* 38)

plus freak species
       "hindquarters web-footed . . .
       [backs] maned with queer spines,"   (*Ibid.,* 66–67)
crazy old witches,
"dwarfish" beings,   (*Ibid.,* 91)
and bizarro things
with "rainbow wings"   (*Ibid.,* 115)

all embellished
by the once institutionalized mind
of a serialized
    paranormal
    space monkey
    junky

whose followers found a cave
so sought a connection
to his lore

      regardless if it's
fiction or not

VI

meanwhile
we kept delving
through crevices, cracks
splits & fissures

wrenching muscles
tearing tendons
squiggling in
and shimmying on

down down
into creepy
claustro town

visions of maddened
miners scrambling

flashes of earthquake
victims wailing

to the first pool room
of amphibious larvae
chilling in the trickle stream

17 to be exact
and 41 in the next;
data recorded
by Destany

In the past
reckless crews
just stomped on through
desecrating ponds of spawn

but now
Salamandria
rises again!

VII

According to the literature
an alias named Branton   (derived from real name <u>Bru</u>ce Al<u>an</u> Wal<u>ton</u>)
published a book entitled
The Underground Empire   (no copyright date
                                                          whatsoever)
          which ain't available anywhere
          except on a bunch of
          self-published files
          posted on a gratis website   (angelfire.com/nm2/aona/branton2.html)
                    (the signature forum
                    of crypto shysters)

Anyway
          "the author of the Branton Files,
          a series of documents
          espousing various conspiracy theories"   (frankensaurus.com)

reported on an expedition
into Blowing Cave
in the fifties

where a "side passage" led
an unverified human named David L
to a "glass cave"
miles under crust

with George Wight
          (or "Wright"
          in other publications)
a bona fide
"UFO buff"   (facebook.com/377858655616927)

to a phosphorescent artery
where following a green fluorescence
          "they . . . found themselves face-to-face with a group of human-like beings who stood
          around 7 to 8 feet tall. 'Their' skin had a faint pale-bluish, almost clay-bluish tint to it
          and their eyes were relatively large and owl-like"

these "direct descendants of Noah"
communicated through
an "electronic 'translator'"
which divulged all sorts
of mind-blowing intel

       that David L brought back to the surface
       along with a "giant cave moth"
       which abruptly crumbled into dust

Ultimately
these discoveries were revealed
to "the now late
Charles A. Marcoux"
while Wight/Wright
stayed below

       According to Branton
       "The peculiar thing about this incident . . . was that shortly after Wight had joined
       [the] underground society all evidence and records of him ever existing began to
       mysteriously disappear from the surface. Birth certificates, school records, computer
       records, bank records, etc. all seemed to vanish, apparently the work of someone in a
       very influential
        position who was able to erase all evidence that Wight had ever lived. Some research-
       ers still retain copies of George Wight's articles from the old UFO periodical, never-
       theless. This would open up the possibility that this underground race closely moni-
       tors events on the surface, and even has 'workers' in various influential positions who
       act as mediators in surface society."
                                        (ufoexperiences.blogspot.com)

       the result being
       all this hoo-ha
       posted in the nineties
       found enough thrust
       to spiral viral

       which is how the blue humans
       became another
       Ozark attraction

for anyone willing
to forego logic

in favor of testing
the improbable Kool-Aid
of the fantastic

VIII

down

down

down

down

in and out
of the Railroad Room
with rusty spikes
nailed in walls
securing lines
for clamber climb

down

down

down

down

back in time

to the center of
the cavern mind

down

down

down

to the Potato Masher
a spasm chasm
of gastric contraction
dropping into
Oblivion

and down

and down

and down

another quarter mile
to the hamburgering of
the Meat Grinder
a nerve mashing
triangular passage
with a twenty two inch
hypotenuse

a brutal
bruising
birth canal
definitely not
for those who fear
the *SKRONCH* of being
skrunched alive

& down

& down

                                                    & down

                                                    & down

                                          to the facts behind
                                                apocrypha

           IX

According to numerous secondhand sources
         "many people believed the [subworld] story . . .
         One of these believers was Charles Marcoux . . .
         [who] appears to have been told
         either by the mysterious David L or Mr. Wight
         that the Blowing Cave was an entrance to
         the underground world described by Shaver"   (drjbn.wordpress.com)

the details then
get muddled and confused:

Marcoux was said
to have led a trek in '66
in which contact was made
with the teros

         the "good" blue humans
         as opposed to the deros
         the "bad guys, so to speak"   (*Shavertron*, Vol. 2, 200)

Now flash forward to the eighties
when such narratives were distributed
through zines prompting
a surge in interest

all at a time
when Marcoux purportedly
held W[r]ight's "'lost' diary"   (*Ibid.*, 92)
confirming Marcoux's rendezvous
with blue humans

Hence
"Marcoux and his wife
 moved to Cushman in 1983"
 with W[r]ight's notes and map
 and a team was formed
 to descend again

but while "visiting the land
around the cave"   (facebook.com/377858655616927)
Marcoux got stung
by a swarm of bees
          launching a fatal
          heart attack
the moral of this story being
any of the hypotheses
espoused by Shaver's
culture of absurdities

          ie
          "We are under mental control
           by underworld peoples using
           ancient telaug devices.

          Hitler was a puppet doing the telaug's bidding.
          Himmler . . . was following orders.
          And Stalin too."   (*Shavertron*, Vol. 2, 206)

          In other words
          take your pick
          of stupid shit

          and pretend there's
          an answer in it

X

                                                   down

down

down

           further underground

              into more
          salamandy pools

      both common cave (tangerine)
and dark-sided (brownish green)
        but always speckled
          with black spots

       where slogging through
      the waist deep current
        sometimes stooping
        sometimes slipping
         but always aqua
           ambulating

        past ceilings studded
        with lines of spiny
           cicle teeth

        thru chambers full
         of flapping bats

         and bright white
          albinopedes
we heard the thrumming
         hum of drums

         along with vague
           wavy voices
warbling from watersounds

         distant drippings
          plipping up

XI

* drip *

       the Cold War notion of space aliens
       being symbolic of "the Other"
       is why the idea
       of extraterrestrials
       held such truck
       during and after
       McCarthyism

           when comic book and sci fi covers
           reflected an US v. them
           mentality

* plip *

       a thought I now
       gotta reject
       when considering the shamans
       of Shaverism

           whose disciples could hardly care less
           about any state of politics

* drip *

       for the amphibians were
       as clear in the stream
       as the fact that
       for the creators of
       blue humans

           Marcoux
           Wight/Wright
           Branton
           Palmer
           Toronto
           the whole bogus cast

              the attraction's totally
              juvenile

* plip *

                                        cuz those ain't names
                                        those are inventions
                                        in it for
                                        the same reason

                                        D&D
                                        roleplaying geeks
                                        create kingdoms
                                        because they can

* drip *

              overgrown
                adolescents
                  still living in
                    their parent's basements

                          though modern
                            mythmakers
                              definitely

                                        striving to leave
                                        a mark on something

XII

having cracked my skull
a couple times
reverberating shock
through noodle spine

with esophageal contortions
cramping up
adding to a weak kneed
wobble gut
that didn't need
no omeprazole in it

I pushed and pulled
and kept on wading
hunched and bent and
late for lunch
stomach full
of busted glass

a tearing
empty
sapping
suck

depleting me
of energy
and bringing on
the Chatterings

but pressing on
for a nuther half hour
gritting
clenching
grinding
dentine

we came upon
some moist formations
layered & labial

in a gray matter grotto
of scintillating shimmer-nodes

a
new Faraway
begging question
of trogging on

but what can you do
when you can't turn back

and what if
cardiac

or broken leg
or strike of stroke

when there ain't no elevator
back to the top

and there ain't no cellular
service neither

and there sure as hell
ain't no wambulance
to be called?

so you swallow your terror
and force it down

XIII

Until Eureka!
the legendary lake
and waterfall—

a third to the heart
of the belly of the beast

and as far as my screeching
stomach would allow

so I sat down and ate
a PB&J

shivering and shuddering
      body temp
      plummeting

in the 58   degree stream
in the 58   degree air

where the chill remains
throughout the year

and it's evident that
the only blue human
in this abyss

is me

XIV

finally took a slug of water
which instantly untwisted
intestinal pretzel

was woozy after that
stumbling drunken
in psychotropic
odyssey out

mashed an ankle
in falling
flailing
trudge
up

drips and plips
still sounding through
the corridors

XV

* drip *

Again the question
of what makes this quest
different than those
from the 1800s?

* plip *

an answer perhaps
in considering that

the oral tradition
is central to both

meaning retelling tales
of gowrows and gollywogs

is just as much an act
of storytelling
as proposing dodgy
blue humans

* drip *

Still   the straight up label
of "science fiction"
should make the latter
matter moot

* plip *

So why all these jokers
opting to believe
that Shaver & co
based fiction
on fact?

* drip *

answer being:

it's the same damn thing
it always is:
            dudes desiring
            stuff to be thus

                        that is
                        we know what's up

                                    but that's just not
                                    sexy enough

* plip *

which is why we have
    a culture of cults
    whose right to remain ignorant

is enough to waste
all of us

consequently
being dreamers
they make junk up

  cuz they can't
  or won't
  or refuse to see

  the true amazing stories
  really going on

  in the true neural tunnels
  of what's really going on

XVII

Personally
after descending into this underworld
and considering these scenarios
so crudely scrawled
on the cave walls
of amateur mass marketing

one's tolerance for make-believe
starts running low
especially when
those who want more
from the immeasurable more
we already have

is reason enough
to flabbergast God

So let's cut the horseshit, people
and get past the man
ufactured distractions

in this toxic
time of crisis

otherwise
we're just spelunking
nothing but our own

selfish

masturbations

of absolute
non-consequence

.

Afterword
Richard Blevins

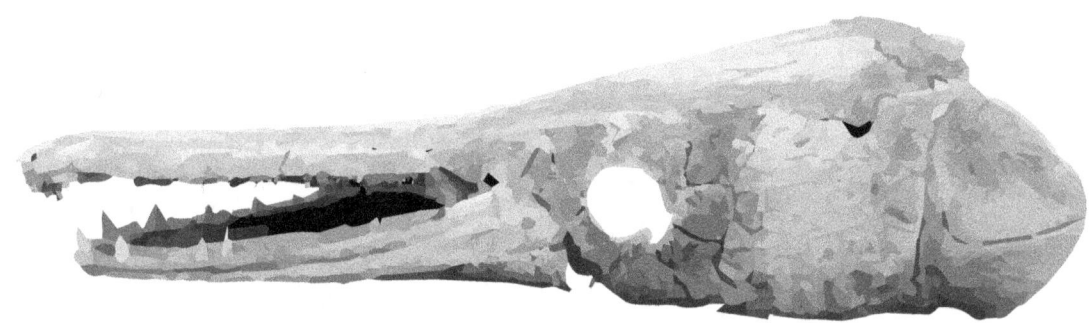

"Consider the Gar"

*I love any discourse of rivers, and fish and fishing--*Izaac Walton.

In person, I am told, the conspirator of the libidinous screeds

    Chum and *CHODE!* and other philippics against boundaries

        was, in fact, perfectly mild and soft-spoken,

            gentle as Jimi Hendrix politely enduring the interview.

I picture Mark Spitzer

"somewhat aloof" from the celebrants, restless to move—

    our very Bulkington ("the land seemed scorching to his feet"),

        Melville's ur-hero who well knows the danger of the lee shore

            equally the liberty of open water although Spitzer's inspiration

is not the sea but rather the river, the lake, and the marsh.

Any moment now, Bulkington will fade unnoticed

    from the party, drive his beat-up 80s wagon thru the stations

        of the night stopping only to sleep in the back seat, to some fishing spot

        only he knows.

Mark's is a Bulkington book, heroic outsider testimony

Mark writes for Donald Harrington Mina Loy Kenneth Irby Laura

    Riding Jackson Tom Kryss Gerrit Lansing Peter Kidd

        Stuart Z. Perkoff was most widely known in Amerika

            as a contestant on Groucho's "You Bet Your Life."

I see an aspirational ruggedness in sportsman's work:

    art made by your best chum who never grew up

        who mainlined Kerouac with mothers milk is now suddenly

            quoting the poète maudit like child's play!

Mark Spitzer elected

to sit by the river with his LINE cast waiting for the day his poetic

    genius will be at length discovered, or not,

        solely on the merits of his poems, eschewing

            NETworks of careerism.

Spitzer's belief in his art must have been unshakable.

He is ever the confident artist; never the con-man.

Returned from his Paris year, it is blindingly clear

as the winter sun glints off David Smith steel

he is not destined to be anybody's poet laureate—

There is no audience… The muse is diffused /

…and the sick and the sad / are our / grand poets, after

he translates Céline's delerium, he castigates Allen Ginsberg's

I saw the best imaginations of my generation

destroyed by stagnance—though well-fed and making it….

Once you read Céline,

you get to see

what Ginsberg and Henry Miller stole,

co-conspirator.

So

he rededicates himself, age 31, to writing authentic poems

to the garfish: *a living fossil*

he had held in his hands at 6. He remembers

a very strange fish—supposedly extinct

yet still I held it

felt it, saw it

twitch its gills

across the lifeline of my palm.

The Gar swims tantalizing just ahead of our reading

in the poems,

more eidedic memory

than motif.

Overkill Omnibus is a fisherman's autobiog,   in *Season of the Gar,*

beginning with juvenilia & tracking the angler's life   S notes ritual garfish

in lure lore bong songs   dances

of fish & fished   by Creek & Chickas

Whatever else Mark may have been (the Gar is the white whale),

he was always a poet and a fisherman. Sometimes more
a fisherman who writes poetry than a poet who happens to fish.
Beautifully Grotesque Fish of the American West
is his U of Nebraska P volume of fishing trips.

I am waiting
to go catch me a garfish…
I go to the swamp
to force a poem. [my line breaks]

You gotta get up pretty early in the morning
to be a fisherman. With him,
fishing is a contact sport—   Native Americans
sometimes you scale the fish   used gar scales
(as in the splendidly detailed "Viscera");   as arrowheads.
sometimes the fish hooks you ("Stuck on Big Sandy").

He records one of
nature's deadly skirmishes
over daily food,

and packing my tackle
I rise like the mammals
that migrated north
centuries ago. ("A Historical Landmark")

MARK HAS PACKED THESE POEMS IN ICE—
THE MOTHERFUCKERS ARE STILL ALIVE!

"**Rivers and the inhabitants of the water elements** are made for wise men to contemplate and for fools to pass by without consideration," Izaac Walton submitted. We know he composed *The Compleat Angler* in his retirement and revised it over his forty remaining years, while Spitzer didn't live to retirement. And Walton's seventeenth-century pastoral has only a graduate studies place in our ecolit. Old Walton could extol at his leisure fly-fishing for the pre-recreation quiet life; Spitzer's "Thomas Hill Lake Contaminants" requires one full page of the collected poems. Walton thought to elevate fishing to the status of an art, since his angler must make a fly to deceive the fish; Pound/academic *poetry is trickery anyway*, Spitzer begins his RANTO series. (I wonder if here's the lesson from Mark's story "Dinner at My Mother's" ending with Berryman's suicide leap missing the river: the real poet's trick is to dive AND survive?) Our critic of the No Bull Shit Reviews was never content to sit on a grassy bank of his flowing poem, but like the angler from "Beneath the Surface" jumped in and "dove / beneath the vegetation," after the fled vision. While this poem's Stupid Fish was too simple to need deception, Mark finds art under the surface of things. Melville (again!) might have identified Spitzer among the deep-divers after the truth, "even though it be covertly, and by snatches." He was thinking of neighbor Hawthorne. For Emerson, the whaling man turned novelist would declare: "I love all men who dive…[the] thought-divers, that have been diving and coming up again with bloodshot eyes since the world began." Mark takes impressive company on the fishing expedition, although he didn't operate in terms of an American canon and remained skeptical of literary hero-types all his life, except for Kerouac and at a formative time for his poetry, Fug and former Olson student Ed Sanders. The late Melville scholar (*Call Me Ishmael*) and failed fishing boat hand Charles Olson made a decisive influence on Spitzer's writing when filtered through Sanders.

(Another Olson student, Ed Dorn, was one of Mark's grad school professors in the 90s, with the result that his grand poems of driving transcontinental USA were begrudgingly inspired, as were mine, by Dorn's vistas and reading lists for field work. I wonder if Ed's grouchy Abhorrence's were evidence of the truth of Celìne for Mark? What is sure is what Olson wrote in *A Bibliography on America for Ed Dorn* and tacked it on Ed's dorm door. "Best thing to do is *to dig one thing or place or man* until you yourself know more abt that than is possible to any other man. It doesn't matter whether it's Barbed Wire or Pemmican or Paterson or Iowa [or garfish]. But exhaust it. Saturate it. Beat it. And then U KNOW everything else very fast: one saturation job…And you're in, forever." The lure is set in the jaw.)

Spitzer made his own the Olson-inspired methodology which Ed Sanders codified around 1970 and employs to this day from Woodstock in divine books of Investigative Poetry, following CO's dictum that the poet must be an 'istorin, one who sees for oneself (itself a derivation of Pound's push to make Louis Agassiz's rotting fish relevant to more than Samuel H. Scudder, and rendering Herodotus' verb as a noun. Spitzer approved Sanders' *America* for *making a new Maximus / what doesn't condescend*). Mark not only looked for his monster fish (the journey out) but he looks *at* it from all angles, in every light (the epistemology in). Note: Lacking a tradition of investigative poetry in their cultures, Bolaño and Sebald had to invent their own detectives. All this is neatly presented in his textbook for teaching *Investigative Creative Writing*). His working syllabus defines ICW as "a free-based collage that incorporates data, history, politics, images, quotes, references, and other bits of textual information, all bound together by a biased sense of humor"; a form good for "investigating monsters in our midst."

--the prehistoric snout he uses for poking into old business.

> *...[W]hat I'm really chasing when I chase fish is beyond the text of what I catch.*
> *What I'm really chasing is the subtext.*
> *It's what I find along the way and what I make of discoveries—*
> *if they're worth it.*
> (Bison Books/U.Neb.Press guest blog, Dec. 18, 2020)

Finally,

        about those translations of yours.

...I burnt myself out trying to decode a language I know nothing about.
Because I made it my goal to fake it. And I faked it so well I learned it.
(*Sick in the Head*, page 1)
Have we come around
to Walton's artful
deception?

No French, reading or writing, so he dives,
head first deep-diver, sold his car for the ticket over,
into Paris and surfaced at Shakespeare & Co, what's left of it,
seeing with his own eyes; trolled the Seine, word by word,
for beautifully grotesque Gar Trek monsters,
              whose flesh is tasty
but the eggs for most are poisonous, hatred-driven poems;
one translates "…I piss on them all
from a great height…"
at risk of
becoming Céline.

I am the greatest translator of my generation
I've done Genet
Céline, Bataille
Cendrars

it started with Rimbaud
went on to Baudelaire
and then there was the Count
de Lautrèamont

what's the point?

the point is I hate French
which is why I don't speak it
or hear it
or—for God's sake—*even understand it*

which is why I am alone
drinking beer
tonight

and feeling sorry for myself

because no one has ever
done what I've done
so of course there's no one
to join me tonight

Oh well
at least I fooled
the world.

With "Alone in Bumfuck Louisiana" Spitzer has written as if his is a brand new Céline piece, having perfectly internalized the master...The poem goes beyond translation...He is solitary as Bulkington...His Izaac's lure can fool the dumb fish...We spot the shadow of the darting Gar in the poem that swallowed the bait called Céline; Céline whose sentences swim heedlessly ahead into the dark with something of the creepy obsessiveness of American sports betting, totem stripped of the tribal rituals of football...The good doctor who taught the Americans to swear. Or Gide masturbating in his jail cell, arrested on made-up charges of petty ribaldry. This is what's left of Paris, loosely translated city. Nowhere is elder statesman Auden walking in his slippers to mass in New York City. It was "the revelation of theft" opened Genet's eyes: there is the matter of the theft: a girl, 1996, apparently framed Spitzer for the theft of Geo Wadsworth's first edition *Ulysses* from the

Shakes & Co bookstore—"…I blame her. I blame myself. I am a thief. This is my myth" (*Sick in the Brain*)--precipitating his flight to Louisiana, land of the monster fish. Like Spenser's Blatant Beast, teamed up with Envy, Spitzer can play the monster to do battle with the award-winning Display Only poets and their Ted Morgan historians, in order "to resume the poet's ancient tradition of describing historical reality" (E. Sanders).

I am a thief, he wrote. Meaning for Mark, only the petty criminal Genet and the anti-Semite physician can be true because they are not hypocrites.

In the spirit of Saint Genet and Waltonian artifice, Mark apparently confesses a crime of deception involving an application for a grant to support translating. He also includes in his collected poems "Apocryphal Rimbaud Forgeries," French and English texts facing, raising the unanswered question of the legitimacy of all translations beginning with Pound's. These poems can raise the titillating question: is the painting you are showing me on your bed room wall a forgery or theft? (Answer: There can be art in both, and the original makes three.)

I easily imagine making friends with Mark, SOMETHING CÉLINE CAN NEVER BE due to their crucial difference: hatred. His translating taught him the poetics of hate, the fantasy of climbing above the fray and someday pissing on everybody. High piss. Not that he loved everybody with power over him behind their closed office doors—he would caricature assassinate the free-range faculty member Dorn in his merciless story "Dinner with Slinger"; *the truth is: we need drama, we need hate. And tragedy—to know we can feel,* he wrote in "Report from Boulder" under Dorn's influence; he called a poem series RANTO—but Mark Spitzer was driven by his vision of the Gar, his work is tempered by that ideal, making him unmoved by the usual illogic of hatred of origin race gender religion politics. He looked to find a way to be a poet who sees for himself in an age of engineers working from home. Mark was born in America in the fusion twilight of the book gods, too late for poetry to matter, so he teaches himself to be the chronicler for timeless monsters. He teaches us: even after the engineers flood the ghost town for the new dam, a trained eye can make out submerged landmarks.

Down Down Down Down Down Down Down, he wrote in *CHODE!*, where *the drop-off suddenly expanded out and into an ancient plane of lava rubble as old as the island itself. And in this rubble: splintered spars and bare-breast sprits, galleons and whaling ships, anchors rusted to the scree, bouillon, armor, cannonry.*

This is where Chud had always gone—not physically, but mentally—since it always made sense to delve these depths, where the creatures of the deep were bastards of chance—just like him.

No wonder he understood fish better than men. And men better than women.

The Descent to the End is Natural.

The best poem in *Overkill Omnibus* is the last—and it's not a poem about fishing—where the poet descends the depths once again, this time exploring Blowing Cave in the Ozarks, *back in time / to the center of / the cavern mind.* It is a scenario out of Poe's *Pym* and features an obstacle to spelunking locally called the Birth Canal, in keeping with Poe's inside-the-earth-is-inside the head Hollow Earth motif. Approaching one thousand pages, the Gar remains the moving target of the poet's hunt, the city of Gloucester on wheels and boats. At last, in the poem "After the Blue Humans," Mark has chased it down to the ground, has followed it underground, waded water and squeezed past rocks, and cornered it *in a gray matter grotto / of scintillating shimmer-nodes. // Until Eureka! / the legendary lake / and waterfall.* And, lo, I see

the Gar is the underground waterfall!

That's a curious epiphany worthy of Poe's only novel--the kind of cracked brain metascience dissertation Mark might well have treasured, a mad neglected masterpiece of blood, ice, wrecks and lurid seas—a trip report of descents into obsession, which breaks off with Pym ushered into the inexplicable presence of the white, shrouded figure. Spitzer is exhausted. It has been a long book. He hasn't encountered Pym's figure or Richard Shaver's blue humans or pushed the button on the garage door opener to where Bruce Alan Walton (the Walton Amerika deserves!) a/k/a Branton's survives in Arkansas Hollow Earth.   Confirmed, he reports: *I sat down and ate / a PB&J.*   Photographs by tourists posted online show the cave's waterfall is about the height the blue humans would be, not that much taller than Mark standing.   He always was more Bulkington, a man of beginnings--multiple masters degrees, moving vans--than Pym.   The Gar would still possess him, had he lived.

> *... [W]hat makes this quest*
> *different from those*
> *from the 1800s?*
> *...*
> *the oral tradition*
> *is central to both*
> *meaning retelling tales*
> *of gowrows and gollywogs*
>
> *is just as much an act*
> *of storytelling*
> *as proposing dodgy*
> *blue humans.*

RICHARD BLEVINS

JANUARY 2023

Acknowledgments

Poems in this collection have appeared in *Poetry Land*, *Cryptozarkia*, *Airborne and Unbelieving*, *Leviathan*, *Inflammatosis: Polemic Poetry, Incendiary Prose, and Other Extremes of Love and War 2008–2018*, *Glurk! A Hellbender Odyssey*, *Crypto-Arkansas*, *Age of the Demon Tools*, *The Pigs Drink from Infinity: Poems 1995–2001*, *Motorhead*, *The Notch of the Sorceress*, *Junkyard*, *En Délire*, *Angry Young Man Rants*, *Fish Stories*, *Poetry School*, *Creatures*, and *Alley Life*. Poems in this collection have also been published in the *Hale School PTA Newsletter*, *Poplars '84*, *Slipstream*, *Gulf Stream Magazine*, *Vowel Movements*, *Wild Muse: Ozarks Nature Poetry*, *Cymbals*, *Limestone*, *Diamond Hitchhiker Cobwebs*, the *Long Beach Guts-ette*, *EIDOS*, *Red Dirt*, *Apo-Eros*, *Sniper Logic*, *Say It With a Fucking Poem*, *Great River Review*, *Chants*, *Steelhead Review*, *Small Time Press*, the *Arizona Unconservative*, *Atom Mind*, *Impetus*, *Rants*, *Bouillabaisse*, *Beatsheet*, *Malcontent*, *Apex Annual*, *Tight*, *Fathoms*, *Crazy Quilt Quarterly*, *Elf*, *Limestone*, *Great River Review*, *Elk River Review*, *Kumquat Meringue*, *Shockbox*, *Kinesis*, *Barbaric Yawp*, *House Organ*, *The Southwestern Review*, *New Delta Review*, *Neologisms*, *New Laurel Review*, *Lucid Moon*, *The San Juan Almanac*, *Many Mountains Moving*, *Exquisite Corpse*, *3 A.M. Magazine*, *Toad Suck Review*, *Journal of American Poetry*, *Blue Mountain Review*, *Coal City Review*, *Unlikely Stories*, *The Mag*, *All Write Then*, *Cokefish*, *The &Now Awards: The Best Innovative Writing*, *Crab Creek Review*, *Kennesaw Review*, *Mad Hatters Review*, *Yellow Mama*, *Slash Pine Press 2010 Poetry Festival Anthology*, *Fish Food and Lava Juice*, *Nerve Cowboy*, *Haz Mat Review*, *The Monitor*, *Truck*, *Amanita Brandy*, *Defunct Magazine*, *New Orleans Review*, *Cimarron Review*, *Struggle*, *Mobius*, *Chiron Review*, *Raven's Perch*, *Where in the West Is Mark Spitzer?*, *Gargoyle*, *Albatross*, limited print-run handmade broadsides by Hot Tomato Press, *The Offbeat*, *Elder Mountain*, *Poetry Motel*, *Reconfigurations*, *Exquisite Corpse Annual*, *Drunken Boat*, *Karamu*, and more.

Photo credits © Nancy MacKenzie, Elva Maxine Beach, David Gessner.

MARK SPITZER lived a life of monstrous passion, continuous inspiration, and constant fascination; but at 57 years, it wasn't long enough. He published nearly forty books: most about fish and the environment, plus novels, memoirs, literary translations, creative writing pedagogy, and, of course, poetry. He was a creative writing professor at Truman State University in Missouri and the University of Central Arkansas where he designed and founded the Arkansas Writers MFA Workshop. He also edited the legendary *Toad Suck Review*, which evolved into the poetry series Toad Suck Éditions. Having lived in the American North, South, Midwest, and West, and having traveled as much of the world as possible, he spent the coda of his most epic poem (his own damn life) loving family and friends in historic Hyde Park, New York.

www.ingramcontent.com/pod-product-compliance
Lightning Source LLC
Chambersburg PA
CBHW080941120626
46546CB00010B/2806